THE GREATER WAR
1912–1923

General Editor
ROBERT GERWARTH

Frontispiece. *Tōkyō Puck*, Volume 13, No. 9, September 1, 1920.

Used by permission of Kawasaki City Museum, Kawasaki, Japan.

Sovereignty at the Paris Peace Conference of 1919

LEONARD V. SMITH

OXFORD
UNIVERSITY PRESS

OXFORD
UNIVERSITY PRESS

Great Clarendon Street, Oxford, OX2 6DP,
United Kingdom

Oxford University Press is a department of the University of Oxford.
It furthers the University's objective of excellence in research, scholarship,
and education by publishing worldwide. Oxford is a registered trade mark of
Oxford University Press in the UK and in certain other countries

First Edition published in 2018

Impression: 1

Published in the United States of America by Oxford University Press
198 Madison Avenue, New York, NY 10016, United States of America

British Library Cataloguing in Publication Data
Data available

Library of Congress Control Number: 2017952709

ISBN 978–0–19–967717–7

Printed and bound by
CPI Group (UK) Ltd, Croydon, CR0 4YY

To my students…

Preface

I routinely tell my junior colleagues that one of the few things that gets easier with age is accepting criticism. After more than two decades of writing about France and the Great War, I decided to take advantage of something else that comes with age: a declining need to prove anything. I would embark on a new kind of project, researching peace rather than war, and international relations rather than France and the French. Further, I would seek, at least in a gingerly way, to deepen the dialogue with International Relations (IR) theory, in hopes of enriching international history in ways parallel to those in which cultural theory enriched the writing of history in the 1990s and beyond. Paradoxically, I argue here, insights from present-day IR theory can help us better understand what debates at the Paris Peace Conference meant at the time.

In bringing this project to completion, I have encountered some strong criticism indeed. An early reader of the book proposal claimed that I clearly did not understand the IR theory I sought to engage. Not all criticism lacked foundation. One reader of a failed grant application found my expansive definition of sovereignty absurd. Another ridiculed me for trying to "reinvent" myself as an international historian in the first place, as though stepping outside of one's graduate training a quarter-century on was intrinsically a bad idea. And those were just the reports I saw. Of course, I received a great deal of positive support and helpful criticism along the way as well. Among other things, tenure can license persistence. I wrote a certain kind of book, and readers will make of it what they will.

Simply put, I claim here that the Paris Peace Conference cannot be reduced either to a realist quest for security or to a duel between realism and idealism. This book is about recapturing some of the "then-ness" of the conference. States and the structures in which they operate do not have timeless, fixed identities, and we can gain something analytically by treating them accordingly. The Paris Peace Conference sought fundamentally to change the way the international system functioned, and did so in highly complicated and historically specific ways. Those ways involved reimagining sovereignty, which I boil down to mean the power or authority to decide what there was to decide in constructing the international system. This book unfolds neither chronologically or geographically, rather conceptually according to problems in and aspects of sovereignty. I consider involved topics such as Upper Silesia and the League of Nations Mandates across several chapters.

I have tried to see things whole, doubtless at the cost of seeing them clearly. Scholars have made careers studying any one of the chapter topics here, and indeed quite a few of the sub-topics. No one could do all the archival research necessary for this book in a lifetime, even with all the necessary language skills. Happily, an army of scholars working for a century has generated a sufficiently vast body of secondary literature to make this kind of book possible. I am interested not so much in corridor politics of politicians and diplomats as in public outcomes, largely knowable through the massive publication of primary documents. In their way, organizations such as the United States Department of State, the Carnegie Foundation for International Peace, the British Foreign Office, and La Documentation internationale followed the Wilsonian aspiration to "open covenants openly arrived at," in making this documentation available decades ago.

Larger-than-life characters such as Woodrow Wilson, Georges Clemenceau, and David Lloyd George appear in these pages. But I focus less on them than on the issues they and others grappled with for months on end. I also "decenter" to some degree the Treaty of Versailles. A surprising number of good historians still refer mistakenly to the "Versailles Peace Conference," and to the entire peace settlement as "Versailles." This book considers peacemaking after the Great War, from the German call for an armistice in October 1918 through the Paris Peace Conference (its proper name in English). It concludes with a treaty not part of the conference, the Treaty of Lausanne signed in July 1923. My geographic and temporal frameworks concur with the goals of a series entitled "The Greater War."

This project has taught me a great deal about the power to name. So apparently simple a matter as capitalization has proved a constant challenge in the various iterations of "council" throughout peacemaking after the Great War. Wherever practical, I have used foreign diacritics in names. Japanese names appear with the family name first. Spellings in the text often differ from those in citations. Some places, particularly in Anatolia and Eastern Europe, have no politically neutral names. Throughout, I adopt usage common in international relations at the time—such as Constantinople rather than Istanbul, Smyrna rather than İzmir, Danzig rather than Gdańsk. Some choices made in the maps may antagonize some readers. I take full responsibility for errors real and imagined. Kate Blackmer's outstanding cartographic skills and a subsidy from Oberlin College made these maps possible. I present only one attempt to map ethnicity, and that with some critical distance. For reasons argued in the text, all attempts to map ethnicity during this period were fanciful in one way or another, and sought to create their own reality. Many books on the Paris Peace Conference seem to contain nearly the same illustrations. I tried to seek out lesser-known images.

One of the happiest tasks in writing a preface is thanking all the people and institutions who provided help along the way. It was my honor to begin this project thanks to an appointment as William F. Podlich Distinguished Fellow at Claremont McKenna College. Particular thanks go to Mr. Podlich and to Gregory Hess. My time in California was immediately followed by a Research Status appointment at Oberlin. A visiting appointment as directeur d'études at the École des Haute Études en Sciences Sociales (EHESS) in Paris in 2012 helped me begin to make sense of this project. Sean Decatur facilitated a second leave in 2014–15. Thanks to Craig Jenkins, Geoffrey Parker, and Alexander Wendt, I had the chance to spend part of that leave as a Visiting Scholar at the Mershon Center for International Security Studies at The Ohio State University. My understanding of the Middle East in the Great War and its aftermath was transformed thanks to a

National Endowment for the Humanities Summer Seminar directed by Mustafa Aksakal and Elizabeth Thompson. I can only express my deepest gratitude.

I have been extremely fortunate in having had the chance to present material from this project in many places. These included the Robert F. Allabough Memorial Lecture at Dartmouth College, the Sally A. Miller Humanities Lecture at the University of Akron, The Rev. Henry Casper, S.J. Lecture at Marquette University, and the Strokheim Lecture at Whitman College. Other venues included Columbia University, The Ohio State University, Claremont McKenna College, the University of Indiana, the University of Wisconsin-Milwaukee, University College and Trinity College, Dublin, Ireland, Oxford University and the University of Nottingham, United Kingdom, Texas A&M University, the University of California at San Diego, Sciences-Po in Paris and Reims, France, New York University-Abu Dhabi, the European University Institute, Florence, Italy, the University of Southern Denmark, Odense, and the IO/IL Working Group of the Northwestern University Buffett Institute. It has been a great honor to speak at all of these fine institutions.

So many people provided intellectual support. I once confessed to Alexander Wendt that if I could drag the historiography of the Paris Peace Conference to where IR was, say, in the late 1980s, I would feel I had succeeded. His own work, so path-breaking in so many ways, inspired this project from beginning to end. I take full responsibility for ways I might have oversimplified and distorted that work. Stéphane Audoin-Rouzeau provided constant friendship and intellectual comradery across a period when our research interests came to diverge, but never to separate. Erez Manela showed himself a steadfast believer in this project, and his support at strategic moments was much appreciated. Other indispensable *compagnons de route* included Luise White, Annemarie Sammartino, Clayton Koppes, Daniel Sherman, Alice Conklin, Jan Lemnitzer, and Bruno Cabanes. Brendan Karch helped me sort out Silesian dialects, Isabel Hull a fine point of international law. Pieter Judson helped me with innumerable points of detail on the Habsburg Monarchy. My dissertation adviser, Robert O. Paxton, saved me from a gaffe in misapplying a term from bridge, in addition to inspiring me for my entire academic career. John and Jeanne Wilson provided a souvenir handkerchief for one of the illustrations. Helen Liggett provided critical help with two photographs.

At a time of great constraint in academic publishing, Oxford University Press granted me the latitude to write the book I wanted to write. Christopher Wheeler offered great encouragement from the beginning, and I think at times understood this project better than I did. The patience and insight of Cathryn Steele have been of immense help in finishing it. Robert Gerwarth encouraged me to include this book in his important series. Drew Stanley did a fine job copyediting the manuscript.

My greatest debt is to my immediate family. In addition to providing over two decades of unceasing love and support, Ann Sherif did me the honor of marrying me as this project came to completion. Over the time it took to finish this project, her son Ian Wilson grew from an obstreperous adolescent to an excellent young man.

I will never be able adequately to express how they have enriched my life, and my love for them. Many scholars are indebted to their pets; relatively few say so. Our cats, Dot and Shnell (d.2016), provided the kind of unconditional affection unique to domestic animals.

I think all historians should dedicate one book to their students sometime in their careers. Teaching, particularly teaching undergraduates, just brings the life of the mind down to earth in ways nothing else ever will. This project began in the classroom, in a new course entitled International Relations Theory for Historians. Teaching that course at Claremont McKenna and at Oberlin has afforded me the chance to teach some of the finest students I have ever encountered. Their curiosity, commitment, and need for clear explanation added to this book in countless ways. It continues to be an honor to teach them.

Cleveland Heights, Ohio
October 2017

Contents

List of Illustrations

List of Maps

Map 1. Germany after the Great War

Map 2. Successor states to the Habsburg Monarchy

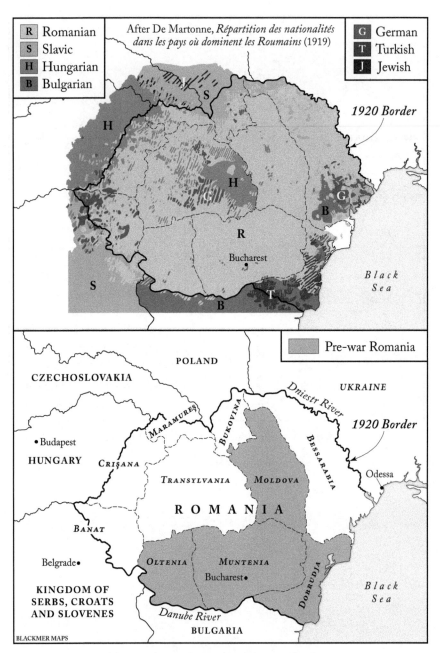

Map 3. Greater Romania: ethnicity and politics

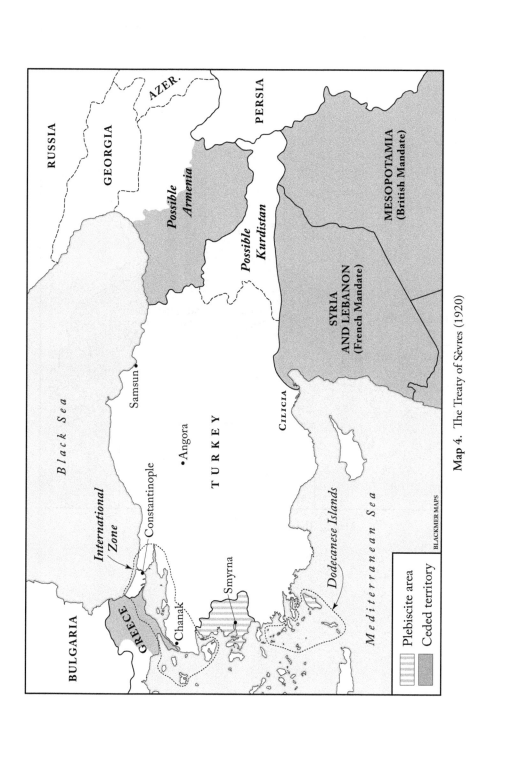

Map 4. The Treaty of Sèvres (1920)

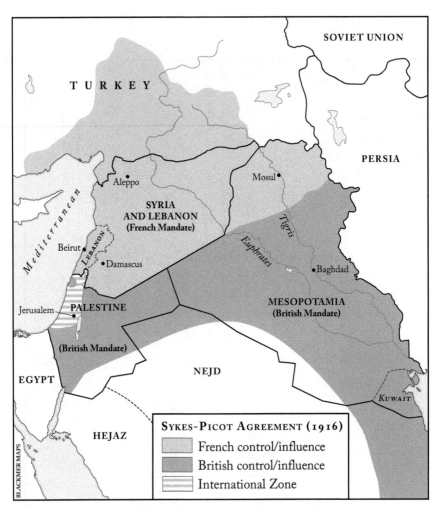

Map 5. The post-Ottoman Middle East: 1923

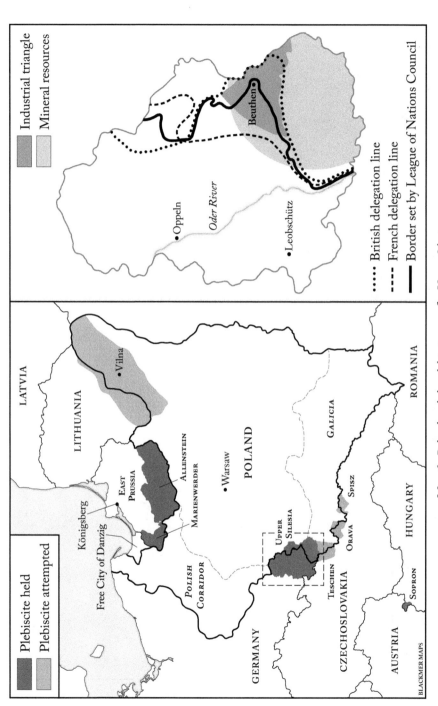

Map 6. Poland and the plebiscite area for Upper Silesia

Industrial triangle

Mineral resources

······· British delegation line

---- French delegation line

— Border set by League of Nations Council

Plebiscite held

Plebiscite attempted

LATVIA

LITHUANIA

Vilna

Königsberg

EAST PRUSSIA

Free City of Danzig

POLISH CORRIDOR

ALLENSTEIN

MARIENWERDER

Warsaw

POLAND

GERMANY

UPPER SILESIA

GALICIA

SPISZ

ORAVA

TESCHEN

CZECHOSLOVAKIA

HUNGARY

ROMANIA

AUSTRIA

SOPRON

BLACKMER MAPS

Oppeln

Oder River

Beuthen

Leobschütz

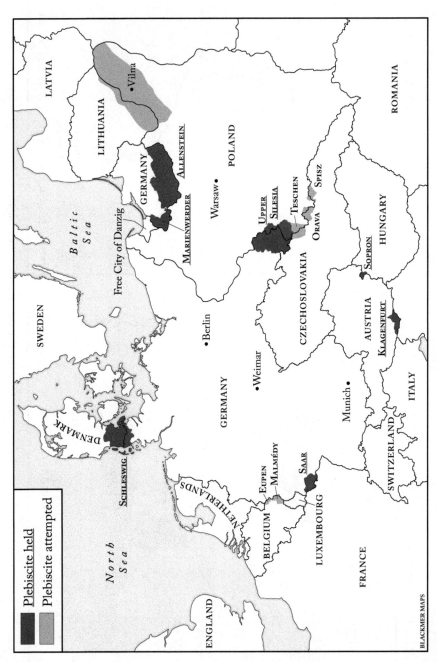

Map 7. Plebiscites after the Great War

Plebiscite held

Plebiscite attempted

North Sea

Baltic Sea

ENGLAND

NETHERLANDS

BELGIUM

Eupen

Malmédy

LUXEMBOURG

SAAR

FRANCE

SWITZERLAND

Munich•

GERMANY

•Weimar

•Berlin

ITALY

AUSTRIA

Klagenfurt

Sopron

HUNGARY

Schleswig

DENMARK

SWEDEN

Free City of Danzig

Marienwerder

Allenstein

GERMANY

Warsaw•

POLAND

CZECHOSLOVAKIA

Upper Silesia

Teschen

Spisz

Orava

Vilna•

LITHUANIA

LATVIA

ROMANIA

BLACKMER MAPS

Introduction

The Riddles of Sovereignty at the Paris Peace Conference

Kitazawa Rakuten, a parent of Japanese *manga*, founded *Tōkyō Puck* as a satirical magazine in 1905. It flourished during the years of "Taishō democracy" in Japan (1912–26), when the enfeeblement of Emperor Yoshihito (the Taishō emperor) created a power vacuum at the center of the quasi-constitutional monarchy created by the Meiji constitution. The cartoon featured as the Frontispiece appeared on September 1, 1920, during the lead-up to the United States presidential election that would determine the successor to Woodrow Wilson. In the background we see a bedridden, frustrated, and brooding Wilson, with his hands clenched in front of him. The contenders struggle for a crown labeled "The American Presidency." The shorter caption above laments "the cripple and the small minded." The longer caption provides the most withering comment: "One can think of the sorry state of the current crop of presidential candidates as really representing the bottom of the barrel of humanity."[1]

The Paris Peace Conference proper had essentially ended by the time this cartoon appeared in print. Yet the work of peacemaking continued; indeed in some respects it had barely begun. The Council of the League of Nations had met for the first time on January 16, 1920. Japan took its seat on the League Council as a permanent founding member. But the United States, having declined to ratify the Treaty of Versailles with Germany, remained notably absent. The last of the five treaties of the conference proper, the soon-moribund Treaty of Sèvres with the captive regime of the Ottoman sultan, had been signed on August 10, 1920. But the war between Greece and a new regime in Anatolia led by Mustafa Kemal continued. A "final" liquidation of the war with the former Ottoman Empire would not occur until the Treaty of Lausanne with the Republic of Turkey in 1923.

But Anatolia was only the most obvious place where victors and vanquished had not achieved peace by September 1920. Nearly two years after a series of armistices intended to end the fighting, the international system, or at any rate the system in Europe, seemed as unstable as it had been in August 1914. Germany, Austria, Bulgaria, Hungary, and Turkey had all been cast as vanquished and criminalized by the treaties. Yet none had been occupied in its entirety by allied forces. How the

---

[1] The cryptic Japanese here, common to political cartoons of the era, is subject to various renderings in English. For this version, I thank my colleague Emer O'Dwyer.

victors intended to enforce any of the punitive articles of the treaties remained an open question.

In Europe east of Germany, where the allies had always had little military power, the treaties demarcated successor states to the multinational empires. But peacemaking up to that time had exacerbated rather than diminished the traditional tension between ethnic and historic boundaries. The aspiration of unitary ethnonational states remained far from fulfilled. Successor states continued to fight over what had been Hohenzollern and Habsburg royal and imperial domains. In Russia, the Bolsheviks had mostly won the civil war that followed the overthrow of the Romanov empire in Russia. Mutual antipathy between the Bolsheviks and the other Great Powers precluded the participation of their regime in the conference. But in the long run, no settlement on the Eurasian continent could stabilize without at least the acquiescence of Russia. As revolutionaries, the Bolsheviks preached world revolution. As Russians, they fought to restore the imperial borders of the tsars. Empires survived, at any rate those empires that had won the war. Yet the outcome of the war had revealed in myriad ways the fragility of empire itself. The British and French empires had never encompassed so much territory, yet never had their futures seemed so uncertain.

My argument reads the cartoon from *Tōkyō Puck* backward in time, as a means of opening up the issues explored in this book. Simply put, I explore a historically specific attempt to create sovereignty over the international system in the aftermath of the Great War. The practice of sovereignty at the Paris Peace Conference was not just about playing a game well or poorly, but about reinventing the game being played. While I explain my use of the term "sovereignty" further below, I invoke it here in a broad sense, as the right or the authority to set the parameters of political society. Such a broad definition has displeased some early readers. But it seems appropriate at this watershed moment in the history of international relations. Sovereignty is about determining not just the answers to what political society constitutes, but the questions. Sovereignty demarcates at the most basic levels what politics is for. This book investigates the myriad discursive attributes of sovereignty, and its variety of loci. The Paris Peace Conference sought to articulate sovereignty over the international system, as well as in the states that inhabited that system.

To the creators of *Tōkyō Puck*, Wilson was not just another Western leader. During the war, artists in the magazine had portrayed him variously as the conqueror of German reaction, the prophet of world justice, and the American imperialist-in-chief.[2] Certainly, *Tōkyō Puck* did not ask its readers to interest themselves in American domestic politics merely for its own sake. After all, the United States had not yet become the global superpower that would remake the world after World War II. Yet what the Great Man had wrought, for good or for ill, would have implications far beyond the United States. Wilson's struggle for democracy clearly sought to transform international relations, in ways that would redefine sovereignty within and among nations.

---

[2] See the images in Frederick R. Dickinson, *War and National Reinvention: Japan in the Great War, 1914–1919* (Cambridge, MA: Harvard University Press, 1999).

As Peter Duus has argued, Japanese political cartoons relied on ambiguity in a frequently repressive political environment.[3] For our purposes, we can read the *Tōkyō Puck* image as pertaining to the United States, Japan, the international system, or all of the above. The crown, a traditional European symbol of monarchical sovereignty, competes with the figure of Wilson for the viewer's attention. One hopes the irony was intentional, because in American democracy the people are sovereign. In contrast, sovereignty in Meiji Japan lay in a divinized emperor. The Meiji constitution implied that the emperor had to rule as well as reign. The liberalization of the Japanese *kokutai* (body politic) during the Taishō period remained fragile and incomplete.[4] But while Japan in 1920 could never be confused with a republic, it had become unclear just who ruled there. It is not difficult to read a parallel between the enfeebled Wilson and the enfeebled Yoshihito. The decline and fall of Wilson sent discomforting messages to those who had hoped to deepen democracy in Japan. It is common to critique one's own nation through critiquing a foreign one. The squabbling would-be successors to Wilson, in fact, look much like Japanese politicians regularly represented in *Tōkyō Puck*.

Resolving the contours of sovereignty within historically inward-looking Japan would likewise have implications far beyond the home islands. Japan had already become the most important military power in East Asia, with expanding colonial interests in Taiwan, Korea, and continental China. The participation of Japan in the Great War, while militarily modest, had earned it a seat at the table of the Great Powers, adding yet more gravitas to its international position after its surprise victory over Imperial Russia in 1905. The evolution of the *kokutai* as that of a Great Power would play an important role in shaping the international system beyond Europe, as would become all too clear by the 1930s under Yoshihito's son Hirohito, the Shōwa emperor.

Historians of the Paris Peace Conference have long considered sovereignty a solved historical problem, thanks to a convergence in explanation provided by realist and liberal international relations (IR) theory. The explanatory framework of realism has proved so powerful that even today historians find it difficult to step outside it.[5] It remains a presence here. Realist storylines revolve around states, often conceived as individuals and represented metonymically through their leaders. To realists, sovereignty within states matters relatively little. Democracies, monarchies, and dictatorships all engage in an endless, Hobbesian competition for "security," most often meaning military dominance over actual and potential enemies. Above states, and driving all realist storylines, lies "anarchy"—the lack of any overarching authority capable of keeping the peace. As a result, under realism an absence essentially determines sovereignty among nations. Some sort of historically specific

---

[3] Peter Duus, "Presidential Address: Weapons of the Weak, Weapons of the Strong: The Development of the Japanese Political Cartoon," *Journal of Asian Studies* 60.4 (2001): 965–97.

[4] Peter Duus, *Party Rivalry and Political Change in Taishō Japan* (Cambridge, MA: Harvard University Press, 1968).

[5] See the fine summary of the historiography of the Versailles Treaty in Patrick O. Cohrs, *The Unfinished Peace after World War I: America, Britain and the Stabilisation of Europe, 1919–1932* (New York: Cambridge University Press, 2006), 20–24.

structure fills this absence, based in the material capabilities of the protagonists. This structure keeps the peace until one or more actors (or agents, to use the more common term from IR) see some advantage in destroying it.

Realism provides a narrative of all-too-inevitable failure in peacemaking after the Great War. Anarchy reigned over the international system, and losers in 1919 would do what they had to in order to become winners. What economist John Maynard Keynes called the "Carthagenian Peace" of the Treaty of Versailles artificially weakened Germany, well below its material capabilities.[6] Sooner or later, Germany would restore its security in a realist sense, first through military equality and eventually through military superiority. Furthermore, the conference also left "victorious" Great Powers such as Italy and Japan unsatisfied with their gains. No successor state to the defeated empires felt safe between the wars, and all schemed against all relentlessly, in a search for security. What became the Axis powers in World War II behaved exactly as realism, or more accurately "offensive realism," would have predicted.[7] For their part, the victors failed to maintain unity, and thus the peace, amidst the structural challenge of anarchy.[8] They had played the game of realism poorly, and would later pay the price.

Liberal IR theory provided a related but distinct emplotment of the Paris Peace Conference. A liberal explanation places at center stage Wilson as philosopher/king, and his cherished project the League of Nations. IR liberals also think of sovereignty over the international system in terms of anarchy, though commonly they construe anarchy as an affliction. The remedy lay in cooperation, generally through international or transnational organizations. Of course, this inevitably would raise the question of whether such an organization would become a locus of sovereignty in its own right. Ever since Ray Stannard Baker's histories of Wilson at the peace conference,[9] Wilsonian liberals have written much of the history of Wilsonianism in Paris. They often have done so in a juridical mode revolving around the conviction or exoneration of those charged with realizing Wilsonian ideals.[10] To liberal historians, World War II proceeded directly from the rejection of a liberal peace after World War I, mostly because of the "selfishness" intrinsic to realism. Certainly, Wilson himself saw the challenges to peace in these terms.

For historians, realist and liberal explanations cooperated in the construction of what elsewhere I have argued is a "metanarrative" of the Great War as tragedy.[11] If the hubris of nationalism proved the fatal flaw that led Europeans to war and

---

[6] John Maynard Keynes, *The Economic Consequences of the Peace* (New York: Harcourt, Brace and Howe, 1920), 56.

[7] On the relationship between IR realism and liberalism, see John Mearsheimer, *The Tragedy of Great Power Politics* (New York: W.W. Norton, 2001), 1–28.

[8] See, for example, Pierre Renouvin, *Le Traité de Versailles* (Paris: Flammarion, 1969).

[9] Ray Stannard Baker, *What Wilson Did at Paris* (Garden City, NY: Doubleday, Page & Company, 1919); and *Woodrow Wilson and World Settlement*, 3 vols. (Garden City, NY: Doubleday, Page & Company, 1923).

[10] For example, see Paul Birdsall, *Versailles: Twenty Years After* (New York: Reynal and Hitchcock, 1941).

[11] "Narrative and Identity at the Front: Theory and the Poor Bloody Infantry," in Jay Winter, Geoffrey Parker, and Mary Habeck, eds., *The Great War and the Twentieth Century* (New Haven, CT: Yale University Press, 2000), 132–65.

mutual massacre beginning in 1914, peacemaking after the Great War further inscribed the flaw. To realists, the victors deluded themselves into believing that they could impose a Carthaginian peace without imposing on their enemies the fate of historic Carthage—complete destruction. To liberals, all-too-human weakness in the form of national pride led nations and the men who led them to refuse the Wilsonian road to the promised land of perpetual peace.

This is not to say that the historiography of the Paris Peace Conference underpinned by realism and liberalism has failed to make great strides since the days of John Maynard Keynes and Ray Stannard Baker. Historians operating within a realist framework have thrown a great deal of new light on some very old questions. Realists such as Mark Trachtenberg and Sally Marks have argued forcefully that the Germans were as much perpetrators as victims in the endless interwar tangles over reparations, before Adolph Hitler the most visible aspect of the German struggle for security.[12] And given the way John Milton Cooper framed the issue, it is difficult to argue with his very liberal contention Wilson was "right"—the United States Senate erred in refusing American participation in the League of Nations.[13] The world's greatest liberal democracy failed to join hands at the pivotal moment with fellow liberal democracies.

Historians have always understood that IR theory is not destiny. Patrick Cohrs has summarized that "recent attempts at reconsidering the negotiations and settlement of 1919 have cast them in a far more benign light."[14] Decades of distance after the global calamity of World War II has encouraged historians to emphasize the constraints on the peacemakers and the simple magnitude of their task in ending the "total" war of 1914–18. As the twentieth century ended, it became less necessary to discern lines of direct causation from 1919 to 1939, and even to make juridical culpability the primary object of historical argument. Moreover, as Zara Steiner has argued, and whatever its flaws, the peace settlement after the Great War became what interwar contingencies made of it.[15] Likewise, Margaret MacMillan concluded in a justly successful narrative history of the Paris Peace Conference: "When war came in 1939, it was the result of twenty years of decisions taken or not taken, not of arrangements made in 1919."[16]

Some of the most promising work early in the new millennium drew more indirectly from realism and liberalism. Erez Manela argued that what the colonized world heard of the liberal aspiration toward "self-determination" proved more

---

[12] Marc Trachtenberg, *Reparation in World Politics: France and European Economic Diplomacy, 1916–1923* (New York: Columbia University Press, 1980); Sally Marks, "Smoke and Mirrors: In the Smoke-Filled Rooms and the Galerie des Glaces," in Manfred F. Boemeke, Gerald D. Feldman, and Elizabeth Glaser, eds., *The Treaty of Versailles: A Reassessment after 75 Years* (New York: Cambridge University Press, 1998), 337–70.

[13] John Milton Cooper, Jr., *Breaking the Heart of the World: Woodrow Wilson and the Fight for the League of Nations* (Cambridge: Cambridge University Press, 2001).

[14] Cohrs, *Unfinished Peace*, 21.

[15] Zara Steiner, *The Lights that Failed: European International History, 1919–1933* (Oxford: Oxford University Press, 2005).

[16] Margaret MacMillan, *Paris 1919: Six Months that Changed the World* (New York: Random House, 2001), 493–94.

important than what Wilson had actually said. "Listening" to Wilson's lofty words became a global process of interpellation and appropriation. A "Wilsonian moment" took the message away from the messenger, and gave focus to anti-colonial movements across the globe. In doing so, the Wilsonian moment helped make the territorial nation-state rather than the multinational empire the normative agent in the international system.[17] Patrick Cohrs argued that inevitably, given the ferocity of the conflict that preceded it, the Versailles Treaty made for an "unfinished peace" with Germany. Consequently, the real work of peacemaking took place not in Paris in 1919, but at the London Conference of 1924 (which began to regularize reparations) and at the Locarno Conference in 1925 (which brought Weimar Germany into the European security system). Indeed, Cohrs continued, formal structures initiated by an emerging Anglo-American partnership by the early 1920s "prefigured those on which more durable Euro-Atlantic stability would be founded after 1945."[18] Adam Tooze has provided an account considering the years 1916 to 1931 as a single period. With an impressively wide geographic and methodological lens, Tooze's compelling story is driven by a "need to understand the origins of the Pax Americana that still defines our world today."[19]

In different ways, Manela, Cohrs, and Tooze continued to rely on foundational assumptions of realist and/or liberal IR theory. Manela normalized the actors or agents. The "self" in search of "self-determination" in the Wilsonian moment is the territorial nation-state, a European concept exported without much alteration around the globe. Cohrs and Tooze, on the other hand, normalized a structure, an international order maintained by Great Power material hegemony. Ideas in both books flow primarily from power. Cohrs tells the story of an Anglo-American duopoly oddly reminiscent of Winston Churchill's World War II dream of united "English-speaking peoples" destined to master the postwar world. Tooze provides a kind of Foucauldian genealogy of the world after 1989. The Great War and its aftermath to the Great Depression constituted the rise and fall, as Tooze put it, of "the first effort to construct a coalition of liberal powers to manage the unwieldy dynamic of the modern world. It was a coalition based on military power, political commitment, and money."[20] Lengthening the time frame provides another forum for debate as to whether to judge the Paris Peace Conference a success or a failure.

My point here is not to malign three very fine books, rather to argue that the history of peacemaking after the Great War can benefit from a broader engagement of thinking about sovereignty as it evolved historically in the international system. Political scientists can rightly assess the results of the Paris Peace Conference in terms of policy-oriented criteria. "Success" and "failure" will always have their lessons. But we have known for quite a long time that the conference "failed," in

[17] Erez Manela, *The Wilsonian Moment: Self-Determination and the International Origins of Anticolonial Nationalism* (Oxford: Oxford University Press, 2007).
[18] Cohrs, *Unfinished Peace*, 7.
[19] Adam Tooze, *The Deluge: The Great War, America, and the Remaking of the Global Order, 1916–1931* (New York: Viking, 2014), 7.
[20] Tooze, *The Deluge*, 511.

the sense that it failed to create a system that prevented the return of war, first to Asia in 1931 and then to Europe in 1939. Historically specific identities created the international system after the Great War, and historically specific identities destroyed it. The question here is not whether the Paris Peace Conference created an effective or ineffective structure for the conduct of international relations, but what kind of structure it created.

Sovereignty at the Paris Peace Conference would evolve not as a solved problem, but as responses to a collection of riddles. What would be the roles of material and discursive power in shaping the new international system? What sorts of agents would rise from the ruins of the defeated multinational empires? What rules would guide the new international system? How did agents produce rules, and vice versa? We can gain something by recapturing some of the genuine interplay of ideas of sovereignty as they produced historically specific identities, much as Mark Mazower has done more broadly in his examination of the competition among liberal democracy, communism, and fascism in twentieth-century Europe.[21] As the 1920 cartoon from *Tōkyō Puck* suggests, the state reimagines itself as it reimagines the international order, and vice versa.

THE STATE AND THE RIDDLES OF SOVEREIGNTY

It was no coincidence that the Great War gave rise to some of the most important twentieth-century definitions of state sovereignty. Nor is it a coincidence that some of the most influential thinking came from Germany, whose state sovereignty the outcome of the Great War did so much to recast. Max Weber gave his famous lecture "Politics as a Vocation" in Munich in January 1919, just as the Paris Peace Conference was getting underway. Sovereignty, according to Weber's famous definition, resided in a monopoly of the legitimate use of violence within a demarcated territory.[22] Strictly speaking, the Versailles Treaty did not seriously compromise German sovereignty according to Weber's definition, considering that the Weimar state had sufficient force at its disposition to secure internal order. But given the treaty's severe restrictions on German military power, its provisions for the continued occupation of the Rhineland, and the structurally incomplete resolution of the instability on Germany's eastern border, one could argue that Germany lacked the means of adequate defense externally. It is thus not surprising that Weber later argued, as a member of the delegation summoned to Versailles, that Germany should refuse to sign the treaty.[23]

---

[21] Mark Mazower, *Dark Continent: Europe's Twentieth Century* (New York: Random House, 1999).

[22] In Weber's words, "a state is a human community that (successfully) claims the *monopoly of the legitimate use of physical force* within a given territory—and this idea of 'territory' is an essential defining feature" (emphasis in original). Max Weber, "Politics as a Vocation," in David Owen and Tracy B. Strong, eds., *The Vocation Lectures*, Rodney Livingstone, trans. (Indianapolis: Hackett Publishing Company, 2004), 33.

[23] Wolfgang J. Mommsen, "Max Weber and the Peace Treaty of Versailles," in Boemeke et al., eds., *The Treaty of Versailles*, 535–46.

Just a few years later, in 1922, Carl Schmitt penned his famous definition: "Sovereign is he who decides on the exception."[24] His immediate concerns were the chronic difficulties of the Weimar Republic in containing its domestic enemies from the Right and Left. At the heart of Schmitt's framing of the issue lay his contention that the true nature of sovereignty reveals itself only in extraordinary circumstances, when the sovereign decides both what is to be decided and how to decide it. Conversely, whoever or whatever decides on the exception is the sovereign de facto. Sovereignty by definition operates inside the law and beyond the law, altering law itself in the process. Conceiving sovereignty in this way led Schmitt to close connections to the Nazi Party in its early years of power, connections that understandably still taint his reputation today.

This book argues that we should take seriously Schmitt's definition of sovereignty in considering the international system after the Great War. For this was not just another European conflict through which stable nation-states rose or fell in cycles according to generally understood behaviors. The Great War made the exception the norm. It had already destroyed the German, Habsburg, Russian, and Ottoman empires, and posed both opportunities for and threats to the formal empires of Britain, France, and Japan, not to mention the informal American empire. A war begun by the preoccupations of nationalism had ended with the transnational phenomena of Wilsonianism and Bolshevism setting the agenda.

Riddles are simply questions without self-evident answers. Sovereign were those who decided upon not just the answers but also the questions of the international order. In different ways, the cartoon from *Tōkyō Puck*, Weber, and Schmitt all described and responded to these riddles. In the cartoon from *Tōkyō Puck*, sovereignty was quite literally up for grabs. The Great Man had declined along with his new vision of sovereignty within nations and among them. But was the alternative really no more than a gaggle of lesser men squabbling over a crown as an antiquated symbol of sovereignty? To Weber, sovereignty remained a living reality for the victors and their protégés, and something unjustly denied to the defeated. To Schmitt, sovereignty was a prediction. Someone, sooner or later, would decide upon the exception in Germany, with consequences for sovereignty over Europe and beyond.

At the heart of the matter lay the territorial nation-state (henceforth referred to as the "state") as the locus of sovereignty, the building block of the international system. Generically, I take the "state" to mean simply a discrete geographical entity in which an identifiable public authority sets the parameters of domestic political society and defines external relations.[25] Andreas Osiander has argued that state sovereignty is not so much a neutral unit of analysis as a self-justifying ideology that, in his words, "had its roots in the transient nineteenth-century heyday of state

[24] *Political Theology: Four Chapters on the Concept of Sovereignty*, George Schwab, trans. (Cambridge, MA: MIT Press, 1985), 5. The key word *Ausnahmezustand* is sometimes translated as "state of exception," though not in this translation.

[25] Thomas J. Biersteker and Cynthia Weber, "The Social Construction of State Sovereignty," in Biersteker and Weber, eds., *State Sovereignty as Social Construct* (Cambridge: Cambridge University Press, 1996), 2.

autonomy."[26] As a result, the state, or at any rate the realist state as the primary agent in international relations, constitutes the IR equivalent of history being written by the winners. Realist state sovereignty evolved as professionalized IR evolved to explain and naturalize it. Indeed, according to Osiander, the two historical developments are inseparable. Nor is it a coincidence that most of the great theorists of state sovereignty wrote in English, German, or French, the languages of the three most powerful Great Powers before 1914.

If we concede the notion that state sovereignty has a history, the Paris Peace Conference constitutes an exceptional episode in that history. From the time of the armistices, the peacemakers after the Great War saw their task as more than settling a realist imbalance within the European state system. They intended to recreate "the world" as a more stable system, though they had diverse views on how to do so. Some, like the would-be successors to Wilson in the cartoon from *Tōkyō Puck*, saw sovereignty as a crown symbolizing a realist state system. Yet before, during, and after the conference, Wilson and Wilsonianism would lurk in the background, from the first to the last days of peacemaking after the Great War. The history of Wilsonianism, I argue throughout this book, is too important to leave to Wilsonians or to anti-Wilsonians.[27] The imaginary of the American president promised not to abolish the state or even the Great Power, but to transform these identities as loci of sovereignty in a transformed international system.

WILSONIAN SOVEREIGNTY
AND RADICALIZED LIBERALISM

Just why the person and rhetoric of Woodrow Wilson took the world by storm in the last months of the Great War remains under-explained. We have long known that Wilson specialized in soaring, eloquently phrased generalities rather than in specifics. The grandeur of Wilsonian rhetoric did not wholly lack skeptics at the time, leading to French premier George Clemenceau's famous if somewhat cryptic remark that whereas the Lord God provided only ten points (otherwise known as the Ten Commandments), Wilson provided his Fourteen Points. For a century, different people have drawn very different conclusions as to just what the specifics of Wilsonianism entailed. Still, the adoration of Wilson expressed by James Shotwell of the American delegation in Paris has resonated across the decades:

> In the darkest hour of disillusionment, he rallied the forces of civilization from their helpless involvement in universal destruction to a task not of rebuilding the outworn structure of the past but of creating a world community of which mankind had until then hardly dared to dream.[28]

[26] Andreas Osiander, "Sovereignty, International Relations, and the Westphalian Myth," *International Organization* 55.2 (2001): 282.

[27] Despite its off-putting chapter title, Tooze strikes a good balance in Chapter 18, "The Fiasco of Wilsonianism," in *The Deluge*, 333–50.

[28] James T. Shotwell, *At the Paris Peace Conference* (New York: Macmillan, 1937), 20.

More successfully than any of his contemporaries (except possibly V.I. Lenin), Wilson offered an explanation of the Great War that went beyond the preoccupations of realism. To Wilson, the war had not really been about expelling the Germans from Belgium, the Austro-Hungarians from Sarajevo, or the Turks from the Arabic-speaking Middle East. Whatever its sordid origins, the war had become a global crusade for democracy. Only a transformation of sovereignty within nations and among them could redeem such a horrible conflict. In its aftermath, Wilson the prophet explained, "the people" throughout the world would become sovereign. The task of the postwar world lay in figuring out just who "the people" were, and building an international system around them. Historians well understand the theological and political roots of Wilsonianism.[29] Less well understood, perhaps, is just how radically Wilsonianism challenged the international system as understood not just by realism, but by IR liberalism.

Wilsonianism never sought to abolish or even weaken the state, rather to give it a new foundation and a new moral compass. Wilson made the individual rather than the state the building block of sovereignty, from the state to the international system itself.[30] The liberal individual was the proper "self" of "self-determination." Nineteenth-century liberalism had many variants, but generally held to a notion of the individual as rational, autonomous, and morally accountable. As imagined in Adam Smith's *Wealth of Nations* (1776), individuals once "free" would make markets a just and efficient means through which to allocate resources. As imagined in John Stuart Mill's *On Liberty* (1859), this individual would guarantee a liberalizing polity through responsible use of the ballot. Under Wilsonianism, properly educated and properly led individuals operating through liberal states could rebuild the world in their image.

Political individuals were people who could make covenants, the connective tissue of Wilsonian sovereignty. "Covenant" was not a term commonly used in American diplomacy either before or after Wilson. Free people make a covenant, as a sacred and irrevocable vow to one another and to God. In so doing, they become a kind of sacralized community. The biblical Hebrews became a people through a covenant, as did the Pilgrims in colonial Massachusetts. Americans became a people through the covenants of the Declaration of Independence and the United States Constitution. Religious or civil, a covenant for Wilson had a quasi-religious quality, and constituted an individualized and totalized commitment to the collectivity. The individual freely bound by covenants constituted the building block

---

[29] On theological influences on Wilson, see Mark Benbow, *Leading Them to the Promised Land: Woodrow Wilson, Covenant Theology, and the Mexican Revolutions, 1913–1915* (Kent, OH: Kent State University Press, 2010); and Milan Babík, *Statecraft and Salvation: Wilsonian Liberal Internationalism as Secularized Eschatology* (Waco, TX: Baylor University Press, 2013). See also Niels Aage Thorsen, *The Political Thought of Woodrow Wilson* (Princeton, NJ: Princeton University Press, 1988); and Thomas J. Knock, *To End All Wars: Woodrow Wilson and the Quest for a New World Order* (New York: Oxford University Press, 1992).

[30] I expand on what follows in "The Wilsonian Challenge to International Law," *Journal of the History of International Law* 13.1 (2011): 179–208. Like many liberals of his day, and notwithstanding his debt to women's votes in the close presidential election of 1916, Wilson largely conflated the individual with the white male. Knock, *To End All Wars*, 101.

of political society, from the smallest locality to the global community. Point I of the Fourteen Points envisioned an international system structured by "open covenants, openly arrived at." At Wilson's insistence, all the treaties produced by the Paris Peace Conference would begin with the Covenant of the League of Nations.[31] To Wilson, victory in the Great War could become complete only by placing covenants at the center of a new international order.

The logic underpinning Wilsonianism had truly radical implications. In the Wilsonian imaginary, all political communities, including the international system itself, would comprise like-minded individuals. This commensurability made possible the subtle but critical shift in Wilson's terminology from 1915 on, from references to "consent of the governed" to "self-determination."[32] The liberal individual, underpinning both concepts, made them expressions of the same thing. Commensurable individuals would make commensurable covenants, in communities ranging from regional religious communities to the community of nations. The Wilsonian state had its origins in the self-sovereign citizens it comprised, according to what Allen Lynch termed "the Anglo-American tradition of civic nationalism."[33] Certainly, difference would not disappear. Some forms, such as religion and ethnicity, would be recognized and legitimized, but would remain bounded by the values of the covenanted community. Other forms of difference, such as race and to some extent gender, could determine whether individuals or categories of individuals were eligible to make a covenant at all.

"World sovereignty" would thus exist at the level of the individual, through a global community of commensurable, self-sovereign citizens. The task of peacemaking after the Great War thus lay in constructing institutions that would properly express this sovereignty. The state, and even Great Powers, would remain as critical loci of formal sovereignty. But in the Wilsonian Promised Land, all states would operate in accordance not just with the wishes of the liberal individuals they governed, but with those of a transnational community of liberal citizens. The first step, Wilson held, was to form a community of states by covenant, the League of Nations. The League, the centerpiece of the new international system, would both draw from and reinforce the inherently liberal character of the peoples of the world, at any rate those peoples liberalism deemed eligible to make covenants.

As a means of organizing the international system, the problem of Wilsonianism was not incoherence, or even its moral hubris, rather its radicalism. Wilson himself tended to speak in grand terms that could obscure the implications of the particulars. He could leap from the general to the specific, leaving it to the listener or the reader to piece together the logic connecting them. For example, in a speech to

---

[31] Widely available documents such as Wilson's Fourteen Points speech and the Treaty of Versailles will not be footnoted.

[32] On this shift in Wilson's rhetoric, see Manela, *The Wilsonian Moment*, 42–3; and Michla Pomerance, "The United States and Self-Determination: Perspectives on the Wilsonian Conception," *American Journal of International Law* 70 (1976): 1–27, esp. 1–3. Hereafter referred to as *AJIL*.

[33] Allen Lynch, "Woodrow Wilson and the Principle of 'National Self-Determination': A Reconsideration," *Review of International Studies* 28.2 (2002): 424–25.

the Senate on January 22, 1917, a few months before the United States entered the war, Wilson stated famously:

> No peace can last, or ought to last, which does not recognize and accept the principle that Governments derive all their just powers from the consent of the governed, and that no right anywhere exists to hand peoples about from sovereignty to sovereignty as if they were property.[34]

Wilson tied the prospects for a peace settlement to a global march toward democracy. From this statement, he proceeded immediately to a brief and seemingly innocuous explanation of the need for an independent Poland. But a stable Poland, and a stable European and international system including Poland, could only exist if "Poland" comprised a functional community of liberal individuals.

Between Wilson's near-apotheosis at his arrival in Europe in December 1918 and the beginning of the Paris Peace Conference the next month, he could scarcely have stated more clearly that the true locus of sovereignty lay with the liberal individual. In Paris, he spoke of "fixed and definite covenants" that would establish a League of Nations. Doing so would give voice to "the conviction of all thoughtful and liberal men," the imagined global community of liberal individuals.[35] In Manchester, he addressed "fellow citizens," and spoke of the peacemakers "obeying the mandate of humanity."[36] He described the task at hand to the Italian Chamber of Deputies:

> ...to organize the friendship of the world—to see to it that all the moral forces that make for right and justice and liberty are united and are given a vital organization to which the peoples of the world will readily and gladly respond.[37]

In their presumed desire for peace and a certain kind of new international order, the logic went, the peoples of the world were one. National leaders had a common constituency beyond and in addition to those of their individual states—that global community of citizens who embodied the legitimate world sovereign.

At home, Wilson had wholly embraced American exceptionalism. He concluded his January 22, 1917 speech by assuring the Senate that: "These are American principles, American policies. We can stand for no others."[38] At George Washington's home in Mount Vernon, Virginia, on July 4, 1918, he told his compatriots: "it is our inestimable privilege to concert with men out of every nation what shall make not only the liberties of America secure but the liberties of every other people as well."[39] Wilson continued to stress American exceptionalism and its attending responsibilities throughout his ill-fated Western tour in the summer and fall of 1919 to win support for the Treaty of Versailles. In Sioux Falls, South Dakota, he

---

[34] "Permanent Peace: Address to the United States Senate, January 22, 1917," *War Addresses of Woodrow Wilson* (Boston, MA: Ginn and Company, 1918), 8. Subsequent references from this collection will refer to address and page number.
[35] "Reply to Socialist Delegation," December 14, 1918, 73.
[36] Free Trade Hall Speech, December 30, 1918, 97, 99.
[37] Speech to the Italian Chamber of Deputies, January 3, 1919, 110.
[38] "Permanent Peace," January 22, 1917, 12.
[39] "No Compromises," July 4, 1918, 119.

described the United States as "the only idealistic Nation in the world." Indeed, "if America goes back upon mankind, it has no other place to turn."[40]

In the United States of the Wilsonian imaginary, "the people" were sovereign, ethnic and even racial difference had been managed peacefully, and sectional strife had been resolved by the outcome of the Civil War. Those excluded by race or gender would be included when they were "ready." Wilsonian liberalism was about the inclusion of those eligible for inclusion, not everyone. By definition, a Great Power held together by covenant among liberal individuals could not threaten its neighbors, and did not need to be contained by a balance of power. Quite the contrary, this greatest of Great Powers had assumed a sacred duty to enlighten the nations and peoples of the world, in the person of its president as teacher-in-chief.[41] Utterly without irony or fear of self-contradiction, Wilson and Wilsonians could speak of a disinterested and unselfish American approach to peacemaking, and of remaking the world in the image of the United States as they saw it.

THE LABORATORY OF SOVEREIGNTY

Tomáš Garrigue Masaryk, the first president of Czechoslovakia, famously described the Paris Peace Conference as a "laboratory built over a vast cemetery."[42] His new country constituted one of the experiments legitimized by that laboratory. Indeed, as we will see, Czechoslovakia became the exemplary experiment as Wilsonian "self-determination" morphed into "national self-determination." My goal is not to judge the "success" or "failure" of Czechoslovakia, or any experiment emerging from the laboratory of the Paris Peace Conference. Rather, I want to explain how the conference sought to redesign sovereignty among and within nations in the ways it did. Like the successors to Wilson in the cartoon from *Tōkyō Puck*, the peacemakers wrestled over a crown, not altogether sure just what the crown signified.

Unlike most books about the Paris Peace Conference, this book unfolds neither chronologically nor geographically. Nor is it a country-by-country narrative of making peace. Rather it is organized around issues of sovereignty in the broad sense deployed here. The first chapter provides an overview of the Paris Peace Conference through the analytical lens of agents and structures, a central problem of IR theory. Evolving structures implied sovereignty over evolving agents, and vice versa. Chapter 2 explores "justice" as a tool of sovereignty—how a discourse of a defeated and criminalized enemy served to articulate victors, vanquished, and the international system itself. Chapters 3 and 4 examine how the Paris Peace

---

[40] *Addresses Delivered by President Wilson on his Western Tour, September 4 to September 25, 1919,* Senate, 66th Congress, 1st Session, Document 120, 87; and Michael J. Hogan, *Woodrow Wilson's Western Tour: Rhetoric, Public Opinion, and the League of Nations* (College Station: Texas A&M University Press, 2006).

[41] Frank Ninkovich, *The Wilsonian Century: U.S. Foreign Policy since 1900* (Chicago, IL: University of Chicago Press, 1999), 67.

[42] There are various versions of Masaryk's expression. Erik Goldstein translates a French version as "a laboratory sitting atop a vast graveyard." See "Great Britain: The Home Front," in Boemeke et al., eds., *The Treaty of Versailles,* 150.

Conference expressed sovereignty over lands and peoples through the drawing of territorial boundaries and the categorization of peoples. Someone had to decide who "the people" were in specific national contexts, where they were to live, and under what conditions. Chapter 5 considers how the peacemakers sought to master revolution as a discourse of sovereignty by instrumentalizing it. The tools at hand included forming the International Labour Organization, the Mandate System, and the recognition and non-recognition of successor states. The last chapter considers the League of Nations as heir to the laboratory of the Paris Peace Conference. Written with assumptions of Wilsonian sovereignty, the League had to function in practice under very different conditions.

1

The Agents and Structures of Peacemaking

> In Eastern Europe there was fighting everywhere, but juridically no war; along
> the Rhine and Danube there was a juridical state of war, but actually no
> fighting. The Austrians and Hungarians claimed that their revolutions had
> made them neutrals and taken them out of the war without a treaty of peace;
> the Poles and Czechs held that their revolutions had made them belligerents
> without a declaration of war. The Serbian Government denied its own
> existence and claimed recognition as the Government of Yugoslavia, an ally.
> The Italian Government denied the existence of Yugoslavia, and regarded the
> Yugoslavs as an enemy people. Clemenceau said he did not know whether
> Luxemburg was a neutral or enemy state, while Miller listed her among the
> Allies. Foch was at a loss to decide whether the Ukraine was an enemy or an
> Ally, although she was juridically neutral, and actually an enemy at Lemberg,
> an Ally at Odessa.[1]

Robert Binkley's 1931 article captured just how much there was to disentangle,
even in a strict legal sense, in the transition to peace after the Great War. In theory,
a series of armistices had ended the fighting and opened the diplomatic path to
peace. Combat had indeed ceased on the Western Front, on November 11, 1918.
But elsewhere, states, their capacities, and their conflicts remained in a state of
confusion. The "Great War" resisted not just closure, but even definition. What
was the relationship between a legal cessation of war and actual fighting? If war is
a state activity, what would happen when war destroyed the states waging it, while
giving birth to new ones? Even which peoples had won and which had lost became
less than self-evident. As its own locus of sovereignty in the international system,
the Paris Peace Conference and the states it comprised had the task of deciding
what there was to decide in making peace, with whom, and how. As its elemental
sovereign act, the conference sought to impose order over the chaos described by
Binkley, and to define itself in the process.

This chapter considers peacemaking after the Great War as a narrative of evolving,
mutually constituted agents and structures. The time frame extends from the
armistices of 1918 to the Treaty of Lausanne in 1923. I rely here on Alexander
Wendt's reformulation of the "agent-structure problem" in international relations

---

[1] Robert C. Binkley, "New Light on the Paris Peace Conference," *Political Science Quarterly* 46.3
(1931): 352–53. See also Robert Gerwarth, *The Vanquished: Why the First World War Failed to End*
(New York: Farrar, Straus and Giroux, 2016).

theory.[2] IR constructivists think of structures in discursive as well as material terms. Such an approach makes possible an exploration of the historical specificity of just what happened in peacemaking after the Great War, and to recapture the dynamic nature of international relations at that time.[3]

Narrative-minded historians could think of agents simply as the characters in the story. For my purposes, realism describes suitably the agents that unleashed war in 1914.[4] It has been common to think of realist states as people writ large. Even if the Great Powers did not foresee the full consequences of a general war prior to August 1914, they understood each other according to well-established rules. For a century, they had sought security under realist anarchy, which in turn produced and reproduced the "security dilemma."[5] With security a zero-sum game, the more armaments and alliances the Great Powers acquired, the more insecure they felt. For example, Germany feared a future in which French capital combined with Imperial Russian manpower. Germany thus provoked a war while there was still time permanently to weaken its rivals and establish a hegemony that would make it safe. In other words, Germany as an agent behaved just as realism, or more precisely "offensive realism," would have predicted.[6]

Structures are not exactly the plot of the story, rather that which determines the plot in the sense of possible outcomes. Under realism, agents compete for security, in predictable ways with predictable outcomes. Competition among agents produces a balance, its stability depending on their relative material capabilities. Historians often write about Europe's "long nineteenth century" between the fall of Napoleon and the outbreak of the Great War as the quintessential realist balance. European states occasionally went to war with one another between 1815 and 1914, but rarely with existential consequences for any of them. Indeed, as Carl Schmitt argued, over the course of the nineteenth century, European Great Powers came to "bracket" war, as one of a variety of tools of international relations.[7] States before 1914 rarely sought to destroy one another.

But the Great War unleashed in 1914 profoundly challenged both realist agents and realist structures. The war became about much more than the distribution of material capabilities, and reframed the most basic questions of political legitimacy among nations and within them. The war destroyed empires and gave birth to new states, most of them based on ethno-nationalism coded as popular

---

[2] Alexander Wendt, "The Agent-Structure Problem in International Relations Theory," *International Organization* 41.3 (1987): 335–70.

[3] Here, the term "structure" applies both to discourse and to forms of political machinery. In other words, "Wilsonianism" is a discursive structure, and the Council of Ten is a formal structure.

[4] For the enduring influence of realism, see William Mulligan, *The Origins of the First World War* (Cambridge: Cambridge University Press, 2010); and Christopher Clark, *The Sleepwalkers: How Europe Went to War in 1914* (New York: Harper Collins, 2013).

[5] See two foundational texts: John Herz, "Idealist Internationalism and the Security Dilemma," *World Politics* 2.2 (1950): 157–80; and Kenneth Waltz, *Theory of International Politics* (Reading, MA: Addison-Wesley, 1979).

[6] John Mearsheimer, *The Tragedy of Great Power Politics* (New York: W.W. Norton, 2001).

[7] Carl Schmitt, *The* Nomos *of the Earth in the International Law of the* Jus Publicum, Europaeum, G.L. Ulmen, trans. (New York: Telos Press, 2003 [originally published in German in 1950]), esp. 140–47.

sovereignty. Wilsonianism provided a radically new discursive structure for international relations. Wilsonianism, in competition with Bolshevism, profoundly destabilized the identities of states and empires as agents. After the Great War, Wilsonianism as a discursive structure and the Paris Peace Conference as a formal structure would create new agents, which would in turn reshape the formal structures of peacemaking. Of course, realism as a competing discursive structure did not go away in Paris, and this book never contends otherwise. But realism cannot fully capture the interplay of the agents and structures making peace after the Great War.

A NEW DISCURSIVE STRUCTURE: THE PARIS PEACE CONFERENCE AND THE "WILSONIAN MOMENT"

Erez Manela's memorable phrase "Wilsonian moment" applies not just to the reception of Wilsonianism across the world, but to the innermost workings of the Paris Peace Conference itself.[8] The German armistice of November 11, 1918 carried with it the collective and public acceptance by the Great Powers of Wilsonianism as the ideological foundation of the peace. The Great Powers formally committed themselves simultaneously to ending the conflicts with the Central Powers and to redesigning the international system itself.

The Great Powers that came together in Paris in January 1919 created something that, at least in its aspirations, went beyond the idea of an "international society" governed by norms as posited by the English school of IR, and even an "international community" inhabited by members sharing ideological commensurability.[9] The Great Powers saw themselves creating nothing less than a provisional world sovereign, tasked with deciding what there was to decide in the new international system. They had come together to do so under Wilsonianism, in surprisingly specific terms. Accepting Wilsonianism meant theoretically accepting a common agency, an abstract notion that proved to have very concrete ramifications. Once accepted, Wilsonianism had implications the Great Powers could not easily renounce, even had they wanted to. Of course, the realist preoccupations of states did not disappear. But through the "Wilsonian Moment" of peacemaking, from the German call for an armistice on October 3, 1918 to the signing of the Treaty of Versailles on June 28, 1919, the Paris Peace Conference would seek to reconcile realism and Wilsonianism.

By the fall of 1918, the Allied and Associated Powers had finally achieved their strategic goal of military predominance over the Central Powers. After four years

---

[8] Erez Manela, *The Wilsonian Moment: Self-Determination and the International Origins of Anticolonial Nationalism* (Oxford: Oxford University Press, 2007).

[9] Hedley Bull, *The Anarchical Society: A Study of Order in World Politics* (New York: Columbia University Press, 1977), esp. 38–52. On the distinction between international society and international community, see David C. Ellis, "On the Possibility of 'International Community,'" *International Studies Review* 11.1 (2009): 1–26.

of carnage, allied[10] pressure on multiple fronts at last overcame the advantage of the Central Powers in the use of interior lines. In a situation of gathering military calamity, the Central Powers one by one appealed for peace. The fighting ceased, at any rate in a legal sense, through a series of armistices running from the Bulgarian Front, to the Middle East and Anatolia, to the Western Front.

By 1918, the armistice had become a well-developed provision of international law.[11] Military commanders would determine a situation-specific set of rules, which would become operative upon ratification by the relevant political officials. As set down in "Land War Regulations" at the Hague Peace Conferences of 1899 and 1907, an armistice suspended military operations by mutual agreement of the belligerents. An armistice did not imply a parity of forces between the belligerents, but it was not surrender. Nor was it a temporary truce, rather the first step toward the making of peace. Any armistice was thus a political as well as a military document. There was no set formula as to who could ask for, grant conditions for, or receive an armistice. Parties would commonly seek an armistice under circumstances such as those of the fall of 1918—when the military outcome was becoming clear, but when for various reasons the protagonists did not wish fighting to continue.

The armistices with Bulgaria and the Ottoman Empire unfolded largely in accordance with established practice.[12] The collapse of Bulgaria in the wake of the French, Greek, and Serbian offensive of September 1918 had opened the paths to Constantinople and ultimately to Hungary.[13] The allied commander in the Balkans, General Louis Franchet d'Esperey, dictated terms without much political direction from his superiors, though the political authorities never repudiated them. The armistice signed on September 29 ended fighting on the Bulgarian Front. The Bulgarian armistice rendered the Ottoman military situation untenable, particularly in combination with the success of the British campaign in Ottoman Syria.

On October 30, the Ottoman commanders concluded the Armistice of Mudros with a British admiral, Arthur Gough-Calthorpe. The armistice gave the allies wide powers, such as the right to occupy any strategic point of their choosing (Article VII), and the surrender of all garrisons throughout Anatolia, the Arabian peninsula, Syria, and Mesopotamia to the nearest allied commanders (Article XVI).[14] Such terms foreshadowed a problem that would haunt peacemaking in the Ottoman lands down to the Treaty of Lausanne in 1923—the disparity between the apparent allied "victory" and actual military capabilities on the ground. How could the allied forces in the field enforce peace throughout the vast former Ottoman realm, even

---

[10] Throughout this book, "allies" (lower case) will be used as shorthand for the Allied and Associated Powers. For an overview of the military situation, see Hew Strachan, "The War Experienced: Command, Strategy, and Tactics, 1914–18," in John Horne, ed., *A Companion to World War I* (Chichester: Wiley-Blackwell, 2010), 35–48.

[11] Ernest Mason Satow, *International Congresses* (London: H.M. Stationery Office, 1920).

[12] On the armistices with Bulgaria and the Ottoman Empire, see Frederick Maurice, *The Armistices of 1918* (London: Oxford University Press, 1943), 14–26.

[13] André Ducasse, *Balkans 14–18: ou le chaudron du diable* (Paris: Laffont, 1964), 182–221.

[14] Gwynne Dyer, "The Turkish Armistice of 1918: I-The Turkish Decision for a Separate Peace, Autumn, 1918," *Middle Eastern Studies* 8.2 (1972): 143–78; and "The Turkish Armistice of 1918: II-A Lost Opportunity: The Armistice Negotiations of Mudros," in ibid. 8.3: 313–48.

before the swift demobilization that immediately followed the armistice? If the power to decide peace in the region did not rest on military force, on what did it rest?

By the fall of 1918, the allies had developed an instrument of military cooperation, the Supreme War Council. This body approved the armistices.[15] It comprised the heads of the British, French, and Italian governments, assisted as necessary by relevant policy aides.[16] Delegates from other powers could be included in discussions of specific issues that directly concerned them. The Supreme War Council would continue to meet during the Paris Peace Conference proper, commonly to oversee administrative enforcement of the armistices. It had no statutory standing as an international organization.

The real challenge to the structure of international relations was discursive, and originated among the vanquished rather than the victors. The German Kaiserreich sought to reverse its fortunes by revolutionizing the ideological content of the peace. Initially, the Germans had wholly realist objectives. The imperial high command sought to avoid complete military defeat, and above all an occupation of the homeland. At first, neither the military command nor the civilian authorities contemplated an internal transformation of the Kaiserreich beyond the imperial decrees of September 1918 that established a more genuine parliamentary democracy than had existed hitherto.[17]

Whatever motivated the German appeal, its content carried with it a sea change in the discursive structure of international relations. The German government addressed not the Supreme War Council nor any of the allied governments, but rather the President of the United States, Woodrow Wilson. On October 3, the Germans did so through an uncoded telegram, which indicated that its true intended audience was transnational public opinion:[18]

> The German Government accepts, as a basis for the peace negotiations, the program laid down by the President of the United States in his message of January 8, 1918 and in his subsequent pronouncements, particularly in his address of September 27, 1918.[19]

These were two of Wilson's most famous speeches, respectively the "Fourteen Points" speech and his speech at the Metropolitan Opera House. The first had

---

[15] F.S. Marston, *The Peace Conference of 1919: Organization and Procedure* (London: Oxford University Press, 1944), Ch. 1, "The Supreme War Council," 1–12; and Maurice Hankey, *Diplomacy by Conference: Studies in Public Affairs, 1920–1946* (New York: G.P. Putnam's Sons, 1946), 10–39.

[16] In keeping with its status as an "associated" power, the United States did not join the Supreme War Council until October 14, 1918.

[17] Shortly before the German appeal for an armistice, an imperial decree had proclaimed a government responsible to the Reichstag. It further placed the military under the control of the government rather than the Kaiser, and abolished the three-tiered voting system in Prussia, designed to underrepresent the parties of the Left.

[18] The *New York Times* published the text on October 7, only one day after its reception by the American authorities. Arthur S. Link, ed., *The Papers of Woodrow Wilson*, 69 vols. (Princeton, NJ: Princeton University Press, 1966–94), 51: 252–53. Hereafter referred to as *PWW*.

[19] *Preliminary History of the Armistice: Official Documents Published by the German National Chancellery by Order of the Ministry of State* (New York: Oxford University Press, 1924), 48.

already come to be taken as his blueprint for the postwar world, and before long the term "Fourteen Points" became shorthand for the entire Wilsonian program. The second speech contained Wilson's insistence that the League of Nations be not just a part, but "in a sense the most essential part, of the peace settlement itself." The League, he argued, "is necessary to guarantee the peace, and the peace cannot be guaranteed as an afterthought." Putting the League at the center of peacemaking meant linking an end to the states of war to the transformation of international relations.

Nineteenth-century structures of peacemaking, discursive or formal, were never going to suffice if the protagonists took Wilsonianism seriously. A parallel note sent by the disintegrating Austro-Hungarian government on October 7 raised the stakes by adding specific mention of Wilson's February 11, 1918 "Four Principles" speech, in which Wilson castigated realism itself, as "the great game, now forever discredited, of the balance of power."

The German and Austro-Hungarian appeals created an exceptional moment in the history of international relations. States on one side of the military conflict had sought an ideological alliance with a head of state on the other side of the military conflict. The German government had appealed to Wilson not as the leader of the allied coalition (which he was not), nor even as the leader of the enemy nation with the most powerful army in the field (which he also was not). Rather, the Germans appealed to Wilson as the arbiter of a certain way of seeing the world. Were this appeal to succeed, it would have the effect of rebuilding the international system according to a new discursive structure. Throughout peacemaking after the Great War, various protagonists, including Wilson himself, would seek to circumvent the radical implications of Wilsonian sovereignty. Abstract language could have very practical implications, if only as a form of what political scientists call "rhetorical entrapment."[20] An explicit commitment to Wilsonianism could create its own reality, with which competing principles would have to contend.

The first state agent to confront the transformative implications of Wilsonianism was Imperial Germany itself.[21] The internal character of the Kaiserreich immediately became an issue. What sort of "Germany" in fact could make a Wilsonian peace? The first American response to the German appeal came through Secretary of State Robert Lansing. He queried whether Germany had indeed sought peace based on the practical application of the Fourteen Points, which were not themselves subject to negotiation.[22] Lansing asked ominously whether "the imperial Chancellor is speaking merely for the constituted authorities of the Empire who have so far conducted the war."

[20] On rhetorical entrapment, see Frank Schimmelfennig, "The Community Trap: Liberal Norms, Rhetorical Action, and the Eastern Enlargement of the European Union," *International Organization* 55.1 (2001): 47–80.

[21] Klaus Schwabe, *Woodrow Wilson, Revolutionary Germany, and Peacemaking: Missionary Diplomacy and Realities of Power*, Rita and Robert Kimber, trans. (Chapel Hill: University of North Carolina Press, 1985 [originally published in German in 1971]), Ch. II, esp. 30–117.

[22] *Preliminary History*, 52.

The "Second Note" from Lansing, dated October 14, 1918, raised the stakes by requiring a peace made "by the action of the German people themselves."[23] By the "Third Note" of October 23, the Americans made clear that the emergence of parliamentary government by imperial decree in September 1918 had not in itself created a truly legitimate regime. Through Lansing, Wilson pronounced himself not satisfied that "the principle of a government responsible to the German people has yet been fully worked out or that any guarantees either exist or are in contemplation that the alteration of principle and of practice now partially agreed upon will be permanent."[24] Only a Germany governed by popular sovereignty could make peace under the new discursive structure. The German High Command and the imperial government soon discovered that they had sown the wind and reaped the whirlwind in calling for a Wilsonian peace. Later, the German delegation would argue that this internal transformation merited recognition in the peace terms.

Hard bargaining continued among the allied Great Powers, to persuade them to accept Wilsonianism as the discursive foundation of the peace.[25] The British and the French insisted on interpreting specific points according to realist concerns for security.[26] The British held that interpretations of Point II ("freedom of navigation upon the seas") could not infringe upon the safety of their empire. The French insisted on leaving open the exact meaning in Points 7 and 8 (calling for "restored" Belgium and occupied France). This anticipated the vexed issue of reparations.[27] Wilsonianism would never banish realism, even at its zenith.

Whether through genuine idealism or a more cynical conviction that realist preoccupations would win out in the end, the broader implications of Wilsonianism did not give rise to much controversy before the conference began. None of the Great Powers questioned the Fourteenth Point, calling for "a general association of nations"—potentially the most transformative element of the Wilsonian program.[28] The note forwarded to the Germans by Lansing on November 5 signaled that the strange bedfellows of President Wilson and the German high command had won on the essential point—the acceptance of Wilsonianism as the ideological foundation for the peace:

> The Allied Governments have given careful consideration to the correspondence which has passed between the President of the United States and the German Government. Subject to the qualifications which follow, they declare their willingness to make peace with the Government of Germany on the terms of peace laid down in the President's Address to Congress of the 8th January 1918, and the principles of settlement enumerated in his subsequent addresses.[29]

---

[23] *Preliminary History*, 68. [24] *Preliminary History*, 114.

[25] Bullitt Lowry, *Armistice 1918* (Kent, OH: Kent State University Press, 1996), 77–100.

[26] For Britain, see David Lloyd George, *The Truth about the Peace Treaties*, 2 vols. (London: Gollancz, 1938), 1: 213–94. For France, see David Robin Watson, *Clemenceau: A Political Biography* (New York: David McKay Company, 1974), 331–35.

[27] For example, see Pierre Renouvin, *L'Armistice de Rethondes* (Paris: Gallimard, 1968), 195–220.

[28] On the provisional inter-allied understanding of the Fourteen Points, see the flurry of telegrams between Edward House and President Wilson, October 29–30, 1918, in *PWW* 52: 495–505; 511–17.

[29] Quoted in Maurice, *The Armistices*, 51–52.

This common commitment to a Wilsonian peace would take on a life of its own as the conference proceeded. As Binkley would put it: "The essential significance of the Fourteen Points as a basis of peace was not their ethical quality but their contractual character."[30] Whatever the intentions of the states who had agreed to the Wilsonian contract, that contract would shape the work of peacemaking after the Great War, from its first days to its last.

Nineteenth-century diplomacy had bequeathed formal structures for making peace. In common usage, a *conference* of plenipotentiaries from the Great Powers would design the peace, whereupon a *congress* of all interested parties (including the recent enemies) would negotiate the remaining fine points of the settlement, then affirm it.[31] In this structure, commensurable agents would make peace as they had made war, over a relatively narrow range of interests. The congress served largely to present publicly the decisions made by the conference.

But nineteenth-century practices were never going to suffice to build the Wilsonianism international system to which the victors had formally committed themselves. The apparently haphazard planning of the conference before it began spoke to this underlying problem. The first written scheme for organizing the conference came from the French Foreign Ministry, and arrived on the desk of David Hunter Miller, legal adviser to the American delegation, shortly after the armistice with Germany.[32] It called for a preliminary conference of Great Powers, followed by a congress of all interested parties. The French proposal split peacemaking into two phases: "1) Resolution of the war strictly speaking; 2) the study of the League of Nations." In effect, the French proposal would have prioritized the security concerns of the Great Powers over redesigning the international system. Indeed, the plan explicitly rejected the Fourteen Points as the foundation for peace, because "they are principles of public law, which can inspire the negotiations, but which do not have the concrete character indispensable to arriving at the precise settlement of concrete provisions." French delegation member André Tardieu later attributed resistance to the French plan to ethnic difference, as reflecting "the instinctive repugnance of the Anglo-Saxons for the systematic constructions of the Latin spirit."[33]

In fact, a much more serious issue was at stake. Nineteenth-century formal structures might well have sufficed to address the realist concerns of the peace—the neutralization of German military power, and perhaps even the geopolitical

---

[30] Binkley, "New Light on the Paris Peace Conference," 338.

[31] As Satow noted, however, "there is no essential difference between a Conference and a Congress...." *International Congresses*, 1. The official American record would use the term "Preliminary Peace Conference" to refer to plenary meetings of the Paris Peace Conference up to the time treaties were presented to the defeated powers. Each meeting at which a treaty was presented and signed was referred to as a "Peace Congress." *Papers Relating to the Foreign Relations of the United States, 1919: The Paris Peace Conference,* 13 vols. (Washington, D.C.: United States Government Printing Office, 1942–47): 3: vii. Hereafter referred to as *FRUS: PPC.*

[32] "Note Sur le Congrès De La Paix," (received November 21, 1918), in David Hunter Miller, *My Diary at the Conference of Paris,* 21 vols. (Privately Printed, 1924), 2: 4–16. Subsequently referred to as Miller, *Diary.* Unless otherwise indicated, all translations from French are my own.

[33] André Tardieu, *La Paix* (Paris: Payot, 1921), 101.

reorganization of the Austro-Hungarian and Ottoman domains in accordance with Great Power interests. If realist preoccupations had in fact taken over the conference, it might have proved a good deal simpler, shorter, and even less acrimonious than it did. But the allies had signed on to a good deal more than a realist peace. Wilson's decision personally to lead the American delegation left little doubt that he would see to it that the conference would undertake writing treaties and redesigning the international system in tandem.[34] The allies had publicly signed on to the Wilsonian program, and theoretically to the radical reconfiguration of sovereignty that program carried within it. Any meaningful conception of the League would have to acknowledge this. The problem of reconciling realism and Wilsonianism presented itself before the larger-than-life persons of the Paris Peace Conference ever met as a group.

The assumption of Great Power predominance over the international system continued to influence planning for the conference, though there was nothing inherently "un-Wilsonian" about this. A group of allied heads of government met in London on December 2–3, though not as the Supreme War Council.[35] David Lloyd George, Georges Clemenceau, and Vittorio Orlando all agreed that an interallied conference should precede a congress.[36] This conference would comprise five Great Powers—Britain, France, the United States, Italy, and Japan. The French would insist on Paris as the location. But exactly what the conference would decide and how the conference would decide it remained open.

Historians of Japan have tended to emphasize its marginalization at the Paris Peace Conference, a marginalization affirmed in the souvenir culture depicted in Figure 1.1.[37] But why did the allies include Japan in the inner circle of the conference in the first place, given its minor military contribution to the war? Japan had not participated in the armistice discussions with Germany, nor had it formally embraced Wilsonianism. In realist terms, Japan merited inclusion because of its Great Power status before the war, its naval alliance with Britain, and the fact that any settlement in Asia (notably the disposition of the German imperial domains in the Pacific) required Japanese assent. From a Wilsonian point of view, including Japan also implied that agents could change through participation in the new

---

[34] At least as early as November 10, Wilson indicated that he planned to attend the conference. "President Wilson to the Special Representative (House)," [Telegram], *FRUS: PPC*, 1: 128. The United States was the only Great Power in which the head of government and the head of state were the same person. Consequently, the head of any American delegation would either outrank his peers, or be outranked by them.

[35] "Notes of an Allied Conversation held in the Cabinet Room, 10, Downing Street, S.W., on Tuesday, 3rd December 1918, at 5:30 PM," United Kingdom, National Archives, CAB 23 First World War Conclusions, CAB 24/42 Original Reference GT 3601–3700, 1917 13 Feb–1918 22 Feb, downloaded July 12, 2010 from: http://www.nationalarchives.gov.uk/cabinetpapers/cabinet-gov/cab24-first-world-war-memoranda.htm#G%20Series,%20Printed%20Papers.

[36] The results of this meeting as presented to the Americans were summarized in "Telegram: The Acting Secretary of State to the Secretary of State," December 7, 1918, *FRUS: PPC*, 1: 340–43.

[37] Frederick R. Dickinson, *War and National Reinvention: Japan in the Great War, 1914–1919* (Cambridge, MA: Harvard University Asia Center, 1999), Ch. 6; and Thomas W. Burkman, *Japan and the League of Nations: Empire and World Order, 1914–1938* (Honolulu: University of Hawai'i Press, 2008), Ch. 4.

Figure 1.1. Embroidering allied victory (minus Japan), souvenir handkerchief, 1918.
From the author's collection.

structure of international relations.[38] If the suppositions of Wilson's speeches were correct, Japan would accept Wilsonianism after the fact, through participating in the conference and joining the League of Nations. In so doing, it would join the other prewar Great Powers in becoming "great" in a moral as well as material sense.[39] The souvenir postcard in Figure 1.2 emphasized just such affinities between the Japanese delegation and the Wilsonian program. The Great Powers would include other states at their discretion, as had been the case with the Supreme War Council. They would consult "smaller allied powers," including formerly occupied states such as Belgium and Serbia, only on questions concerning them. President

[38] The minutes of the January 12 meeting noted the future participation of Japan almost in passing. "Secretary's Notes of a Conversation Held in M. Pichon's Room at the Quai d'Orsay on Sunday, January 12, 1919, at 4 p.m.," *FRUS: PPC*, 3: 506. Japanese representatives appeared the next day.
[39] At one point, Wilson had to be reminded by Baron Makino Nobuaki that Japan had never formally accepted the Fourteen Points. Wilson countered with the basic argument made above. "Secretary's Notes of a Conversation Held in M. Pichon's Room at the Quai d'Orsay, Paris, January 22, 1919, at 15 Hours 15," *FRUS: PPC*, 3: 678–79.

Figure 1.2. Souvenir postcard of the Japanese delegation to the Paris Peace Conference. From the author's collection.

Wilson insisted that he approve final arrangements after his arrival in Europe, but never took issue with the fundamental organization approved at the London meeting.[40] Immediately thereafter, the French considered matters evolved sufficiently to begin issuing invitations.[41]

Yet considerable uncertainty remained in the highest quarters as to just what anyone had been invited *to*. Arguably, the heads of the French, British, American, and Italian delegations convened "the Paris Peace Conference" on January 12, 1919 at 2:40 p.m. Allied Supreme Commander Marshal Ferdinand Foch began by discussing progress made in carrying out the armistice with Germany. Wilson inferred that he was present at a meeting of the Supreme War Council.[42] Lloyd George responded that this could not be the case because he had brought no military advisers with him. Clemenceau agreed, and discussion shortly terminated. In another version of the minutes, Wilson argued that in the conference that would emerge from the present meeting, "they must have an organization of all the nations, otherwise they would run the risk of having a small number of nations regulate the affairs of the world, and the other nations might not be satisfied."[43] This led Clemenceau to ask, a bit scornfully, whether "there can be

---

[40] "Telegram: Secretary of State to the Acting Secretary of State," December 8, 1918, 5:00 PM, *FRUS: PPC*, 1: 343.

[41] Marston, *The Peace Conference of 1919*, 50.

[42] "Procès verbal of the Meeting of the Supreme War Council Held in M. Pichon's Room at the Quai d'Orsay, Paris, on Sunday, January 12, 1919, at 2:30 PM," *FRUS: PPC*, 3: 477.

[43] "Notes of a Meeting of the Supreme War Council Held at the Quai d'Orsay at 2:30 on January 12, 1919," Tasker Bliss Papers, reprinted in *FRUS: PPC*, 3: 505.

no question however important it may be for France, England, Italy or America upon which the representative of Honduras or of Cuba shall not be called upon to express his opinion?"

A second meeting the same day continued the discussion. Wilson remained confused enough to ask: "What was the Conference to which the discussions on representation related?"[44] Clemenceau's response seems obvious only in retrospect: "they were the preliminary Peace Conference which all the world was awaiting." Reversing his prior position, Clemenceau now opined that with or without supporting staff, they sat as the Supreme War Council until the Peace Conference properly convened, presumably at the first plenary. Clemenceau continued that he envisaged three levels of meetings reflecting three concentric circles of power at the conference: the present informal and confidential conversations; a more formal conference of all the allied states; followed by a formal peace congress.

After several days of discussion among themselves, the Great Powers presented the "Rules of the Preliminary Peace Conference at Paris" at the first plenary session on January 18, 1919 (see Figure 1.3). The written rules constituted the first public documentation of the Paris Peace Conference as a formal structure. Much in the

Figure 1.3. First plenary meeting of the Paris Peace Conference, January 18, 1919.
Held by the Library of Congress (public domain).

[44] "Secretary's Notes of a Conversation Held in M. Pichon's Room at the Quai d'Orsay on Sunday, January 12, at 4 p.m.," in *FRUS: PPC*, 3: 493.

document would have been familiar to readers a century earlier. The rules made no mention of the Fourteen Points or indeed of any Wilsonian principles:

> The Conference summoned with a view to lay down the conditions of peace, in the first place by peace preliminaries and later by a definitive Treaty of Peace, shall include representatives of the Allied or Associated Powers.[45]

Sovereignty over making peace lay with the collectivity of states that had won the war. But there had been no prior consultation with any of the twenty-seven other states that ultimately would sign the Treaty of Versailles. The rules specified a clear hierarchy. The British Empire, France, Italy, the United States, and Japan declared themselves "belligerent Powers with general interests," which would participate in "all sessions and commissions."

The rules made no explicit provision for the continued meeting of the Great Powers as such, though their self-designation suggested that whenever they did so, they constituted the sovereign power over the proceedings. Other invitees would participate at the discretion of the Great Powers, and would fall into three subcategories. "Belligerent Powers with special interests" included states as diverse as Belgium, the Serb-Croat-Slovene State, the Czecho-Slovak Republic, the British Dominions, as well as countries little touched by the war such as Liberia, Nicaragua, and Honduras. States such as Bolivia and Ecuador, which had simply broken diplomatic relations with the Central Powers, would attend only those sessions of direct concern. The same would hold true for neutrals and unrecognized states "in process of formation," which would present their views only as deemed necessary.

The council of Great Powers would adopt various names to describe itself.[46] But it never doubted its self-created role as provisional world sovereign, representing in its way "the people" of the world. According to a member of the Italian delegation, on June 27, 1919, the eve of the signing of the treaty with Germany, Clemenceau opined: "We are a league of the people." Wilson agreed enthusiastically, referencing absolutist French King Louis XIV: "*L'état c'est nous.* [We are the state.]"[47] There was nothing inherently "un-Wilsonian" about a world order in which Great Powers decided what there was to decide and how to decide it. With its deep roots

---

[45] *AJIL* 13, Supplement: Official Documents (1919); 109–12.

[46] When speaking generically, particularly concerning the early phases of the Paris Peace Conference, I will use the term "council of Great Powers." Formally, from January–March 1919, this council met as the Council of Ten, comprising the heads of delegations and the foreign ministers of the five Great Powers. Beginning in late March, a Council of Four (the heads of delegations, now excluding Japan most of the time) and the Council of Five (the foreign ministers, and including Japan) met separately. The Council of Five made recommendations, particularly on territorial matters, sent to the Council of Four for disposition. For clarity, I most commonly use the term "Supreme Council" to refer to the Council of Four. Marston, *The Peace Conference of 1919*, Ch. 8, "The Councils of Four and Five," 164–76.

[47] Luigi Aldrovandi Marescotti, *Nuovi Riddordi e frammenti de diario per far séguito a Guerra diplomatica (1914–1919)* (Milan: A. Mondadori, 1938), 102. The Italian reads: "La liga dei popoli siamo noi."; and "E poi, in francese: 'Lo Stato siamo noi.'" French translator Paul Mantoux's version has Clemenceau saying "*l'État c'est nous*," with no rejoinder from Wilson. "Conversation between President Wilson, MM. Clemenceau and Lloyd George, and Barons Sonnino and Makino," June 27, 1919, 4 PM, in Arthur Link, ed. and trans., *The Deliberations of the Council of Four (March 24–June 28, 1919): Notes of the Official Interpreter, Paul Mantoux*, 2 vols. (Princeton, NJ: Princeton University Press, 1992 [originally published in French in 1955]), 2: 580. Hereafter referred to as Mantoux, *Deliberations*.

in the Progressive tradition, Wilsonianism in no way precluded a handful of men deciding the fate of the world, provided they followed the proper moral compass. In the Wilsonian imaginary of moral absolutes, power was something to be steered in the right direction rather than balanced. Power under Wilsonianism could become as concentrated as circumstances warranted, provided those who exercised it remained accountable to the true global sovereign, the global community of self-sovereign individuals.

From the outset, the council of Great Powers prioritized the League of Nations, ahead of even the treaty with Germany. On January 13, Wilson proposed an uncontested agenda making the League the first item of business. Clemenceau added that the agenda required an early meeting of the plenary, "to give the Delegates a mandate to start work."[48] The world had to be present at its own re-creation through designing the League. For our purposes here, it matters little whether Clemenceau endorsed Wilson's priorities out of genuine idealism, as a concession to American material power, or cynically as a means of rendering the plenary harmless by occupying it with an institution unlikely to mean much anyway. The priority given to designing the League had structural implications for the conference.

The plenary unanimously approved the establishment of a commission to establish a League of Nations at its second session on January 25.[49] This meeting made clear the hierarchical structure of the conference. João Pandiá Calógeras, head of the Brazilian delegation, took seriously the first sentence of the written procedures of January 12, which described the "Conference" as the complete assembly of the Allied and Associated Powers. He protested that the proposed League commission would comprise two members each from the Great Powers, and five members total from the rest of the conference:

> It is with some surprise that I constantly hear it said: "This has been decided, that has been decided." Who has taken a decision? We are a sovereign body, a sovereign court. It seems to me that the proper body to take a decision is the Conference itself. (190)

Clemenceau, as president of the conference, gave a pointed response with a surprisingly nuanced rationale. On the one hand, he left no doubt just where sovereignty lay at the proceedings:

> With your permission, I will remind you that it was we who decided that there should be a Conference at Paris, and that the representatives of the countries interested should be summoned to attend it. I make no mystery of it—there is a Conference of the Great Powers going on in the next room. (196)

The authority of the Great Powers, military and moral, lay in their having won the war. Might had legitimized right in deciding what there was to decide. "We have had dead," he continued, "we have wounded in the millions, and if we had not kept before us the great question of the League of Nations we might perhaps have been selfish enough to consult only each other. It was our right" (196–97).

[48] "Secretary's Notes, January 13, 1919," *FRUS: PPC*, 3: 537.

[49] "Preliminary Peace Conference, Protocol No. 2, Plenary Session of January 25, 1919," in *FRUS: PPC*, 3: 190.

But immediately thereafter, Clemenceau admitted in so many words the influence of the Wilsonian contract. The peacemakers held themselves accountable to something beyond their national communities. The legitimacy of the whole project of making peace lay with "the people," defined in transnational terms. Wilson himself could not have put the matter more plainly:

> Now, Gentlemen, let me tell you that behind us is something very great, very august and at times very imperious, something which is called public opinion. It will not ask us whether such and such a State was represented on such and such a Commission. That interests nobody. It will ask us for results, ask us what we have done for the League of Nations. (197)

Here too, we need not believe in Clemenceau's sincerity to take his words seriously. Whatever he meant, he expressed the views of the Great Powers in Wilsonian language. This language recognized the ultimate sovereignty of the peoples of the world in structuring the new international order, and the leaders of the Great Powers as accountable to that sovereignty.

The committee designing the League of Nations carried out its work with dispatch, and presented a draft Covenant to the plenary conference on February 14.[50] The League reflected the structure of the conference, though not completely. It would comprise a Council and an Assembly (representing all League members), assisted by a Secretariat. Membership on the League Council would include the five Great Powers plus four other rotating members, to be selected by the Assembly. In other words, the Great Powers would have only a bare majority on the League Council. The Covenant described the writ of both the League Council and the Assembly in exactly the same terms. Both "may deal at its meetings with any matter within the sphere of action of the League or affecting the peace of the world" (Articles 3 and 4). Theoretically, the League Council could bring matters to the Assembly, and vice versa.

On most matters, the League Council remained the senior body. It would advise on the fulfillment of Article 10, perhaps the most sweeping provisions of the Covenant, which guaranteed the "territorial integrity and existing political independence of all Members of the League." The League Council would manage international disputes, and recommend further action if diplomacy and arbitration should fail (Articles 12–17). It would also make recommendations to protect collective security arrangements (Articles 16–17), according to which an attack on any member of the League would be considered an attack on all. Under Article 15, any dispute under examination could be brought before the Assembly, at the request of either of the parties in the dispute.

As written, the Covenant called for a new form of common state interaction. Political scientist John Ruggie has argued that under certain circumstances, states can act according to "collective intentionality," something more than the sum of

---

[50] See the overview by David Hunter Miller, *The Drafting of the Covenant*, 2 vols. (New York: G.P. Putnam's Sons, 1928).

individual intentions, less than a collective conscious.[51] For example, each violinist in an orchestra plays according to an individual intentionality, but that intentionality exists as such only in relation to the common enterprise of playing symphonic music. The League as written would function in a like manner. States, above all Great Powers, would continue to exist. But the agency of a given state would formally structure that system through the agency of other states.

Only collective intentionality makes sense of Article 5 of the Covenant, which established the requirement of unanimity in League Council and Assembly decisions.[52] This requirement presupposed a transnational community of self-sovereign individuals to which states would recognize themselves as accountable. Transnational popular opinion, in turn, would guarantee collective intentionality. Article 5 imagined a radical relocation of the locus of real sovereignty in the state system. Wilson put the matter plainly in presenting the draft Covenant to the Conference:

> The significance of the result, therefore, has that deepest of meanings, the union of wills in a common purpose, a union of wills which cannot be resisted, and which I dare say no nation will run the risk of attempting to resist.[53]

States could conform their interests to those of the global citizenry. In this radical liberal vision, "the world," once properly educated and informed, would speak with one voice in international relations. Collective intentionality could rule only if the states became the geographically specific organizers of popular sovereignty in commensurable states around the globe.

Sovereignty within states and sovereignty among them would become two sides of the same coin. Contemporaries understood full well how profoundly the world was supposed to change. Wilson even made an oblique reference to Jeremy Bentham as a precursor to liberalism. Although he never used Bentham's term, he envisaged the Panopticon as a model for the League, as: "the eye of the nations, to keep watch upon the common interest—an eye that did not slumber, an eye that was everywhere watchful and attentive."[54] The panoptical League, the instrument of the sovereign citizens of the world, would maintain surveillance, determining inclusion in and exclusion from the international system.

At the February 14 plenary meeting, Wilson's colleagues went out of their way to echo his vision. The usually understated Baron Makino Nobuaki of Japan praised "what is, perhaps, the most important document ever compiled by man."[55] Lord Robert Cecil of the British Empire delegation drew attention to collective intentionality, without using the term. The prospects of the League would depend on the

---

[51] John Ruggie, "What Makes the World Hang Together?: Neo-utilitarianism and the Social Constructivist Challenge," *International Organization* 52.4 (1998), esp. 869–70.

[52] My view runs counter to arguments that Article 5 emerged to constrain the League from the beginning. Cromwell A. Riches, *The Unanimity Rule and the League of Nations* (Baltimore, MD: The Johns Hopkins Press, 1933), 1–36.

[53] "Preliminary Peace Conference, Protocol No. 3, Plenary Session of February 14," *FRUS: PPC*, 3: 211.

[54] "Preliminary Peace Conference, Protocol No. 2, Plenary Session of January 25, 1919," *FRUS: PPC*, 3: 179.

[55] "Plenary Session of February 14," 224.

shared, enacted belief "that the interest of one is the interest of all, and that the prosperity of the world is bound up with the prosperity of each nation that makes it up" (217). Italian Prime Minister Orlando addressed most forthrightly the problem of state sovereignty in the new world order. He argued that the conference had effected a "dialectical impossibility," the reconciliation of state sovereignty and restraint on state behavior. He spoke of a "'self-constraint,' a spontaneous coercion, so that states will in the future be brought under the control of the public opinion of the whole world, voluntarily to recognize the restraint imposed on them for the sake of universal peace" (218). French delegation member Léon Bourgeois, here as later, argued that the Covenant laid the foundation for a supranational organization that as its own locus of sovereignty would prepare responses to future aggression (223–24).

In short, the Covenant of the League of Nations as written would established a new formal structure of international relations. Territorial states would continue to organize sovereignty, but on new terms. Great Powers would continue to play the leading role in the international system, as its moral and material guardians. But all states would become accountable to a transnational community of self-sovereign citizens that would ensure world peace. States would become a new kind of agent in the international system.

The council of Great Powers had undertaken the concurrent task of writing a treaty of peace with Germany, by far the most dangerous of the Central Powers. As we will see in Chapter 2, a complicated discourse emerged of "justice" crafted by the Supreme Council and embraced in a certain manner by the Germans themselves. Here, it suffices simply to assert that the Treaty of Versailles cast Germany as a criminalized once-and-future Great Power, unsuited for an indeterminate period to participation in the international system. Whether or not one agrees with Utada Mehta or Joan Scott that liberalism actually depends on exclusion rather than simply permits it, surely liberalism in the early twentieth century accommodated exclusion comfortably.[56] Wilson owed his presidency, after all, to the Jim Crow South. In Paris, the liberal international system defined itself in part through the criminalization and exclusion of Germany and its allies.

Most notoriously, Article 231 became known as the *Kriegsschuld* or "war guilt" clause. It established the "responsibility of Germany and her allies for causing all the loss and damage" resulting from the war. As we will see, the post-Kaiserreich regime in Germany embraced Article 231 of the treaty as its centerpiece, arguably as much as the victors. In doing so, that regime began a protracted struggle that would affirm German unity against the allied "Other." Whatever else divided Germans during the entire interwar period, a shared hatred of the Treaty of Versailles united them as a national community in search of some kind of self-determination. The treaty made Germany a successor state.

[56] Utada Mehta, "Liberal Strategies of Exclusion," in Frederick Cooper and Ann Laura Stoler, eds., *Tensions of Empire: Colonial Cultures in a Bourgeois World* (Berkeley: University of California Press, 1997), 59–86; and Joan Wallach Scott, *Only Paradoxes to Offer: French Feminists and the Rights of Man* (Cambridge, MA: Harvard University Press, 1996), esp. 5–9.

The Treaty of Versailles also deprived Germany of the material attributes of a Great Power—a large army and navy, overseas colonies, even control over its own borders. It limited the German army to 100,000 men, and greatly reduced its feared navy. Germany could possess no submarines or military aircraft at all (Articles 159–213). German colonies and German extraterritorial rights, most notably in Shandong, China, were expropriated without compensation (Articles 118–58). The treaty imposed new borders—notably the return of Alsace and Lorraine to France, and the cession of parts of Prussia to Poland. Germany also lost smaller territories to Belgium and Czechoslovakia (Articles 27–30). The Saar would go into receivership under the League of Nations, its mines ceded to France as reparations (Articles 45–50). The allied occupation of the Rhineland would continue in some areas for as long as fifteen years (Articles 428–32), and the left bank of the Rhine would remain demilitarized in perpetuity (Articles 42–44). The treaty excluded Germany from the League of Nations until further notice.

Yet had Germany actually been as dangerous as wartime rhetoric had proclaimed, the peace conference might well have decided upon its dismemberment and occupation—the fate of Germany after World War II. But the peacemakers of 1919 went to considerable lengths to preserve German unity and independence, notably in opposing French efforts to detach the Rhineland. As we will see, only *in extremis* did the Great Powers agree to Marshal Foch's perilous scheme to invade and separate the south German states should a unitary Germany decline to sign the treaty. As the Poles would later point out with some bitterness, the Great Powers did not even provide for the protection of ethnic minorities in postwar Germany, the one place where the allies had some capacity to do so by force.

Whether because of their own fading military strength, a desire to maintain a bulwark against Bolshevism, or both, the allies left Germany mostly intact and mostly unoccupied. The treaty identified Germany as a Great Power, retrospectively and prospectively. Indeed, the treaty seemed to presume German "greatness" to be inevitable, precisely what made the military provisions and the Rhineland occupation necessary. Only this inevitability explains the insistence of France on separate, bilateral treaties with Britain and the United States, signed the same day as the Versailles Treaty.[57] The mere existence of such guarantees, of course, sowed doubt as to the efficacy of the League as the future guarantor of world peace. Moreover, Article 5 of the treaty with Britain stipulated: "The present treaty shall impose no obligation upon any of the Dominions of the British Empire until and unless it is approved by the Parliament of the Dominion involved." Scarcely noticed at the time, this provision established autonomy for the British Dominions in foreign affairs that would have very real consequences in the endgame of peacemaking in Anatolia.

Clemenceau's simple remark about the Treaty of Versailles spoke volumes: "It is what it is." Perhaps more disconcerting was Wilson's casual comment that he

---

[57] "Agreement between the United States and France Providing for Assistance to France in the Event of Unprovoked Aggression by Germany," and "Agreement between England and France Providing for Assistance to France in the Event of Unprovoked Aggression by Germany," *AJIL* 13, Supplement: Official Documents (1919): 411–16.

looked forward actually to reading it.[58] For all the rancor and sheer confusion that the treaty excited, the peacemakers had largely done what they had set out to do at the time of the armistice with Germany. The Covenant of the League of Nations designed a new formal international structure, based on a radically new discursive structure. The conference had also written a treaty with Germany conferring on it a specific new identity. Doing so contributed to the construction of a more generic state identity that would transform the conference itself—the successor state. New agents would ultimately create a new structure.

THE STRUCTURE CREATES AGENTS: SUCCESSOR STATES IN POST-IMPERIAL EUROPE

The last plenary meeting of the Paris Peace Conference took place on June 28, 1919, with the ceremonial signing in the Hall of Mirrors of the Treaty of Versailles. President Wilson left Paris that same day, to join what would prove the losing battle for the League of Nations in the Senate. The departure of the president began the long exit of the United States from the conference. Yet there remained a great deal of peace to make, and the conference continued as a formal structure of international relations. The discursive power of the conference remained undiminished. Up to the Treaty of Sèvres of August 1920, nothing overtly displaced Wilsonianism as the formal ideological foundation of the Paris Peace Conference. The Covenant of the League of Nations, the blueprint for the new international order, would serve as a preamble to the four remaining treaties produced by the conference.

There is in fact no clear date for the "end" of the Paris Peace Conference. Certainly after June 28, the "Paris Peace Conference" and the council of Great Powers in its various subsequent iterations became essentially the same thing. According to a plan proposed by Lloyd George in December 1919, "large questions of policy" would be handled by communications among governments, while "questions of detail," specifically carrying out the provisions of the treaties, would fall to a Council of Ambassadors operating in Paris.[59] The Supreme Council ceased meeting regularly in January 1920, about the same time as the first meeting of the League Council.[60] Ad hoc conferences, such as San Remo in April 1920 and Spa in July 1920, would revive the Supreme Council to decide basic issues such as the distribution of mandates. The Council of Ambassadors would continue to meet

---

[58] Margaret MacMillan, *Paris 1919: Six Months that Changed the World* (New York: Random House, 2001), 460.

[59] Resolution B, "Secretary's Notes of a Conference Held at 10, Downing Street, London, S.W.1, on Saturday, December 13, 1919, at 4:30 p.m.," *FRUS: PPC*, 9: 858.

[60] The exactitude of nomenclature declined beginning in the summer of 1919. Confusingly, a Council of Heads of Delegations and a Council of Foreign Ministers most of the time referred to the same officials. Occasionally, the group used the terms "Supreme Council" and the "Council of the Heads of Government." Marston marks the "end" as the Spa Conference of July 5–16, 1920, the last time "Supreme Council" was used in official records. *The Peace Conference of 1919*, 215–27.

until 1931, resolving more day-to-day issues of the treaties.[61] In this increasingly state- and empire-oriented formal structure, remnants of the Paris Peace Conference and its claimed sovereignty over the new international system would live on well into the interwar period. To the extent that the conference survived through the League of Nations, it would "end" only with the dissolution of the League in favor of the United Nations in April 1946.

In the meantime, peacemaking had to move beyond Germany. The Supreme Council had to rely increasingly on discursive power, if only because day by day it had less material power. The speed and extent of allied demobilization remains an underappreciated dimension of peacemaking after the Great War. France had mobilized over 8 million men over the course of the war, and had the most powerful army on the Western Front at the armistice of November 11, 1918. But it had demobilized nearly 5 million soldiers by September 1919.[62] As of April 1919, with none of the treaties finished, the French had some 1,170,000 men on the former Western Front, with another 1,132,000 (including colonial soldiers) in the interior and in the French territories around the world. Of these, the French had 127,000 soldiers in the Armée de l'Orient in southeastern Europe, and 25,000 in the Levant.[63] Apart from the increasingly meager yearly contingents in the metropole, reinforcements could come mostly from the French empire. Depending on colonial troops for the security of the metropole would always prove a politically fraught expedient.[64] The British army on the Western Front shrank even more dramatically, from some 3.5 million men at the armistice to some 900,000 men at the signature of the Versailles Treaty.[65] At the time of the Mudros armistice, British imperial forces in the Middle East numbered nearly 1.1 million men, many from the Army of India. By the time of the signature of the Treaty of Sèvres, they numbered only about 320,000.[66] In this context, the rapid demobilization of the American army along the former Western Front was in fact quite typical—some 3.7 million men on November 11, reduced to some 1 million men at the signature of the Versailles Treaty.[67] Military power, of course, is always relative rather than absolute. But even in the absence of state-organized resistance, allied forces could

[61] Gerhard P. Pink, *The Conference of Ambassadors (Paris, 1920–1931)* (Geneva: Geneva Research Centre, 1942). In the historiographical literature, "Conference of Ambassadors" and "Council of Ambassadors" are often used interchangeably to refer to the same body. To emphasize continuity with preceding councils, I use "Council of Ambassadors" here.

[62] Bruno Cabanes, *La Victoire endeuillée: la sortie de guerre des soldats français, 1918–1920* (Paris: Seuil, 2004), 277.

[63] Antoine Prost, *Les Anciens Combattants et la société française, 1914–1939*, 3 vols. (Paris: Presses de la fondation national des sciences politiques, 1977), 1: 49.

[64] General Jean Bernachot, *Les Armées françaises en Orient après l'Armistice de 1918*, 2 vols. (Paris: Imprimerie Nationale, 1970), esp. 2: 313–73.

[65] Stephens Richard Graubard, "Military Demobilization in Great Britain Following the First World War," *Journal of Modern History* 19.4 (1947): 304, 309.

[66] David Fromkin, *A Peace to End All Peace: The Fall of the Ottoman Empire and the Creation of the Modern Middle East* (New York: Henry Holt and Company, 1989), 404; and John Darwin, *Britain, Egypt, and the Middle East: Imperial Policy in the Aftermath of War, 1918–1922* (New York: St. Martin's Press, 1981), 172.

[67] Edward M. Coffmann, *The War to End All Wars: The American Military Experience in World War I* (Madison: University of Wisconsin Press, 1968), 357.

only occupy so much space. As we will see, paramilitary violence infested Central and Eastern Europe, further complicating efforts to settle boundaries and establish states.

These depleted and dispersed allied forces faced a vacuum of sovereignty in former multinational empires. Sovereignty in these empires had lain in monarchical states whose legitimacy depended on the imperial crowns. To topple the monarchy was to dissolve the empire—precisely what happened in the Imperial Russian, Habsburg, and Ottoman lands in 1917 and 1918. Replacing imperial authority constituted the problem of sovereignty in Central and Eastern Europe, and in the Middle East. Wilsonianism as a discursive structure had created a ready-made solution to this problem that the peacemakers would never be able fully to control: the successor state. The structure had created an agent.

The terms "national," "ethnic," and "racial" came to be used in Paris almost interchangeably. In part under pressure from the Bolsheviks in Russia, Wilson's "self-determination" morphed over the course of the conference into the far better known "national self-determination." Ultimately, the Paris Peace Conference naturalized a doctrine articulated by Stéphane Pierré-Caps as "to each nation, its state."[68] States were simply legitimized nations within demarcated boundaries. "Nation" came mostly to mean ethnicity, defined by some combination of language, culture, and religion. "National" boundaries determined who could belong to the political community under what circumstances, and were thus cultural as well as territorial. "Historic" boundaries had been territorial, and mostly dynastic in origin. "Bohemia," for example, comprised the lands of the Crown of St. Wenceslaus, "Hungary" the lands of the Crown of St. Stephen. By definition, of course, "historic" and "national" boundaries were constructed—the former by royal and imperial houses, the latter by politicians, ethnographers, linguists, and activists. As such, boundaries were subject to mutually inconsistent interpretations.

In accepting "national self-determination," the Paris Peace Conference legitimized the "successor state." This is a common term used here to mean a historically specific kind of agent. Here a "successor state," is a state structured by an impossibility—a unitary, sovereign state that combined "national" and "historic" boundaries.[69] For example, the lands and peoples of any "Poland" had been divided among Imperial Russia, Germany, and Austria-Hungary. Successor Poland could have a majority of people construed as ethnic Poles, or could reclaim territorial boundaries preceding the partitions of the eighteenth century. But by definition, and however much Polish nationalists so desired, it could not do both, at least not without a dislocation of populations on a scale not widely thinkable in 1919.

Constructing successor states over the former Hohenzollern, Habsburg, Romanov, or Osman imperial domains would thus prove a muddy, zero-sum game. Any successor state could fully realize its national and historic boundaries only at the expense of its neighbors. Some successor states, notably Czechoslovakia and the

[68] Stéphane Pierré-Caps, "Karl Renner et l'État multinational: Contribution juridique à la solution d'imbroglios politiques contemporains," *Droit et Société* 27 (1994): 423.

[69] On the wartime origins of successor state-building, see Pieter Judson, *The Habsburg Empire: A New History* (Cambridge, MA: Belknap Press of Harvard University Press, 2016), 385–441.

Kingdom of the Serbs, Croats, and Slovenes, had never existed as such prior to 1919.[70] Others, such as Germany, Greece, or Romania, had successor state identities overlaid onto existing ones. Most successor states most of the time saw "injustices" inflicted by the peace conference as existential challenges. Of course, in polyglot Central and Eastern Europe, no one could even presume to draw purely "national" boundaries without requiring the vigorous ethnic classification of peoples who had managed to live together for centuries in ethnic confusion.

The discursive construction of the successor state began during the war itself. Throughout the war, Great Powers stoked nationalist ambitions toward imperial ends. As early as August 1914, Imperial Russian Commander-in-Chief Grand Duke Nicholas appealed to the Poles of Germany and Austria to fight for a "united" Poland under the tsar.[71] This inaugurated a bidding war for a quasi-sovereign Poland integrated into one or more of the multinational empires.[72] By 1915, British colonial entrepreneurs in Egypt saw to the establishment of an Arab Bureau to foment nationalist uprisings in the Ottoman domains.[73] Émigré nationalists pressed claims for ethnic and historic boundaries in foreign capitals years before Wilson proclaimed the Fourteen Points.

As Arno Mayer argued many years ago, the competition between V.I. Lenin and Woodrow Wilson helped radicalize the identity of the successor state.[74] Through twin globalized attempts to confer meaning on the Great War, the Bolshevik and the liberal made "national self-determination" the Pandora's Box of peacemaking after the Great War. The Bolshevik Peace Decree of October 26, 1917 posited (in somewhat complicated syntax) that the world owed liberation to any nation that did not possess "the right to determine the form of its State life by voting and completely free from the presence of troops of the annexing or stronger State and without the least pressure."[75] The Bolsheviks sought to destabilize all empires, and so to pave the way for the proletarian revolution.

On national self-determination as on much else, Wilson's Fourteen Points constituted what Mayer called a "counter-manifesto" to the Bolshevik Peace Decree.[76] The Fourteen Points were less categorical, but also less internally consistent.[77] Majority German-speaking Alsace and Lorraine would revert to France (Point VIII),

[70] The term "Kingdom of Yugoslavia" dates only to 1929. However, contemporaries used "Yugoslavia" as a shorthand term, a practice I will adopt on occasion here.

[71] Robert Machray, *Poland, 1914–1931* (London: George Allen & Unwin, 1932), 51.

[72] See the decree from the German and Habsburg emperors of November 5, 1916 establishing an "autonomous" Polish state in Stanislas Filasiewicz, ed., *La Question polanaise pendant la guerre mondiale*, 2 vols. (Paris: Section d'Études et de publications politiques du comité national polonais, 1920), 2: 57–58.

[73] Aaron Kleiman, "Britain's War Aims in the Middle East in 1915," *Journal of Contemporary History* 3 (1968): 237–51; and Bruce Westrate, *The Arab Bureau: British Policy in the Middle East, 1916–1920* (State College: Penn State Press, 1992), 14–21.

[74] Arno Mayer, *Political Origins of the New Diplomacy, 1917–1918* (New Haven, CT: Yale University Press, 1959), esp. "Epilogue: Wilson vs. Lenin," 368–93.

[75] "The Declaration of Peace (November 8, 1917)," in John W. Wheeler-Bennett, *Brest-Litovsk: The Forgotten Peace, 1918* (London: Macmillan and Co., 1938), 376.

[76] Mayer, *Political Origins*, 329–67.

[77] Trygve Throntveit, "The Fable of the Fourteen Points: Woodrow Wilson and Self-Determination," *Diplomatic History* 35.3 (2011): 445–81.

as a matter of righting a historic wrong rather than self-determination. Point XIII prefigured the perils of peacemaking in Poland by calling for an "independent Polish State" that would comprise "territories inhabited by indisputably Polish populations" but with "free and secure access to the sea." Strictly speaking, Wilson's counter-manifesto never explicitly called for the breakup of either the Habsburg Monarchy or the Ottoman Empire. Rather, it evoked nebulous concepts such as the "freest opportunity of autonomous development" (Point X). Nationalists across Europe and around the world saw what they wanted to see in the Fourteen Points. The open-endedness of Wilsonianism helped legitimize the identity of the successor state.

Claims in the name of "national self-determination" rose within the Supreme Council itself. Italy, for example, claimed Fiume, a deep-water port adjacent to Habsburg Croatia on the Adriatic.[78] Part of the Venetian trading empire in the Middle Ages, Fiume and its hinterlands had belonged to the Hungarian crown since the late eighteenth century. The secret Treaty of London (April 1915) had lured Italy into the war on the allied side, though it did not promise Fiume to the Italians. Flush with victory in 1918, the Italians now sought to unite "history" and ethnicity, based on their own judgment as to just who lived in and around Fiume. Italian claims directly conflicted with those of the new Serb-Croat-Slovene State.

As we will see in Chapter 3, no one had reliable figures as to who lived in and around Fiume in 1919. Most observers assumed that the city itself had an Italian majority, the hinterlands a Slavic majority comprising mostly Slovenes and Croats. Giving the port to one state and the hinterlands to another would tear the local economy asunder. Wilson generally supported South Slav claims, and made Fiume a test case for what by then had become "national self-determination." By April 1919, conflict between Wilson and the Italians made the workings of the Supreme Council increasingly unstable by the day. Italian demands, Wilson noted, exceeded even those granted secretly in London. Italy had supposedly renounced secret agreements by endorsing the Fourteen Points. Efforts to mediate on the part of Lloyd George and Clemenceau proved fruitless.

As tempers flared by late April, Wilson impugned the motives of his Great Power ally: "Baron [Sidney] Sonnino led the Italian people into war to conquer territories. I did it by invoking the principle of justice. I believe my claim takes precedence over his."[79] Shortly thereafter, Wilson appealed directly, if quixotically, to the Italian peoples over the heads of their leaders. In protest, the Italian delegation left the conference altogether for several crucial weeks as the treaty with Germany was coming to completion. While Italy would return to the Supreme Council, the matter remained incompletely resolved long thereafter.

The Supreme Council tried to control the identity of the successor state through subsidiary treaties protecting minorities. As we will see in Chapter 5, according to

---

[78] For a succinct summary of the Fiume affair, see Frances Kellor and Antonia Hatvany, *Security against War*, 2 vols. (New York: Macmillan Company, 1924), 236–45.

[79] Meeting of the Supreme Council, April 22, 1919, quoted in H. James Burgwyn, *The Legend of the Mutilated Victory: Italy, the Great War, and the Paris Peace Conference, 1915–1919* (Westport, CT: Greenwood Press, 1993), 278.

the constitutive theory of recognition in international law, these treaties in some sense "created" the new states through public acts of making treaties. The treaties came from the Supreme Council rather than the Paris Peace Conference proper, and bound the five allied Great Powers and the new or newly expanded states in question.[80] The treaty with Poland, commonly known as the Polish Minority Treaty or the "Little Versailles" treaty, was signed the same day as its namesake.[81] As Carole Fink has shown, it would guide treaties with seven other successor states.[82] The Polish treaty illustrated the discursive power of the Supreme Council as provisional world sovereign, but by definition highlighted its material weakness. As we will see in Chapter 4, the treaty envisaged a Poland guided by civic nationalism, in which the new state would protect religious and ethnic difference within the community. Jews, notably, could become Poles and remain Jews, just as Jews had long been both American and Jewish in the United States.

The guarantor of minority protections in Poland lay beyond the national state. Article 12 of the Polish treaty stipulated that the preceding protections "constitute obligations of international concern and shall be placed under the guarantees of the League of Nations." This directly implicated the League in Polish domestic law. Nationalists throughout Central and Eastern Europe considered such provisions an affront to the very concept of state sovereignty to which "national self-determination" was supposed to give expression. Any nation not fully sovereign over domestic law could not consider itself fully independent. Though none dared say so, Wilson would never have agreed to take orders from the League of Nations about Jim Crow. Moreover, as many an enraged nationalist pointed out, the Great Powers did not require Germany to sign a minority treaty. The Polish delegates fought ferociously to weaken the treaty until the day before they signed it.[83]

The apparently arbitrary nature of peacemaking after the Treaty of Versailles spoke not to the material strength of the victors, but to their material weakness overlaid with discursive strength. The increasing gulf between discursive and material power meant that the Council would decide upon anything at all only by taking sides—among successor states it had here legitimized and there criminalized. The most important discursive power held over the successor states lay in what in a very different context Hope Olsen would call the "power to name."[84] In myriad ways, the lands and peoples of Central and Eastern Europe did not fall into self-evident categories of friend and foe. The successor state most favored by

[80] Carole Fink has argued that the Great Powers acted in their own names because the plenary would never have approved the treaties. *Defending the Rights of Others: The Great Powers, the Jews, and International Minority Protection, 1878–1938* (Cambridge: Cambridge University Press, 2004), 133–264.

[81] "Treaty of Peace between the United States of America, the British Empire, France, Italy, and Japan and Poland," *AJIL* 13, Supplement: Official Documents (1919): 423–40.

[82] Carole Fink, "The Minorities Question at the Paris Peace Conference: The Polish Minority Treaty, June 28, 1919," in Manfred Boemeke, Gerald Feldman, and Elisabeth Glaser, eds., *The Treaty of Versailles: A Reassessment after 75 Years* (Cambridge: Cambridge University Press, 1998), 249–74.

[83] "Conversation between President Wilson, MM. Clemenceau and Lloyd George, and Barons Sonnino and Makino," June 27, 1919, in Mantoux, *Deliberations*, 2: 578–82.

[84] Hope A. Olson, *The Power to Name: Locating the Limits of Subject Representation in Libraries* (Dordrecht: Kluwer Academic, 2002).

the conference, Czechoslovakia, had been entirely enemy territory during the war. Serbia had been an ally, Croatia and Slovenia enemies. Poles had fought on both sides. The Supreme Council would name some successor states as allies, such as Czechoslovakia, Poland, and the Serb-Croat-Slovene State, and its inhabitants as oppressed peoples. It would name Austria, Hungary, Bulgaria, and post-Ottoman Turkey as criminalized residuals of the defeated empires, whose peoples owed reparations to the victors.

Norman Davies used an old Polish expression "God's Playground" (*Boże igrzysko*) to describe a land "where fate has frequently played mischievous tricks."[85] The power to name could never control the dramas of interwar Poland. Those dramas helped demarcate the limits of the sovereignty of the Paris Peace Conference. Through it all, the allies had little direct military influence anywhere near Poland. At the time of the armistice with Germany, the Polish Legion, serving in France under General Józef Haller, comprised some 100,000 recruits.[86] The new regime in Poland sought to transfer those troops to Polish national territory. The quickest way to do so would have been to move them by sea through Danzig, at that time an incontestably German city. The allies hesitated to do so, as this would have required a direct occupation of the city amidst the threat of a German uprising. Not until early April 1919 did the Supreme Council work out an agreement to send Haller's troops and much-needed supplies through Germany by rail.[87] That the Council proved so unsure of its authority even in defeated Germany provided an early indication of the limits of its writ in Central and Eastern Europe.

The Supreme Council proved less and less able to support Poland materially over time. In October 1919, the Polish government sent an urgent appeal for winter clothing for no fewer than 600,000 men. Unless the Council acted immediately, the plea went, the Polish army would prove "extremely liable to become imbued with the dangerous revolutionary doctrines by which they were surrounded."[88] Italian Foreign Minister Tomaso Tittoni curtly observed at the Council meeting: "the size of the Polish army must be reduced, as there was no way to pay for it." In the end the Council decided officially to receive the report, and send it to Marshal Foch for execution. It provided no further direction as to just how he might do so.

The limits of the authority of the provisional world sovereign became all too clear by the spring of 1920, when successor Poland provoked what became an existential struggle with Bolshevik Russia. The Council could not control Poland or its war aims once the Poles briefly occupied the Ukrainian capital of Kiev.[89] As the fortunes of war turned in favor of the Bolsheviks, the British made vague

[85] See the explanation of the term in Norman Davies, *God's Playground: A History of Poland*, 2 vols. (Oxford: Oxford University Press, 2005 [originally published in 1982]), 1: xv–xvi.

[86] Davies, *God's Playground*, 2: 287.

[87] Piotr S. Wandycz, *France and Her Eastern Allies, 1919–1925: French-Czechoslovak-Polish Relations from the Paris Peace Conference to Locarno* (Minneapolis, MN: University of Minnesota Press, 1962), 32–34.

[88] "Notes of a Meeting of the Heads of Delegations of the Five Great Powers Held in M. Pichon's Room at the Quai d'Orsay, Paris, on Monday, October 20, 1919, at 10:30 AM," *FRUS: PPC*, 8: 711.

[89] Wandycz, *France and Her Eastern Allies*, 144–45; Davies, *God's Playground*, 2: 292–94; and Norman Davies, *White Eagle, Red Star: The Polish-Soviet War, 1919–1920* (London: Orbis Books, 1983).

threats to intervene should the Red Army take Warsaw. But it remains difficult to see just what the British could have done about it.[90] Most scholars dismiss the mythology that French General Maxime Weygand, then adviser to the Polish army, had been the chief architect of the victory that stopped the Red Army at the Battle of Warsaw on August 16, 1920.[91] Successor Poland could not reverse the Bolshevik Revolution, and the Bolsheviks could not, or did not immediately want to, restore Poland to Russian rule. The Treaty of Riga of 1921 was a bilateral agreement between Polish and Bolshevik Russian successor states, not a product of the Paris Peace Conference.[92]

As we will see in Chapter 2, the Supreme Council developed a template for a defeated and criminalized Great Power for the German treaty—for better or worse the paramount exercise of its power to name. As peacemaking moved east, the Council continued to apply that template, even though neither Bulgaria, nor Austria, nor Hungary, nor Turkey was likely to emerge as a Great Power in the post-war world. The Treaty of Neuilly, signed with Bulgaria in November 1919, created a defeated successor state over whom the victors had or desired little actual control.[93] The treaty affirmed the critical loss of Western Thrace, and thus direct access to the Aegean coast, as well as smaller territorial losses to the South Slav state. The reparations provisions based themselves on guilt by association. Article 121 stipulated that "by joining in the war of aggression," with Germany and Austria-Hungary, Bulgaria had caused the Allies "losses and sacrifices of all kinds, for which she ought to make complete reparation." In principle, the treaty obligated Bulgaria to pay 2.25 billion gold francs in reparations. Indeed, the entire reparations regime (Articles 121–30) in its detail and its absurdity, given the remoteness and penury of Bulgaria, emphasized the pro forma character of the arrangements.[94] We will examine in Chapter 4 a convention appended to the treaty providing for a "voluntary" exchange of populations between Greece and Bulgaria.

A.J.P. Taylor, simplistically but not altogether inaccurately, described successor Austria and Hungary as having "paid a penalty for retaining their former imperial names."[95] Neither successor state much resembled its namesake half of the Habsburg Monarchy. Opinions differed as to just how to categorize the various former Habsburg heartland. At a meeting of the Supreme Council on May 26, 1919, James Headlam-Morely of the British delegation posited: "The present

[90] Norman Davies, "Lloyd George and Poland, 1919–1920," *Journal of Contemporary History* 6.3 (1971): 154.

[91] M.B. Biskupski, "Paderewski, Polish Politics, and the Battle of Warsaw, 1920," *Slavic Review* 46.3–4 (1987): 503–12; and Pytor Wandycz, "General Weygand and the Battle of Warsaw of 1920," *Journal of Central European Affairs* 19.4 (1960): 357–65.

[92] Stanislaw Dubrowski, "The Peace Treaty of Riga," *The Polish Review* 5.1 (1960): 3–34; and Jerzy Borzecki, *The Soviet-Polish Peace of 1921 and the Creation of Interwar Europe* (New Haven, CT: Yale University Press, 2008).

[93] R.J. Crampton, *A Concise History of Bulgaria* (Cambridge: Cambridge University Press, 2005), 137–45.

[94] Article 127, for example, required among other things the delivery to Greece of 15 bulls (age 18 months–3 years), 60 to Romania, and 50 to the Serb-Croat-Slovene State.

[95] A.J.P. Taylor, *The First World War: An Illustrated History* (London: Hamish Hamilton, 1963), 190.

Austria is only a part of the former empire; she isn't the former empire diminished."[96] If Austria was an entirely new state, there was no justification for criminalizing it. If Austria was not a new state, exactly what was it? "Self-determination" complicated the matter yet further. Many in Paris and beyond held to the common if not wholly accurate assumption that most inhabitants of the Austrian crownlands wanted unification (*Anschluss*) with Germany.[97] But Germany could hardly emerge from defeat augmented in territory and population.

Clemenceau's famous quip: "*l'Autriche, c'est ce qui reste* [Austria, that's what's left over]" illustrated the discursive power of the Supreme Council to name in this much-reduced corner of Europe. But here, the Council would temper "justice" with mercy. The Treaty of Saint-Germain, signed on September 10, 1919, rendered Austria a criminalized residual. As per Article 177, the new Austrian Republic accepted responsibility "for causing the loss and damage to which the Allied and Associated Governments and their nationals have been subjected as a consequence of the war...." The treaty created an elaborate reparations regime, about as unrealistic as that in the Treaty of Neuilly. Article 88 of the Austrian treaty explicitly prohibited *Anschluss* with Germany. Yet as early as July 1919, the Supreme Council indicated that Austria might be accorded early admission to the League of Nations.[98] This served the purpose of according "Germans" a form of international status distinct from Germany. Recognizing an independent Austria through the League also created in a mild way a decriminalized and materially weak "German" state, as a foil to the criminalized, once-and-future German Great Power.

Successor Hungary, neither more nor less responsible for the war than successor Austria, proved much more problematic for all concerned parties. Habsburg Hungary had been its own multinational kingdom as the lands of the Crown of St. Stephen. These lands included Slovakia, Croatia-Slavonia, and Transylvania. Before 1945, no Hungarian nationalist leader, Left, Center, or Right, would willingly accept boundaries short of those of "historic" Hungary. According to the 1910 census, the last taken before the war and widely distrusted by non-Magyars, fewer than half of the inhabitants of historic Hungary counted themselves Magyar.[99] The National Council of Hungary signed its own armistice with French and Serbian commanders in Belgrade on November 13, distinct from the

---

[96] "Conversation between President Wilson and MM. Clemenceau, Lloyd George, and Orlando," May 26, 1919, Mantoux, *Deliberations*, 2: 214–17.

[97] On Austrian ambivalence, see Karl R. Stadler, *The Birth of the Austrian Republic, 1918–1921* (Leyden: A.W. Sijthoff, 1966), 62–70. On allied views, see Alfred D. Low, *The Anschluss Movement (1918–1919) and the Paris Peace Conference* (Philadelphia, PA: American Philosophical Society, 1974), 229–332.

[98] "Reply of the Allied Powers to the Austrian Note on the League of Nations," July 8, 1919, in *The Treaty of St. Germain: A Documentary History of Its Territorial and Political Clauses*, Nina Almond and Ralph Haswell Lutz, eds. (Stanford, CA: Stanford University Press, Hoover War Library Publications No. 5, 1935), 269–70. Hereafter referred to as *Treaty of Saint-Germain*. Austria would join the League in December 1920, in the first extension of membership beyond the original signatories to the Covenant.

[99] In 1910, 48.1% of people in all the Hungarian lands designated themselves as Magyar, 54.5% excluding semi-autonomous Croatia-Slavonia. Calculated from *A magyar szent korona országainak 1910. évi népszámlálása. Első rész. A népesség főbb adatai* (Budapest: Magyar Kir. Központi Statisztikai Hivatal [KSH], 1912).

Villa Giusti (or Padua) armistice signed with "Austria-Hungary" on November 3.[100] This armistice gave the allies the rights to occupy strategic points in Hungary of their choosing (Article 3). Yet Article 17 stipulated: "The Allies shall not interfere with the internal administration of affairs in Hungary." Pending a final peace settlement, any government operating out of Budapest would take "Hungary" to include Slovakia and Transylvania, which remained under Magyar administration.[101] Successor Czechoslovakia and successor Romania would take the armistice to mean something else altogether.

The emergence of no fewer than three mutually antagonistic regimes in Hungary before the signing of the Treaty of Trianon made it a more than usually unstable successor state. Little joined these regimes except the imperative of creating an ethno-national state within the boundaries of historic Hungary. All three regimes faced severe economic dislocation, Magyar refugees from lands occupied by other successor states, and paramilitary violence.[102] In just over a year and a half, successor Hungary would try left-leaning liberal democracy under Count Mihály Károlyi (November 1918–March 1919), a Soviet regime under Béla Kun (March–July 1919), and a counter-revolutionary regency under a former Habsburg admiral, Miklós Horthy (c. November 1919–c.1944). The Horthy regime provided enough stability for Hungary to sign the Treaty of Trianon on June 4, 1920. This treaty applied the template of the criminalized residual state developed in the Austrian and Bulgarian treaties. Horthy himself became regent for a vacant throne, still imagined as uniting all the lands of the crown of St. Stephen.

Having legitimized the identity of the successor state in the cases of Czechoslovakia and Poland, among others, the Supreme Council found it could not deny that identity to Hungary simply through writing a treaty that created it as a criminalized residual. The Supreme Council fretted throughout about its inability to decide anything in Hungary by military force. On July 5, 1919, Clemenceau derided Marshal Foch's scheme for an inter-allied crusade against the Kun regime as "a plan more ambitious than that of Napoleon's march on Moscow."[103] But the alternative amounted to isolating the Béla Kun regime, in the hope that it would eventually collapse of its internal contradictions. "This might be inglorious," Clemenceau concluded wistfully on July 26, "but there was little glory in fighting without men, or in making threats that could not be carried out."[104]

[100] Bogdan Krizman, "The Belgrade Armistice of 13 November 1918," *Slavonic and East European Review* 48, No. 110 (1970): 67–87.

[101] Croatia-Slavonia had enjoyed some autonomy under the Kingdom of Hungary, and its separation caused relatively little conflict.

[102] Bela Bodo, "Paramilitary Violence in Hungary after the First World War," *East European Quarterly* 38.2 (2004): 129–72. A thoughtful if partisan account of the vicissitudes of Hungarian politics in this period remains Oscar Jászi, *Revolution and Counter-Revolution in Hungary* (London: P.S. King, 1924 [originally published in German in 1924]). Jászi had been minister for minorities under the Károlyi regime.

[103] "Notes of a Meeting of the Heads of Delegations of the Five Powers Held in M. Pichon's Room at the Quai d'Orsay, Paris, on Saturday, July 5, 1919, at 3 p.m.," *FRUS: PPC*, 7: 25.

[104] "Notes of a Meeting of the Heads of Delegations of the Five Great Powers Held in M. Pichon's Room at the Quai d'Orsay, Paris, on Saturday, July 26, 1919, at 3:30 p.m.," *FRUS: PPC*, 7: 319.

As we will see in Chapter 5, the Supreme Council was reduced to playing a game of recognition among competing successor states that probably delayed the making of peace. The conflict between successor Hungary and successor Romania showed that the Supreme Council could not control the successor state identities it had legitimized. "Victorious" Romania proved more difficult for the Council to contain than "defeated" Hungary. The Supreme Council ratified decisions effectively made elsewhere.

While the very name "Romania" suggests Roman ancestry, a fully sovereign, modern Romania distinct from the Ottoman Empire dated only from the Treaty of Berlin of 1878.[105] "Romanians" before 1918 comprised an array of peoples. In addition to the Romanian-speaking majority, these peoples included Jews, Romani (Roma speakers), Bulgarians, Magyars, Armenians, and many others. The central, but by no means the only, historic and ethnic territorial claim of Romania lay in Transylvania, held to have been unjustly seized by the Hungarian crown at various disputed dates in the Middle Ages, "returned" with the Ottoman advance of the sixteenth century, then seized again late in the seventeenth century, as the Habsburgs as kings of Hungary wrested Transylvania from the Ottoman Empire.

In August 1916, the allies coaxed Romania into the war through the secret treaty of Bucharest.[106] This treaty promised Transylvania, the Banat, and Bukovina in the event of an allied victory.[107] However, Romania's military position gradually became untenable after the victory of the Central Powers on the Eastern Front in 1917. The May 1918 Treaty of Bucharest with Germany and Austria-Hungary took Romania out of the war until November 10, 1918, when it reclaimed its allegiance to the allied cause and rejoined the war. The British delegation, for one, asked whether Romania's departure from the war through the 1918 Treaty of Bucharest with the Central Powers further called into serious question the legitimacy of the earlier treaty, a question deepened by Wilson's distrust of secret diplomacy.[108]

But in word and deed, Romania never considered itself bound by the hierarchy of states established by the conference. The Romanians reminded their once and present allies of Article VI of the 1916 Treaty of Bucharest, which declared that Romania "shall enjoy the same rights as the Allies in all that concerns the preliminaries of the peace negotiations, as well as the discussions of the questions which will be submitted to the decisions of the Peace Conference." At his first meeting with the Supreme Council on February 1, 1919, Ion I. C. Brătianu, head of the Romanian delegation, claimed: "Neither legally, practically, nor morally, were the Roumanians ever really at peace with the enemy."[109] Like every other successor

---

[105] Keith Hitchins, *A Concise History of Romania* (Cambridge: Cambridge University Press, 2014); and his *Ion I.C. Brătianu: Romania* (London: Haus Publications, 2011).

[106] Sherman David Spector, *Rumania at the Paris Peace Conference: A Study of the Diplomacy of Ioan I.C. Bratianu* (New York: Bookman Associates, 1962).

[107] For the English text, see Charles Upson Clark, *Greater Roumania* (New York: Dodd, Mean and Company, 1922), 171–77.

[108] "Secretary's Notes of a Conversation Held in M. Pichon's Room at the Quai d'Orsay on Sunday, January 12, at 4 p.m.," *FRUS: PPC*, 3: 486.

[109] "Secretary's Notes of a Conversation Held in M. Pichon's Room at the Quai d'Orsay, Paris, on Saturday, February 1, 1919, at 3 p.m.," *FRUS: PPC*, 3: 844.

state, Romania evoked its own understanding of Wilsonianism. In the 1916 agreement, "the Allies undertook to ensure the national unity of Romania." His nation claimed Transylvania, the Banat, Bukovina, and Bessarabia simply to become whole:

> The claims of Roumania, as recognized by her [1916] treaty of alliance had never been of an imperialistic character. Her claims had only represented the manifestation of the national aspirations of the people and the desire of the Roumanians to be once more united on the ethnical territory assigned to them by history.[110]

Unlike most successor states, Romania also had a viable military, and had not even nominally recognized the authority of allied commander-in-chief Marshal Foch. As we will see in Chapter 5, Romania in the second half of 1919 would invade and occupy not just Transylvania, but much of residual Hungary including Budapest. The discursive weapon of recognition became the only weapon the Supreme Council could use to restrain successor Romania.

With the signing of the Treaty of Trianon with Hungary in June 1920, the juridical work of the Paris Peace Conference in making peace in Central and Eastern Europe came to an end. Employing Wilsonianism as discursive power served to expose its internal contradictions. Having legitimized the successor state as a particular kind of agent, the conference as a formal structure could never wholly control the many manifestations of that identity. Military force could be useful only at the margins, and was fraught with risks even then. East of Germany, war had continued beyond the practical control of the conference. At times with the cooperation of the conference and at times despite it, the successor states themselves built the new international system in the region, as they all sought to realize the impossible concurrence of ethnic and historic boundaries.

AGENTS, STRUCTURES, AND EMPIRES

In Europe, empires were sites over which peace was made. Beyond Europe, empires were the agents making peace. As an agent in the international system, what is an empire? According to Jane Burbank's and Frederick Cooper's definition: "Empires are large political units, expansionist or with a memory of power extended over space, polities that maintain distinction and hierarchy as they incorporate new people."[111] They are thus the opposite of the principle of one nation, one state. Empires as agents hierarchically and permanently structure difference. They are thus in a sense both agents and structures. The permanent nature of difference helps distinguish empires from nation-states, even expansionist ones.[112] For example, "British India" would always remain "British India," never becoming a part of the

---

[110] "Secretary's Notes," February 1, 1919, *FRUS: PPC*, 8: 845.

[111] Jane Burbank and Frederick Cooper, *Empires in World History: Power and the Politics of Difference* (Princeton, NJ: Princeton University Press, 2010), 8.

[112] Krishan Kumar, "Nation-states as Empires, Empires as Nation-States: Two Principles, One Practice?," *Theory and Society* 39.2 (2010): 119–43.

United Kingdom. Even in assimilationist and republican France, the colonial doctrine of "association" would recognize difference as forever. The permanence of difference has also given empires considerable flexibility and durability over time. As Burbank and Cooper have noted, empires have a much longer history than the territorial nation-state, largely a creation of Europe in the nineteenth century.

Each empire in the Great War combined lands and contracts in a unique way.[113] Some empires meant little beyond the dynasties that ruled them. Imperial Russia, the Habsburg Monarchy, and the Ottoman Empire collapsed with the deposition (or in the case of the Osmans, the de facto incarceration) of their imperial houses. "Blue water" empires with vast overseas possessions were likewise diverse composites. The British Empire, the world's largest empire in 1919, existed as such through a variety of personal political links to the British crown. Strictly speaking, the only "imperial" title held by George V was Emperor of India. As we will see, the self-governing Dominions could pull in separate ways at a highly problematic moment for the metropole.

Just what held the French Empire together beyond the aspirational slogan "*mission civilisatrice*" and Great Power competition never seemed altogether clear.[114] Just what the colonies of France contributed by way of profit or security remained a matter of contention. The Japanese Empire, ostensibly dynastic, expanded across water and land, with generally more assimilationist aims than its European counterparts. The United States, originally a collection of British colonies, held an official disdain for formal empire. Yet in 1919 it exercised sovereignty over lands as diverse as Alaska, Hawaii, Puerto Rico, the Panama Canal Zone, and the Philippines, to say nothing of powerful influence over nominally independent states such as Cuba, Haiti, Honduras, and Mexico.

As agents, empires constitute a specific case in the long tradition in realist IR of treating states as individuated persons.[115] Empires are emotive and perpetually discontented entities. They crave unconquered territories, and covet domains of rival empires. Above all, like states, they fear for security. An empire can feel safe only by making its rivals less safe. Moreover, structural stresses on empires give them a life cycle. States can reincarnate while preserving some continuity of identity. "France" has remained "France" through a monarchy, two empires, and five republics. Empires, on the other hand, are born, grow strong, overextend, age, weaken, and ultimately die. From this point of view, the Great War accelerated the aging process of the European empires. Some died as a result, others aged prematurely.

As with states, realism describes accurately enough the empires that fought the Great War. During the war as well as prior to it, empires competed and bargained in order to enhance their security, directly or indirectly. Japan, for example, took

[113] Robert Gerwarth and Erez Manela, eds., *Empires at War, 1911–1923* (Oxford: Oxford University Press, 2014). This section draws from my contribution, "Empires at the Paris Peace Conference," 254–76.

[114] Alice L. Conklin, *A Mission to Civilize: The Republican Idea of Empire in France and West Africa, 1895–1930* (Stanford, CA: Stanford University Press, 1997).

[115] Alexander Wendt, "The State as Person in International Theory," *Review of International Studies* 30.2 (2004): 289–316.

advantage of instability in Europe to extend its interest in China.[116] The Japanese presented the Twenty-One Demands to a nominally independent China in January 1915. These demands included Chinese consent to the Japanese seizure of the valuable German concessions in Shandong province, taken in November 1914 by Japan in its only significant military engagement in the Great War. The demands also included expanded leasehold and extraterritorial rights along the South Manchurian Railway.[117] The status of these arrangements would become a major source of conflict at the Paris Peace Conference. Chinese delegates argued for "self-determination," while Japanese delegates argued for the same kind of asymmetrical contracting underpinning imperial expansion in China that Europeans had practiced for many decades.

During the war, the European allies had also made an array of imperial agreements among themselves. The Treaty of London (April 1915) with Italy had promised territories that blended national and imperial expansion, in German-speaking Tyrol and particularly along the Adriatic.[118] The Sykes–Picot Agreement of May 1916 divided much of the Arab domains of the Ottoman Empire between the British and the French. The St. Jean de Maurienne Agreement of April 1917 brought the Italians into these arrangements.[119]

Imperial contracting had always been diverse. In the Middle East, wartime arrangements little noted at the time would have implications later. Within the demarcated areas of the Sykes–Picot Agreement, the British and the French agreed "to recognize and protect an independent Arab state or confederation of Arab states." This "independence" would remain subject to traditional forms of indirect rule, such as European loans and exclusive rights to "supply advisers and foreign functionaries." But the insistence so early on the term "independent" would have implications for the classification of the Middle East mandates.

No example of wartime imperial contracting would have more implications than the Balfour Declaration of November 1917. In a personal letter to the Second Baron Rothschild for distribution to British Zionists, Foreign Secretary Arthur James Balfour promised, rather vaguely: "His Majesty's Government view with favor the establishment in Palestine of a national home for the Jewish people," subject to protection of the "civil and religious rights" of existing non-Jewish communities.[120] Such a homeland could hardly be established without interjecting the transnational politics of European Jews into the region, or without the expansion of European power. Of course, "self-determination" could easily be grafted on to this mix, on the part of both Jews and Arabs, thereby setting the stage for decades of conflict.

[116] Xu Guoqi, *Asia and the Great War: A Shared History* (New York: Oxford University Press, 2016), 38–58.

[117] Xu Guoqi, *China and the Great War: China's Pursuit of a New National Identity and Internationalization* (Cambridge: Cambridge University Press, 2005), 93–98; and Dickinson, *War and National Reinvention*, 85–92.

[118] See the map in René Albrecht-Carrié, *Italy at the Paris Peace Conference* (New York: Columbia University Press, 1938), 23. The text of the accord appears on pages 334–38.

[119] On the Sykes–Picot Agreement, see Fromkin, *Peace to End All Peace*, 188–99. The text of the St. Jean de Maurienne Agreement appears in Albrecht-Carrié, *Italy at the Paris Peace Conference*, 345–46.

[120] Jonathan Schneer, *The Balfour Declaration: The Origins of the Arab-Israeli Conflict* (New York: Random House, 2010).

The historiography of the Mandate System has tended to emphasize continuities with European imperial rule. As Susan Pedersen put it, the mandates "began as a project of imperial reconciliation and legitimization."[121] As such, it contributed to what she called the "crisis of empire." As administered, the Mandate System produced colonies under another name, and contributed to the injustice, overextension, and ultimate decline of European imperial rule. At a practical level, neither the conference nor the League sought to abolish empire, any more than they sought to abolish the nation-state. While this position dismayed anti-colonialists everywhere, it should not have surprised them.

The Fourteen Points had said little about empire, apart from a less than lucid claim in Point V that in all questions of sovereignty concerning colonial claims "the interests of the populations concerned must have equal weight with the equitable claims of the government whose title is to be determined." The Mandate System outlined in Article 22 of the Covenant of the League of Nations referred only to the former German and Ottoman imperial domains, not to those of any of the victorious empires. Nor did the Mandate System apply to any lands and peoples in Europe formerly under imperial rule. White Europeans, by definition, merited self-determination right away.[122] Nevertheless, the subtle but profound discursive challenge Wilsonianism posed to empire would gradually become clear.

Mandates constituted a particular species of imperial contracting that would challenge the practice of imperial contracting itself. Pilfering a phrase originally made by Edmund Burke, the Covenant referred to the mandates as a "sacred trust of civilization."[123] Just where sovereignty lay in the mandates would never be wholly clear, though presumably it would ultimately lie with the peoples living there.[124] The Covenant established the former domains of Germany and Ottoman Turkey as lands "inhabited by peoples not yet able to stand by themselves under the strenuous conditions of the modern world." The very term "not yet able" indicated that with time these peoples held intrinsically not just the ability but also the right to stand by themselves. In the meantime, sovereignty over them was to be administrated, but not actually held, by the mandatory powers. These powers, in turn, became accountable to the League. Mandatory rule had within it a presumption of independence and thus an implicit expiration date.

As we will see, the classification system of mandates had little to do with actual peoples. At Wilson's insistence, no territories would be ceded as colonial annexations, and the Mandate Principle would apply throughout the former German and Ottoman lands. Classification emerged as a compromise between advocates of annexation and advocates of the Mandate Principle. Article 22 of the Covenant stipulated that "certain communities formerly belonging to the Turkish Empire," were held "to have reached a stage of development where their

---

[121] Susan Pedersen, *The Guardians: The League of Nations and the Crisis of Empire* (Oxford: Oxford University Press, 2015), 403.

[122] Only former Boer commander General Jan Smuts of South Africa had even dared suggest that Europeans could benefit from mandatory administration. See his *The League of Nations: A Practical Suggestion* (London: Hodder and Stoughton, 1918), 11–12.

[123] Burke had coined the phrase in a speech on an East India bill on December 1, 1793.

[124] Quincy Wright, "Sovereignty of the Mandates," *AJIL* 17.4 (1923): 691–703.

existence as independent nations can be provisionally recognized." Mandatory rule in what would become Class-A mandates was supposed to be practical and short. Other lands and people, notably "those of Central Africa, are at such a stage that the Mandatory must be responsible for the administration of the territory under conditions which will guarantee freedom of conscience and religion." The mandatory power would be responsible for prohibiting the slave trade, traffic in arms and liquor, and the militarization of the territories in question. Independence in these Class-B mandates would occur at some indefinite point in the future. Still other territories, notably the former German South West Africa, and the South Pacific islands formerly occupied by Germany, became Class-C mandates. These would most closely resemble colonies of old, "best administered under the laws of the Mandatory as integral portions of its territory."

But whatever its caprices, the Mandate System as written posed uncomfortable questions about empire all over the world. The acceptance of the Empire of Japan into the inner circle of the Great Powers, which pre-dated the Great War, had already shown that empires did not need to be "white." Mandates further undermined European and American racial assumptions underpinning empire. What made some peoples eligible for independence sooner rather than later, and commensurate peoples ruled by the allied powers eligible for independence never? Empires simply did not make sense in the same way as agents after the establishment of the Mandate System. Imperial sovereignty became a specific case of what Stephen Krasner called "organized hypocrisy."[125] In accepting the Mandate System, imperial agents accepted a discursive structure that undermined their own legitimacy.

As much as the Mandate System, the disposition of the former German concessions in Shandong showed how difficult it would be to incorporate empire into a Wilsonian international system. As Fiume was to the victorious successor state, Shandong was to the victorious empire—a site at which realist Great Power politics and Wilsonianism proved irreconcilable. All the protagonists—Japan, China, and the other Allied and Associated Powers—agreed that Shandong was "China," meaning Chinese national territory. For that reason, Shandong was never a territorial issue per se.[126] The issue, rather, was the status of the German concessions. A modified version of the Twenty-One Demands became formal treaties between China and Japan in May 1915 and September 1918. Under these agreements, Japan inherited "all rights, interests and concessions, which Germany, by virtue of treaties or otherwise, possesses in relation to the province of Shantung."[127] Moreover, Britain and France endorsed Japan taking over German concession rights in Shandong in an exchange of notes in February and March 1917.

[125] Stephen Krasner, *Sovereignty: Organized Hypocrisy* (Princeton, NJ: Princeton University Press, 1999).

[126] Amos S. Hershey, "The Shantung Cession," *AJIL* 13.3 (1919): 530–36; and Charles Burke Elliott, "The Shantung Question," *AJIL* 13.4 (1919): 687–737.

[127] Document No. 1, "Japan's Twenty-One Demands," in *The Shantung Question: A Statement of China's Claim together with Important Documents Submitted to the Peace Conference in Paris* (San Francisco, CA: Chinese National Welfare Society in America, 1919), 33.

The Chinese delegation, led by Wellington Koo, argued that the German concessions expired with the Kaiserreich.[128] Further, any wartime agreement between Japan and China on Shandong had been coerced, and thus had no validity. Moreover, the Chinese Republic had declared war on Germany and Austria-Hungary in 1917, and Chinese labor, particularly in France, had contributed substantially to the allied war effort.[129] China as victor and China as self-determined republic could not countenance the transfer of illegitimate German concession rights to Japan.

Throughout the peace conference, the Japanese delegation would insist that its understandings with China constituted binding agreements between fully sovereign states. China had signed these agreements of its own free will, and its colleagues at the conference had no business interfering. As Viscount Chinda Sutemi put it:

> The question is simple: a definite agreement exists between China and Japan; so there is no cause for a long discussion, and we cannot be convinced that a dilatory solution can be of any advantage at all.[130]

If China were sovereign, the agreements it signed had the same force as other agreements. If China were not sovereign, how could any other imperial concessions, likewise signed with a supposedly sovereign "China," have any legal standing? How could the allies denounce the wartime agreements between Japan and China, and stand by their own?

Shandong as an example of "organized hypocrisy" put national self-determination and the sanctity of treaties on a collision course. The preamble of the Covenant of the League of Nations itself had declared "a scrupulous respect for all treaty obligations in the dealings of organized peoples" as an essential condition for "international peace and security." In the end, Wilson, the self-proclaimed scourge of secret diplomacy, felt compelled to assure the Japanese: "I respect all international agreements, even when I should prefer that they had not been signed, and that I am not at all proposing to hold them null and void."[131] Article 156 of the Treaty of Versailles accorded Japan the German concessions in their entirety, without an expiration date.[132] The discursive structure of Wilsonianism proved circumscribed by Great Power imperial interests.

AGENTS, STRUCTURES, AND EMPIRES IN THE MIDDLE EAST AND ANATOLIA

As peacemaking turned to the former Ottoman lands, the Supreme Council morphed into a conference of European empires. These empires largely sought to

---

[128] Xu, *China and the Great War*, 258–70.

[129] Xu Guoqi, *Strangers on the Western Front: Chinese Workers in the Great War* (Cambridge, MA: Harvard University Press, 2011).

[130] "Conversation between President Wilson and MM. Clemenceau and Lloyd George," April 22, 1919, 11 AM, Mantoux, *Deliberations*, 1: 322.

[131] "Conversation," April 22, 1919, 11 a.m., Mantoux, *Deliberations*, 1: 323.

[132] After the Washington Naval Conference of 1921–22, Japan returned formal sovereignty over Shandong to China, where chronic instability facilitated Japanese expansion in the 1930s.

operate as realist states writ large, adjudicating imperial claims through assigning League of Nations Mandates. Yet Wilsonianism would remain lurking in the background, as it would in the image from *Tōkyō Puck*. "National self-determination," and in the case of post-Ottoman Turkey, the identity of the successor state, had spread to the Middle East and Anatolia. The results would demarcate the limits of empire in the region, and in the case of the British, interrogate the identity of empire itself.

Britain and France had complicated their own imperial claims by formally and publicly endorsing a Wilsonian peace in the Middle East. The Anglo-French Declaration of November 7, 1918 captured the millenarian fervor that infused the last weeks of the Great War:

> The goal envisaged by France and Great Britain in prosecuting in the East the war let loose by German ambition is the complete and final liberation of the peoples who have for so long been oppressed by the Turks, and the setting up of national governments and administrations deriving their authority from the free exercise of the initiative and choice of the indigenous populations.

Woodrow Wilson himself could not have put the matter more forcefully. Like most of the Fourteen Points, and the Balfour Declaration, the Anglo-French Declaration avoided an explicit promise of full state sovereignty. But in effect, these two imperial great powers had endorsed the formation of successor states-in-the-making. How then to reconcile the very public statement of the Anglo-French Declaration and the wartime agreements—notably the Sykes–Picot Agreement of May 1916 and the agreement of St. Jean de Maurienne of August 1917, which partitioned parts of Anatolia and much of the Arabic-speaking Ottoman domains among France, Britain, and Italy?

In the Arabic-speaking lands, the British and French sought to square the circle of Wilsonianism and wartime agreements through supporting powerful local notables, who could facilitate the transition from Ottoman to European rule. In the Arabian Peninsula, the British had been subsidizing two rival families, that of the Hashemite Emir of Mecca (Hussein) and the House of Saud.[133] As the fortunes of the former came to wane in the peninsula in favor of the latter in the spring of 1919, the attention of the British turned to redeploying the Hashemites in the Levant. But enthroning Hussein's son Faisal in Syria potentially conflicted with French claims. Faisal had spent months in Paris pleading the Arab cause. He came to an arrangement with Clemenceau in April 1919, according to which Faisal would rule a nominally independent Syria (including Lebanon) under a loose French mandate.[134] The British decided to accept these arrangements, provided the French endorsed a British mandate in Palestine that would help fulfill the Balfour Declaration. But it soon became clear that matters were not wholly under the control of the French, the British, or even Faisal.

---

[133] Hussein at one point complained that he had to spend half of his £12,000 per month subsidy fending off attacks from Saudi forces. Fromkin, *Peace to End All Peace*, 424.

[134] Meir Zamir, "Faisal and the Lebanese Question, 1918–1920," *Middle Eastern Studies* 27.3 (1991): 409–10.

Nationalists in the Middle East, as elsewhere, took the Wilsonian discursive structure of international relations seriously.[135] A Syrian National Congress called by Faisal in June 1919 sought to create a unitary, self-determining "Greater Syria," encompassing present-day Syria, Lebanon, Jordan, Palestine, and Israel.[136] But Faisal could not control the Congress he himself had supported.[137] In March 1920, the Congress declared Syrian independence with Faisal as king. This put Faisal in an untenable position. He could antagonize either his European patrons or his independence-minded Syrian "subjects." Most pan-Arab nationalists proved willing to overlook the fact that Faisal was a native of Mecca, not Syria. But majority decisions in the Congress rested on a complicated and fragile coalition.

The imperial powers continued to undermine the Anglo-French Declaration by implementing their own plans through the evolving Mandate System. At the Conference of San Remo of April 1920, the allies agreed on a French mandate in Syria (including Lebanon) and a British mandate in Palestine and Trans-Jordan. In July 1920, the French Armée du Levant occupied Damascus, closed down the Syrian National Congress, and forced Faisal into exile.[138] But the matter could hardly end there. Pandora's Box of self-determination in the French mandates would not close throughout the turbulent and often violent mandate period.

The disposition of former Ottoman Mesopotamia showed the outer limits of British and French efforts to merge imperial acquisition with Wilsonianism, geographically as well as discursively. "Mesopotamia" comes from ancient Greek, meaning "the land between rivers," specifically the Tigris and the Euphrates. The Arabic term "Iraq" means simply "fertile" or "deep-rooted" land. Diverse people have always inhabited Mesopotamia. Alongside Sunni and Shia Arabs (each group divided along many tribal lines) lived a large Kurdish population interested in self-determination. Exactly how "Mesopotamia" or "Iraq" would self-determine remains an unresolved question today.

Susan Pedersen has argued that the British first pursued a mandate in Mesopotamia and in 1931 granted "Iraq" a dependent form of "independence" for largely the same reasons—access to oil and a cost-effective, expanded zone of influence protecting the route of passage through the Suez Canal to India.[139] The Government of India and the India Office lobbied relentlessly to expand empire in the Middle East. The issue became doing so in an increasingly austere budgetary climate. The cost of maintaining some 100,000 troops in the region gave rise to ferocious debates, both within Westminster and between Westminster and the

[135] Elizabeth Thompson, *Justice Interrupted: The Struggle for Constitutional Government in the Middle East* (Cambridge, MA: Harvard University Press, 2013).

[136] Moshe Ma'oz, "Attempts at Creating a Political Community in Modern Syria," *Middle East Journal* 26.4 (1972): 389–404.

[137] On Faisal and the Syrian National Congress of 1920, see the somewhat adoring biography, Ali A. Allawi, *Faisal I of Iraq* (New Haven, CT: Yale University Press, 2014), 271–75.

[138] Dan Eldar, "France in Syria: The Abolition of the Sharifian Government, April–July 1920," *Middle Eastern Studies* 29.3 (1993): 487–504.

[139] Susan Pedersen, "Getting out of Iraq—in 1932: The League of Nations and the Road to Normative Statehood," *American Historical Review* 115.4 (2010): 975–1000.

Government of India.[140] In the end, the political solution involved setting the then-unemployed Faisal on an Iraqi throne under a British mandate. The British and the French came to an understanding about the oil in the Mosul region.[141] Like the French in Syria, the British in Iraq would rely on a brutal but frugal policy of terrorizing the population through the latest military technology, notably airplanes, tanks, and armored vehicles.[142] In quasi-independent Iraq, as in Syria, terror proved a tactic of the weak, and in its way showed the lack of effective imperial control.[143]

For all the labors of the British and French empires, the Wilsonian discursive structure would trouble the sleep of imperial rulers throughout the mandate period. The peoples of the region would never forget the difference between a Class-A mandate and a colony, much as the British or the French might seek to do so. Arab–Jewish riots in Jerusalem and a major tribal revolt in Iraq in 1920,[144] followed by revolts in Syria and Lebanon in 1925,[145] meant that the peoples of these lands would pursue their own interpretations of "national self-determination" with all the means at their disposal. Indeed, the conference had created a collection of successor states-in-the-making in the former Ottoman lands as unstable as anything it created in Europe.

The Great War in the Ottoman Empire came to a legal close through a unique combination of agents and structures. The remnants of the Paris Peace Conference writing what became the Treaty of Sèvres would drive Wilsonian principles unashamedly in the direction of realist imperialism. The regime of the Sultan would sign the treaty on August 10, 1920. But by then, the effective locus of sovereignty in Anatolia had shifted from the captive multinational sultanate to two ethnically based successor states—a new ethno-national state in Turkey and a newly irredentist state in Greece. The conflict between these two states demarcated the limits of empires in the region. A new formal structure would result from this outcome connecting empires and a largely victorious Turkish successor state. The Conference of Lausanne, distinct from the Paris Peace Conference, would produce the Treaty of Lausanne, signed on July 24, 1923.

---

[140] Briton Cooper Busch, *Britain, India, and the Arabs, 1914–1921* (Berkeley: University of California Press, 1971), esp. Ch. 8–9.

[141] The de facto Kurdish capital, oil-rich Mosul, lay in the French zone under Sykes–Picot. See Luigi Scassieri, "Britain, France, and Mesopotamian Oil, 1916–1920," *Diplomacy and Statecraft* 26.1 (2015): 25–45.

[142] On the role of the Royal Air Force, see David E. Omissi, *Air Power and Colonial Control: The Royal Air Force, 1919–1939* (Manchester: Manchester University Press, 1990). The British seriously considered using poison gas, though they did not actually do so. R. M. Douglas, "Did Britain Use Chemical Weapons in Mandatory Iraq?," *Journal of Modern History* 81.4 (2009): 859–87.

[143] Priya Satia considers the matter from the point of view of environmental history in "A Rebellion of Technology: Development, Policing, and the British Arabian Imaginary," in Diana K. Davis and Edmund Burke III, eds., *Environmental Imaginaries of the Middle East and North Africa* (Athens: Ohio University Press, 2011), 23–59.

[144] John J. McTague, Jr., "The British Military Administration in Palestine," *Journal of Palestine Studies* 7.3 (1978): 55–76.

[145] Joyce Laverty Miller, "The Syrian Revolt of 1925," *International Journal of Middle East Studies* 8.4 (1977): 545–63.

As we saw, the Mudros Armistice of October 30, 1918 encouraged the mistaken belief that the allied forces had material control over Anatolia. A modest force of some 3,500 allied (mostly British) troops entered Constantinople as an unofficial occupying force.[146] But as work began on a treaty with Ottoman Turkey, an ethnic Turkish successor state gradually emerged, independent of allied supervision. In May 1919, the hero of the Gallipoli campaign, Mustafa Kemal, took up the innocuous-sounding position of inspector of the 9th Army. He placed his headquarters in Samsun along the Black Sea, well beyond the reach of allied military power. In February 1920, the last Ottoman parliament in Constantinople adopted the Misak-i Millî (National Pact). This document declared national independence in ways that directly challenged the sovereignty of the conference. The pact laid the foundation for a Turkish successor state.[147]

The Misak-i Millî prefigured a Turkey shorn of any opprobrium from the Ottoman defeat. Article 1 renounced any notion of a restored Ottoman Empire. It proposed self-determination, either through immediate independence or through plebiscites, for most of the Arabic-speaking lands. Other historically Turkish areas, such as Armenia and the Allepo and Mosul Vilayets, would remain in Turkey. Like the other successor states, this post-Ottoman Turkey promised to protect minorities, on its own terms. Article 5 posited something of a "golden rule" concerning national minorities. Protections such as those envisaged in the other treaties "shall be confirmed and assured by us," provided neighboring countries did the same with Muslim minorities. The declaration in Article 4 assented to freedom of navigation and free trade through the Straits, provided Constantinople and the Sea of Marmora remained "protected from every danger."

On the other side of the Aegean, Greece adopted a successor state identity after the Mudros armistice. Like Italy in Fiume, Greece resolved to reconcile ethnic and historic claims on the Anatolian peninsula by deciding the identity of the people who lived there. Greek participation in the Allied offensive in the Balkans in 1918 fostered what Michael Llewellyn Smith called the "Ionian Vision," of a Hellenic successor state.[148] The pre-1914 boundaries would constitute simply, in the expression of Eleftherios Venizelos, the "backbone" of a much greater Greece, which would encompass most of the remaining Ottoman territory in Europe (including Constantinople), the territories on both sides of the straits, and the Anatolian peninsula itself up to the Central Plateau.[149] The vast majority of the inhabitants, the

---

[146] Andred Mango, *Atatürk: The Biography of the Founder of Modern Turkey* (Woodstock: Overlook Press, 1999), 196; and Nur Bilge Criss, *Istambul under Allied Occupation, 1918–1923* (Leiden: Brill, 1999).

[147] English and French versions appear in Arnold J. Toynbee, *The Western Question in Greece and Turkey: A Study in the Contact of Civilizations* (London: Constable and Company, 1922), 207–10.

[148] Michael Llewellyn Smith, *Ionian Vision: Greece in Asia Minor: 1919–1922* (London: Allen Lane, 1973).

[149] Dynastic instability in 1920–21 encouraged Greek irredentism. King Alexander died on October 25, 1920 from an infection caused by a monkey bite, to be succeeded after a referendum by his exiled, pro-German father, King Constantine I. Venizelos resigned following a general election of November 1, 1920. Both events strengthened irredentist opinion. Venizelos would re-emerge in late 1922 to lead the Greek delegation in Lausanne.

Ionian vision held, were unredeemed "Greeks," whatever their claimed religious or linguistic affiliations.

As the Supreme Council worked on the Turkish treaty, it began to fracture over competing imperial interests. With the mythology of a *vittoria mutilata* (mutilated victory) continuing to develop as the Council resisted Italian claims to Fiume along the Adriatic, Italy sought to assert its identity as an empire.[150] Article 8 of the St. Jean de Maurienne Agreement had accorded Italy a share of Anatolia, in the interest of "Mediterranean equilibrium."[151] On this basis, and without consulting the other Great Powers, the Italians on May 2, 1919 landed troops in Smyrna. In response, the Supreme Council (with Italy absent) on May 6 authorized the Greeks to do the same.[152]

Successor Greece subsequently became the proxy instrument for protecting the allied victory in Anatolia. With allied permission and logistical support, the Greeks attacked—not the Italians, but the Turks—from their foothold in Smyrna in June 1920. Shortly thereafter, the Greeks found themselves in a full-fledged war with the successor state emerging in far-off Angora (later Ankara). All the while, the Supreme Council insisted that the sultan's regime remained the viable locus of sovereignty over the Anatolian peninsula, and that to control him was to control post-Ottoman Turkey. The allies made their de facto occupation of Constantinople official in March 1920 by dissolving Parliament, and assuming control of the former Ottoman War Office and the mail and telegraph services.[153] In response, the Grand National Assembly in Angora elected Kemal its speaker, thereby making the emergence of the new regime official. The assembly declared the sultan the prisoner of the allied powers, and his acts as Turkish sovereign invalid.

In such an environment, the signing of the Treaty of Sèvres parodied the actual situation in Anatolia.[154] The treaty characterized a criminalized former Great Power as unfit to play a legitimate role in the international system. But unlike defeated Germany, Austria, Hungary, and Bulgaria, post-Ottoman Turkey would fall into allied receivership through losing control over its finances. By joining the war on the side of Germany and Austria-Hungary, according to Article 231, Turkey had caused "losses and sacrifices of all kinds for which she ought to make complete reparation." As with Germany, the allies recognized that this would be well beyond the capacity of the post-Ottoman Turkey to pay, particularly given the loss of the Arabic-speaking lands. Accordingly, in order "to afford some measure of relief and assistance to Turkey," the treaty set up a Financial Commission comprising one representative each from France, the British Empire, and Italy, with a Turkish

---

[150] Robert L. Hess, "Italy and Africa: Colonial Ambitions in the First World War," *Journal of African History* 4.1 (1963): 105–26.

[151] "St. Jean de Maurienne Agreement," April 19–21, 1917, in Albrecht-Carrié, *Italy at the Paris Peace Conference*, 345–46.

[152] Burgwyn, *Mutilated Victory*, 292–95.

[153] Paul C. Helmreich, *From Paris to Sèvres: The Partition of the Ottoman Empire at the Peace Conference of 1919–1920* (Columbus: Ohio State University Press, 1974), 281.

[154] A.E. Montgomery, "The Making of the Treaty of 10 August 1920," *The Historical Journal* 15.4 (1972): 775–87.

representative serving in a consultative capacity. This commission had control over the government budget (Article 232), and authority over future government loans (Article 234). None of the other treaties required such compromised sovereignty, in the name of reparations or anything else.

While the Treaty of Sèvres preserved nominal Turkish sovereignty over Constantinople and did not interfere in the religious position of the sultan as caliph of Islam, it set in motion a process likely to result in the partition of the Anatolian peninsula and the straits.[155] A French, British, and Italian commission would make recommendations for an autonomous Kurdistan within six months of the signing of the treaty (Article 62). Sovereignty around Smyrna (technically still Turkish as per Article 69) would finally be determined by plebiscite after five years of direct rule by Greece (Article 83). The treaty immediately established an independent, if amorphous, Armenia (Article 88). Its eventual boundaries would be determined through arbitration, improbably enough, led by the president of the United States (Article 89).[156] Minorities in vestigial Turkey proper would enjoy protections similar to those in the other treaties (Articles 140–51). But minority rights would be guaranteed not by the League of Nations, but by the allies in consultation with the League Council.

Of some 160,000 allied troops in Anatolia at the signature of the Treaty of Sèvres, some 90,000 were Greek.[157] The British, French, and Italians all had concentrated their forces around the straits and Constantinople. The allies thus tied their fortunes in Anatolia to the outcome of the war between the Greek and Turkish successor states. After the failed London Conference of February 1921, the Great Powers approved a renewed Greek offensive designed to topple the Angora successor regime.[158] While the initial success of this campaign brought the Greek forces to within some 60 miles of Angora, the badly overextended Greeks shortly found themselves in retreat. By September 1922, Smyrna was in flames, and violent exchange of population between the Greek and Turkish successor states had begun. Turkish forces began to close in on the straits and Constantinople. This situation in turn produced the Chanak Crisis of September–October 1922, which brought successor Turkey and the British Empire to the brink of war.[159]

As all this transpired, the conference of empires for practical purposes disintegrated. As early as October 1921, the French made an agreement with the Turkish Republic, granting it de facto recognition by a Great Power. This agreement

---

[155] As per Article 36, an international zone administered by an inter-allied Commission of the Straits would guarantee freedom of movement in these strategic waters.

[156] On the politics of Armenia in the late Wilson administration, see Lloyd E. Ambrosius, "Wilsonian Diplomacy and Armenia: The Limits of Power and Ideology," in Jay Winter, ed., *America and the Armenian Genocide of 1915* (New York: Cambridge University Press, 2004), 113–45.

[157] Nur Bilge Criss estimates 100,000 Greek soldiers, 30,000 British, 18,000 French, and 2,000 Italian. *Istambul Under Allied Occupation*, 70.

[158] Peter Kincaid Jensen, "The Greco-Turkish War, 1920–1922," *International Journal of Middle East Studies* 10.4 (1979): 553–65.

[159] A.L. Macfie, "The Chanak Affair: September–October 1922," *Balkan Studies* 20.2 (1979): 309–41.

resolved the border between Cilicia and the French mandate in Syria.[160] Italian imperial interests in former Ottoman lands contracted to the occupation of the Dodecanese islands, a policy unaltered by Benito Mussolini's March on Rome of October 1922. By the time of the Chanak Crisis, both France and Italy for some months had actually been delivering war material to the Angora regime.[161] Their small contingents of troops had been withdrawn to Constantinople, leaving the British Empire as the sole defender of allied sovereignty in the straits.

During the Chanak Crisis, the British Empire itself would cease to function as a unitary imperial agent. On September 15, 1922, Westminster sent a telegram to the Dominions requesting support in the event of war with Turkey over the straits. Colonial Secretary Winston Churchill released the telegram to the British press on a Saturday, which allowing for the time difference meant that it reached most of the Dominions through local newspapers before it could be officially decoded the following Monday.

The little-noted though long-remembered Article 5 of the 1919 security treaty between Britain and France, which established the requirement of prior consultation with Dominion parliaments, had sudden relevance. Canada and Australia overtly declined military assistance. Newfoundland agreed with the policy, but did not agree to send troops. South Africa chose silence, an unusual response for the normally loquacious Prime Minister Jan Smuts. New Zealand offered assistance, but only a battalion with the possibility of a brigade later. In the end, an armistice agreement at Mundanya on October 11, 1922 headed off armed conflict between the British and Turkish forces, and paved the way for renewed peace negotiations for a revised treaty. But Lloyd George fell from power on October 19, the last of the wartime leaders of the Great Powers to do so.[162] Clearly, the time had come for a new recognition of structures and agents to make peace in the region.

Even before the Chanak debacle, British Foreign Minister Lord Curzon[163] contemplated convening a new conference to write a new treaty more reflective of the actual situation.[164] After Chanak, a new conference became a necessity. This new conference met in Lausanne, Switzerland, between November 1922 and July 1923. The term "Allied and Associated Powers" passed from usage in the official record. Soviet Russia was invited to send representatives, the British Dominions were not. Successor Turkey participated in the negotiations from the beginning, as a legal equal. The Conference of Lausanne was not a continuation of the Paris Peace Conference, rather a new formal structure created by a configuration of new agents.

The signing of the Treaty of Lausanne on July 24, 1923 constituted the proper end of formal peacemaking after the Great War. Kemal proclaimed the treaty

---

[160] Yücel Güçlü, "The Struggle for Mastery in Cilicia: Turkey, France, and the Ankara Agreement of 1921," *International History Review* 23.3 (2001): 580–603, esp. 593–603.

[161] Criss, *Istambul under Allied Occupation, 1918–1923*, 141.

[162] J.J. Darwin, "The Chanak Crisis and the British Cabinet," *History* 65, No. 213 (1980): 32–48.

[163] George Nathaniel Curzon, First Marquess Curzon of Kedleston, hereafter Lord Curzon.

[164] Erik Goldstein, "The British Official Mind and the Lausanne Conference, 1922–23," in Erik Goldstein and B.J.C. McKercher, eds., *Power and Stability: British Foreign Policy, 1865–1965* (London: Frank Cass, 2003), 192–93.

"a political victory unequalled in the history of the Ottoman era," a theme echoed in nationalist historiography long thereafter.[165] Article 59 replaced any mention of an Ottoman *Kriegsschuld* with a statement that Greece owed Turkey reparations for "the acts of the Greek army or administration which were contrary to the laws of war." Yet the new regime in Turkey, its sovereignty over Anatolia now uncontested, formally renounced any such claims in consideration of the dismal financial condition of the Hellenic state. The allied Financial Commission disappeared, along with restrictions on the size of Turkish military forces. Gone was any mention of an autonomous Kurdish region, to say nothing of an independent Armenia. Today's Armenia drew its territory from the Russian Armenia.

Yet in intriguing ways, successor Turkey carefully articulated its sovereignty within an international system demarcated by the Paris Peace Conference. The simple act of writing a new treaty, of course, was essential to the new regime attaining recognition in that system. The Great Powers who led the conference still ruled vast swaths of the world, and controlled much of its capital. Unlike the Bolshevik successor state in Russia in its early days, republican Turkey wanted to join that system, not overthrow it. The residual structure shaped the agent, just as the agent shaped the new structure.

The Treaty of Lausanne qualified the sovereignty of successor Turkey in nontrivial ways. A convention on the straits guaranteed a Wilsonian "freedom of the seas" in peace and in war (Articles 1–2, with the Annex).[166] The agreement created a demilitarized zone on both sides of the straits (Articles 4–6), overseen by an international commission operating under the auspices of the League of Nations (Articles 12, 15). Further, Turkey would rejoin the system of international finance through involved provisions for restructuring and paying the Ottoman public debt (Part II, Financial Clauses). Article 28 explicitly banned the extraterritorial capitulations that privileged Western nationals and institutions. But a declaration from the republican government issued the same day as the signing of the treaty declared its intention to study the Ottoman legal system "with a view to the institution of such reforms as may be rendered advisable by the development of manners and civilization."[167] Turkey would employ foreign jurists from non-belligerent countries to advise in the modernization of Turkish law. These foreign employees of the national Ministry of Justice would be eligible to receive complaints and petitions on a wide range of civil and criminal matters in Turkey (Article 2).

The apparently contradictory statements made in the Lausanne settlement about religious and ethnic minorities will be explored below. Most notoriously, a bilateral convention between Greece and Turkey appended to the treaty provided

---

[165] Quoted in Mango, *Atatürk*, 388. For a nationalist echo, see Yücel Güçlü, "Turkey's Entrance into the League of Nations," *Middle Eastern Studies* 39.1 (2003): 186–206.

[166] "Convention Relating to the Regime of the Straits," *AJIL* 18, Supplement, No. 1: Official Documents (1924): 53–62. Article 2, Annex, Section I (c) of the Straits Convention gave Turkey "full power to take such measures as she may consider necessary to prevent enemy vessels from using the Straits." The convention did require continued access for "neutral" shipping.

[167] "Declaration Relating to the Administration of Justice," *AJIL* 18, Supplement, No. 2: Official Documents (1924): 97–98.

for a mandatory exchange of Greek and Turkish populations.[168] Historians, sociologists, and political scientists now consider the exchange an early example of "ethnic cleansing."[169] The convention discerned ethnic identity exclusively by religion. Christians were Greeks, Muslims were Turks. In the end, the exchange legitimized the uprooting of some 1.1 million Greeks, and over 350,000 Turks.[170] Yet even this brutal population exchange after the Great War was not total. It specifically excluded populations of some 110,000 "Greeks" in Constantinople and over 100,000 "Turks" in Western Thrace.[171] In addition, the Treaty of Lausanne retained most of the language of minority protection found in other treaties. Article 38 guaranteed freedom of religion, and "full and complete protection of life and liberty to all inhabitants of Turkey without distinction of birth, nationality, language, race or religion."

Perhaps more remarkably under the circumstances, Article 44 stipulated that minority protection would "constitute obligations of international concern and shall be placed under the guarantee of the League of Nations," which Turkey did not even join until 1932.[172] However, these protections would not have standing in domestic law, as in Eastern Europe. The Great Powers (named as the British Empire, France, Italy, and Japan) agreed simply not to "withhold their assent" to any modification "assented to by a majority of the Council of the League of Nations." Lerna Ekmekçioğlu has argued that much as in Eastern Europe, the Turkish state remained its own master in minority affairs.[173]

The peace finally made among successor Turkey, successor Greece, and the allies reflected a certain configuration of agents and structure. The Great Powers needed the Great War to end, and a stable regime in Anatolia. Lacking the material power to enforce borders or protect the peoples living inside them, the Great Powers assented to the population exchange, so long as they could keep it at arm's length through a bilateral convention that did not bear their names. Greece needed peace to recover from domestic political turmoil and its defeat in Anatolia.

---

[168] "Convention Concerning the Exchange of Greek and Turkish Populations," *AJIL* 18, Supplement, No. 2: Official Documents (1924): 84–90.

[169] Michael Mann, *The Dark Side of Democracy: Explaining Ethnic Cleansing* (New York: Cambridge University Press, 2005), 67–68; and Philipp Ther, *The Dark Side of Nation-States: Ethnic Cleansing in Modern Europe*, Charlotte Kreutzmüller, trans. (New York: Berghahn Books, 2014 [originally published in German in 2011]), 74–81.

[170] Raoul Blanchard, "The Exchange of Populations between Greece and Turkey," *Geographical Review* 1 (1925): 455. These figures are generally accepted in the essays in Renée Hirschon, ed., *Crossing the Aegean: An Appraisal of the 1923 Compulsory Population Exchange between Greece and Turkey* (New York: Berghahn Books, 2003).

[171] Alexis Alexandris, "Religion or Ethnicity: The Identity Issue of the Minorities in Greece and Turkey," in Hirschon, ed., *Crossing the Aegean*, 118, 122. The exemptions took several years to adjudicate, and considerable variations exist in estimates of the numbers of people involved. An important early study gave figures of some 300,000 Greeks in Constantinople and 130,000 Muslims in Western Thrace. Stephen P. Ladas, *The Exchange of Minorities in Bulgaria, Greece and Turkey* (New York: Macmillan Company, 1932), 400.

[172] Before then, Turkey would make skillful use of Article 17 of the League Covenant, which made it possible to "join" the League on an issue-by-issue basis in order to resolve specific disputes. See Güçlü, "Turkey's Entrance into the League of Nations."

[173] Lerna Ekmekçioğlu, "Republic of Paradox: The League of Nations Minority Protection Regime and the New Turkey's Step-Citizens," *International Journal of Middle East Studies* 46.4 (2014): 657–79.

For its part, successor Turkey needed to establish itself as a fully sovereign state within its desired borders and simultaneously acquire acceptance into the international system. It could admit minority protection in the Treaty of Lausanne precisely because it had appropriated the authority to decide who was "Turk" and who was "Greek." Successor Turkey in victory could make a public face of generosity toward minorities in the name of modernization—a goal clearly signaled in the Misak-i Millî.[174] The Turkish state would govern its role in the international system largely on its own terms.[175]

This chapter has recounted the mutual evolution of agents and structures over the course of the Paris Peace Conference. States and empires recognizable as nineteenth-century realist agents began the process of making peace as military decision loomed in 1918. Imperial Germany sought to stave off defeat through appealing to a discursive structure, Wilsonianism. When the allies endorsed this structure, they created a provisional world sovereign that promised to redesign the international system itself. Through legitimizing "self-determination," the conference legitimized the identity of the successor state, an identity the provisional world sovereign could nowhere completely control. As the Great Powers demobilized, the disconnect between discursive and material power became more and more pronounced. In Central and Eastern Europe, the Supreme Council played some successor states off against others, further confusing the already tangled Wilsonian discursive structure.

As peacemaking moved beyond Europe, realist empires sought to operate in the Wilsonian discursive structure through the mandates. Yet the very logic of the mandates undercut the legitimacy of empire, and undermined empires as agents. Pandora's Box of "national self-determination" would remain open around the globe. Along the Aegean and in Anatolia, the formal structures of the Paris Peace Conference broke down. Indeed, the British Empire itself ceased to function as a unitary agent. Peacemaking also broke down, as the Greek and Turkish successor states returned to war. Defeated empires and successor states, not the Paris Peace Conference, would meet in Lausanne finally to end the Great War in Anatolia. Yet successor Turkey, while jealously protective of its self-determined sovereignty, wanted the international recognition that only the Great Powers could provide. It selectively appropriated various aspects of the Wilsonian structure toward its modernizing project. Structures and agents had shaped each other in peacemaking after the Great War, from beginning to end.

---

[174] J. Edgar Turlington, "The Settlement of Lausanne," *AJIL* 18 (1924): 699–700.
[175] Lerna Ekmekçioğlu, *Recovering Armenia: The Limits of Belonging in Post-Genocide Turkey* (Stanford, CA: Stanford University Press, 2015).

2

The Sovereignty of Justice

If Wilsonianism meant anything, it meant replacing realist security with "justice" as the organizing principle of the international system. Toward that end, the Paris Peace Conference presented the German delegation with the draft Treaty of Versailles at a plenary session on May 7, 1919. As president of the conference, Clemenceau spoke first. The time had come for justice, construed as compensation: "The hour has struck for the weighty settlement of our accounts. You asked us for peace. We are disposed to give it to you."[1] By requesting an armistice back in October 1918, the Germans had asked for a peace on the terms of the Allied and Associated Powers. Justice meant making restitution for the war. On this occasion, Clemenceau made no explicit statement of the morality of the matter one way or another, though he certainly had his views. The conference as sovereign power had drafted the treaty, and now ceremonially presented it. The Germans would have fifteen days to respond, but could do so only in writing, and only in French and English. Clemenceau then asked if anyone had comments.

The head of the German delegation, Foreign Minister Count Ulrich von Brockdorff-Rantzau (pictured in Figure 2.1), rose to make a speech that constituted the debut of post-Imperial Germany on the international stage.[2] Thanks to press leaks and to reports from German diplomats with discreet contacts in Paris, Brockdorff certainly knew the general direction of the treaty.[3] In any event, he had decided before he spoke how to interpret a document he could not yet have seen in its entirety.[4] Also aware that French newspapers had referred to the arranged position of the German delegates as the "prisoners' dock," he spoke seated rather than standing. The count also spoke in German, though as a career diplomat and an aristocrat he would have spoken excellent French. This meant that the speech had to be translated, sentence-by-sentence, into the two official languages

[1] "Peace Congress (Versailles), Protocol No. 1, Plenary Session of May 7, 1919," *FRUS: PPC*, 3: 413–20.

[2] Sally Marks has shown that Brockdorff-Rantzau's arguments were well familiar in the German cabinet long before May 7. "Smoke and Mirrors: In Smoke-Filled Rooms and the Galerie des Glaces," in Manfred F. Boemeke, Gerald D. Feldman, and Elizabeth Glaser, eds., *The Treaty of Versailles: A Reassessment after 75 Years* (New York: Cambridge University Press, 1998), 337–70, esp. 349–52.

[3] Klaus Schwabe, *Woodrow Wilson, Revolutionary Germany, and Peacemaking, 1918–1919*, Rita Kimber and Robert Kimber, trans. (Chapel Hill: University of North Carolina Press, 1985), 300–02.

[4] The count had prepared three other (less confrontational) drafts of his speech. "Three Preliminary Drafts of the Speech of Count Brockdorff-Rantzau for the Session at the Trianon Palace Hotel, Versailles, May 7, 1919," in Alma Luckau, ed., *The German Delegation at the Paris Peace Conference* (New York: Columbia University Press, 1941), 213–20.

Figure 2.1. The German delegation arrives in Paris (Count Brockdorff-Rantzau center, grey raincoat).

gallica.bnf.fr/Bibliothèque nationale de France.

of the conference, French and English. The listeners had plenty of time to absorb every word. He began with an admission of German helplessness in the present situation: "We cherish no illusions as to the extent of our defeat—the degree of our impotence."[5]

But Brockdorff argued for peace based on a very different kind of justice. Brockdorff and not Clemenceau would focus on guilt (*Schuld*) for the war as the centerpiece of the unjust draft treaty. Germany would be willing to settle accounts in a legal or technical sense, but would reject any specific guilt for the catastrophe of the Great War. In so pointedly rejecting guilt, he made guilt the issue. Brockdorff thus heralded an approach to the Paris Peace Conference and its results that would sustain German foreign policy until the Nazi regime destroyed the settlement altogether. He raised the moral stakes of the matter, as a way of asserting the sovereignty of a fledgling German regime in the making of peace. Appalled and misjudged Germany had a moral duty to fight an unjust treaty, and to return "justice" in peacemaking to its original, Wilsonian foundations.

The count placed war guilt on the international system itself, rather than on any one state. A constructivist *avant la lettre*, Brockdorff described a prewar

---

[5] Brockdorff-Rantzau used the word *Ohnmacht*, in today's less gendered parlance more commonly translated as "powerlessness." Graf Brockdorff-Rantzau, *Dokumente* (Berlin: Deutsche Verlansgesellschaft für Politik und Geschichte, 1920), 113.

international system comprising mutually constituted agents, who collectively had created the structure that led to war:

> During the last fifty years the imperialism of all European States has chronically poisoned the international situation. The policy of retaliation and that of expansion as well as disregard of the rights of peoples to self-determination, contributed to the disease of Europe, which reached its crisis in the world war. (417)

According to Brockdorff, if the Great Powers all constructed one another, all shared equal guilt for the tragedy that followed. By 1914, the states of Europe had formed a self-destructive system that needed only the assassination of an archduke to explode. Germany had played its role in the catastrophe—specifically the regrettable if militarily necessary violation of Belgian neutrality and the destruction of northeastern France. Germany expected to pay for its share of the physical damage, but no more. Properly understood, "justice" meant limited material compensation shorn of moral judgment.

Brockdorff intervened in an evolving relationship between justice and morality that had existed since the German call for an armistice back in October 1918. Then, he argued, Germany had sought to point the way to a better international system by asking for a Wilsonian peace. The Allied and Associated Powers had signed on to the same discursive structure. In doing so, as Brockdorff put it, they had "abandoned the idea of a peace of violence and inscribed the words 'Peace and Justice' on their banner" (418). While he never used the word "covenant," his argument suggested that the armistice of November 11 constituted a sacred pact committing all the Great Powers—friend and foe—to one another: "The conscience of the world is behind it; no nation will be permitted to violate it with impunity" (418).

Indeed, Wilson had compromised his own ideals by agreeing to a treaty based on singular and unjust incrimination. German guilt, Brockdorff accused, had driven the entire conference up to that time: "we have heard the passionate demand that the victors should both make us pay as vanquished and punish us as guilty" (417). In resisting the treaty, Germany sought to direct peacemaking back to its true path: "You yourselves have brought us an ally: Justice, which was guaranteed to us by the agreement relating to the bases of Peace" (418). The solution lay in referring "the principal questions individually at the earliest possible moment to a special Commission of experts, for discussion on the basis of the draft presented by you" (419). Such a commission, the argument implied, would swiftly set aside the vindictive peace laid out in the draft treaty.

Matters would thus return to where the Germans had left them back on November 11. Of course, this amounted to setting aside the entire peace conference and starting afresh. Brockdorff concluded with a thinly veiled threat should the allies decline to do so: "A Peace which cannot be defended in the name of justice before the whole would continually call forth fresh resistance" (420). No state could sign such an unjust treaty with a clear conscience, and no state would take up the guarantees necessary to fulfill it.

A red-faced Clemenceau adjourned the meeting shortly after Brockdorff finished.[6] Wilson called the remarks "the most tactless speech I have ever heard," proving that "the Germans really are a stupid people." The count had flustered Lloyd George enough for him to break an ivory penknife during the speech. He regretted that Clemenceau had given the German the chance to speak at all, though doing so enabled Lloyd George, for the first time, fully to understand the hatred of the French for Germany. Brockdorff's speech sought not only to reinterpret the war, but to change its outcome and lay the groundwork for a peace among equals.

As with so much else, the Great War radicalized the very meaning of "justice," and the role of "justice" in demarcating sovereignty over the international system. Certainly "justice" overflowed the confines of international law as it had existed in 1914. "Total" war had led millions to expect "total" peace, underpinned by a new morality that would guide new definitions of justice in international relations. Nothing had heightened those expectations more than the millenarian rhetoric of Wilsonianism. Peacemakers in 1919 could hardly follow their forebears of 1815, who had blamed the turmoil of the French Revolution on dead revolutionaries and Napoleon, recognized the changed regime in France, exacted a financial penalty owed by the loser to the winners, and swiftly restored post-Revolutionary France as a partner in the international system.

In 1918 and 1919, Wilsonianism achieved the global resonance it did precisely because it placed a certain idea of justice at the center of the new world order. But doing so raised more questions than it answered. The Paris Peace Conference would have to grapple with amorphous and radical concepts of "justice" that would ask more from states than a system based on realist security. Had there been nothing wrong with the international system before 1914, there would have been no need to redesign it, as the victors had committed themselves to doing. Clearly, the matter had to go beyond exacting restitution from the states guilty of starting the conflagration in August 1914, some of which no longer existed. The victors would have to change themselves.

As Brockdorff's remarks suggested, "justice" in international relations could take two directions—a direction of compensation analogous to civil law, and a direction of inculpation analogous to criminal law. We will see that as a procedural matter, the conference went to some trouble to keep the two directions separate. It would charge one commission with considering reparations, another with considering responsibility for the war. But as per the very circumstances creating the conference, this proved not so simple. Wilsonianism had made morality a public preoccupation of international relations. Compensation without explicit moral judgment had a long history. But a peace of morality suggested a peace of new law. War guilt could not remain an abstract principle, because the conference had to write specific treaties with specific defeated powers.

---

[6] See the description of Brockdorff-Rantzau's speech in Margaret MacMillan, *Paris 1919: Six Months that Changed the World* (New York: Random House, 2001), 463–65.

Deciding justice after the Great War would decide a foundational issue of sovereignty over the international system. The Paris Peace Conference never defined a precise relationship between morality and justice, and its participants would often use the terms more or less interchangeably. Discussions on reparations veered time and again toward the moral. Discussions on responsibility for the war veered time and again toward the legal. Compensatory and criminal approaches to justice would become increasingly muddled as the Paris Peace Conference proceeded. The Germans would play an active role keeping morality at center stage. Skillful use of the discursive tools at hand made them partners in creating the new international system, much to the consternation of the victors. As Sally Marks has argued, once the Germans themselves made war guilt the defining issue of the Treaty of Versailles, the allies would find themselves hard pressed to do otherwise.[7] Moreover, the template for the criminalized Great Power became more and more confused and internally inconsistent as applied to the other defeated Central Powers: Austria, Bulgaria, Hungary, and Turkey.

THE MORALITY OF REPARATIONS

The compensatory path to a peace based on justice led to reparations. No one offered more assistance to Brockdorff's moralizing of reparations than John Maynard Keynes. Keynes had served in the British delegation to the Paris Peace Conference, specializing, among other things, in the issue of German financial responsibility. He had seized on Wilsonianism in 1918 as a cure-all for the pathologies that had caused the war. Later, appalled at the draft treaty with Germany, he resigned from the British delegation.[8] Keynes immediately set to work on *The Economic Consequences of the Peace*, published in December 1919. Within six months, it had sold some 100,000 copies, and had made Keynes a transatlantic public intellectual. As German power grew and became more malevolent in the 1930s, Keynes acquired the status of prophet.[9]

Keynes added a moralistic component to realist interpretations of the Paris Peace Conference. The peace helped turn the Great War into a tragedy, a narrative form common to realism. Hubris had led the allies to abandon Wilsonianism in favor of a "Carthaginian" Treaty of Versailles.[10] Keynes drew biting, insider portraits of Clemenceau, Wilson, and Lloyd George that shape our impressions of them to this day. In different ways, each became a tragic hero, a great man undone by fate, which exposed his fatal flaws. The men who had won the war would lose the peace,

---

[7] Marks, "Smoke and Mirrors," 231.

[8] On Keynes and the war, see Robert Skidelsky, *John Maynard Keynes*, 2 vols. (New York: Viking, 1983), 1: 305–75.

[9] Skidelsky, *Keynes*, 1: 394.

[10] The term "Carthaginian Peace" is variously attributed to Keynes and his friend in Paris, General Jan Smuts. Smuts had written in a letter of "the most reactionary [peace] since Scipio Africanus dealt with Carthage." Smuts to M.C. Gillett, May 19, 1919, *Selections from the Smuts Papers*, W.K. Hancock and Jean Van der Poel, eds., 7 vols. (Cambridge: Cambridge University Press, 1966–73), 4: 979.

through their own inner failings. Keynes positioned himself as morally superior witness to the tragedy, the narrator who could tell the story and identify its moral.

Clemenceau, "dry in soul and empty of hope," nevertheless "felt about France what Pericles felt of Athens—unique value in her, nothing else mattering."[11] Wilson's failings complemented those of Clemenceau. Few heroes fell from such lofty heights. The American president arrived in Europe with "a prestige and a moral influence throughout the world unequaled in history," such that "the Allied peoples acknowledged him not as a victor only but almost as a prophet." Yet Keynes found the flesh-and-blood Wilson a figure "lacking that dominating intel-lectual equipment which would have been necessary to cope with the subtle and dangerous spellbinders" (39), notably Lloyd George. Keynes trod a bit more care-fully around the British prime minister, at the time still at the height of his power. Yet no one contributed more than Keynes to the image of Lloyd George as the wily Welshman: "Never could a man [Wilson] have stepped into the parlor a more perfect and predestined victim to the finished accomplishments of the Prime Minister" (41). Yet Lloyd George had himself become a prisoner, of his own radicalized rhetoric to "make Germany pay," which had bought him electoral victory in December 1918. Lloyd George could only seek to take the hindmost for Britain, as his electors had commanded. As Keynes put it, this toxic trio wrote a peace directed to "the future enfeeblement of a strong and dangerous enemy, to revenge, and to the shifting by the victors of their unbearable financial burdens on to the shoulder of the defeated" (56).

To Keynes, this morality tale had practical economic consequences. The notori-ously open-ended reparations regime established in the treaty did not even call for a final figure until 1921. The treaty made only one glancing reference to the German capacity to pay, and none to German economic growth, which alone could provide for payment at all. The absurdity of the template developed for Germany became increasingly clear as applied in the subsequent treaties, to the shattered economies of Austria, Hungary, Bulgaria, and Turkey. This spread the tragedy across Eastern Europe and beyond.

The theory and practice of reparations from Germany after the Great War have generated a vast secondary literature. The basic paradigm remains the judgmental one put in place by Keynes.[12] Most, but not all, historians concur with a "Carthaginian peace," at least in the intentions of the peacemakers.[13] The question has remained assigning blame for the debacle that followed. Among specialists, Keynes's characterization of a vindictive France has been softened considerably. Marc Trachtenberg has argued that the French turned to a severe position on

[11] John Maynard Keynes, *The Economic Consequences of the Peace* (New York: Harcourt, Brace and Howe, 1920), 38.

[12] Alan Sharp, *The Versailles Settlement: Peacemaking in Paris, 1919* (Houndmills: Macmillan, 1991), Ch. 4, 77–101; and Leonard Gomes, *German Reparations, 1919–32: A Historical Survey* (Houndmills: Palgrave, 2010).

[13] For example, see Norman A. Graebner and Edward M. Bennett, *The Versailles Treaty and Its Legacy: The Failure of the Wilsonian Vision* (New York: Cambridge University Press, 2011). Sally Marks contextualizes the literature on reparations in "Mistakes and Myths: The Allies, Germany, and the Versailles Treaty, 1918–1921," *Journal of Modern History* 85.3 (2013): 632–59.

reparations only after attempts failed to continue wartime allied economic cooperation, notably on war debt.[14] Such an argument would make the British or the Americans the villains of the piece. Antony Lentin blamed the Anglophones, and seldom noted that the French were even present.[15]

Other historians have distributed blame for the failure of the reparations regime on domestic politics more broadly. Bruce Kent faulted "conservative liberal democracies" (including Weimar Germany) for using nineteenth-century economic policies to pay for a twentieth-century "total" war.[16] The United States and Britain deserve proportionally more blame as the most powerful players in international finance. Gerald Feldman argued that the Weimar Republic had such chaotic instruments of foreign and economic policy in its early years that it scarcely mattered what reparations regime the victors decided upon.[17] The defeated Great Power gave a performance of unjust reparations full of sound and fury that signified little.

Other historians emphasize German bad faith and incessant efforts to split Britain and France, in order to prevent the meaningful enforcement of any reparations regime. Weimar ruthlessness extended to provoking the French and Belgian occupation of the Ruhr and to sacrificing the German middle class through hyperinflation. Stephen Schuker and Marc Trachtenberg have shown how the French confronted endless German stonewalling and evasion.[18] Marks has argued for an essentially workable reparations regime, behind what she called the "smoke and mirrors" of unrealistic allied demands and German subterfuge.[19] On this point, a wry Feldman agreed: "No one has accused the Germans of honestly and forthrightly attempting to fulfill their obligations under the Treaty, and there is a general consensus that the policy of fulfillment had, as its purpose, the demonstration that fulfillment was not possible."[20]

Rather than seeking to assign yet more guilt, the discussion here asks why the reparations regime under Articles 231 and 232 took on the form it did. No regime could fulfill the galloping expectations of the populations of the victorious states. No regime could even claim to do so under the prewar rules of the international system. Much as the conference tried to avoid saying so, the whole notion of

[14] Marc Trachtenberg, "Reparations at the Paris Peace Conference," *Journal of Modern History* 51.1 (1979): 24–55.

[15] Anton Lentin, *Lloyd George, Woodrow Wilson and the Guilt of Germany* (Baton Rouge: Louisiana State University Press, 1984), and a précis "Germany: A New Carthage?," *History Today* 62.1 (2012): 20–27.

[16] Bruce Kent, *The Spoils of War: The Politics, Economics, and Diplomacy of Reparations, 1913–1932* (Oxford: Clarendon Press, 1989).

[17] Gerald Feldman, *The Great Disorder: Politics, Economics, and Society in the German Inflation, 1914–1924* (New York: Oxford University Press, 1993).

[18] Stephen A. Schuker, *The End of French Predominance in Europe: The Financial Crisis of 1924 and the Adoption of the Dawes Plan* (Chapel Hill: University of North Carolina Press, 1976); Marc Trachtenberg, *Reparation in World Politics: France and European Economic Diplomacy, 1916–1923* (New York: Columbia University Press, 1980).

[19] Marks, "Smoke and Mirrors."

[20] Gerald Feldman, "The Reparations Debate," in Conan Fischer and Alan Sharp, eds., *After the Versailles Treaty: Enforcement, Compliance, Contested Identities* (London: Routledge, 2008), 70.

compensation would need enhanced moral content. Toward this end, the conference created the identity of a criminalized state by muddling compensatory and criminal approaches to "justice."

Simple indemnities following European wars had a well-established history. After the final defeat of Napoleon, France owed the victors an indemnity of 700 million francs, payable over five years. The French would raise much of this money through issuing bonds, thereby linking compliance to their preciously guarded credit rating. Partial allied occupation further solidified the guarantee, with withdrawal progressively linked to payment.[21] After the Franco-Prussian War, the Treaty of Frankfurt of 1871 stipulated an indemnity of 5 billion gold francs, payable over three years, likewise linked to the withdrawal of German troops from French territory.[22] But these were simply fines for lost wars, and compensation to the victors for the costs incurred in winning them. The victors exacted indemnities from other states simply because they could do so.[23] Such indemnities morally judged neither states nor peoples.[24]

Organizationally, the Paris Peace Conference at first adopted this model, and carefully separated compensation and responsibilities. At a meeting of the Council of Ten on January 23, 1919, Lloyd George submitted proposals to establish separate commissions on reparations and on breaches in the laws of war.[25] Presented to the plenary on January 25, the proposal gave rise to a lively discussion on representation. Paul Hymans believed Belgium, as the original target of German aggression in August 1914, deserved representation on both bodies.[26] But neither he nor anyone else present questioned the wisdom of taking separate compensatory and criminal tracks. The resolutions passed by the plenary on January 25 established two commissions. A commission on "reparation for damage" would investigate what the defeated powers should pay, as well as what they would be capable of paying. Another commission "relative to the responsibility of the authors of the war" would focus on responsible individuals and the formation of an appropriate tribunal for trying them.

This procedural clarity took shape against the backdrop of gathering uncertainty as to just what compensation would mean. The Fourteen Points had been more

[21] André Nicolle, "The Problem of Reparations after the Hundred Days," *Journal of Modern History* 25.4 (1953): 343–54.

[22] Marks, "Smoke and Mirrors," 347–49; and Christian Tomuschat, "The 1871 Peace Treaty between France and Germany and the 1919 Peace Treaty of Versailles," in Randall Lesaffer, ed., *Peace Treaties and International Law in European History: From the Late Middle Ages to World War One* (New York: Cambridge University Press, 2004), 382–96.

[23] Richard M. Buxbaum, "A Legal History of International Reparations," *Berkeley Journal of International Law* 23.2 (2005): 314–46.

[24] Since World War II, debates about reparations have shifted away from states toward what Elezar Barkan has called "classes of people deserving reparation," such as indigenous peoples and descendants of slaves. "Introduction: Reparation: A Moral and Political Dilemma," in Jon Miller and Rahul Kumar, eds., *Reparations: Interdisciplinary Inquiries* (Oxford: Oxford University Press, 2007), 18.

[25] "Secretary's Notes of a Conversation Held in M. Pichon's Room at the Quai d'Orsay on Thursday, January 23, 1919, at 10:30 a.m.," Appendix C: "Draft Resolution in Regard to Reparation; Draft Resolution in Regard to Breaches of the Laws of War," *FRUS: PPC*, 3: 698–99, 703.

[26] "Preliminary Peace Conference, Protocol No. 3, Plenary Session of January 25, 1919," *FRUS: PPC*, 3: 176–203.

than usually clear in calling for targeted reparations. Point VII had decreed that Belgium "must be evacuated and restored." Point VIII required the same for northeastern France, as did Point XI for Romania, Serbia, and Montenegro. The term "restoration" had a generally accepted meaning of restitution for material damages suffered by the civilian population from direct military action.[27] But the Lansing Note of November 5, 1918 had implied the possibility of casting a broader net. The allied governments had agreed "that compensation will be made by Germany for all damages caused to the civilian population of the allies and their property by the aggression of Germany by land, by sea, and from the air."[28] For their part, the French insisted on leaving open just what "restoration" would mean at the time they accepted Wilsonianism as the foundation of the peace.

It was always possible to read the Lansing Note of November 5 not as a ceiling for reparations, but as a floor. All allied lands and peoples touched by German aggression, one could argue, merited compensation. Such an understanding made of capital importance the exact meaning of "German aggression," whether it meant specific material damage done during the German invasion, or the sum total of material harm done during the entire "war of aggression". The first sentence of Article 19 of the armistice agreement of November 11 had not clarified matters:

> With the reservation that any subsequent concessions and claims of the Allies and United States remain unaffected, the financial conditions are imposed:
>
> Reparations for damage done.[29]

During the war, some of the best legal minds in France argued for *réparations intégrales*, meaning full restoration of all material harm done to civilians in the invaded areas.[30] The British countered that focusing on these areas would exclude the substantial losses to civilian British shipping caused by submarine warfare.[31] American David Hunter Miller had written an extensive report in July 1918 that sought to bring the fine points of Wilsonianism to bear on the matter.[32] To Miller, the invasion of Belgium in August 1914 had so blatantly violated international law that it called for special means of redress.[33] Martyred Belgium could claim "restoration" as

---

[27] See Philip Mason Burnett, *Reparation at the Paris Peace Conference from the Standpoint of the American Delegation*, 2 vols. (New York: Columbia University Press, 1940), 1: 3–8.

[28] Quoted in Frederick Maurice, *The Armistices of 1918* (London: Oxford University Press, 1943), 52.

[29] English version quoted in Frederick Maurice, *The Armistices of 1918* (London: Oxford University Press, 1943), 97. The authoritative French reads:

Sous réserve de toute revendication et réclamation ultérieure de la part des Alliés et des Etats-Unis;
Réparation des dommages.

[30] See Ferdinand Larnaude, *La Guerre et la réparation des dommages* (Paris: Comité National d'Action pour la réparation intégrale des dommages causés par la guerre, 1916).

[31] Foreign Office, Political Intelligence Department, "Memorandum on President Wilson's Speeches as a Basis for Negotiation," October 12, 1918, in Miller, *Diary*, 2: 59–68, esp. 64–65.

[32] David Hunter Miller, "The American Program and International Law: Draft Memorandum," Miller, *Diary*, 2: 391–400.

[33] On the legal controversies that swirled around the invasion of Belgium, see Isabel V. Hull, *A Scrap of Paper: Breaking and Making International Law during the Great War* (Ithaca, NY: Cornell University Press, 2014), 16–50.

meaning compensation for the sum total of all financial damages suffered by the Belgian people. "Restoration" from this point of view had to mean restoration to the economic position Belgium would have enjoyed had its neutrality been respected.

The argument that Belgium constituted an exceptional case led to a slippery logic. The German armies had hardly limited their destruction to Belgium, or even to the Western Front. Theoretically, Germany and its allies could become liable for all the war costs of all the victorious powers. Not all of Miller's American colleagues agreed with him. John Foster Dulles argued in Paris for a more conservative approach based on compensation for direct physical damage.[34]

Clearly, any reparations regime in 1919 would need more explanation than had seemed necessary in 1815 or 1871. At the first meeting of the commission on reparations, the French presented a position paper justifying integral reparations drawing from the Imperial German civil code. Article 823 of the code protected the "life, body, health, liberty, and the property" of all the subjects of the Kaiser. Article 246 required the liable party "to reestablish the order of things that would have existed if the circumstances that gave rise to the obligation had not happened."[35] Millions of men, women, and children, as well as their property, had suffered destruction and damage from Germany's war. The allies, from this point of view, could satisfy justice simply by applying German standards to Germany: "Germany must make reparation for the integrality of the damage it has caused."

On February 10, 1919, the reparations commission had a lively exchange of views that would do much to shape the subsequent debate on reparations.[36] William Morris ("Billy") Hughes, prime minister of Australia and member of the British Empire delegation, argued for an expansive view of reparations, "based on the idea of justice and not on the idea of vengeance. When a wrong has been committed, the author must right that wrong up to the extreme limit of his resources."[37] Moreover, Hughes continued, "in good logic, as in justice, we cannot distinguish between restoring the devastated regions and claims for general damages."[38] Such a logic could swiftly spin out of control. According to American commission member Bernard Baruch, Hughes argued that Australian homeowners who took out mortgages to buy war bonds deserved compensation (presumably for the risk assumed), on the same terms as French homeowners whose houses had been burned by the invaders.[39] Two British Empire representatives, Lord Sumner and Lord Cunliffe, would become known as the "heavenly twins," because of their sky-high expectations from the reparations regime.

---

[34] "Proposed Principles of Reparation," *c.* February 7, 1919, in Miller, *Diary*, 5: 154.

[35] "Annexe au Procès-verbal de la séance du 3 février," in Albert Gouffre de LaPradelle, *La Paix de Versailles*, 13 vols. (Paris: Les Éditions internationals, 1929–1939), 4: 17. An English version may be found in Burnett, *Reparations*, 2: 283–84.

[36] Commission de Réparations des dommages, "Séance du 10 février 1919," in LaPradelle, *Paix de Versailles*, 4: 46.

[37] "Hughes' Speech before the Commission on the Reparation of Damage, February 19, 1919," in Burnett, *Reparations*, 1: 553–57. On Hughes and reparations, see Neville Meaney, *Australia and the World Crisis, 1901–23* (Sydney: Sydney University Press, 2009), 313–404.

[38] "Séance du 10 février," LaPradelle, *Paix de Versailles*, 4: 46.

[39] Bernard Baruch, *The Making of the Reparation and Economic Sections of the Treaty* (New York: Harper & Brothers, 1920), 6.

At the February 10 meeting, the delegations submitted general position papers. The American views proved those of an isolated minority.[40] The Italians extended the expansive concept of liability to the other Central Powers. The Poles claimed liability to individuals for damages to "their lives, their capacity to work, or their liberty, resulting from acts of the enemy" (57). All the Allied and Associated Powers deserved compensation, they argued, for "all expenditures involved [*la réparation intégrale*]" for acts resulting from the declaration of war (57). The Serbs likewise claimed full compensation, for a war "desired, premeditated, and provoked by the enemy powers toward goals of conquest, domination, and plunder [*lucre*]" (58). The British submitted a carefully reasoned, legalistic document drawing from transnational understandings of civil liability. But at the end of the day, the British concurred: "We have the absolute right to demand full payment for the cost of the war" (56).[41] As always, the British chose their words carefully. The right to demand full payment did not necessarily carry with it the right to receive.

In the days that followed, debates within the commission irretrievably entangled the issues of why Germany should pay and what Germany could pay. The Americans held to the limited position of "restoring" the occupied territories outlined in the Fourteen Points. Only the Belgians supported this position, because of the high proportion of total reparations allocated to Belgium under the American plan.[42] The British sought to "play the percentages," as the expression of the time had it, because only including some measure of total war costs would give the British what they considered their fair share of whatever amount Germany, in the end, would actually pay. Finally, on February 19, the commission reached a unanimous decision, or rather a unanimous non-decision. It would defer to the Supreme Council the question of whether the right to "integral reparations" was contrary to the intentions of the Supreme War Council in accepting the Lansing Note of November 5, 1918.[43] Because of President Wilson's absence in America and the organizational shift from the Council of Ten to the Council of Four, serious discussion of reparations did not resume until late March 1919.

In the interim, the Council had established an inter-allied committee to assess the ability of Germany to pay. Their report, submitted on March 20, made for disappointing reading for maximalists.[44] Based on prewar figures adjusted for wartime losses and likely losses of territory, the commissioners concluded that Germany would require twenty to thirty years to pay reparations even according to the strictest interpretation of the Lansing Note of November 5. If the final treaty required more than this, Germany "might, within a few years, repudiate the entire obligation as having been an imposition, and the moral opinion of the world

---

[40] "Annexes," LaPradelle, *Paix de Versailles*, 4: 55–67.

[41] The French reads: "*le droit absolu d'exiger le paiement intégral du coût de la guerre.*"

[42] See Baruch, *The Making of the Reparation and Economic Sections*, 21–22.

[43] For the rather involved precise French wording, see "Séance 19 février 1919," LaPradelle, *Paix de Versailles*, 4: 129–30.

[44] "Report, March 29, 1919, made by Norman H. Davis, R. Hon. E.S. Montagu, and Louis Loucheur Regarding the Reparation Settlement, with Special Reference to Germany's Capacity to Pay," in Ray Stannard Baker, *Woodrow Wilson and the World Settlement*, 3 vols. (Garden City, NY: Doubleday, Page & Company, 1923), 3: 376–79.

might support her in this" (378). Germans might well prefer occupation should the allies overplay their hand.

The stalemate continued once the Council of Four (or Supreme Council) sought to resolve both why Germany should pay and what Germany could pay. The British Empire delegation sent particularly confusing signals. They kept insisting on the inclusion of pensions, conspicuously unmentioned in the Fourteen Points. General Smuts of South Africa made this case again before the Council in a well-circulated memo of March 31, by arguing that death and injury to soldiers extended the damage to their families. Germany owed pensions to widows and their dependents as reparations for "civilian" damage.[45]

But in what became known as the March 25 "Fontainebleau memo" from Lloyd George, he warned that "in the end if she [Germany] feels that she has been unjustly treated in the peace of 1919 she will find means of exacting retribution from her conquerors."[46] Two days later, he reminded Clemenceau at a meeting of the Supreme Council that in 1815, the Duke of Wellington and Viscount Castlereagh had moderated Prussian demands, as it would have been "a great error to seek to destroy France, whose presence was necessary for civilization and European stability." At the same meeting, Wilson agreed that "we must avoid giving our enemies even the impression of injustice."[47]

As tempers began to flare, the conversation morphed into a discussion of just why Germany should pay at all. Clemenceau connected justice and coercion. "The Germans are a servile people," he argued, "who need force to support an argument." They would never accept responsibility for their actions until compelled to do so. He disagreed with the Napoleonic adage that nothing permanent could be based on force: "I am not sure of that; for it is enough to look at the great nations of Europe and the United States itself to have doubts." "Justice" would have to be unilateral, something imposed by the Allied and Associated Powers on a Germany incapable of sincere repentance: "We must do everything we can to be just toward the Germans; but as for persuading them that we are just towards them, that is another matter."[48]

The next day, March 28, a discussion about reparations melded with a discussion about French claims over the Saar, and resulted in Clemenceau directly confronting Wilson. Justice meant one thing among moral equals, another among morally superior and morally inferior parties. Clemenceau scolded the American president:

> You seek to do justice to the Germans. Don't believe they will ever forgive us; they seek only the opportunity for revenge. Nothing will extinguish the rage of those who wanted to establish their domination over the world and who believed themselves so close to succeeding.[49]

[45] Jan Smuts, "Notes on Reparation," in Baruch, *The Making of the Reparation and Economic Sections*, 29–32.

[46] "A Memorandum by David Lloyd George," March 25, 1919, *PWW*, 56: 260.

[47] "Conversation between President Wilson and MM. Clemenceau, Lloyd George, and Orlando," March 27, 1919, Mantoux, *Deliberations*, 1: 31.

[48] "Conversation," March 27, 1919, Mantoux, *Deliberations*, 1: 33.

[49] "Conversation between President Wilson and MM. Clemenceau, Lloyd George, Orlando, and Tardieu," March 28, 1919, Mantoux, *Deliberations*, 1: 63.

As the conversation reheated, Clemenceau further moralized reparations. French losses in blood and treasure had created a national sentiment that reparation "isn't only a matter of material repairs. The need for moral redress [*réparations morales*] is no less great" (62). "Justice" had to go beyond the material payments: "This is the reason we must arrive, not at a mathematical justice, but at a justice which takes feeling into account" (64). Of course, such a position raised the uncomfortable question of how such a concept of justice could ever be satisfied.

All along, lower-level diplomats had been seeking a practical exit from the impasse. As early as February 22, John Foster Dulles submitted draft articles on reparations that recognized in the abstract German responsibility for all war costs. But the victors would recognize "that the ability of the German Government and nation to make reparation is not unlimited, which renders the making of such complete reparation impossible."[50] According to a revised draft four days later, "the German Government recognizes complete legal and moral responsibility for all damage and loss." The plan included a set payment schedule, with a Claims Commission to adjudicate claims and a Finance Commission to adjudicate actual payment.[51] Eventually, this solution trickled up to the Supreme Council. As Norman Davis of the American delegation put it: "We can write that Germany is morally responsible for the war and all its consequences and that, legally, she is responsible for damages to property and persons, according to the formula provided."[52] Disagreements in the Council continued, not just as to the specific wording, but as to the amounts and modalities of payment. Discussions again became fraught, and at one point, Wilson summoned his ship the *George Washington* to the harbor at Brest, threatening to leave the conference altogether. But by April 7, the Supreme Council agreed to what would become Articles 231 and 232 of the Treaty of Versailles.

Historians have long known that Article 231 and Article 232 existed in direct relation to each other. As early as 1926, two American scholars suggested that the whole problem revolved around translation.[53] The original translation used by the German delegation referred to Germany as *als Urheber* (the instigator or pre-meditated author) of the war. The more appropriate translation, the scholars argued, would have been *Verursacher*, a more restrictive term meaning the agent of immediate cause. The "cause" in this case was simply the invasion of Belgium. The Germans themselves had admitted as much, what they saw as the military necessity of the invasion notwithstanding. Three years later, Robert Binkley developed what has become the standard explanation—the sole purpose of Article 231 was to

---

[50] "Draft of Mr. Dulles," February 22, 1919, in Miller, *Diary*, 6: 25–26.

[51] "Redraft by Mr. Dulles," February 26, 1919, in Miller, *Diary*, 6: 56.

[52] "Conference among MM. Clemenceau, Lloyd George, Colonel House, Baruch, Davis, Lamont, Lord Sumner, Klotz, Loucheur, De la Chaume, and Crespi," April 5, 1919, in Mantoux, *Deliberations*, 1: 147–48.

[53] Robert C. Binkley and A.C. Mahr, "A New Interpretation of the 'Responsibility' Clause in the Versailles Treaty," *Current History*, January 1, 1926, 398–400. The level of linguistic expertise in the German Foreign Ministry makes this argument problematic.

establish legal liability for reparations.[54] It was thus more about compensation than inculpation. In 1932, Camille Bloch and Pierre Renouvin lent their considerable prestige to a similar set of conclusions.[55] In 1940, Phillip Burnett described a solved historical problem: "The language of Article 231 in the final Treaty with Germany, then, originated in the American desire to reconcile British and French Political necessities with the American requirement of abiding by the terms of the [Lansing] Note of November 5, 1918."[56]

Any international agreement becomes what the signatories make of it. For their part, the representatives of the Allied and Associated Powers took German war guilt as a given, morally as well as legally.[57] Consequently, they could write of it in narrow, legalistic terms, and bury explicit mention of war guilt a full 231 articles into a lengthy treaty. For the Germans, however, the entire concept of war guilt provided not just an insult, but an opportunity. War guilt provided Germany with a way to continue the war through diplomatic means.

Taken together, the mutually dependent Articles 231 and 232 decided what there was to decide on the reparations, morally and legally. Any system of compensation has some sort of moral foundation. The foundation inherited from the previous century was morally non-judgmental. Losers paid simply because they lost. The game of realist competition would continue as before, the material capabilities of the players adjusted through the settlement. But after the Great War, a "total" war brought forth a new discourse of "total" reparations. The British Empire, France, and Belgium had all called for the inclusion of civilian damages on that moral basis. The more legalistically minded Americans, who had suffered relatively little, supported an older notion of compensation.

At the discursive level, the compromise among the allies created a distinction between payable and unpayable German debts, both underpinned by a moral criminalization of Germany. Article 232 suggested an undefined but practical limit to the amount that Germany would ever pay. Financial reparations would eventually come to an end, at a point to be worked out through normal diplomatic machinery. But an unpayable moral debt justified that material debt. To recall Clemenceau's words, exactly how would Germany pay *réparations morales*, and at what point could the world consider the account paid in full? Would Germany remain a criminalized once—and future—Great Power forever? Brockdorff understood very well the tangled and problematic relationship between morality and reparations in the treaty, and for that reason he placed it at the center of his attack on the entire enterprise of the Paris Peace Conference.

---

[54] Robert C. Binkley, "The 'Guilt' Clause in the Versailles Treaty," *Current History*, May 1, 1929, 294–300.

[55] Camille Bloch and Pierre Renouvin, "L'Art. 231 du Traité de Versailles: sa genèse et sa signification," *Revue d'Histoire de la guerre mondiale*, 19 (1932): 1–24.

[56] Burnett, *Reparations*, 1: 69.

[57] The Commission on Responsibilities specifically excluded war guilt from consideration, in order to focus on the criminal responsibility of individuals. See Bloch and Renouvin, "L'article 231," 6–9.

THE LEGALITY OF RESPONSIBILITY

Before 1945, war crimes under international law concerned states rather than individuals. For that reason, the Paris Peace Conference took a separate track for discerning criminality by establishing a Commission on Responsibilities. Historians of international law have considered "responsibilities" after the Great War in terms of evolving individual accountability for state actions. This makes the commission part of what James Willis called a "prologue to Nuremberg," which would prefigure the war crimes trials after World War II.[58] I take a related but distinct tack here in examining "responsibilities" as a means of articulating the sovereignty of justice.

The Commission on Responsibilities provided some of the most sophisticated discussions of state sovereignty to be found at the Paris Peace Conference. The task of the commission seemed obvious. The sub-commission tasked with establishing the facts of the outbreak of the war was hardly going to arrive at any other conclusion than that "Germany" had caused the Great War. But who was "Germany," and whom could the victors find criminally liable for what "Germany" had done? "Responsibility" had to involve the articulation of new international law. Like those of the Commission on Reparations, the recommendations of the Commission on Responsibilities constituted a compromise—a grandiose but ill-defined scheme for pursuing individual perpetrators for crimes of state.

No academic conference could have brought together a more impressive array of international lawyers than the Commission on Responsibilities. The president of the commission, United States Secretary of State Robert Lansing, had been a founder of the *American Journal of International Law* (*AJIL*), as well as a prominent lawyer in arbitration cases before entering public service in 1914. His colleague James Brown Scott had been an American delegate to the second Hague conference in 1907. Fernand Larnaude was dean of the law faculty at the University of Paris, and his colleague Albert Gouffre de LaPradelle had directed various international law journals and served as legal counsel to the French Foreign Ministry. Ernest Pollock of Britain was a Member of Parliament and solicitor general, the second ranking legal officer for England and Wales after the attorney general. Nikolaos Politis, foreign minister of Greece, had taught international law in Paris before the war. Edouard Rolin-Jaequemyns of Belgium had directed the Institut du Droit International, which had been awarded the 1904 Nobel Peace Prize for its work promoting international law.

The original language setting up the Commission on Responsibilities provided a vast mandate. The conference charged the commission with: investigating "the responsibility of the authors of the war" and the facts of "the breaches of the laws and customs of war"; assigning degrees of responsibility, "however highly placed"; the establishment of the appropriate tribunals in order to prosecute the resulting

[58] James F. Willis, *Prologue to Nuremberg: The Politics and Diplomacy of Punishing War Criminals of the First World War* (Westport, CT: Greenwood Press, 1982). See also Kate Parlett, *The Individual in the International Legal System: Continuity and Change in International Law* (Cambridge: Cambridge University Press, 2011), 234–41; and Mark Lewis, *The Birth of the New Justice: The Internationalization of Crime and Punishment, 1919–1950* (Cambridge: Cambridge University Press, 2014), 27–63.

cases; and "any other matters cognate or ancillary to the above," meaning most anything the commission wished to consider.[59] At its first meeting on February 3, the commission elected Lansing its president, as the highest-ranking delegate present.[60] Doing so would have considerable implications for how the commission structured its task. At its second meeting on February 7, it established three sub-commissions—on "criminal facts [*faits criminels*]," "war responsibilities [*responsabilités de la guerre*]," and "responsibilities for violations of the law and customs of war [*responsibilité des violations des lois et coutumes de guerre*]" (22).

Considerable wrangling immediately ensued within the commission about the sequence of proceedings and jurisdiction. Did the facts need to be established before any of the work of the commission could proceed? States could not be put on trial. Did this, for example, make "Germany" reducible to the now-exiled Kaiser, or the "Ottoman Empire" to the captive Sultan? In any event, as Kate Parlett has affirmed, in 1919 "there was no developed conception of individual criminal responsibility under international law."[61] A doctrine of sovereign immunity dating from the Middle Ages protected heads of state.[62] Previously, war crimes had been tried in national courts under national procedures. The international prosecution of war criminals would require new law and new institutions. But an ancient maxim common to both continental and Anglo-American law stipulated *nullum crimen, nulla poena sine lege* [no crime, no penalty without law].[63] Prosecuting a former head of state for crimes that did not exist as such at the time they were committed presented formidable legal hurdles.

At the heart of the matter lay fundamental differences as to the sources and purposes of international law. The French often made arguments based in natural law, a timeless, knowable, and absolute set of principles to which all states and all humanity could be held accountable, before and after the fact.[64] Clemenceau appeared to support such a position at the first plenary meeting of the conference, borrowing the Wilsonian notion that the victors were simply the instruments of universal principles. Those principles themselves had produced the allied victory, leading to an argument that could prove itself: "If it is wished to establish law in the world," he argued, "penalties for the breach thereof can be applied at once, since the allied and associated powers are victorious."[65]

Clemenceau drew the attention of the conference to an article written by Larnaude and LaPradelle on the criminal liability of the Kaiser.[66] Nationals of a

---

[59] "Secretary's Notes," January 23, 1919, 699.

[60] Commission sur les Responsabilités des auteurs de la guerre et sanctions, "Lundi, 3 février 1919," in LaPradelle, *Paix de Versailles*, 3: 10.

[61] Parlett, *The Individual in the International Legal System*, 230.

[62] George W. Pugh, "Historical Approach to the Doctrine of Sovereign Immunity," *Louisiana Law Review* 13.3 (1953): 476–94.

[63] Aly Mokhtar, "Nullum Crimen, Nulla Poena Sine Lege: Aspects and Prospects," *Statute Law Review* 26.1 (2005): 41–55, esp. 41–47.

[64] On the French delegation and natural law, see Willis, *Prelude to Nuremberg*, 72–73.

[65] "Preliminary Peace Conference, Protocol No. 1, Session of January 19, 1919," *FRUS: PPC*, 3: 169.

[66] Fernand Larnaude and Albert Geouffre de LaPradelle, "Examen de la responsabilité pénale de l'Emperer Guillaume II," in LaPradelle, *Paix de Versailles*, 9–1 (Supplement): 5–27.

country that knew something about the theatrics of criminal trials, Larnaude and Gouffre de LaPradelle argued that in order to provide "the solemn and purifying sanction demanded by the public conscience, higher jurisdiction is necessary, more resounding debates, a grander stage" (15). Wilhelm II had personal criminal liability as warlord (*Kriegsherr*): "The emperor possessed an absolute prerogative that he exercised personally through his war cabinet, without the necessity of going through the War Ministry" (19). Because of the victory, "a new international law is born" (16). Natural law had always been morally right. The victory provided new means of articulating and enforcing it through new international law.

Lansing, on the other hand, operated within a positivist paradigm that predominated in the *AJIL*.[67] Under positivism, states are the elemental units of the international system. International law can be neither more nor less than what states determine it to be. While law may be guided in some sense by abstract principle, it is the creation of what states do, incrementally and in concert with one another. This organic, Burkean conception of international law saw no law-making role for non-state actors (such as a peace conference), least of all in making international criminal law.

Lansing, while not a major thinker on state sovereignty, had written extensively on the subject before the war.[68] As a positivist, he believed sovereignty preceded law, the reverse of a natural law paradigm. International law operated along a track of civil law rather than criminal law—until such time as states chose to delegate sovereignty over criminal law to supranational bodies. On certain reprehensible activities, such as piracy or the slave trade, states de facto had reached broad consensus. But even for these "international" crimes, actual prosecution could take place only in national courts. International judicial bodies in the present existed for arbitration, not prosecution. While positivists could be friendly toward an organic concept of "world government," the consensual, state-driven means of building it would do so over an indefinite period of time.

Lansing as president of the Commission on Responsibilities would ferociously support *nullum crimen, nulla poena sine lege*. Law could not be created after the fact, nor could tribunals be created to enforce such law. Above all, the Allied and Associated Powers could not try Kaiser Wilhelm without destabilizing state sovereignty itself. Having already lost a sub-commission confrontation on establishing tribunals on February 25,[69] Lansing proposed on March 12 before the full commission a declaration to be appended to a peace treaty that would displace the whole matter to the political realm.[70] Because of the "immunity from accusation and trial enjoyed by a monarch who is head of state," the Kaiser would be

[67] See Leonard V. Smith, "The Wilsonian Challenge to International Law," *Journal of the History of International Law* 13.1 (2011): 179–208, esp. 182–89.

[68] Three articles by Lansing written between 1907 and 1913 were published as *Notes on Sovereignty: From the Standpoint of the State and of the World* (Washington, D.C.: Carnegie Foundation for International Peace, 1921).

[69] See the protracted discussion in Troisième Sous-Commission, "25 février 1919," in LaPradelle, *Paix de Versailles*, 3: 312–24.

[70] "Project de resolution" and "Proposition de la delegation américaine," from "12 mars 1919," in LaPradelle, *Paix de Versailles*, 3: 331–32.

condemned politically and morally (but not legally) by a newly constituted commission of inquiry. That commission would affirm publicly that German motives had violated "morality and international justice." But the matter would end there. Lansing defended his position in an argument he had made virtually verbatim before the war: "the essential character of sovereignty is the absence of responsibility toward any other person" (334).[71] The Germans, for better or worse, had conferred their sovereignty on the Emperor-King Wilhelm II. State and crown were inextricable. Other states could legally make war on Wilhelm, and conceivably kill him in the process. But legally, they could not try him for any act of state.

Larnaude, predictably, responded that either they had assembled in Paris to create a new and more just international order, or they had not. No one, not even a Kaiser, could be above legal responsibility in the new world. A clearly irritated Larnaude continued: "If we suppress this responsibility, particularly considering such a rigid structure of the German army, how could we possibly pursue others— soldiers, officers, staff officers, who could be even more guilty than the Kaiser—it is possible—but who could not however be pursued and punished if the Kaiser was not?" (336). Given the distance between Larnaude and Lansing, the latter quickly brought the session to a close, without the adoption of his proposal.

British arguments sought to combine natural law and positivist approaches to international law, with an inclination toward the latter. Ernest Pollock, presiding over a meeting of the second sub-commission (on general responsibilities) on February 17, counseled caution on practical grounds in seeking to invent new law on unleashing aggressive war. A thorough investigation of the calamity of 1914 would have to go back many years, and include detailed archival research in various countries. Such an inquest "would necessarily involve many arduous and complicated problems what are better left to historical research and men of state than to a tribunal charged with judging violators of the laws and customs of war" (369). On the other hand, and in contrast to Lansing, Pollock believed that the peace conference provided a catalytic moment for the transformation of international law along positivist lines. He argued on March 17: "We consider the present situation as providing an occasion to develop the law" (370). Working together, he argued, the victors should seize the exceptional historical moment. Pollock particularly supported the establishment of international tribunals for accused war criminals. Britain, after all, in the previous century had led the movement to establish mixed commissions to suppress the slave trade.[72]

Throughout the commission and sub-commission meetings, Pollock zealously advocated bringing Wilhelm II to international justice. Lloyd George, caught up in his own inflamed rhetoric during the "khaki election" of December 1918, had long called for a trial.[73] Yet the matter was always more complicated than it looked. Wilhelm II, after all, remained the eldest grandson of Queen Victoria. While the Kaiser had certainly played a role in the national war effort, so had

---

[71] "12 mars 1919," in LaPradelle, *Paix de Versailles*, 3: 334. For the prewar explanation, see Robert Lansing, "Notes on Sovereignty in a State," Part I, *AJIL* 1.1 (1907): 107.

[72] Lewis, *New Justice*, 14–15.   [73] See Willis, *Prelude to Nuremberg*, 49–64.

King George V.[74] However much the king personally disliked his first cousin, he never supported putting him on trial. In any event, the Kaiser had fled to the Netherlands before the armistice. The Dutch had a long tradition of granting political asylum, and refused any requests to turn the Kaiser over to the allies.[75] As a result, Pollock and Lloyd George could call loudly for a trial of the Kaiser, secure in the knowledge that it stood little chance of actually taking place.

On March 29, 1919, the Commission on Responsibilities submitted its report, followed on April 6 by minority reports from the American and Japanese delegations.[76] The commission concluded to the surprise of no one that through "a dark conspiracy against the peace of Europe" (4), Germany and Austria-Hungary, followed by Turkey and Bulgaria, had provoked a premeditated war. The report broke new if vague legal ground by asserting personal criminal liability on the part of those leading the defeated powers, including heads of state (20). In response to the crime of violating the neutrality of Belgium and Luxembourg, the report concluded that "it would be right for the Peace Conference, in a matter so unprecedented, to adopt special measures, and even to create a special organ in order to deal as they deserve with the authors of such acts" (23). The commission did call for specific penal sanction for future such infractions. The report provided detailed recommendations for the establishment of a future High Tribunal to prosecute "Violations of the Laws and Customs of War and of the Laws of Humanity" (23–26). Future law would include treatment of civilians and prisoners of war, and submarine warfare. An international tribunal comprising representatives of the Allied and Associated Powers would define procedures, and write specific statutes.

The American dissent, written by Lansing and Scott, unambiguously endorsed *nullum crimen, nulla poena sine lege*, and sovereign immunity. "An act could not be a crime in the legal sense of the word," they held, "unless it were made so by law, and that the commission of an act declared to be a crime could not be punished unless the law prescribed the penalty to be inflicted" (74). Because the peace conference could not create new criminal law on waging war, it could not create new institutions to enforce it. Violating the neutrality of Belgium and Luxembourg were political rather than legal offenses, and "matters for statesmen, not for judges" (66). Further, they contended, "no precedents are to be found in the modern practice of nations" (65) for prosecuting heads of state. They saw endeavoring to do so as a political attempt directed toward a certain individual, the former Kaiser. Heads of state could not be held accountable to any law but their own: "subordinating him [the sovereign] to foreign jurisdictions to which neither he nor his country owes allegiance or obedience, thus denying the very conception of sovereignty"

---

[74] For example, the king had gone out of his way to protect General Sir Douglas Haig in 1917 and 1918. See Ian Beckett, "King George V and His Generals," in Matthew Hughes and Mark Seligmann, eds., *Leadership in Conflict, 1914–1918* (Barnsley: Leo Cooper, 2000), 247–64.

[75] Nigel J. Ashton and Duco Hellema, "Hanging the Kaiser: Anglo-Dutch Relations and the Fate of Wilhelm II, 1918–20," *Diplomacy & Statecraft* 11.2 (2000): 53–78.

[76] *Violations of the Laws and Customs of War: Reports of Majority and Dissenting Reports of American and Japanese Members of the Commission on Responsibilities, Conference of Paris, 1919*, Carnegie Endowment for International Peace, Division of International Law, Pamphlet No. 32 (Oxford: Clarendon Press, 1919).

(65–66). A brief report from the Japanese supported the American position. As subjects of a constitutionally divinized emperor, they particularly stressed the need to exempt heads of state from any conceivable criminal liability (80).

The Council of Four held two impassioned discussions of the report, on April 2 and April 8.[77] Wilson, Lloyd George, and Clemenceau held forth to each other as politicians on fine points of international law over which renowned experts differed greatly. None brought new legal arguments to the table. Rather, they began with a shared moral assumption of German responsibility, and debated the proper legal means of bringing that responsibility into the peace treaty. Consequently, the debate became a moral and political discussion of the law.

The members of the Supreme Council held close to the positions provided by their national delegations. Clemenceau echoed Larnaude and LaPradelle. Also echoing Schmitt *avant la lettre*, Clemenceau argued for their responsibility as provisional world sovereign to decide upon the exception—to make new law as victors in an exceptional war. They had gathered together to change the world. Changing the nature and reach of international law in accordance with universal principles provided the opportunity to do so: "For me, one law dominates all others: that of responsibility. Civilization is the organization of human responsibilities" (193). All responsible Germans, including the ex-Kaiser, should be tried according to new law by new international tribunals.

For Wilson, war responsibilities proved a rare area of agreement in the otherwise troubled relationship between himself and Lansing. Wilson, in fact, had made it known to Lansing that he wanted an American minority report opposing a criminal trial of the Kaiser.[78] Wilson, as the only head of state on the Supreme Council, had his successors to think of. The president hastened to remind his colleagues, "it is Congress [and not the president] that declares war in the United States" (119). Just as he opposed any kind of international armed force for the League, so too did he oppose international juridical power in criminal matters.

Lloyd George likewise remained true to form—speaking grandly with different positions on different days. He commented as though he were still on the campaign trail: "We have the right to say that, for us, the war won't be ended so long as the enemy hasn't handed over those who are judged guilty of certain crimes" (192). He scornfully represented to his colleagues the Japanese objection to trying the Kaiser based on a parallel to their own emperor: "the Mikado is a god who cannot be held responsible" (119). Wilson joined him in rejecting what Wilson called this "ridiculous principle" (120), even though he had made the same argument for non-divinized heads of state. The British prime minister came around on the matter shortly thereafter by conceding: "the Japanese principle is the English principle— that the King can commit no crime" (120). Had Germany won the war, the prime minister would have been held responsible, not the king. Lloyd George understood full well the complications of trying the cousin of his sovereign.

[77] "Conversation between President Wilson and MM. Clemenceau, Lloyd George, and Orlando," April 2, 1919, 4 p.m.; and "Conversation between President Wilson and MM. Clemenceau, Lloyd George, and Orlando," April 8, 1919, 3 p.m., in Mantoux, *Deliberations*, 1: 118–23; 187–95.

[78] Willis, *Prologue to Nuremberg*, 75.

Orlando, the only career jurist on the Supreme Council, agreed with Lansing that criminal law belonged to national sovereignty: "Crime is essentially a violation of the domestic law of each national entity, a violation of a subject's obligation towards his sovereign. To create a different precedent is a serious thing" (191). Even the Belgians, the violation of whose neutrality had constituted the core of the case against the Kaiser, declined to lead any prosecution against him. On April 18, Clemenceau reported that Albert I, King of the Belgians, "as the representative of a country with a monarchical constitution ... doesn't accept the arraignment of a sovereign."[79] With two Great Powers and a directly concerned small power opposed to the stated British and French positions, the peacemakers needed to find an exit strategy.

The relevant articles in the Treaty of Versailles exemplified obfuscation, arguably more so than Articles 231 and 232. As per Article 227, the Allied and Associated Powers took it upon themselves to "publicly arraign" the former Kaiser for "a supreme offense against international morality and the sanctity of treaties." They would form a tribunal of five judges, one from each of the victorious Great Powers. This tribunal would be guided by "the highest motives of international policy," and would emphasize "the validity of international morality." It could fix unspecified punishments it considered appropriate. The powers would make an extradition request to the Netherlands. Such stipulations, of course, implied two possible all-or-nothing outcomes. Either the new tribunal would essentially invent a new, enforceable body of international criminal law, or no trial would happen at all. Diverse sides in the debate all could read their desired outcomes into Article 227.

Article 228 provided for other categories of perpetrators. Individuals who had violated the "laws and customs of war" were to be extradited and tried by military tribunals under the codes of the countries in which the alleged infractions had taken place. But as Mark Lewis has argued, this outcome included important concessions to the American, Italian, and Japanese positions.[80] Most importantly, the accused would be tried by existing, national institutions of military justice in the country against which the alleged offense took place rather than by inter-national tribunals (Article 229).[81] Such an outcome arguably had some prior standing, given that courts martial traditionally could try foreign nationals in their custody in wartime. But by definition, the proposed trials would take place in peacetime. Extradition of the accused could hardly be taken for granted, notwith-standing Article 230, which required the extradition of inculpated persons and the transfer of all relevant documentation.

The articles in the Treaty of Versailles covering reparations and responsibilities had distinct origins at the Paris Peace Conference. The articles in both categories reflected non-trivial differences among the allies on principles of peacemaking and international law. Reconciling these differences led to articles that said very

---

[79] "Conversation between President Wilson and MM. Clemenceau, Viscount Chinda, Balfour, Lansing, and Baron Sonnino," April 16, 1919, 4 p.m., in Mantoux, *Deliberations*, 1: 269.

[80] Lewis, *New Justice*, 50.

[81] If nationals of more than one country were involved, the concerned parties would form a mixed tribunal.

different things to different people. The Germans would seize on these ambiguities in a campaign to instrumentalize the criminalized identity created by the Treaty of Versailles. In attacking the injustice of that identity, Germany could seek to undermine the legitimacy of the Paris Peace Conference itself. Doing so became the cornerstone of recasting German sovereignty in the new international order.

THE GERMANS COUNTERATTACK:
EMBRACING DEFEAT AND VICTORY

Brockdorff's speech on May 7 proved no more than the daring opening round of a determined campaign on the part of the German delegation to seize discursive control over the sovereignty of justice. States can make inventive use of adverse circumstances. John Dower coined the term "embracing defeat" to describe how postwar Japan sought to restore its sovereignty by pursuing a role as the key ally of the United States in Cold War Asia.[82] In the case of Germany, such rhetoric embraced the defeat of the Kaiserreich and the victory of Wilsonianism, to re-establish German sovereignty as that of a Great Power.

Criminalizing Germany mattered as much to Germany as it meant to the Allied and Associated Powers. Embracing this identity enabled the new regime to set the stated values of the new international system against it. Between 1919 and 1945, nothing drew Germans together so much as resisting the hated Treaty of Versailles. In placing a self-caricatured, criminalized Germany at the heart of the new international system, the German delegation could impugn the entire postwar settlement. By the 1930s, they and their successors surely had done so.

As we have seen, millenarian thinking had pervaded mobilization and remobilization throughout the Great War. Michael Geyer showed how a specifically German "catastrophic nationalism" emerged as the military situation worsened in the fall of 1918.[83] Calls for a *Volkserhebung* (popular insurrection) to face the Allied forces had some surprising supporters, among them Walter Rathenau, a centrist liberal who had masterminded German economic mobilization. Some military commanders endorsed an *Endkampf* (Final Battle). On the ground, this meant a scorched-earth retreat from Belgium and an apocalyptic fight to the death in the Rhineland. At sea, the notion of an *Endkampf* produced an actual plan. On October 26, 1918, a group of senior commanders in the Admiralty went so far as to issue orders to the Imperial Navy to confront the British Navy on the high seas.[84]

The point of such Wagnerian scenarios was not the material defeat of the allied forces, an outcome even their supporters considered highly unlikely. Rather, the imaginary of catastrophic nationalism centered on, as Geyer put it, the "desperate hope of being carried from the shadow of defeat into the light of redemption and

---

[82] John Dower, *Embracing Defeat: Japan in the Wake of World War II* (New York: W.W. Norton & Company, 1999).

[83] Michael Geyer, "Insurrectionary Warfare: The German Debate about a *Levée en Masse* in October 1918," *Journal of Modern History* 73.3 (2001): 459–527.

[84] The scheme provoked mutiny, strikes, and the fall of the Kaiserreich within a few days.

rebirth" (509). Germany, having lost the war on the ground, could continue the war discursively. Glorious annihilation could enter the realm of myth, from which a new Germany could arise like the phoenix.

Ernst Troeltsch famously described the interval between armistice and the presentation of the Treaty of Versailles as "*das Traumland der Waffenstillstandsperiode* [the dreamland of the armistice period]."[85] The overthrow of the Kaiserreich, the outbreak of peace, the global expectations of Wilsonianism, and the absence of an actual allied invasion all encouraged the German national community to believe anything was possible. Soldiers marched home in what appeared to be perfect order. Acting president Friederich Ebert famously assured his compatriots that "no enemy has vanquished you." Germany still occupied vast territories to its east. Germans at all ranks of the social and political order found it possible to assure themselves that the armistice had not marked a defeat, but a new beginning. Germany had embraced the Fourteen Points and the new international order it seemed to promise. Shorn of the Kaiser and the imperial regime, democratic Germany could resume its place in the inner circle of the Great Powers, its standing in the world none the worse for wear.

In his remarks to the plenary on May 7, Brockdorff sought to make the "dreamland" a reality by opening a discursive counterattack on the Paris Peace Conference itself. On May 29, after weeks of frantic effort, the German delegation continued the counterattack through extensive counterproposals to the draft treaty.[86] In signing the armistice, their argument went, Germany had embraced neither defeat nor criminalization, but admission to an international contractual community based on Wilsonianism. The Paris Peace Conference had unjustly excluded Germany from that community. "We were grieved," the delegation wrote in its cover letter to Clemenceau as president of the conference, "when reading this document to see what conditions victorious Might demanded of us."[87]

From this perspective, Germany had a duty to restore the integrity to the peace, which the misguided peacemakers had so sadly permitted to fall away. The Great War was a dispute among moral equals that had not ended in victory for anyone. The relatively disadvantageous military position of Germany at the armistice implied some concessions. But above all, Germany had to be treated as an equal in peacemaking, as it had been an equal in accepting the armistice: "Germany has a right to the discussion of the terms of peace. This discussion can only extend to the application of the Fourteen Points and of the subsequent proclamations of Mr. Wilson."[88] The Germans, in short, proposed nothing less than returning to the murky business of interpreting Wilsonianism.

---

[85] Quoted in Klaus Schwabe, "Germany's Peace Aims and the Domestic and International Constraints," in Boemeke et al., eds., *The Treaty of Versailles*, 42.

[86] Indeed, so extensive were the counterproposals (some 100 printed pages) that there had not been time to translate them into French and English, as Clemenceau's instructions of May 7 had required. Luckau, *German Delegation*, 87.

[87] Covering Letter to the German Counterproposals of May 29, 1919, in Luckau, *German Delegation*, 302.

[88] "German Counterproposals of May 29, 1919," in Luckau, *German Delegation*, 308.

To be sure, by accepting the Lansing Note of November 5 as a prelude to the armistice, the Germans had accepted the ominous term "aggression" and the need to pay for its consequences. As an original guarantor of Belgium, Germany would accept responsibility for paying for the damage caused to civilians resulting from the regrettable if necessary invasion of 1914 (348). To show its good faith, Germany would even offer some compensation for the damage caused in northern France, as well as the war loans raised by Belgium, "as a voluntary concession" (349). But even this limited liability would have to be adjudicated by a neutral international commission. The German response scorned the proposed Reparations Commissions, which would "have the power to administer Germany like the estate of a bankrupt" (313). While the German delegation abjured the exiled Kaiser, it protested the idea that "German citizens be handed over to courts of the enemy Powers" (313). Brockdorff's cover letter re-emphasized his previous demand for "a neutral examination of the responsibility for the war and crimes committed during the war" (305). Victors' justice was both immoral and illegal.

According to the German counterproposals, "national self-determination" meant a territorial settlement in which ethnic Germans who so chose could live in Germany. Even in Alsace and Lorraine, under French military occupation since the armistice, Germany could right the "wrong done to France" in Alsace and Lorraine as per Point VIII of the Fourteen Points by allowing a plebiscite. The delegation did admit that "an injustice was committed in 1871" (330) by not holding a plebiscite after the Prussian victory. But two wrongs could not make a right, and post-Imperial Germany would do better. Inhabitants could choose among annexation by France, the status of a Free State within Germany, or complete independence (330). As for German-speaking Austria, "German cannot pledge herself to oppose the desire of her German brothers in Austria, as the right of self-determination should apply universally and not only to the disadvantage of Germany" (332). The same presumably applied to the Germans of Bohemia and Moravia, though the counterproposals did not even mention the lands that had become Czechoslovakia.

The delegation castigated any likely settlement in Poland as a special travesty of Wilsonian principles. The assignment of Upper Silesia to Poland in the draft treaty "constitutes a quite unjustifiable inroad into the geographical and economic structure of the German Empire" (333). According to the German delegation, anyone who mattered in Upper Silesia—intellectuals, landowners, skilled workers, labor leaders—"are, without exception, German" (334). As to the industrial riches of the region: "Germany cannot dispense with Upper Silesia, whilst Poland is not in need of it" (334). Moreover, the outlandish demand for reparations meant that "Germany can meet her liabilities resulting from the world war only in conjunction with Upper Silesia, and never without her" (334–35).

The idea of a "Polish Corridor," providing access to the sea, necessarily involved mutilating Prussia, and creating a forsaken island of Germany in East Prussia. Likewise, "the attempt to make Danzig a free city, and to surrender its means of communication and the representation of its rights abroad to the Polish state, would lead to violent opposition and to a continuous state of war in the east"

(336). Instead, the "free and secure access to the sea," assured to Poland in Point XIII of the Fourteen Points, could be guaranteed through German territory and German ports. The world could count on democratic, post-Imperial Germany to stand by the Fourteen Points, by clear implication more so than the authors of the draft treaty.

Interestingly, the counterproposals made scant mention of the military provisions, proposing simply that in the transitional period to the new regime, "Germany retains the right to maintain such forces as are required to preserve internal order, which is so much shaken at the present time" (322). German agreement to demobilize would simply provide a further gesture of German good will, as a prelude to the global disarmament envisioned under Point IV of the Fourteen Points. Presumably the League of Nations once created would lead this effort, with Germany as a charter member.

Colonies remained a priority. Germany "has acquired them lawfully and has developed them by means of incessant and fruitful toil and at the cost of many sacrifices" (340). Before 1914, the other Great Powers had never contested Germany's right to them. Colonies would remain vital as markets, sources of raw materials, and as possible sites of emigration (340–41). Simply removing them from German custody as punishment would defy Point V of the Fourteen Points, which called for "a free, open-minded, and absolutely impartial adjustment of all colonial claims." Germany would, however, agree "to administer her colonies according to the principles of the League of Nations—possibly as the mandatory of the latter" (343) provided it immediately acceded to League membership.

Charter membership in the League under a rewritten Covenant became the linchpin of recognizing post-Imperial Germany as a Great Power. The delegation argued that the proposed Covenant provided simply "a continuance of the present hostile coalition which does not deserve the name of 'League of Nations'" (315). Rather audaciously under the circumstances, the delegation had submitted its own proposal for a League of Nations on May 10.[89] As the German delegation pointed out, Germany could hardly sign a treaty establishing an international organization that the very same treaty precluded it from joining. However, Germany did show itself willing to negotiate the future form of the League based on the Covenant as it then appeared, "under the condition that Germany shall enter the League of Nations as a power with equal privileges as soon as the peace document agreed upon has been signed" (321).

Such an experienced German delegation could scarcely have been surprised at the vehemence of the response from the Supreme Council delivered on June 16.[90] This response completed the conflation of compensatory and criminal approaches

---

[89] "Proposals of the German Government for the Establishment of a League of Nations," May 10, 1919, in Luckau, *German Delegation*, 226–33.

[90] This response comprised two documents, a letter from Clemenceau entitled "Allied Reply to the German Counterproposals, June 16, 1919" and a collective document titled "Reply of the Allied and Associated Powers to the Observations of the German Delegation on the Conditions of Peace," both in Luckau, *German Delegation*, 411–73.

to justice. The allies anthropomorphized Germany as both a sociopath and a spoiled, petulant adolescent. "The protest of the German Delegation," the Council scolded, "shows that they utterly fail to understand the position in which Germany stands today" (411). "Not satisfied with that growing prosperity and influence to which Germany was entitled," they continued, the leaders of the Reich "required that they should be able to dictate to and tyrannize over a subservient Europe, as they dictated and tyrannized over a subservient Germany" (411). The war had shown that German "security" had required hegemony: "The whole history of Prussia has been one of domination, aggression, and war" (440). As Prussia had conquered Germany, Prussianism sought to conquer the world: "Germany for decades has steadily pursued a policy of inspiring jealousies and hatred and of dividing nation from nation in order that she might gratify her own selfish passion for power" (441). Once defeated, the sociopath had to be contained and the adolescent disciplined.

Thus, reparations and trials at last became two sides of the same coin of justice: "There must be justice for the dead and for those who have been orphaned and bereaved that Europe might be freed from Prussian despotism" (414). Because "reparation for wrongs inflicted is the essence of justice" (414), the wrongs of the Great War had pushed compensation, crime, and punishment in new directions. Past practice and existing conventions would not suffice. War criminals, however highly placed, would be pursued: "Those individuals most clearly responsible for German aggression and for those acts of barbarism and inhumanity which have disgraced German conduct of the war, must be handed over to a justice which has not been meted out to them at home" (414). As with any punishment, restitution would also deter:

> If the German people themselves, or any other nation, are to be deterred from following in the footsteps of Prussia, if mankind is to be lifted out of the belief that war for selfish ends is legitimate to any state, if the old era is to be left behind and nations as well as individuals are to be brought beneath the reign of law, even if there is to be early reconciliation and appeasement, it will be because those responsible for concluding the war have had the courage to see that justice is not deflected for the sake of convenient peace. (414)

Precisely because the League would provide the keystone of the new international system, a criminalized Germany could not join it at its origins. The Council considered the overthrow of the Kaiserreich a necessary but insufficient condition for making peace: "The German revolution was postponed to the last moments of the war, and there is as yet no guarantee that it represents a permanent change" (418). The League itself once created would continue to judge Germany, specifically whether it "shall have given clear proofs of its stability as well as of its intention to observe international obligations—particularly those obligations which arise out of the treaty of peace" (423). The sooner Germany by deeds admitted its guilt by fulfilling the treaty, the sooner it could find rehabilitation and join the League.

Like a frustrated parent disciplining a truculent teenager, the Supreme Council relied on its position more than on the consistency of its arguments. As the executive body of the Paris Peace Conference, the Council had appropriated the power to decide what there was to decide—on the very meaning of justice itself. The stipulations of the treaty were just because the Supreme Council had articulated them. Because "the German Delegation have greatly misinterpreted the reparation proposals of the treaty" (417) the text would remain unchanged. Further, Germany had shown itself a bad imperial parent. Its "cruel methods of repression, the arbitrary requisition and the various forms of forced labor" in its administration of German East Africa and the Cameroons, not to mention the massacres of the Herero people of German South West Africa between 1904 and 1907,[91] all revealed a Germany unfit for colonial rule, particularly colonial rule reinvented as mandatory tutelage (434). The sovereignty of the Supreme Council over key territorial issues did not require explanation, let alone justification. The French re-annexation of Alsace and Lorraine (428), and the forbidden *Anschluss* with Austria (432) required no explanation as to why "national self-determination" did not apply.

Further, in establishing Poland, the Supreme Council had simply righted historic wrongs. It swept away specious German ethnographic claims to former West Prussia (429) and Danzig (432). Even East Prussia, which would remain a non-contiguous part of Germany, had been "wrested from its original inhabitants by the German sword" (431). Making East Prussia contiguous to the rest of Germany did not provide a reason why "the dismemberment and partition of another nation [Poland] should be continued." Successor Poland could not become successor Poland without direct access to the sea, which could not be assured except through unfettered access to the port of Danzig. As it was, putting the city under League rather than Polish sovereignty constituted a considerable concession to the German ethnographic character of the city. Only in Upper Silesia, where the Supreme Council in fact would make a major concession in allowing a plebiscite, would it permit Germany to raise doubt that "separation from Germany is not in accordance with the wishes or the interests of the population" (430).

Within Germany, the debate over whether to sign the treaty recapitulated the debate about *Volkserhebung* (popular insurrection) preceding the armistice. The German delegation had argued that Germany would no longer be Germany if it signed the treaty without major revisions. It had been given no reason to expect that the Allied and Associated Powers would agree revisions on the scale Germany required. As early as May 9, just two days after his address to the plenary, Brockdorff informed the Supreme Council in writing: "The draft treaty includes demands which are intolerable for any nation. Furthermore, in the opinion of our experts, many of these demands cannot be met."[92] On May 27, Brockdorff sent what became known as the "professorial memorandum," in which such luminaries from the delegation as Hans Delbrück, Max Weber, and Albrecht

---

[91] On the Germans and the Herero, see Isabel V. Hull, *Absolute Destruction: Military Culture and the Practices of War in Imperial Germany* (Ithaca, NY: Cornell University Press, 2005), 5–90.

[92] "German Note of May 9, 1919, on the General Content of the Conditions of Peace," Luckau, *Deliberations*, 225.

Mendelssohn-Bartholdy protested "the peace conditions presented in defiance of solemn promises to the people of a Germany recreated on a democratic basis."[93]

But had the treaty in fact constituted so dire an existential threat to Germany, the logical move might have been to refuse to sign it, provoke an allied invasion, and let the chips of direct occupation fall where they may. Such indeed appeared to constitute the original response to the treaty in Germany. If Rathenau had called for *levée en masse* to fight the invader in October 1918, Brockdorff-Rantzau's determined opposition to the treaty laid the foundation of a *union sacrée*. Protests against the treaty broke out in all major cities, and newspapers throughout Germany competed to publish the most scathing editorials. On May 12, Chancellor Philip Scheidemann announced to the Weimar National Assembly to thunderous applause: "The treaty is, according to the conception of the national government, unacceptable."[94] Scheidemann later famously opined: "What hand would not wither which placed this chain upon itself and upon us?"[95] Brockdorff and the German delegation left France, never to return, shortly after the allied response of June 16. Scheidemann and his entire cabinet resigned on June 20, deadlocked over whether to sign the treaty. But theatrically protesting was one thing, accepting certain foreign invasion would prove quite another.

Within the Supreme Council, Clemenceau's offhand remark of May 10 proved prophetic: "I think that the negotiation will have its ups and downs, but that they [the Germans] will sign in the end."[96] Nevertheless, on that same day, the Council discussed military contingencies with Marshal Foch. On May 10, Foch expressed great confidence that the forces still at his disposition could launch a secure drive from the Rhine first to Weimar and then to Berlin, to compel signature of the treaty. Within just a few weeks, the marshal's confidence had declined, and fault lines in allied unity deepened.

On June 2, a more than usually mercurial Lloyd George laid out the position of the British Empire should Germany decline to sign the treaty. After extensive consultations, his colleagues in the Cabinet along with representatives of the Dominions reported: "if certain provisions to the treaty are not changed, they could agree neither to having the British army advance into Germany nor to having our fleet secure the blockade."[97] He proceeded to list various shortcomings of a treaty that he himself had played such a central role in framing. Rumor had it that earlier in the conference, Lloyd George had said he would no sooner award Upper Silesia to Poland than "he would give a clock to a monkey."[98] With a draft

---

[93] "Observations on the Report of the Commission of the Allied and Associated Governments on the Responsibilities of the Authors of the War," May 27, 1919, in Luckau, *Deliberations*, 299.

[94] Quoted in Ralph Haswell Lutz, *The German Revolution, 1918–1919* (Stanford, CA: Stanford University Press, 1922), 149.

[95] Quoted in MacMillan, *Paris 1919*, 465.

[96] "Conversation between President Wilson and MM. Clemenceau, Lloyd George, and Orlando," May 10, 1919, Mantoux, *Deliberations*, 2: 19.

[97] "Conversation between President Wilson and MM. Clemenceau and Lloyd George," June 2, 1919, in Mantoux, *Deliberations*, 2: 269.

[98] Quoted in Norman Davies, *God's Playground: A History of Poland*, 2 vols. (Oxford: Oxford University Press, 2005), 2: 291.

treaty doing just that now in German hands, he demanded a plebiscite. Having fought so hard to include pensions in reparations, Lloyd George opined that "everyone agrees that we are asking of Germany more than she can ever pay. But what they criticize the most is the indefinite and unlimited character of the debt imposed on Germany."[99] He also complained about the cost of a sustained occupation of the Rhineland. Following some fraught discussions, Clemenceau and Wilson agreed to the plebiscite in Upper Silesia, and Lloyd George agreed to leave the reparations provision intact.

On June 16, Foch presented a changed and highly unfavorable military situation before the Supreme Council.[100] He now dwelled on the degree to which the allied armies had demobilized, the size of the German population, and the distance from the Rhineland to Berlin. He had at his disposition a total of 39 divisions (18 French, 10 British, 6 Belgian, and 5 American) to subdue a population of 65 million people. Berlin was some 480 kilometers from the French border, meaning long lines of communication across hostile territory. Allied forces would have to cross "the most populated, best organized, most militaristic part of Germany" (463). Of course, neither the geography nor the population of Germany had changed since May 10, when he claimed only 40 divisions at his disposal.[101] Now, however, Foch argued that an invasion, not to occupy Berlin but to separate southern Germany from northern Germany, constituted the only strategic option. Whatever Italian, Czechoslovak, and Polish forces could be mustered would exert further pressure from the south and east.

So experienced a commander as Foch could not have failed to realize that his plan shifted the political as well as the military strategy. The allies would have to deal with Baden, Württemberg, and Bavaria, presumably with diminished responsibility for the war as their price of separation. As Lloyd George observed: "We must choose: either we will deprive ourselves of what they owe us as an integral part of Germany, or, if we treat them like the rest of Germany, I don't see why they should come over to us" (464). Pressed by Wilson to explain just what had changed militarily since May 10, Foch responded vaguely: "The Germans could have manufactured war materials. German morale has certainly stiffened" (466).

Later the same day, and without Foch present, Wilson renewed his puzzlement as to what had happened to change the situation. An exasperated Clemenceau responded curtly: "Nothing has happened."[102] Clemenceau, Lloyd George, and Wilson all agreed that the real agenda of Foch was political—the dismemberment of Germany toward the end of French hegemony on the continent.[103] As commander-in-chief, Foch served at the collective pleasure of the French, British,

[99] "Conversation," June 2, 1919, Mantoux, *Deliberations*, 2: 270.

[100] "Conversation between President Wilson, MM. Clemenceau and Lloyd George, and Baron Sonnino," June 16, 1919, 4 p.m., Mantoux, *Deliberations*, 2: 461–69.

[101] Foch had specified 40 divisions in "Conversation," May 10, 1919, Mantoux, *Deliberations*, 2: 20.

[102] "Conversation between President Wilson and MM. Clemenceau and Lloyd George," June 16, 1919, 6:30 p.m., Mantoux, *Deliberations*, 2: 472.

[103] See Jere Clemens King, *Foch versus Clemenceau: France and German Dismemberment* (Cambridge, MA: Harvard University Press, 1960).

and American governments. But removing the most renowned military commander in the world posed substantial political risks. Lloyd George feared a propaganda victory for the Germans: "the Germans will soon say: 'He left because he judged the thing impossible'" (475). Clemenceau countered: "On the other hand, it is dangerous to allow him to return to the field if it is to carry out a policy in Germany which is not our own." The provisional world sovereign fretted that it could live neither with Foch nor without him.

A meeting of the Supreme War Council comprising the French, British, American, and Italian heads of government and their head military advisers decided the matter at a special session held on June 20. Marshall Foch explained again his strategy of invading southern Germany and making separate armistice agreements with Baden, Württemberg, and Bavaria. He cast the matter in even graver terms than he had four days previously:

> Without this cutting up of Germany, and if we are obliged to maintain our position toward southern Germany at the same time that we aim at Berlin, our forces will not be sufficient and our anemic offensive will be forced to stop halfway.[104]

In the best of worlds, after the first three German states were brought into submission, the initial invading force would link up with Italian, Czechoslovak, and Polish forces for a "concentric march on Berlin" (495). The Supreme War Council discussed no other plan, which in effect meant that Foch had prevailed should Germany decline to sign the treaty. Clemenceau held no illusions about the real import of Foch's plan: "It is certain that the entire treaty would then have to be rewritten" (501).

The new German government under Gustav Bauer would make one more effort to gain concessions on June 21, just two days before the allied ultimatum expired.[105] It restated Brockdorff's confession of material helplessness coupled with an attempt to shame the allies on Wilsonian grounds. "In view of the attitude of the Allied and Associated Governments," the chancellor pleaded on his first day in office, "the German people has no other force in its hands save to appeal to the eternally inalienable right to an independent life which belongs to the German people as to all peoples" (479). His government lacked the material means to defend the Fatherland, and "can lend no support to this sacred right of the German people by the application of force" (479). Overtly donning the Wilsonian discursive mantle, he continued: "The Government can only hope for support through the conscience of mankind" (479).

Nevertheless, he continued, with certain reservations the German government "yields to force" (479) in agreeing to sign the treaty. These reservations subtly capped the German struggle to place the criminalization of Germany front and center. Germany's signature would not apply to Article 231, meaning it would: "decline to recognize that the burdens should be placed upon her on the score of

---

[104] "Supreme War Council," June 20, 1919, Mantoux, *Deliberations*, 2: 494–95.
[105] "German Note of June 22, 1919, Accepting the Treaty with the Exception of Articles 227 to 231," Luckau, *German Delegation*, 478–81. The note itself is dated June 21, but presumably was received by the allies on June 22.

the responsibility for the war which has unjustly been placed at her door" (480). Likewise, the German signature would not apply to Articles 227–30, which called for the international trials (political or criminal) of the Kaiser and other individuals to be named. The reservations underscored the idea of the "responsibility" articles as the core of the entire treaty.

The immediate and predictable response from Paris, fewer than twenty-four hours before the ultimatum expired, indicated that the Allied and Associated Powers would enforce their disciplinary authority over unruly Germany by unspecified material means.[106] Because the most recent note "presents no arguments or considerations not already examined," the Allied and Associated Powers decreed simply that "the time for discussion has passed." A German signature would mean that the powers "must hold Germany responsible for the execution of every stipulation of the treaty."

In its way, the allied insistence itself affirmed that Articles 227–31 constituted the central articles of the treaty. Germany thus won the first round of a discursive battle that would continue for many years. For the time being, the centrifugal forces won out over the centripetal forces, as the Weimar National Assembly reluctantly voted to sign the treaty without conditions. Consequently, the Foch plan to invade southern Germany—which would have eviscerated the treaty rather more than any last-minute German reservations—was never carried out. Redemptive annihilation would have to wait until the Third Reich.

The staged drama of signing the Treaty of Versailles notwithstanding, something had changed in the international system. In 1815 and 1871, it mattered who won and who lost wars among Great Powers much more than it mattered who caused them. Even in 1919, the Paris Peace Conference began on separate tracks to create a "just peace"—one to determine reparations, another to assign responsibilities. But new varieties of cultural mobilization had sustained a different kind of war. The delirious early enthusiasm for Wilsonianism could not wholly transform or redirect this mobilization. Someone would have to pay, in material and discursive senses, for the ruin spread by the Great War. Fraught populations would accept no less. Perhaps it was never realistic to expect that civil and criminal approaches to "responsibility" would remain separate. In the end, the two mixed in an array of compromises among the Allied and Associated Powers.

Struggles to un-mix civil and criminal approaches continued throughout the interwar years, with maximal tensions and minimal results. The Dutch would never extradite the ex-Kaiser, and the Allied and Associated Powers would never seek a theatrical trial *in absentia*. No international tribunals would be established for others accused of war crimes. In February 1920, the allies made public a list of 855 suspects for whom it sought extradition.[107] Germany offered a "compromise" of trials under the Criminal Senate of the Reichgericht in Leipzig. The British

---

[106] "Allied Note of June 22, 1919, in Reply to the German Note of June 22," Luckau, *German Delegation*, 481.

[107] See John Horne and Alan Kramer, *German Atrocities, 1914: A History of Denial* (New Haven, CT: Yale University Press, 2001), 345–55.

accepted these arrangements, while the French and the Belgians rejected them. The Reichgericht ultimately produced nine judgments—five acquittals and four convictions, none of officers. The French and the Belgians held largely meaningless military tribunals *in absentia*. No international tribunals for war crimes would be established until after World War II. The tug of war over reparations would continue for years, until payments came to a practical halt because of the Great Depression and to a formal halt when the Nazis took power.[108]

For the international system, the effects of inventing justice as an exercise of sovereignty helped structure the international system between the wars. Before the Great War, status in the international system had been primarily a matter of material power. States permitted access to the system enjoyed moral as well as legal equality, as each was understood under international law at the time. However, through the Treaty of Versailles, the Paris Peace Conference had created a criminalized once and future Great Power. Germany, as we have seen, actively participated in the construction of this identity through specific challenges to allied "justice." Germany, in other words, embraced defeat in order to continue the war at the level of discourse.

THE SOVEREIGNTY OF JUSTICE BEYOND GERMANY

The Treaty of Versailles had been written almost as though Germany had been the only enemy belligerent. The Supreme Council closely monitored turmoil elsewhere—from Ukraine, Russia, and the Baltics, to Hungary, to the Balkans, to Anatolia. But seldom did the Allied and Associated Powers speak of Germany as part of an alliance. Just as the allies had considered the Western Front the decisive front in the Great War, so too would they consider the peace with Germany the decisive document for the peace of the world. Passing judgment on a perpetually dangerous Germany by a jury of its Great Power peers at least had a coherent explanation, whether one agreed with the justice produced or not. Compensatory and criminal approaches to justice became ever more muddled as peacemaking moved east.

What did a "peace of justice" mean beyond Germany? It certainly meant confronting a transformed geography. As Great Powers, "Austria-Hungary" and the "Ottoman Empire" had already paid the supreme penalty of annihilation. Neither Austria nor Hungary nor Turkey was going to emerge from the war as a Great Power. Wartime imperial intrigue among the allies had paved the way to a partitioned and dependent Anatolia, in which post-Ottoman Turkey, like post-Habsburg Austria, would survive as a residual. Bulgaria, having lost much in the Balkan Wars of 1912–13, would lose its Aegean coast as a result of the Great War.

---

[108] West Germany would resume payments after 1945, and a reunified Germany would make a final payment of nearly £59 million to holders of reparations bonds in October 2010. "Germany Ends World War One Reparations after 92 Years with £59m Final Payment," *Daily Mail*, September 28, 2010.

The template of the criminalized state developed for Germany looked increasingly awkward when applied elsewhere. The very idea of a "state" presumes a kind of somatic unity of lands and peoples. The Paris Peace Conference saw its very task as recognizing states that combined lands and peoples in new and more just ways. This raised the perplexing issue of just what to criminalize. Was "Hungary" to share the guilt for unleashing the war, or were Magyars? Not all Magyars lived within the borders of successor Hungary, far from it. Why should Magyars in successor Hungary toil to pay for reparations, and not their ethnic siblings in Transylvania (annexed to Romania)?

The conference made no serious effort to hold any of the other heads of state accountable for the war. The most promising candidate of all, Habsburg Emperor-King Francis Joseph, had died in November 1916. His grandnephew and successor Charles had become heir presumptive only upon the assassination of Archduke Franz Ferdinand in June 1914. As Lloyd George put it: "He wasn't there when war was declared, and his responsibility is nil."[109] In 1921, the Great Powers would exile Charles to Madeira, not because of anything he had done during his two-year reign, but because of his continued quest for restoration as king of Hungary. In Bulgaria, defeat led to the abdication of Tsar Ferdinand I. But he relocated to peaceable exile in Germany, where the allies declined to pursue him. The Bulgarian monarchy lived on in a curtailed form under his son, Boris III. The Treaty of Sèvres provided for the survival not just of the sultanate, but of the sitting sultan, Mehmed VI. Personal responsibility for the war ended with Kaiser Wilhelm II.

The reception of the treaties by the successor states adopted a generic form developed by Germany. The delegations would protest the treaties as unacceptable, pointing out their many inconsistencies and anti-Wilsonian provisions—not, after all, a very daunting rhetorical task. The Supreme Council would decline to make changes, and the delegations would sign anyway. Explanations from the Council seemed ever more self-proving—the treaties were just because the Paris Peace Conference produced them. Surreal reparations regimes emerged. The absence of international tribunals meant that prosecutions for war crimes would have to take place in the national courts of new states, if at all. This embroiled the sovereignty of justice in the politics of successor states and victorious empires.

As we saw in Chapter 1, the Paris Peace Conference criminalized the two named successor states to "Austria-Hungary." In the Treaty of Saint-Germain with Austria, Articles 177 and 178 repeated more or less verbatim Articles 231 and 232 of the Treaty of Versailles. As with Germany, a Reparations Commission would set a final bill in May 1921 (Article 180). An annex provided details of remarkable specificity for payments in kind, including 1,000 heifers to Italy, 300 to the Serb-Croat-Slovene State, and 500 to Romania.[110] Contemporaries understood the dim prospects for collection. "It is obvious to the most superficial observer," wrote Herbert Hoover, head of the American Relief Organization, to Lansing on

---

[109] "Conversation between President Wilson and MM. Clemenceau, Lloyd George, Orlando, and Baron Sonnino," May 8, 1919, Mantoux, *Deliberations*, 2: 6.

[110] Part VIII (Reparations), Annex 4, Section 6.

July 11, 1919, "that the present economic resources of the State of German-Austria are incapable of supporting the population of seven and one-half million people for at least another year."[111] How could such an Austria pay reparations?

The new borders further complicated the already problematic task of trying war crimes through national tribunals. What about accused perpetrators who did not live in successor Austria or successor Hungary? As Wilson noted before the Supreme Council on May 12, "we can't compel Austria to turn over men who are no longer under her jurisdiction." Orlando appreciated the problem: "It wouldn't be fair for a submarine commander, because he was born in Bohemia, not to be punishable, whilst he would be had he been born in Vienna."[112]

Ultimately, the Supreme Council granted jurisdiction to the state wherein the accused held nationality.[113] In other words, the theoretical submarine commander would be prosecuted by Czechoslovakia had he been born in Bohemia, by Austria had he been born in Vienna. Whether he was prosecuted at all depended largely on the whims of a state that had not existed at the time of his birth. Both Austria and Czechoslovakia were new states.[114] By definition, the commander would be tried under national law that had not existed at the time of the alleged crimes. Prosecutions became a matter of national politics in the volatile successor states. The treaties of Saint-Germain and Trianon contained virtually identical procedures for setting up the prosecution of war crimes.[115] Austria established a tribunal in 1920, which tried and acquitted two Habsburg generals for mistreating prisoners of war.[116] Hungary did not even bother to establish a tribunal.

On receiving the draft treaty of Saint-Germain on June 2, 1919, Karl Renner, chancellor of the Republic of Austria, made a speech to the plenary that sharply contrasted in tone to Brockdorff's speech of May 7. Renner spoke in French, and deferentially. "We are aware, Gentlemen," he observed, "that it is you, the victors, who will impose on us the Conditions of Peace, and we are determined loyally to examine any proposal which you make to us and any counsel which you will offer."[117]

Renner took the rhetorical tack of separating the culpability of states and peoples. He offered a counter-narrative to the end of the war in the Habsburg Monarchy. The House of Habsburg had indeed committed a "terrible crime" in igniting the Great War, but that constituted "a crime of the former governors, not

---

[111] Herbert Hoover to Robert Lansing, July 11, 1919, in Nina Almond and Ralph Haswell Lutz, eds., *The Treaty of St. Germain: A Documentary History of Its Territorial and Political Clauses* (Stanford, CA: Stanford University Press, 1935), 104.

[112] "Conversation between President Wilson and MM. Clemenceau, Lloyd George, and Orlando," May 14, 1919, in Mantoux, *Deliberations*, 2: 66.

[113] "Resolution (Annex VI to CF-42)," May 30, 1919, *FRUS: PPC*, 6: 129.

[114] In the event, the matter would have been more complicated still, as the submarine commander could likely have claimed Austrian, German, or Czechoslovak nationality.

[115] See "Résolution presentée au Conseil Suprême des Principales Puissance alliées et associées au sujet des conditions de la paix avec la Hongrie [Annexe au Procès Verbal No. 15]," July 31–August 5, 1919, in Conference de la Paix, 1919–1920, *Recueil des Actes de la Conférence*, Partie IV (Paris: Imprimerie Nationale, 1922), 280.

[116] Willis, *Prologue to Nuremberg*, 150.

[117] "Peace Congress (Saint-Germain), Protocol No. 1, Plenary Session of June 2, 1919," *FRUS: PPC*, 3: 430.

of the peoples." On November 12, the day of the proclamation of the Austrian Republic, the Dual Monarchy ceased to exist. Into the vacuum stepped a host of small successor states, "bereft of all public organization, which on a day's notice, have created their own Parliaments, Governments and armies, and thus formed states which reflect the peculiar genius of each one" (428). Austria was simply one of several heirs to the estate of deceased Austria-Hungary, the moral equal of Czechoslovakia, Poland, or the Kingdom of the Serbs, Croats, and Slovenes. Austria "is therefore in no greater degree than they are, the successor of the former Monarchy" (428). It made no more sense to criminalize "Austria" for the war than the others. No less than they did Austria deserve "the inalienable right of free self-determination" (349). He never mentioned reparations by name, simply his hopes for "a just and democratic peace [that] restores to us the indispensable means of economic existence" (430).

The Austrian delegation submitted detailed counterproposals on July 25.[118] Post-Habsburg Austria, the counterproposals argued, "cannot, under any sense of the word, be identified with the former Austrian-Hungarian Monarchy or with former Austria [meaning the former Austrian Empire]" (237). Not only did the proposed boundaries make for a non-viable Austrian state, the destruction of the free trade area within the Habsburg Monarchy would invoke the economic and political ruin of Central Europe: "the collapse of our economic existence must perforce destroy all public authority situated in the heart of the continent and also bring about the dismemberment of the State and political and social anarchy" (209).

As an alternative, the delegation proposed various plebiscites to determine the borders of Austria. If all self-declared Germans could not live in "Germany," all Austrian Germans where they constituted the majority ought to be permitted to live in "Austria"—notably German-speakers in former Western Hungary and in the border regions of Bohemia and Moravia eventually known as the Sudetenland (281–87). German-speaking Tyrol should become not Italian, but quasi-independent and neutral, under the protection of the Great Powers (353). Further, any just peace settlement would preserve the trade patterns and economic unity of the Austrian half of the Dual Monarchy. The Austrians neglected to mention that this would have preserved the position of ethnic Germans and Jews as the traditional commercial class throughout the successor states.

In response, the Supreme Council, predictably if less than logically, insisted on "Austria" as one of two exclusive heirs to the Habsburg Monarchy.[119] In combination with a similarly construed "Hungary," Austria bore "responsibility for the ills which Europe has suffered in the course of the last five years" (225). "Austrians" had acclaimed the war from the moment Emperor-King Francis Joseph declared it, and did "nothing to separate itself from the politics of its government and of its allies

---

[118] "List of Counter Proposals Submitted by Austrian Delegation to June 2 Draft of the Treaty," July 25, 1919, in Almond and Lutz, *Treaty of Saint-Germain*, 211–12. The actual proposals appear throughout the volume.

[119] "Note of the Allied and Associated Powers Accompanying the Peace Conditions of September 2, 1919," in Almond and Lutz, *Treaty of Saint-Germain*, 225–31.

until their defeat on the field of battle" (226). This accusation applied only to ethnic Germans within the borders of post-Habsburg Austria and to the Magyars of post-Habsburg Hungary. German-speakers in Bohemia, and even Magyars in Slovakia and Romania, would remain blameless. The argument assumed that only ethnic Germans and ethnic Magyars within the boundaries of the Austrian and Hungarian successor states had ever supported the Habsburg cause.

Moreover, the Supreme Council held, the monarchy itself degenerated into an anti-Slav conspiracy, "destined to maintain the supremacy of the German and Magyar peoples over the majority of the inhabitants of the Austro-Hungarian Monarchy" (226). The allies appreciated the economic frailty of post-Habsburg Austria. Indeed, the Reparations Commission "will receive instructions to acquit itself of the functions with which it is entrusted in an eminently humanitarian spirit" (228). But Austria should not expect any change in the basic parameters of the treaty, least of all on the territorial decisions "made after months of profound studies" (229). The Austrian delegation would have five days to provide "a declaration making known that it is ready to sign the Treaty as it stands" (230).

Bulgaria likewise presented a sophisticated if foredoomed attempt to seize the discourse of war guilt, by throwing the innocent Bulgarian people before the mercy of the conference.[120] "Justice," for the Bulgarians as for the Austrians, required the separation of states and peoples. Teodor Todorov, head of the Bulgarian delegation, addressed the conference on September 19.[121] Like Renner, he spoke in deferential French. War guilt lay with the Bulgarian regime overthrown at the end of the war: "In contradiction with the feelings of her people, with the traditions of her policy, and with the manifest interests of her future, Bulgaria was plunged, under compulsion by ill-starred powers, into a senseless war" (436). Bulgarians remained blameless: "The Bulgarian people is, in its vast majority, innocent of the evil which has been done in its name, the Bulgarian State is responsible for it" (437). The Bulgarian people deserved mercy from the conference. Todorov omitted mentioning the continuity of the Bulgarian monarchy, with the crown of Ferdinand I simply passing to his son, Boris III. Todorov hailed the conference as creator of a new and more just world. The equation of "justice" and the "rights of peoples," he argued, made the moral authority of the conference absolute: "In your exalted sense of justice you have, from the outset, placed it [the rights of peoples] in an unassailable position. It is therefore permissible for a guilty State also, even a vanquished state, to invoke it" (437–38). His one request was that the borders of Western Thrace be adjusted only by plebiscite rather than by fiat.

Successor Bulgaria would affirm its bona fides through the aggressive pursuit of war criminals: "We have bound ourselves to punish the authors of those excesses pitilessly" (437). This admission dovetailed with an effort within the Commission on Responsibilities during the summer of 1919 to establish international tribunals

---

[120] R.J. Crampton, *Aleksandur Stamboliiski: Bulgaria* (London: Haus Histories, 2009), esp. 44–109.

[121] "Peace Congress (Paris), Protocol No. 1, Plenary Session of September 1919," *FRUS: PPC*, 3: 435–41.

in the treaty with Bulgaria.[122] Led by Nikolaos Politis, the commission submitted draft articles on July 22 establishing such tribunals, accompanied by a memo from the Americans reminding the Supreme Council that it had already rejected similar articles for the German treaty.[123] Larnaude of France presented the report to the Council: "He did not see why there should be any difference between the two countries [Germany and Bulgaria] and that justice should be applied everywhere in the same manner."[124] The Supreme Council duly declined to reconsider the matter.

The Bulgarian delegation produced detailed counterproposals to the Treaty of Neuilly on October 25.[125] "The Bulgarian nation," Todorov reminded the allies yet again, "was not in favor of a German alliance and accepted that pact under constraint."[126] The real problem was unfinished business from the Balkan Wars, particularly the Second Balkan War of 1913. In that conflict, Greece and Serbia, later joined by Romania, sided against their erstwhile ally in the First Balkan War. In the second war, Bulgaria lost Southern Dobrudja, an important territorial gain from the First Balkan War, to Romania. The irredentism of the victorious states in the Second Balkan War had driven Bulgaria into the arms of the Central Powers: "Neither Belgrade, nor Bukarest nor Athens adopted at the critical juncture in sufficient measure the generous ideas which, by the reconstruction of the Balkan League, hoped to associate Bulgaria with the policy of the Entente" (15, awkward syntax in the original).

The Entente had to bear its share of the blame. Neglect after the Second Balkan War by the now-victorious Great Powers "left in the mind of the Bulgarian people a feeling of bitterness which was cleverly exploited by the ill-omened politicians who chained Bulgaria to the German policy" (16). This argument, of course, suggested that state and people in Bulgaria had not been so gravely separated from each other after all. The Bulgarians dismissed the reparations regime: "Many errors and unjust dispositions, due to clauses literally borrowed from the Treaty with Germany, might have been avoided by means of verbal explanations or appropriate elucidations from competent persons" (109). Bulgaria was willing to pay reparations, but in a way "truly proportional to the resources of the country" (96). For the war-ravaged economy, the total sum of 2.25 billion gold francs coupled with huge payments in kind was simply "impossible" (111).

---

[122] Willis, *Prelude to Nuremberg*, 150–52.

[123] "Conditions of Peace with Bulgaria: Appendix to Minutes of Fourteenth Meeting, Annex II," July 22, 1919, in *Commission on the Responsibility of the Authors of the War and on the Enforcement of Penalties*, 204–05. This is a printed English version of the minutes found in the Frank Lyon Polk Papers, MS 656, Yale University Archives.

[124] "Notes of a Meeting of the Heads of Delegations of the Five Great Powers Held in M. Pichon's Room at the Quai d'Orsay, Paris, on Friday, July 25, 1919, at 3:30 p.m.," *FRUS: PPC*, 7: 260.

[125] "Notes of a Meeting of the Heads of Delegations of the Five Great Powers held in M. Pichon's Room, Quai d'Orsay, Paris, on Saturday, October 25, 1919, at 10:30 PM," in E.L. Woodward and Rohan Butler, eds., *Documents on British Foreign Policy, 1919–1939* (London: HM Stationery Office, 1948), First Series, 2: 65–66. Hereafter cited as *DBFP*.

[126] *Conditions of Peace with Bulgaria: Observations of the Bulgaria Peace Delegation* (Paris: Imprimerie H. Elias, 1919), 15.

Beneath its surface deference, the Bulgarian delegation sought to alter the outcome not just of the Great War, but of the Second Balkan War. Todorov's "just" peace would require territorial losses among the victors. Southern Dobrudja (then occupied by Romania) deserved incorporation into defeated Bulgaria, because the loss had been the cause of "an incurable wound to the Bulgarian soul and an injury to the general equilibrium to the nation" (23). Likewise, the Bulgarians advocated an independent Macedonia, at the expense of Serbia and Greece, as the best way to protect the diverse peoples living there, notably the "Bulgarian mass which continues to remain the predominant ethnical force in the province" (30).

To the Bulgarians, the greatest injustice of the draft Treaty of Neuilly lay in the transfer of Western Thrace to Greece, which would deny Bulgaria access to the Aegean Sea. Bulgarian trade henceforth would have to occur through the Black Sea and the contentious Straits of the Dardanelles. Article 48 provided only vague assurances of Bulgarian access to the Aegean, and certainly nothing like the "corridor" to the Baltic given to Poland. Transferring Western Thrace to Greece "inflicts an injury to the sacred right of peoples, for it takes from Bulgaria a territory which is the lawful patrimony of its race" (27). The delegation appealed to "the high wisdom and the sovereign equity inherent to its mission and of which it has given so many brilliant proofs, to reach a settlement based on the true reality of things, on the freely expressed will of populations, and the needs of a lasting peace" (26).

The Supreme Council asserted its full sovereignty over a just peace in Bulgaria. The allies declined point-blank to engage the thesis of mitigated responsibility based on the unwilling alliance with Germany: "The eloquence of facts is sufficient for them."[127] Perhaps less plausibly, the stipulations on reparations were "just and lenient" (162). By this time, little pretense remained of distinguishing between compensatory and criminal approaches to justice. The Supreme Council would apply the identity of the criminalized state to the weak as well as the strong: "Bulgaria will undoubtedly have heavy liabilities to bear. These will not, however, be the result of the Conditions of Peace, but of the war of aggression in which she voluntarily took part, into which she entered of her own free will, in a spirit of domination and conquest" (162). Nor could criminalized Bulgaria expect territorial concessions. The allies had set boundaries "only after an attentive study taking into account all the elements of the problem" (169). Given the outcome of the war, "the Dobrudja question is out of place" (169). The Council expressed some sympathy on the matter of access to the Aegean Sea. But like a child who had misbehaved, Bulgaria would have to accept punishment and promise better behavior in the future. However, "if Bulgaria loyally accepts this solution, the future will show that the guarantees which have been given her will be in no manner illusory" (169).

For its part, successor Bulgaria would bide its time and seek opportunities. More than any of the other defeated Central Powers, Bulgaria actively pursued prosecutions of accused war criminals, though surely with domestic preoccupations in

---

[127] "Reply of the Allied and Associated Powers to the Observations of the Bulgarian Delegation on the Conditions of Peace," November 3, 1919, *DBFP*, First Series, 2: 157.

mind. The new agrarian regime under Alexander Stamboliski arrested some 200 individuals on November 4, 1919, including several cabinet ministers.[128] A special war crimes tribunal arraigned eleven men in October 1921. After trials lasting for nearly a year and a half, the tribunal handed down sentences of long terms in prison, six for life. A Major Kulchin was even executed for the murder of civilians. But by that time, prosecutions for war crimes had become mired in Stamboliski's agrarian revolution. A counter-revolution began to take shape beginning in the officer corps.[129] Stamboliski's calls for more and more trials further muddled boundaries between criminal justice and domestic revenge. A "Thermidorian" reaction led by the army led ultimately to the murder of Stamboliski himself in June 1923. By that time, Bulgaria had returned to the margins of peacemaking. Even the "voluntary" population exchange with Greece would be overshadowed by the far larger "compulsory" exchange between Greece and Turkey.

The conference would finally make peace with Hungary through the Treaty of Trianon, signed on June 4, 1920, the path to which will be explored further in Chapter 5. The identity of Hungary remained in play for an extended period, even to President Wilson. Perhaps thinking of Democratic votes in American cities from the Magyar diaspora, an absent-minded president remarked before the Supreme Council on March 25, 1919: "Nominally, we are friends of the Hungarians, and even better friends of the Rumanians." A clearly annoyed Clemenceau curtly reminded him: "The Hungarians are not our friends but our enemies."[130] Like post-Habsburg Austria, the conference would create post-Habsburg Hungary as a criminalized residual, with substantial portions of its former lands and peoples absorbed by competing successor states.

The Hungarian delegation would protest the Treaty of Trianon along what by then had become familiar lines. Count Albert Apponyi, head of the delegation, made an impassioned plea to the Supreme Council on January 16, 1920.[131] He expressed outrage at a treaty that took from historic Hungary two-thirds of its territory and nearly two-thirds of its people: "Can it be meant as a sentence passed against Hungary?" (540). Less than convincingly, Apponyi found the very idea of punishing Hungary hurtful given that in August 1914 Hungary was "not in full possession of its independence and was at most capable of exercising some degree of influence on the affairs of the Austro-Hungarian monarchy" (540). Hungary had tried to steer the aged emperor-king off the suicidal path he had chosen.[132] Apponyi claimed that abandoning Magyars in Transylvania and elsewhere to Romanian rule assaulted civilization itself: "I should imagine that the transference

---

[128] Willis, *Prelude to Nuremberg*, 152–53.

[129] See John D. Bell, *Peasants in Power: Alexander Stamboliski and the Bulgarian Agrarian National Union, 1899–1923* (Princeton, NJ: Princeton University Press, 1977), 154–241.

[130] "Conversation between President Wilson and MM. Clemenceau, Lloyd George, and Orlando, March 25, 1919, 3:30 P.M.," Mantoux, *Deliberations*, 1: 12.

[131] "Address of the President of the Hungarian Peace Delegation, Count Apponyi, to the Supreme Council, January 16, 1920," in Francis Deák, *Hungary at the Paris Peace Conference: The Diplomatic History of the Treaty of Trianon* (New York: Columbia University Press, 1942), 539–49.

[132] Under dualism, any declaration of war required the approval of both the Austrian and the Hungarian governments.

of national hegemony to an inferior grade of civilization could not be a matter of indifference to the great cultural interests of humanity" (542). The only winner in such a peace would be the "still burning fire of Bolshevism" (547). Months of political maneuvering followed, with the Hungarian delegation trying to improve its position through the Poles, the British, and the French.[133]

The final response came in a letter from the Supreme Council to the Hungarian delegation of May 6, 1920.[134] The Council, now under the presidency of Clemenceau's successor Alexandre Millerand, affirmed Hungary as a criminalized residual. The post-Habsburg Kingdom of Hungary, now under the regency of Admiral Miklós Horthy, would have to assume co-responsibility for "the imperialistic policy pursued by the Dual Monarchy" (551). As with Austrians, the "Hungarians" who had to pay the price were not all Magyars, but the residents of the new state.

At the same time, the response to the Hungarians came about as close as the Supreme Council ever got to acknowledging its own caprices. With regret, the allies conceded "that it is indeed impossible for the political frontiers in their total extent to coincide with the ethnical frontiers" (552). A great many Magyars would have to live outside post-Habsburg Hungary, whatever the peacemakers did. In most of the border disputes, the Council held, probably correctly, that a plebiscite "would not offer a result differing sensibly from those which they [the allies] have arrived at after a minute study of the ethnographic conditions of Central Europe and of national aspirations" (552). Neither could post-Habsburg Hungary hope to return to its borders of 1914: "A state of affairs, even when millennial, is not meant to exist when it has been recognized as contrary to justice" (552). All borders resulting from the peace treaties one day could be revised in the future under the auspices of the League of Nations. But for the time being, the solution of the Supreme Council constituted "justice" because the Supreme Council had decided it. The representatives of Hungary had ten days to decide whether to sign the Treaty of Trianon as written.

A few weeks earlier, on May 11, 1920, the Supreme Council presented representatives of the Ottoman sultan with the Treaty of Sèvres. Millerand rose to make the only speech.[135] By "ceding to foreign pressure," he scolded, the Ottoman Empire had "caused the prolongation of a cruel war, perhaps for several years." Consequently, the allies had taken "all efficacious precautions" so that "such grave peril" would not recur. Further, the terms would fulfill the stated goal "to install in Turkey a peace founded on the principles of the right, of liberty, and of justice, for which the allies had fought." The main features of that peace comprised well-known allied war aims—the "freedom of the straits" and maintaining the regime of the sultan in Constantinople. The Turkish government had one month to respond, and could do so only in writing.

---

[133] See the narrative in Deák, *Hungary at the Paris Peace Conference*, 253–338.
[134] "Concerning Letter of the Reply of the Allied Powers to the President of the Hungarian Peace Delegation, May 6, 1920," in Deák, *Hungary at the Paris Peace Conference*, 551–54.
[135] Quoted in *Correspondance d'Orient*, No. 239, June 15, 1920, 513–14.

The delegation would make what by then had become the familiar protest, followed by counterproposals.[136] Post-Ottoman Turkey resigned itself to partition and inter-allied receivership: "The mutilated Ottoman Empire would be shorn of all the attributes of internal and external sovereignty, all the while remaining responsible for fulfilling the Treaty of Peace and the international obligations incumbent on every state." True to its own script, the Supreme Council would refuse any major revisions. Delegates signed the Treaty of Sèvres on August 10, 1920.

For a time, the regime of the sultan tried to reinvent itself as junior partner in the post-Ottoman Middle East, through pursuing prosecutions for war crimes.[137] In addition to supporting the Armenians, at least indirectly, the British also sought redress for the thousands of British Empire prisoners who had died in Turkish hands, notably after the capture of Kut-el-Amara in Mesopotamia in 1916. Mehmet VI promised wide prosecutions. Under the direction of Grand Vizier Damad Ferid Pasha, the sultan's regime established a tribunal that sentenced Major Tevik Bey to fifteen years' labor, and Kemal Bey to death, for crimes against the Armenians. Like Stamboliski in Bulgaria, Ferid used tribunals to pursue political opponents, notably prominent Young Turks.

The new regime in Anatolia taking shape under Mustafa Kemal would neither support nor continue such prosecutions. Evidence of Greek atrocities accompanying the landings at Smyrna in May 1919 made the prosecution of war crimes under the Ottomans still more problematic.[138] The British continued to try Ottoman prisoners they had removed to Malta, which led the new regime to take prisoners of its own. These included Lieutenant-Colonel Alfred Rawlinson, the brother of Henry Rawlinson, commander-in-chief of British forces in India. Eventually, the prisoner exchange that took place in 1921 seemed like the only viable exit strategy. By this time, prosecution for war crimes had become a matter of mutual compensation. The definitive peace for Anatolia made in 1923 through the Treaty of Lausanne contained no provisions for prosecuting Ottoman war crimes.

This chapter has considered the discourse of "justice" at the Paris Peace Conference as discourse of sovereignty. "Justice" in Paris drew from two legal traditions: compensation from civil law and prosecution from criminal law. The initial organization of the Paris Peace Conference established two organizational tracks toward that end, one for reparations and another to determine responsibilities. But the "total peace" required to end the "total war" melded civil and criminal approaches to making a just peace. Because no existing provisions of international law would suffice politically to provide compensation for so costly a conflict, moralistic judgement infused all attempts to establish reparations regimes. Attempts to assign responsibility, from heads of state to individuals guilty of war crimes, foundered on legalities, international as well as domestic.

---

[136] *Observations Générales presentées par la Délégation ottomane à la Conférence de la Paix* (no publisher, no date, but sometime between May and August 1920), 3.

[137] Willis, *Prelude to Nuremberg*, 153–63.

[138] See Peter M. Buzanski, "The Interallied Investigation of the Greek Invasion of Smyrna, 1919," *The Historian* 25.3 (1963): 325–43.

The early German republic sought to capitalize on the muddled civil and criminal approaches to embrace the identity of the criminalized state, as a means of resisting both the material effects of reparations and the artificial suppression of its identity as a Great Power. By discrediting the peace itself, interwar Germany could reassert its national sovereignty and its status in the world. This reassertion drove German nationalism until the crushing of the Nazi regime in 1945. Other defeated Central Powers would likewise seize on what they construed as unjust features of the just peace, as a means of creating and asserting successor state identities. The Hungarian cry of *Nem, Nem Soha* (No, No, Never [the Treaty of Trianon]) simply became one famous articulation of embracing defeat in order to reverse it. In the end, the Supreme Council went to great lengths to preserve its exclusive domain over the sovereignty of justice. But doing so highlighted almost numberless internal contradictions within the treaties themselves.

3

The "Unmixing" of Lands

Georges Clemenceau remarked upon his election as president of the Paris Peace Conference: "we have no longer to make peace for territories more or less large; we no longer have to make peace for continents; we have to make it for peoples."[1] In what today looks like an obvious statement, Clemenceau made sweeping and new claims for the sovereignty of the conference. The conference would seek to build an international system inhabited by states each expressing a somatic unity of lands and peoples in a proper "body politic." It would build this system materially through the demarcation of territory and discursively through the categorization of peoples. In demarcating new or changed states, the conference could either draw boundaries to suit peoples, or define peoples to suit boundaries. Chapters 3 and 4 examine how it did both.

Eric Weitz has argued that in the broad century between the Congress of Vienna of 1815 and the Paris Peace Conference of 1919, a "tectonic shift" occurred in the kinds of settlements within the international system. The statesmen at Vienna had focused on "dynastic legitimacy and state sovereignty within clearly defined borders." In Paris, in contrast, peacemakers "focused on populations and an ideal of state sovereignty rooted in national homogeneity."[2] The international system would structure a new territoriality, based in the unity of lands and peoples.

"Territory," Charles Maier has reminded us, "is not just land, even extensive land. It is a global space that has been partitioned for the sake of political authority, space in effect empowered by borders."[3] Territoriality, a term from biology applied to geography and political theory, refers simply to rule in its various forms over geographic space.[4] Under the Vienna system, monarchies had arranged territoriality in a straightforward manner. Emperors and kings divided territories according to dynastic legitimacy and a balance of material capabilities within the system. Lands mattered a great deal, peoples hardly at all. Populations "were" what the crowned heads of Europe said they were, subjects of national or multinational monarchies. According to Weitz's argument, by 1919 territoriality acquired a new level of

[1] "Preliminary Peace Conference, Protocol No. 1, Session of January 18, 1919," *FRUS: PPC*, 3: 168–69.

[2] Eric D. Weitz, "From the Vienna to the Paris System: International Politics, and the Entangled Histories of Human Rights, Forced Deportations, and Civilizing Missions," *American Historical Review* 113.5 (2008): 1313–43. All citations here come from pages 1313–14.

[3] Charles S. Maier, *Once Within Borders: Territories of Power, Wealth, and Belonging since 1500* (Cambridge, MA: Belknap Press of Harvard University Press, 2016), 1.

[4] Robert Sack, *Human Territoriality: Its Theory and History* (Cambridge: Cambridge University Press, 1986); and Stuart Elden, *The Birth of Territory* (Chicago, IL: University of Chicago Press, 2013).

meaning, whose construction had been underway for more than a century. Lands would become a function of peoples, rather than the reverse. Reconciling lands and people provides the linchpin to stability under the Paris System.

Lord Curzon, British foreign secretary in the latter stages of the Paris Peace Conference, reputedly coined the phrase "unmixing of peoples" to describe territoriality after the Balkan Wars of 1912–13.[5] I use the expression ironically here, to explore first how the conference sought to draw borders to suit peoples based on expert advice. Experts, diplomats, and politicians sought to "unmix" peoples by defining them. Where and when it proved impossible to draw boundaries to suit defined peoples, the conference turned to tailoring populations to borders—through plebiscites, minority treaties, and ultimately population exchanges. While the "unmixing" of lands and peoples occurred simultaneously, they remain distinct practices that I will examine in distinct chapters.

Of course, "unmixing" implied a primordial order of things that history had later confused.[6] For example, "unmixing" the populations of Poland and Czechoslovakia implied that once upon a time, there had existed a "Poland" and a "Czechoslovakia" inhabited by "Poles" and "Czechoslovaks." Multinational monarchies, this argument went, had mixed peoples together for centuries for their own selfish purposes, with tragic results. The victory of the Allied and Associated Powers offered the chance to right these ancient wrongs. Conceived in this way, peacemaking looked backward, to the restoration of "true" boundaries as they had existed in a distant past.

In fact, "unmixing" meant imposing varieties of political clarity on lands and peoples that had managed to live without it for centuries. Doing so brought together different foundational principles of political geography in Britain, France, and the United States. All schools of political geography agreed that properly categorized peoples would produce proper territorial boundaries. But the role of "the people" in determining the identity of a given territory, and even just who "the people" were, meant different things to different geographers. Necessarily, these differences politicized expertise. From the outset, the council of Great Powers operated as a sovereign court weighing competing claims to lands and peoples.

"OFFICIAL MINDS" AND POLITICAL GEOGRAPHY

Knowledge and power at the Paris Peace Conference depended too much on one another to argue that one border was determined "scientifically," and another "politically." In any event, the "scientific" expertise of the experts was often of very recent vintage. Further, expertise based itself on empirical data that everyone knew to have highly problematic origins. Realism also ringed the discursive sphere of

[5] For a standard attribution, see Michael R. Marrus, *The Unwanted: European Refugees in the Twentieth Century* (New York: Oxford University Press, 1985), 41.

[6] Walter Pohl, "National Origin Narratives in the Austro-Hungarian Monarchy," in Patrick J. Geary and Gábo Klaniczay, eds., *Manufacturing Middle Ages: Entangled History of Medievalism in Nineteenth-Century Europe* (Leiden: Brill, 2013), 13–50.

expertise. For example, it became clear eventually that "Kurdistan" would not become a state, whatever experts said about the Kurds, because no Great Power would guarantee it. During the war, the Americans, the British, and the French all built new machineries of expertise in planning for peace. In each of the three Great Powers, the wartime state developed a new "official mind," distinct from the standing foreign ministries. Most commonly associated with historians of British imperialism, the term "official mind" speaks to that which informs permanent state interest beyond the vicissitudes of high politics.[7]

Woodrow Wilson never had cordial relations with the State Department, notwithstanding his lack of experience in foreign policy before becoming president. Lloyd George probably had even more disdain for the Foreign Office than Wilson for the State Department.[8] He preferred to plan for peace through the War Cabinet, notably through former Boer commander General Jan Smuts and the War Cabinet secretary, Maurice Hankey. He had not even bothered to include his own foreign secretary, Arthur James Balfour, in the War Cabinet. In France, Clemenceau thoroughly dominated foreign policy.[9] Through two terms as foreign minister under Clemenceau (1906–11 and 1917–20), Stephen Pichon remains known primarily for his personal loyalty to his master. Olivier Lowczyk has argued that only André Tardieu exercised real authority alongside Clemenceau, based on many years of experience maneuvering within the French state. Yet he too remained Clemenceau's vassal.[10] But for Clemenceau, as for Wilson or Lloyd George, it would be a mistake to overemphasize the personal nature of making foreign policy. No one individual could fully understand all the issues at stake at the Paris Peace Conference. Broader knowledge had to come from somewhere.

Organizational commonalities joined the ways that Britain, France, and the United States planned for peace. All three drew in collections of academic luminaries, whose prior expertise seldom coincided with the specific knowledge that planning for peace had called on them to produce. National traditions in political geography brought expertise to experts. Political geography shaped both specific solutions and, perhaps more importantly, how issues got raised in the first place.[11] Indeed, national cultures produced distinct meanings of "geopolitics."

[7] Ronald Robinson, John Gallagher, and Alice Denny, *Africa and the Victorians: The Official Mind of Imperialism* (London: Macmillan, 1961); and John Darwin, "Imperialism and the Victorians: The Dynamics of Territorial Expansion," *English Historical Review* 112, No. 447 (1997): 614–42.

[8] M.L. Dockrill and Zara Steiner, "The Foreign Office at the Paris Peace Conference in 1919," *The International History Review* 2.1 (1980): 55–86; and Roberta M. Warman, "The Erosion of Foreign Office Influence in the Making of Foreign Policy, 1916–1918," *The Historical Journal* 15.1 (1972): 133–59.

[9] See Jean Jacques Becker, *Clemenceau, chef de guerre* (Paris: Armand Colin, 2012), 150–52.

[10] On the French delegation, see Olivier Lowczyk, *La Fabrique de la paix: du Comité d'Études à la conference de la paix, l'élaboration par la France des traits de la première guerre mondiale* (Paris: Economica, 2010), 17–126. A Comité consultative de la délégation française led by Tardieu informed Clemenceau's decisions. See Volker Prott, *The Politics of Self-Determination: Remaking Territories and National Identities in Europe, 1917–1923* (Oxford: Oxford University Press, 2016), 31–32. Tardieu wrote his own account, *La Paix* (Paris: Payot, 1921), 113.

[11] This section expands on my argument in "Drawing Borders in the Middle East after the Great War: Political Geography and 'Subject Peoples,'" *First World War Studies* 7.1 (2016): 5–21.

As proprietors of the world's most extensive empire, the British state particularly prided itself on a long tradition of global strategic thinking. The Foreign Office never ceased trying to gain political ground under Lloyd George, on many fronts.[12] What became the 174-volume *Peace Handbooks* originated in the Admiralty, a traditional guardian of British global strategic interests. The Ministry of Blockade established in 1916 established the War Trade Intelligence Department, which began to develop specifically economic intelligence. In 1918, the Directorate of Military Intelligence established M.I. 2 (e), which reported to the Imperial General Staff. Under the direction of Lord Charles Hardinge, permanent under-secretary in the Foreign Office and a former viceroy of India, the Foreign Office gradually centralized these diverse efforts, culminating in the formation of the Political Intelligence Department.

Wartime planning for peace had gathered together a glittering cast of academic characters with close ties to Oxford and Cambridge Universities. Not all, however, had prior expertise in the fields in which they were about to become experts. Harold Temperley of Cambridge was a diplomatic historian by training, and before the war had written books on George Canning and Prussian–Habsburg relations in the late eighteenth century.[13] James Headlam-Morely, a classicist by training at Cambridge, had written about Germany under Bismarck. R.W. Seton-Watson of Oxford had long been a major Anglophone voice on Central and Eastern Europe. A close friend of Tomáš Masaryk, he had founded a periodical, *The New Europe*, in 1916.[14] This publication advocated something recognizable as Wilsonianism in the Habsburg lands well before the Fourteen Points.[15] Louis Namier, one of the great British political historians of the twentieth century, had made his name as a historian of British domestic politics and the time of the American Revolution. Born in Poland as Ludwik Bernsztajn vel Niemiorowski, Namier had immigrated to Britain only in 1907.[16] Arnold J. Toynbee, a classicist by training, had become a resident expert on the Middle East during the war. He would achieve his greatest fame after the war as author of the multi-volume *A Study of History* (1934–59).[17]

Expertise grappled with well-known strategic concerns of the British Empire. The British Empire existed to further the global interests of the United Kingdom of Great Britain and Ireland. That kingdom required global trade to prosper. It also required outposts, whether self-governing settler Dominions, the "sub-empire" of

---

[12] Erik Goldstein, *Winning the Peace: British Diplomatic Strategy, Peace Planning, and the Paris Peace Conference, 1916–1920* (Oxford: Clarendon Press, 1991), 9–119.

[13] Temperley is perhaps best known for *A History of the Peace Conference of Paris*, 6 vols. (London: H. Frode and Hodder and Stoughton, 1920–24).

[14] For a succinct intellectual biography, see Lázló Péter, "R.W. Seton-Watson's Changing Views on the Nationality Question in the Habsburg Monarchy and the European Balance of Power," *Slavonic and East European Review* 82.3 (2004): 655–79.

[15] Harry Hanak, "The New Europe, 1916–20," *Slavonic and East European Review* 39, No. 93 (1961): 369–99.

[16] See Linda Colley, *Lewis Namier* (New York: St. Martin's Press, 1999).

[17] Michael Lang, "Globalization and Global History in Toynbee," *Journal of World History* 22.4 (2011): 747–83.

India, or the array of crown colonies. Imperial trade and imperial defense lived in symbiosis. Most experts seemed convinced that empires have life cycles. Imperial Britain early in the twentieth century lived with the challenges of what Paul Kennedy called a "mature power."[18] As the British Empire aged, consolidation and development took precedence over further expansion. Realism loomed large over imperial policy, guided by the article of faith that the British Empire could survive only if it held more economic and military capacity than its rivals. As in the nineteenth century, protecting empire could sometimes mean expanding it, even if strategic stasis remained the ideal.

No one did more to shape the official mind of the British Empire in the era of the Great War than Halford J. Mackinder, one of the founders of the London School of Economics.[19] In 1904, as part of the wave of imperial introspection in the aftermath of the Anglo-Boer War, Mackinder published a highly influential article positing that in the new century, power on land would come to dominate sea power.[20] He argued for the existence of a land-based "pivot area" beginning in European Russia and extending into Central Asia and Siberia. Control over the pivot area would determine control over the "World Island," the combination of Europe, Africa, and Asia. The Great War, he wrote in February 1919, "has established, and not shaken, my former points of view."[21] The disintegration of Imperial Russia had put the pivot area (now renamed the Heartland) in play, making it more strategic than ever. Mackinder explained the matter in his most famous three lines:

> Who rules East Europe commands the Heartland:
> Who rules the Heartland rules the World-Island:
> Who rules the World-Island rules the World.[22]

These three simple axioms had redefined protecting the decidedly "blue water" British Empire. While seafaring Britain could not itself control the "Heartland," it would have to make sure that no other Great Power did so, whether a resurgent Germany or Bolshevik Russia. Only a strategically integrated British Empire, combined with an alliance of democracies perpetuated through the League of Nations, could preserve British interests through the perils of the twentieth century.[23] Mackinder's political geography prioritized lands over peoples. Indeed, peoples mattered at all only to the extent that they aided or impeded rule over territories.

---

[18] Paul Kennedy, *The Rise and Fall of the Great Powers: Economic Change and Military Conflict* (London: Unwin Hyman, 1988), 224–32; and John Darwin, *The Empire Project: The Rise and Fall of the British World-System, 1830–1970* (Cambridge: Cambridge University Press, 2009).

[19] See Brian W. Blouet, *Halford Mackinder: A Biography* (College Station: Texas A&M University Press, 1987).

[20] H.J. Mackinder, "The Geographical Pivot of History," *The Geographical Journal* 23.4 (1904): 421–44.

[21] H.J. Mackinder, *Democratic Ideals and Reality: A Study in the Politics of Reconstruction* (London: Constable and Company, 1919), Preface.

[22] Mackinder, *Democratic Ideals and Reality*, 194.

[23] Lucian M. Ashworth, "Realism and the Spirit of 1919: Halford Mackinder, Geopolitics, and the Reality of the League of Nations," *European Journal of International Relations* 17.2 (2010): 279–301; and Darwin, *Empire Project*, 359–417.

The question became refining rule over lands and seas to ensure stability around a vast border region running from Scandinavia to Japan.

Imperial security from this point of view required a stable Europe, preferably without a sustained British military presence on the continent. This meant maintaining the alliance with France. Above all, the allies after the war could not permit criminalized Germany and outcast Bolshevik Russia to ally with each other to dominate the Heartland. Revolutionary fever would need to be calmed throughout the Heartland.[24] Britain as empire and as European Great Power needed strong, anti-German, and anti-Bolshevik successor states in Central and Eastern Europe.

Imperial balance would prevail in Africa and the Pacific through the distribution of mandates. Dominions such as Australia and South Africa would become mandatory powers, further subcontracting empire. Britain would have to negotiate its maritime interests in the Pacific with Japan and the United States, two allies doubling as rivals.[25] India, which had contributed massively in blood and treasure to the victory, would require a palliative through some form of self-government. The British Empire would expand in the Middle East, to fill the vacuum created by the disintegration of Ottoman authority. An ever-expanding notion of just what it meant to guarantee access to India through the Suez Canal, the need for access to oil in Mesopotamia, the Arabian Peninsula, and Persia, and the Balfour Declaration would all mean substantial new imperial commitments.[26]

This overall strategic perspective informed the 174-volume collection of *Peace Handbooks*, the most extensive monument extant to any state's official mind in planning for peace after the Great War. G. W. Prothero, editor of the prestigious *Quarterly Review*, supervised the enterprise.[27] Written in wartime, the handbooks had to draw primarily from prewar published sources, almost entirely in English, French, and German. Most handbooks are long on assertion, short on documentation or statistics. Some end abruptly, while others contain "general remarks" with more explicit recommendations. Almost none identified individual authors.

The *Peace Handbooks* characterized peoples around the world primarily according to how they might serve or impede the geopolitical interests of the British Empire. For example, the authors simply adjusted "self-determination" in Alsace and Lorraine to match British geostrategic requirements for a strong France. Despite more than four decades of German-managed economic prosperity, it turned out that the people of Alsace "resented being torn from France; they resented being annexed to Germany; but, above all, they resented being treated like chattels, as if

---

[24] As High Commissioner to South Russia in 1919–1920, Mackinder took up the unenviable task of trying to unite the Whites in opposition to the Bolsheviks. Blouet, *Mackinder*, 172–77.

[25] See J. Chal Vinson, "The Imperial Conference of 1921 and the Anglo-Japanese Alliance," *Pacific Historical Review* 31.3 (1962): 257–66.

[26] See John Fisher, *Curzon and British Imperialism in the Middle East, 1916–1919* (London: Frank Cass, 1999).

[27] On the writing of the *Peace Handbooks*, see Goldstein, *Winning the Peace*, 30–51.

their opinions counted for nothing."[28] British interests sufficed to render the people of Alsace and Lorraine "French."

France and Britain would continue to compete around the globe, notably in dividing up the Arabic-speaking domains of the former Ottoman Empire. In the Middle East, the *Peace Handbooks* reproduced an "official mind" familiar to anyone who understood the Sykes–Picot agreement. Here, Mackinder's concerns of land and sea power came together. The Mediterranean would remain a shared maritime space, in which France, Italy, Spain, and Greece would all have spheres of influence.[29] But Britain would still hold the chokehold points of access, through Gibraltar and the Suez Canal. Some sort of circumscribed post-Ottoman Turkey would survive the war, not least because the nationalist project of the Young Turks had fatally divided pan-Islamic movements in the Arabic-speaking domains.[30]

It remained to guarantee British interests in the strategic land bridge between Anatolia and India. In contrast to prevailing views from the Government of India, the authors of the handbooks did not particularly extend British interests to Mesopotamia and the Arabian Peninsula. Both were sparsely populated with uncivilized peoples. The generic Arab of Mesopotamia was "slovenly and uncreative in practical matters, and is lacking in the power of co-operation and sustained labour in the face of difficulties." The Kurds "have little tribal cohesion, and are addicted to blood feuds."[31] The Arabs of the peninsula, though physically "one of the finest races in the world," were likewise "deficient in organizing power and capacity for combined action, while they have an instinctive dislike of all kinds of governmental control." Bedouins seemed more promising, "especially among such as form part of a federation under the control of the greater Emirs or the King of the Hejaz."[32] Surprisingly, the authors paid no attention to the vast oil resources of both Arabia and Mesopotamia known to exist at the time. Instead, they focused on limited prospects for economic development. Apart from their location, Arabia and Mesopotamia offered little threat and little promise for the British Empire. With minimal forms of suzerainty, Britain could leave them largely as they were.

"Syria," however, would prove another matter altogether, because of its strategic location. In Mackinder's terms, if the Eurasian landmass was the pivot of world history, Syria constituted the pivot of the British presence around that landmass. Ottoman Syria (including present-day Syria, Lebanon, Israel, Jordan, and Palestine) provided the key to the British presence around the Eurasian landmass. The French had made claims to what the handbook with palpable derision called *la Syrie intégrale* (Greater Syria) based on what the British considered dubious assertions of France as the protector of all Christian communities in the Middle East.[33] As per

---

[28] *Alsace-Lorraine* (Handbooks Prepared Under the Direction of the Historical Section of the Foreign Office, No. 30) (London: H.M. Stationery Office, 1920), 53. Subsequent citations will refer only to title and volume number.

[29] *Italian Libya*, No. 127; and *Greece with the Cyclades & Northern Spora*, No. 18.

[30] *Pan-Islamism*, No. 57, 54–62.   [31] *Mesopotamia*, No. 63, 10.

[32] *Arabia*, No. 61, 10. The volume carefully avoided choosing sides between the Hashemite and al-Saud families.

[33] *France and the Levant*, No. 66, 22.

the Sykes–Picot Agreement, British imperial stability could best be achieved through the partition of Syria, into a French "Syria" and a British "Palestine."

Geopolitical requirements in the region determined this "unmixing" of lands, with the "unmixing" of peoples to follow. To the Romans and the Ottomans, "Syria" had been simply "the country that lies between the eastern shore of the Mediterranean and the deserts of Arabia." Diversity characterized the peoples of Syria—religious, linguistic, ethnographic. The assumption of diversity could create categories that required only assertions, such as the peculiar contention that "the peoples west of the Jordan [River] are not Arabs, but only Arab-speaking."[34] Given the diversity of peoples in Roman and Ottoman Syria, it scarcely mattered how the Great Powers "unmixed" them.

If "Syria" had only geographic meaning, there could be no problem dividing it for reasons of imperial balance between French "Syria" and British "Palestine." As in the last century, imperial rivalry need not preclude imperial cooperation. The new British domain would reinvent a very old concept: "In modern usage the expression Palestine has no precise meaning, but is best taken as being the equivalent to Southern Syria."[35] The British Empire could protect its access to interests in the Arabian Peninsula and Mesopotamia, and to India beyond, through a Jewish "homeland," beholden to the British and adjacent to the protectorate of Egypt and the Suez Canal. The Balfour Declaration had never been entirely about a humanitarian concern for the world's Jews.[36] Jews recently arrived from Europe would establish a settler colony of European Zionists in the newly reinvented "Palestine." The British could speak loudly of Faisal's friendly attitude toward Jewish settlement, as a means of developing lands subject to malevolent neglect under the Ottomans. They could speak softly of European Zionists' intent that "the Jewish population would rapidly increase until the Jew became the predominant member in the combination."[37]

The authors of the *Peace Handbooks* seemed genuinely perplexed as to how to draw boundaries in Central and Eastern Europe. They did not assume a priori the breakup of the multinational empires. An independent Poland, if history were any judge, would have bleak postwar prospects. In addition to habitual Great Power meddling, or worse, Poland had never developed a Third Estate: "In the country all power lay in the hands of the nobles, in the towns in the hands of the Jews."[38] The nobility cared only for its class interests, while anti-Semitism had tainted the very idea of commerce throughout Polish society. Neither nobles nor Jews fostered economic development or the development of a liberal polity. Readers could only infer that a truly modern Poland would have to break the power of both groups.

While they did not mention Mackinder, the authors of a volume on Bohemia and Moravia wrote of a race war whose ultimate outcome would determine the fate

---

[34] *Syria and Palestine*, No. 60, 56.   [35] *Syria and Palestine*, No. 60, 1–2.
[36] Jonathan Schneer, *The Balfour Declaration: The Origins of the Arab-Israeli Conflict* (New York: Random House, 2010).
[37] *Zionism*, No. 162, 47.   [38] *Poland: General Sketch of History, 1569–1815*, No. 43, 18.

of the Heartland: "Here the age-long struggle between Teuton and Slav first broke out, and here, as many Germans assure us, it will be decided."[39] Yet the volume on Slovakia emphasized the polyglot demography, and economic underdevelopment caused by the underdevelopment of Hungary.[40] Nowhere did either volume assume the formation of "Czechoslovakia." Likewise, there was no assumption that ethnically tangled Transylvania and Banat would or should be taken from Hungary. Nor did the authors assert this was even the desire of the Romanian-speaking Vlachs, the single most numerous ethnicity in both provinces.[41] Britain would need strong successor states (or successor empires), but prudent minds would remain open as to how peacemaking would demarcate them.

The realist concerns of the French did not differ much from those of the British—strong successor states to contain Germany, and expansion of the empire where necessary or practical. But the French offered different explanations through a specifically French school of geography, which seemed tailor-made for designing new states in its concern for the unity of lands and peoples.[42] In February 1917, premier Aristide Briand established the Comité d'Études to plan for peace. A committee of some thirty persons met into the spring of 1919, in the exclusive manner of an eighteenth-century *salon*. Members presented papers to one another and commented on them. A list of academic luminaries represented the permanent intellectual guardians of the Republic. Many were not geographers; though all were influenced by French geography. The Comité stood above and beyond the shifting fortunes of ministries under the Third Republic. Historian Ernst Lavisse laid out the mission of the Comité at its first meeting on February 28, 1917: "This is not about coming up with solutions, but about creating a series of dossiers useful to those who will have the responsibility for representing France at the Peace Conference."[43] Unsurprisingly, the Comité reports supported well-known French war aims. It would be up to the generals, the politicians, and the diplomats to draw the borders once peace came. It was up to the Comité to demarcate what there was to discuss.

Like their British counterparts, the French experts comprised accomplished individuals rapidly retooling themselves to plan for peace. Charles Benoist of the École libre des sciences politiques (forerunner of today's Sciences-Po) had written widely on political history from the Middle Ages to the twentieth century. Ernst Lavisse had come to embody the entire Republican educational project, both as the author of standard textbooks in French history and as director of the École Normale Supérieur.[44] Alphonse Aulard was the first occupant of the chair at the Sorbonne in the history of the French Revolution. Charles Seignebos, a

---

[39] *Bohemia and Moravia*, No. 2, 37.   [40] *Slovakia*, No. 3.

[41] *Transylvania and the Banat*, No. 6, 5.

[42] Vincent Berdoulay, *La Formation de l'école française de géographie* (Paris: Editions du Comité des travaux historiques et scientifiques, 1995).

[43] *Travaux du Comité d'Études*, Tome I, *L'Alsace-Lorraine et la fontière du Nord-Est* (Paris: Imprimerie nationale, 1918), and Tome II, *Questions européennees* (Paris: Imprimerie nationale, 1919), 1: iv. Subsequent references will cite article, volume, and page numbers.

[44] Pierre Nora, "Lavisse, instituteur national," in Pierre Nora, ed., *Les Lieux de mémoire*, 3 vols. (Paris: Gallimard, 1997 [originally published 1984–86]), 1: 239–74.

student of Lavisse, had been a renowned historian of ancient civilizations and historical methodology.

Three geographers on the Comité particularly influenced territorial recommendations. Paul Vidal de la Blanche had essentially founded the French school of geography.[45] He died in April 1918, but two of his students kept his influence alive throughout the conference. Emmanuel de Martonne was known for emphasizing physical geography, the impact of land on human civilization. He served on the Comité as well as on various commissions and sub-commissions of the conference.[46] As a specialist in Romanian geography, he would wield considerable influence in the territorial settlement there. His colleague Albert Demangeon emphasized human geography, the adaptation of civilization to the land.

Most of the findings of the Comité were published in 1918 and 1919 in two lavishly produced volumes plus annexes, including high-quality color maps. The entire first volume considered the eastern borders of France, and comprised nearly 150 pages on Alsace and Lorraine alone.[47] No government-sponsored academic body was going to question that the "Lost Territories" had always remained "French," whatever language their inhabitants spoke.[48] Considering Alsace and Lorraine as geographic spaces also opened a gateway to a much larger expanse of the former Kaiserreich that, the Comité argued, had not been "Germany" in the same sense as Prussia or Saxony. French geography could argue for the ambiguous territoriality of the Rhineland and the Saar. The key to doing so through French geography lay in uncovering the intimate connections between lands and peoples.[49] Rivers, plains, mountains, climates, and peoples formed "natural" combinations remarkably consistent with anticipated French policy. Ethnography became a sub-field of geography, discoverable by professionals much like the features of topography.

To this way of thinking, the Rhineland constituted a natural topography for the extension of a certain kind of civilization, stretching back to Antiquity. A zone of "Gallic" and "Celtic" peoples, forebears of the French, had settled a broad strip of land running from present-day Belgium and Luxembourg,[50] through the Rhineland, through what became Baden and Württemberg. Lands drew peoples, and through them Roman civilization: "A zone of more civilized life, on the left bank of the Rhine, separated the rest of Gaul from the still-barbarian Germany."[51] Particularly after the solidification of French rule in Alsace and Lorraine in the eighteenth century, the Saar and the Rhineland joined the economic hinterland of

---

[45] See, for example, Geoffrey Parker, "Ratzel, the French School and the Birth of Alternative Geopolitics," *Political Geography* 19.8 (2000): 957–69.

[46] See Gilles Palsky, "Emmanuel de Martonne and the Ethnographical Cartography of Central Europe (1917-1920)," *Imago Mundi* 54.1 (2002): 111–19.

[47] Ernest Lavisse and Christian Pfister, "La formation d'Alsace-Lorraine," 1: 3–30; and Première Partie, "La Frontière d'Alsace-Lorraine," 57–150.

[48] On debates among the French about Alsace and Lorraine, see Prott, *Politics of Self-Determination*, 54–82.

[49] Berdoulay, *La Formation de l'école.*

[50] On the Comité and the complicated politics of postwar Luxembourg and Belgium, see Lowczyk, *Fabrique de la paix*, 223–42, 245–66. See also Albert Demangeon, "Le Port d'Anvers," 2: 31–82.

[51] Camille Jullian, "Les Populations rhénanes dans l'antiquité," 1: 353.

France.[52] The unification of the Reich in 1871 unnaturally tore this unity asunder by separating these lands. General Robert Bourgeois, the one serving military officer on the Comité, grafted human geography onto military science, and argued that France could remain safe only through subduing the Rhineland militarily, as it had already done economically and culturally.[53]

The essays on the border with Germany maintained a strict silence as to the precise political status of the peoples of the Rhineland and Saar after the war. As Lowczyk has argued of the Comité members, such impartial servants of the Republic would not stoop to advocating annexations of any sort in so many words. French geography could simply explain the "natural" contours of French influence. The conclusions of the Comité also hinted at hybrid forms of sovereignty, such as a suspiciously prescient suggestion of French mineral rights in a Saar legally still part of Germany, as well as a demilitarized, occupied, or even "independent" Rhineland.

What of the lands where Hohenzollern, Habsburg, and Romanov authority had disintegrated? Physical geography could show the preconditions of viable economies. Human geography could articulate the relationships of peoples to lands. All categorization of peoples in Central and Eastern Europe had to draw on prewar population figures, generated by the multinational empires. The Comité certainly understood the politics of the census machinery in the Habsburg Monarchy. For example, the monarchy considered Jews as members of a religion rather than an ethnic group, and Yiddish as a form of slang rather than its own language. Consequently, census takers categorized the massive Jewish population of Galicia mostly as "Polish," even though Jews lived much of their lives in Yiddish.[54] Recognizing Jews as Polish, the Comité observed, served artificially to augment the number of Poles, as a group of Slavs to set against others in endless Habsburg strategies of divide and rule. Likewise, Habsburg census takers in the Kingdom of Hungary relied on "mother tongue [*langue maternelle*]," counted in ways to maximize the Magyar population. A Magyar-born mother invariably had Magyar children, whatever the primary language of the family.[55]

Nevertheless, the Comité had only Habsburg census figures to work with, and no other figures available at the time could prove less imaginary. Were the Comité to set Habsburg figures aside, de Martonne argued, "we risk depriving ourselves of all serious basis for discussion, and we risk falling into flights of fancy." He believed data on religion could provide additional assistance disentangling peoples in the Hungarian lands, particularly Magyars from Romanians. De Martonne admitted the obvious, however, that religion could separate peoples only up to an ill-defined point. Roman Catholics could be Magyars, Romanians, or most anything else. Uniates could be either Ruthenes/Ukrainians or Romanians; Serbs either Uniates or Orthodox.[56] Inevitably, mapping ethnic categories made French political geographers the creators of the very situation they claimed to observe. De Martonne,

[52] Christian Pfister, "La Frontière économique, rapport préliminaire," 1: 195–206.

[53] General Robert Bourgeois, "La Frontière militaire du Nord et du Nord-Est," 1: 307–27; and "Le Rhin, frontier militaire," 1: 329–40.

[54] Jules-Eugène Pichon, "Le Recensement des populations en Autriche-Hongrie," 2: 198.

[55] Pichon, "Recensement des populations," 2: 200–01.   [56] "Discussion," 2: 202–03.

second only to Vidal in his reputation as a geographer and a specialist on Romania, wrote four essays justifying a Greater Romania comprising the Banat, Transylvania, and Bessarabia.[57]

In the end, French geography supported the French goal of strong successor states in Eastern Europe that could replace the alliance with Imperial Russia. "Czechoslovakia," a wholly new political entity, would play a vital role keeping Germany in check. The new state would comprise historic Bohemia, Moravia, and Slovakia, even though a good third of the population would be neither Czech nor Slovak. Only historic boundaries, French geographers held, could give the new state economic and strategic viability.[58] All peoples in geographic Czechoslovakia should be given a full ten years to decide whether to accept Czechoslovak citizenship. Czechs and Slovaks resident elsewhere in the former monarchy would be given the same ten years to move to Czechoslovakia and become full citizens there.[59]

Successor Poland would also prove critically important to French security, but represented a far more delicate subject.[60] Poland had no "natural," defensible frontiers to its east or west, precisely what had made it so difficult to resist partition in the eighteenth century. French geographers on the Comité hedged their bets, and managed to find a Polish "unity" in both the "small," ethno-religiously exclusionary Poland advocated by Roman Damowski, and in the "greater," more federal and multi-ethnic Poland advocated by Józef Piłsudski. Whatever the differences among the twelve Comité papers on Poland, seven of which made it to publication, they all affirmed the obvious, that successor Poland could either have its borders from prior to the partitions of the eighteenth century, or it could have an ethnically "Polish" population. It could not have both.

In the Mediterranean, the Comité expected the demise and likely partition of the Ottoman Empire to reconfigure the balance in the region among the victors. Some sort of internationalized entity would manage the Straits of the Dardanelles, in the name of "Mediterranean" unity.[61] The Comité encouraged a friendly Greece, expanded into western Anatolia. The Hellenic kingdom should acquire some form of sovereignty over the Dodecanese Islands, Smyrna, and its hinterland. Given the certain non-Greek majority beyond Smyrna proper, the border would need to be drawn carefully, and the access to the sea guaranteed for the peoples of inland Anatolia. Reciprocal guarantees could exist for Greek minorities elsewhere.[62] Long-suffering Armenia presented a particularly difficult "Mediterranean" problem,

---

[57] "La Question du Banat," 2: 533–78; "La Transylvanie," 2: 579–624; "La Bessarabie," 2: 625–42; and "La Dobroudja," 2: 643–82.

[58] Jules-Eugène Pichon, "Les Frontières de l'État Tchéco-Slovak," 2: 105–24.

[59] Jules-Eugène Pichon, "Les Allemands de Bohème et de Moravie," 2: 143.

[60] See Lowczyk, *Fabrique de la paix*, 301–54. See also the lively discussion of Poland in "Procès verbal de la séance du Comité d'études, 3 décembre 1918," in Georges-Henri Soutou, ed., *Les Experts français et les frontières d'après guerre: les procès-verbaux du comité d'études* (Paris: Société de Géographie, 2015), 162–64.

[61] Albert Demangeon, "Formation territorial d'un état international des détroits," 2: 753; and Paul Masson, "Constantinople et les détroits, leur rôle eonomique," 2: 709–50.

[62] Paul Masson, "Smyrne et l'hellénisme en Asie mineur," 2: 822–23.

in the sense of commanding access to Iran and Central Asia: "The Armenian question extends, in some way, the question of the Straits."[63] But the establishment of a large Armenia would prove central to the recasting of Post-Ottoman "Turkey" which would become a residual, much as envisaged by the Sykes–Picot agreement. One major revision of Sykes–Picot, however, involved preserving the contours of Roman and Ottoman Syria. France could continue to share the Mediterranean with other states so long as they accepted a Greater Syria under French rule.[64]

American political geography sought to put the lofty ideas of Wilsonianism into practice. As "self-determination" morphed into "national self-determination," this meant seeking coherence with a minimum of self-contradiction. American planning for peace was vast yet secretive, remarkably so given that Wilson had called for a new international order based on open covenants, openly arrived at. The Inquiry, as the planning apparatus became known, employed some 126 people at its peak. It generated some 2,000 reports, ranging from a few pages to hundreds of pages in length.[65] A ninety-eight-page summary known as the Black Book, delivered to President Wilson in January 1919, originally existed in only forty copies.[66]

In September 1917, Wilson established a planning apparatus distinct from the State Department under the supervision of Colonel Edward House.[67] House chose as director his brother-in-law, Sidney Mezes, a philosopher of religion by training and president of the City College of New York. Its core members comprised mostly Ivy League faculty who lived within commuting distance from New York City. As in the British and French cases, The Inquiry selected its members more for their academic positions than for their demonstrated expertise in the matters at hand. As pro-Wilson journalist Walter Lippman put it:

> What we are on the lookout for is genius—sheer, startling genius because nothing else will do because the real application of the President's ideas to those countries requires inventiveness and resourcefulness which is scarcer than anything.[68]

Charles Homer Haskins, dean of the graduate school at Harvard University, had trained in medieval European history. Charles Seymour of Yale had written on the franchise in nineteenth-century England and Wales. Frederick Jackson Turner of Harvard, known for his thesis on the American frontier, and William Dunning

---

[63] Antoine Meillet, "La Nation arménienne," 2: 841.

[64] See Smith, "Drawing Borders in the Middle East," esp. 9–12.

[65] Lawrence E. Gelfand, *The Inquiry: American Preparations for Peace, 1917–1919* (New Haven, CT: Yale University Press, 1963), 45, 110.

[66] See Wesley Reisser, *The Black Book: Woodrow Wilson's Secret Plan for Peace* (Lanham, MD: Lexington Books, 2012), 129. Reisser overstates the secrecy of the Black Book, which was published in its entirety as "Outline of Tentative Report and Recommendations Prepared by the Intelligence Section, in Accordance with Instructions, for the President and the Plenipotentiaries, January 21, 1919," *Miller Diary*, 4: 209–67. Subsequent references to the Black Book will appear in the text as page numbers in Miller.

[67] The Inquiry would play an important role in developing the specifics of the Fourteen Points. See Neil Smith, *American Empire: Roosevelt's Geographer and the Prelude to Globalization* (Berkeley: University of California Press, 2003), 123–25.

[68] Walter Lippman to Ray Stannard Baker, May 16, 1918, in Gelfand, *Inquiry*, 48.

of Columbia University, a historian of Reconstruction, served on the advisory committee. James Shotwell, also of Columbia and later a guiding light behind the International Labor Organization (I.L.O.), had written a dissertation on the history of the Eucharist. Some thirty experts from The Inquiry accompanied President Wilson to Europe on the *George Washington*. En route, the president famously told his entourage: "Tell me what's right, and I'll fight for it; give me a guaranteed position."[69] Wilson had provided the general principles, and relied on the newly minted experts to provide him with the details.

A self-proving logic of legitimacy underpinned The Inquiry. Since the United States had no territorial ambitions in the war, knowledge produced in its name was inherently neutral politically. The Inquiry produced neutral knowledge because the Inquiry produced it. The "American" goal for the Inquiry, therefore, was to mobilize knowledge to refute the inherently selfish claims of friend and foe alike, and to provide unselfish alternatives. A report on The Inquiry's activities from March 1918 counseled: "The American negotiators must be in a position to judge whether a claim put forward by a power is supported by the democracy at home, or whether it is merely a traditional diplomatic objective or the design of an imperialistic group."[70]

Some of the conclusions in The Inquiry's reports must have seemed peculiar even at the time. Robert J. Kerner had taught European history at the University of Missouri, and would later help found Slavic Studies at the University of California at Berkeley. He argued for recasting multinational Central Europe, but with Slavs rather than the Germans as the *Staatsvolk*, the glue holding the rest together. Kerner construed as the main impediment to such a scheme a conspiracy joining the Catholic Church (the church of millions of Slavs), international Jewry, and pacifists as a deadly fifth column.[71] The researchers of The Inquiry generally wished Bolshevism in Russia away, preferring to ruminate on how a democratic, post-Romanov regime would interact with the former imperial domains.[72] Nor were comments about the Ottoman world always helpful. "Syphilitic diseases" afflicted the Turks. Further, they suffered from a conspicuous "lack of executive ability," an odd insult to people who had ruled such a vast empire for so long.[73] Kurds were "avaricious, utterly selfish, shameless beggars, and have a great propensity to steal."[74] Their only hope lay in Christian missionaries.

Isaiah Bowman would wrest effective control of The Inquiry from Mezes, to emerge as the principal author of the Black Book. No one took more seriously Wilson's call on the *George Washington* for "a guaranteed position." Further, no one would adopt a more straightforward approach to drawing boundaries as essentially a technical matter. To Bowman, politicians and diplomats determined policy, to be implemented on maps by geographers. Political geography, by definition, created

---

[69] Gelfand, *Inquiry*, 174.

[70] "Report on the Inquiry: Its Scope and Method," Inquiry Document No. 889, March 20, 1918, *FRUS: PPC*, 1: 55.

[71] Gelfand, *Inquiry*, 200–02.   [72] See Gelfand, *Inquiry*, 211–14.

[73] J.K. Birge, "The Ottoman Turks of Asia Minor," quoted in Gelfand, *Inquiry*, 247.

[74] Arthur I. Andrews, "The Koords," February 20, 1918, quoted in Gelfand, *Inquiry*, 243.

certainty. Bowman became Wilson's chief advisor on boundaries in Paris.[75] The Black Book comprised a series of decisions imposing certainty on an uncertain world, and left little room for doubt. The multinational empires had disintegrated, and self-determined, ethnographically discerned nation-states had to take their place. No-nonsense political geography balancing the competing good intentions of Wilsonians would provide the key to unmixing lands after the Great War.

Shortly after returning from Paris, Bowman wrote an influential textbook on political geography published in many subsequent editions. Its preface began: "Whether we wish to do so or not we are obliged to take hold of the present world situation in one way or another."[76] A man of his later words, Bowman drew borders according to stripped-down, basic principles. Practically speaking, language determined ethnicity, which in turn determined nationality. The bold lines of the Black Book indicated that clear linguistic/ethnic/national boundaries were there for the drawing, whatever the quality of the prewar data. Such boundaries could be adjusted to guarantee strategic viability (as in the case of Czechoslovakia) or to guarantee trade (as in providing access to the sea through a "Polish Corridor"). Peoples in the new states would be expected to assimilate into the public spheres of their respective new states.[77] Bowman strongly opposed specific protections for religious or ethnic minorities, as sites of resistance that would trouble the formation of clear national communities.

Bowman certainly understood that drawing boundaries meant imposing ethno-national boundaries on multinational lands. His duty as he saw it therefore lay in following political directions as closely as practically possible. For example, the conference could legitimately reduce historic Hungary to the Danube lowlands because there lay the largest single concentration of Magyars. Except for Slovakia and Transylvania, according to the Black Book, "no large compact masses of Magyars would be placed under alien control" (245). Islands of Magyars elsewhere, however vast, would have to live in lands demarcated by the "vital economic needs of neighboring states" (255). Political geography should decide the proper balance between ethnicity and economics. As self-determination morphed into national self-determination, the perfect could not be the enemy of the good.

Bowman was widely credited with the idea of the "Polish Corridor" through former German East Prussia.[78] Here too, Bowman construed the matter as technical rather than political. Point XIII of the Fourteen Points might have been self-contradictory, but it could not have been clearer. Poland was supposed to be "indisputably Polish," and "be assured a free and secure access to the sea." Were the conference to cede all East Prussia to Poland, some 1.6 million Germans would live under Polish rule. But if the conference left prewar East Prussia intact, some 600,000 Poles would live under German rule. Further, the Black Book

[75] On Bowman in Paris, see Smith, *American Empire*, 139–80.
[76] Isaiah Bowman, *The New World: Problems in Political Geography* (Yonkers-on-Hudson, NY: World Book Company, 1921), v.
[77] See Smith, *American Empire*, 171, 493 fn. 76.
[78] On Bowman and Polish questions, see Geoffrey J. Martin, *American Geography and Geographers: Toward Geographical Science* (New York: Oxford University Press, 2015), 620–26.

reported, the 20 million Poles in Poland "will probably have but a hampered and precarious commercial outlet" under the authority of hostile Germans (226). Properly drawn, the Polish Corridor could fulfill Wilsonian principles, at least well enough, by minimizing minorities in the new states while still providing a port for successor Poland.

For the Black Book, the Fourteen Points either constituted the basis of the peace, or they did not. "Selfish" claims, such as those of the Italians to Fiume, would prove a crucial test of whether Wilsonianism guided American peacemaking or not. As shown in Figure 3.1, the Black Book offered two possible solutions to the boundary between Italy and Yugoslavia in the Istrian Peninsula (241–42). Both gave Italy more territory than it deserved according to the confidently drawn "linguistic boundary" between Italians and Croatians. But neither gave Fiume to Italy. Habsburg Croatia, and indeed the Dual Monarchy itself, had relied on two deep-water ports, Trieste and Fiume. To encourage economic growth through competition under free trade, it made sense to grant Trieste to Italy and Fiume to Yugoslavia. Bowman supported Wilson's intransigence on the issue, by granting no credence whatsoever to Italian claims to Fiume on either ethnographic or economic grounds.[79] In what became known as the "experts memo" sent to the president on April 17, 1919, Bowman and his colleagues pleaded with the president to accept the verdict of political geography over expedience. Italy, the experts argued in words shortly paraphrased by Wilson in the Supreme Council, "*entered* the war with a demand for loot."[80] If the British and French could acquiesce to Italian greed for their own selfish reasons, Wilson could not, for the sake of the world.

American experts beyond The Inquiry shared Bowman's passion for clarity. The United States sent missions to various trouble spots to acquire more immediate local knowledge, and to alleviate the need to rely on prewar and other suspect sources. The Coolidge Mission, headquartered in Vienna from January–May 1919, sent to Paris a stream of intrinsically fascinating reports.[81] Archibald Cary Coolidge, professor of history at Harvard, had earned his doctorate at the University of Freiburg and had served in the diplomatic service before the war.[82] A diplomatic historian, Coolidge numbered among the relatively few experts with prior expertise in the issues at hand.

A March 1919 memo by Coolidge showed how local knowledge could disrupt the certainty of the Black Book. He claimed that even though "the official statistics of population at our disposition are partisan and not to be trusted implicitly, nor are the estimates made by the rival nationalities worthy of confidence any

---

[79] Smith, *America's Empire*, 158–63.

[80] Memo to President Wilson signed by Isaiah Bowman, W.E. Lunt, Clive Day, Douglas Johnson, Charles Seymour, Allyn A. Young, April 17, 1919, in Ray Stannard Baker, *Woodrow Wilson and the World Settlement*, 3 vols. (Garden City, NY: Doubleday, Page & Company, 1923), 3: 278–80. Emphasis in original.

[81] On setting up the Coolidge Mission and its first reports, see *FRUS: PPC*, 2: 218–37. Its subsequent reports appear in *FRUS: PPC*, 12: 240–523.

[82] Harold Jefferson Coolidge, *Archibald Cary Coolidge: Life and Letters* (New York: Houghton Mifflin, 1932).

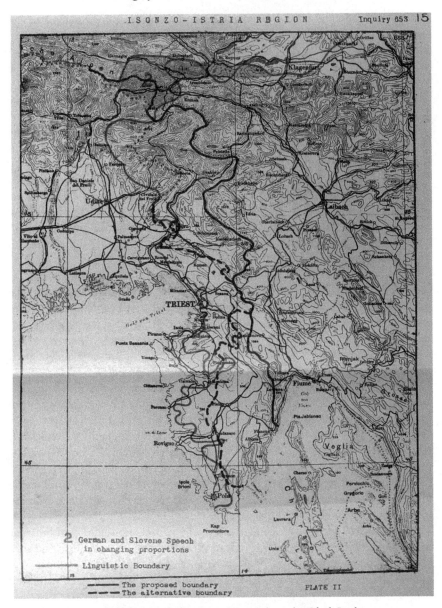

Figure 3.1. Imposing certainty on the Istrian Peninsula in the *Black Book*.
David Hunter Miller, *My Diary at the Conference of Paris* (privately printed and never copyrighted, 1924).

more than are their readings of history."[83] Nevertheless, Coolidge felt he could still make confident recommendations. These included detaching the Sudetenland from future Czechoslovakia, and granting Pressburg (today's Bratislava) to Hungary

---

[83] Professor A.C. Coolidge, "The New Frontiers in Former Austria-Hungary," *FRUS: PPC*, 12: 272.

rather than Slovakia. Neither recommendation would appeal to influential Czechoslovak nationalists such as Tomáš Masaryk or Edvard Beneš.

The King–Crane Commission remains probably the best-known project in American planning for peace outside of The Inquiry.[84] The co-chairs exemplified the Wilsonian ideal of diplomacy as too important to leave to diplomats. Charles Crane, an heir to the Crane plumbing fixtures fortune, had been a Wilson campaign contributor and a private foreign policy freelancer. Henry Churchill King, president of Oberlin College, had long been a major voice in reformist Christian higher education. In the summer of 1919, the commission traveled as an American rather than an inter-allied mission because the British and the French declined to send representatives.[85]

The King–Crane Commission carried to their conclusion the radical implications of Wilsonianism by recommending American mandates from Mesopotamia, to Greater Syria, to Constantinople. Like the Comité d'Études, the King–Crane Commission called for a multinational, multi-confessional, secular state in Greater Syria. But Americans advocated creating a micro-version of the United States itself. King–Crane portrayed Faisal as almost an Arab George Washington. The commission pointedly rejected not just the Balfour Declaration, but any large-scale Jewish immigration to the Middle East. The report waxed even more passionate on Armenia, whose people looked to America to protect them as they rebuilt their shattered national life.

Planning for peace in Britain, France, and the United States created national variants of the "official mind" that would provide the intellectual infrastructure for drawing of boundaries after the Great War. For the British, geopolitics prized lands over peoples, in the interest of preserving an aging empire. For example, British planners hoped that Jews and Arabs would live together peaceably in Palestine. Whether they did so or not would always be secondary to the need for a British-ruled territory further securing the Suez Canal. French geography emerged at the conference as a *science humaine*, making politically useful claims of unity among lands and peoples. American geographers took Wilsonianism as seriously as anyone at the Paris Peace Conference. Wilsonianism provided the intellectual as well as the moral compass for political geography. Politicians and diplomats would both accept and reject the conclusions of American political geography according to the political processes of the peace conference itself.

THE THEATER OF GEOGRAPHY IN PARIS

The infrastructure of planning for peace largely would demarcate the thinkable in "unmixing" lands. Between the infrastructure and the actual drawing of boundaries

---

[84] On the establishment of the commission and the report itself, see *FRUS: PPC*, 12: 745–863.

[85] Andrew Patrick, *America's Forgotten Middle East Initiative: The King-Crane Commission* (London: I.B. Tauris, 2015); and Leonard V. Smith, "Wilsonian Sovereignty in the Middle East: The King-Crane Commission Report of 1919," in Luise White and Douglas Howland, eds., *The State of Sovereignty: Territories, Laws, Populations* (Bloomington: Indiana University Press, 2009), 56–74.

lay a political process largely invented on the spot, by politicians, diplomats, nationalist activists, and experts. The more knowledge all these actors created in the name of the conference, the more self-contradictory and less controllable that knowledge seemed to become. After opening the door to expert advice, the Council began to receive presentations from nationalist leaders, each of which extolled his own data and castigated the irredeemably compromised data of his rivals.

From the first to the last days of the Paris Peace Conference, the council of Great Powers sought to preserve its sovereignty over the drawing of borders. Early in the conference, the council established itself as a sovereign court, which would hear pleas and decide among them. To support its efforts, the council in its various incarnations developed an elaborate network of territorial committees, which actually made many of the key decisions. They did so largely through endorsing conclusions drawn from one school or another of political geography.

The Council of Ten quickly devised means of mediating knowledge. The January 18, 1919 rules of the Paris Peace Conference had authorized delegations to bring "duly accredited Technical Delegates," who would "supply information when called upon" (Article III). Article XIII authorized the conference as it "shall think fit" to entrust "the study of any particular question from a technical point of view" to committees of Technical Delegates, who could report back to the conference and "suggest solutions." As Volker Prott has shown, this formal structure laid the groundwork for considerable collaboration among national experts.[86]

The evolution of the Council of Ten into a sovereign court on "unmixing" lands proved somewhat haphazard. On January 23, the Council decided to invite all claimants to submit their cases in writing within the next ten days. Sidney Sonnino of Italy recommended that each delegation plead its case in person. The Council should set up a schedule of hearings, so that "a complete picture of the whole problem would then be available."[87] On January 30, Clemenceau as chair announced, seemingly in passing, that Ion I.C. Brătianu of Romania would appear before them the next day. This led Lloyd George to ask if Clemenceau meant to begin a serious discussion of European territorial questions, and if so, under what circumstances.[88] Clemenceau responded that they had to begin somewhere: "If it were decided not to hear the Roumanian case the following day, well, let it be so; but they must have courage to begin with those questions one day or another." After some discussion, the Council agreed to hear Brătianu on January 31.

At least for a time, the Council became the sovereign power by treating itself as such, and by being treated as such by those making national claims. Performances from charismatic nationalists provided some of the best theater to be had at

---

[86] *The Politics of Self-Determination*, 40–53, 113–19. Prott convincingly argues against earlier conclusions that experts had little influence in Paris. See Dimitri Kitsikis, *Le Rôle des experts à la conférence de la paix de 1919: gestation d'une technocratie en politique internationale* (Ottawa: Éditions de l'Université d'Ottawa, 1972).

[87] "Secretary's Notes, January 23," *FRUS: PPC*, 3: 699–700.

[88] "Secretary's Notes of a Conversation Held in M. Pichon's Room at the Quai d'Orsay, Paris, on Thursday, January 30, 1919, at 15 Hours 30," *FRUS: PPC*, 3: 813–15.

the conference. As Bowman would remark scornfully: "Each one of the Central European nationalities had its own bagful of statistical and cartographical tricks."[89] News of what transpired in supposedly secret sessions often reached the public through press releases, leaks, and innuendo. Consequently, and against the intentions of the Council, these presentations satisfied what Clive Day of the American delegation later called "the demand of the public for the spectacular."[90] The petitioners well understood the power of the Council to grant its own form of recognition, and thus to help turn their cases into territorial sovereignty.

The Council saw petitioners virtually almost daily between the second and third plenary meetings of the conference (January 25–February 14). Petitioners comprised a "Who's Who" of nationalists. Some, such as Paul Hymans of Belgium and Eleftherios Venizelos of Greece, represented prewar states making claims as victorious allies. Brătianu of Romania would present some of the most expansive demands of any petitioner. Edvard Beneš of Czechoslovakia represented the state most likely to succeed in its claims of matching ethnic and historic boundaries. Nikola Pašić, Milenko Vesnić, and Ante Trumbić represented a new South Slav kingdom in which Serbs had been on one side during the war, and Croats and Slovenes on the other. Poles likewise had fought on both sides. The Council authorized two carefully preselected non-Europeans to appear before it—the British-subsidized Faisal of Mecca and Chekri Genem, a Francophile Lebanese who directed the influential colonial periodical *Correspondance d'Orient*.

Claimants told structurally similar narratives of "subject peoples" rooted in nineteenth-century Romanticism. Multinational imperial houses had subjugated national identities. Germans suppressed Czechs and Poles, Magyars suppressed Romanians and Slovaks, Turks had suppressed Greeks, etc. However, irresistible national consciousness—expressed in music, poetry, and much else—arose over time. Victory in the Great War had at last made it possible to create states based on the "natural" union of lands and nationally conscious peoples. For existing states such as Romania or Greece, fulfilling just irredentist claims would make the nation whole. In most cases, the unity of nation and state would have to be "restored," notwithstanding the historically fragile claims that these states had ever existed in a modern sense previously.

Presenters marshaled discourses of history, demography, ethnography, geography, and economics to justify their cases. They spoke as representatives of always-having-existed nations that needed simply international recognition as states, usually in maximally demarcated territories. The knowledge they presented legitimized itself. The voice of the people did not need documentation, and always countermanded prewar information originating with the oppressors. Each claimant could have echoed the words of Beneš: "All the Nation wanted was to control its own

---

[89] Isaiah Bowman, "Constantinople and the Balkans," in Edward House and Charles Seymour, eds., *What Really Happened at Paris: The Story of the Peace Conference, 1918–1919* (New York: Charles Scribner's Sons, 1921), 142.

[90] Clive Day, "The Atmosphere and Organization of the Peace Conference," in House and Seymour, *What Really Happened*, 16.

destinies."[91] Perhaps inadvertently, his very choice of the plural term "destinies" hinted at more instability within the "Nation" than he wished to convey.

Most petitioners stressed history as the decisive discourse. Nationalist history assumes concurrence between moralistic and "scientific" approaches to history.[92] It collects facts and arranges them into a story with a moral. History could explain how illegitimate regimes came to oppress foreign peoples, as well as how peoples could come to lose their own identities. Nationalist history could even explain how peoples came to live where they did not "belong." Historical consciousness provided a means of restoring national identity. Nationalist history, by definition, serves pedagogical purposes in nation building. Proper citizens, above all in ethnically based republics, are people who "know their history." The stakes of presenting historical narratives in Paris, therefore, could not have been higher.

The wrongs of history most often wore specific imperial faces. The houses of Hohenzollern, Habsburg, and Romanov had partitioned Poland late in the eighteenth century, tearing the Polish nation asunder. Oppressive nationalities had embraced monarchy, and vice versa. For centuries, both Osmans and Habsburgs had oppressed South Slavs. Hungarian kings had torn the Banat and Transylvania from their rightful places as parts of Serbia and/or Romania. The Habsburgs, as emperors of Austria and kings of Hungary, schemed for centuries to prevent the unity of Czechs and Slovaks. In seizing "Greek" lands, the Ottomans, both as "Orientals" and as Muslims, had oppressed hundreds of thousands of Christian Greeks in need of redemption through an expanded Greek state.

History looked ahead as well as back. Petitioners reminded the Council relentlessly of its role in altering the very course of history. As Faisal argued for the Arabic-speaking peoples: "He hoped the Conference would regard them [the Arabic-speaking peoples] as an oppressed nation which had risen against its masters." History could also provide a moral compass for the future: "For 400 years," Faisal added, "the Arabs had suffered from violent military oppression, and as long as life remained in them, they meant never to return to it."[93] Belgium sought to mobilize very recent history to support territorial claims against the Netherlands. The Treaty of 1839 establishing Belgium gave the Netherlands sovereignty over the mouth of the Scheldt, between Belgian Antwerp and the sea. Paul Hymans justified Belgian claims to the west bank by the fact that in the fall of 1918, the "neutral" Netherlands had permitted some 75,000 to 100,000 Germans to cross through Limburg on their way back to Germany.[94]

[91] "Secretary's Notes of a Conversation Held in M. Pichon's Room at the Quai d'Orsay, Paris, on Wednesday, 5 February 1919, at 3 p.m.," *FRUS: PPC*, 3: 877.

[92] J.C.D. Clark, "National Identity, State Formation and Patriotism: The Role of History in the Public Mind," *History Workshop* 29.1 (1990): 95–102.

[93] "Secretary's Notes of a Conversation Held in M. Pichon's Room at the Quai d'Orsay, Paris, on Thursday, 6 February, 1919, at 3 p.m.," *FRUS: PPC*, 3: 892.

[94] "Minute of a Conversation Held in M. Pichon's Room at the Quai d'Orsay, Paris, on Tuesday, 11 February, 1919, at 3 p.m.," *FRUS: PPC*, 3: 962–63.

The claims of history extended to ethnography and demography. For example, Venizelos pleaded for the historic "Greek-ness" of 120,000 "Greeks" in Northern Epirus who spoke only Albanian:

> After the experience gained in this war, neither race, nor language, nor skull, could be taken by itself as determining nationality; national conscience alone must decide.[95]

Consciousness had become conscience. In the ethnography of Venizelos, neither language nor phrenology could determine "national conscience." But neither could individuals choose, or necessarily even understand, their own historic conscience, at least not in Northern Epirus. Greeks living in Greece needed to tell these Albanian speakers why deep down they still had the national conscience of Greeks.[96]

Before the war, the petitioners held, demographers and statisticians served oppressive monarchies through systemic ethnic misclassification. But in the present, "the people" knew their actual identities, or could through their representatives in Paris. Further documentation was both impossible and unnecessary. For example, Brătianu produced population figures for Transylvania provided by the Hungarian government, only to denounce them as "fanciful figures, varying according to the political situation and the degree of acuteness of political struggles." The Hungarian figures counted 1 million Magyars and 2.5 million Romanians in Transylvania excluding the Banat, whereas the "real" (if undocumented) figures would count 687,000 Hungarians and 2.9 million Romanians.[97]

For Anatolia, Venizelos so impugned Ottoman figures that he preferred German ones, supplemented by what he considered more reliable numbers from the Greek patriarch in Constantinople. Even so, he applied one set of criteria for the "Greekness" of Albanian speakers in Northern Epirus on one day (national conscience, defined by Greeks living in Greece), only to apply another the next day, to justify Greek claims in Western Anatolia. In the parts of the peninsula claimed by Greece (excluding Constantinople), he counted 1,132,000 Greeks and 943,000 Muslims (mostly Turks). However, including 100,000 Jews and Armenians as "Greek" based on their religion would further bolster the Greek majority to nearly 1,250,000 Greeks.[98] Religion, in this case, sufficed to distinguish Greek from Turk. As we will see, using religion as the mark of ethnicity would have dramatic consequences in the population exchanges.

According to Beneš, Habsburg census takers had made a science of demographic manipulation in Bohemia, Moravia, and Austrian Silesia.[99] For the reviled 1910

[95] "Secretary's Notes of a Conversation Held in M. Pichon's Room at the Quai d'Orsay, Paris, on Monday, 3 February, 1919, at 11 a.m.," *FRUS: PPC*, 3: 859–60.

[96] Triadafilos Triadafilopoulos, "Power Politics and Nationalist Discourse for 'Northern Epirus': 1919–1921," *Journal of Southern Europe and the Balkans* 2.2 (2000): 149–62.

[97] "Secretary's Notes of a Conversation Held in M. Pichon's Room at the Quai d'Orsay, Paris, on Saturday, 1 February, 1919, at 3 p.m.," *FRUS: PPC*, 3: 846.

[98] "Secretary's Notes of a Conversation Held in M. Pichon's Room at the Quai d'Orsay, Paris, on Tuesday, 4 February 1919, at 11 O'clock a.m.," *FRUS: PPC*, 3: 871. Most Armenians claimed affiliation with the ancient Armenian Apostolic Church, distinct from Greek Orthodox Christianity.

[99] "Secretary's Notes of a Conversation Held in M. Pichon's Room at the Quai d'Orsay, on Wednesday, 5 February, 1919, at 3 p.m.," *FRUS: PPC*, 3: 879.

Habsburg census, officials warned villages that individuals would be classified ethnically "on the lines of spoken language, not of mother tongue." Consequently, if a worker spoke to his employer in German, the census taker would record him as German, whatever language he spoke at home or elsewhere. Given the prominence of German speakers among employers, the argument went, this vastly overestimated the German population—by nearly 1 million in Bohemia alone (2.4 million by Habsburg figures, 1.5 million by otherwise unidentified "Czech" figures). "The same method," Beneš assured the Council, "had been employed in the territories of other mixed populations in the Austro-Hungarian Kingdom."

Few doubted that the defeated monarchies had their own demographic axes to grind. But nationalist spokesmen expected acceptance of their own figures on faith, based in the inherent virtue of the oppressed. For the Council, judging population figures meant judging successor regimes. All figures, it bears repeating, involved imposing clarity on centuries of linguistic and thus ethnic ambiguity. What did reliable information even mean in parts of the world where everyday people routinely could transact business in two, three, or more languages?

From its first days to its last, the council of Great Powers fretted about the quality of the demographic information it received. The peacemakers certainly understood well enough the limitations of the data at hand. On January 29, 1919, the council dispatched its first specially created commission, to investigate continued instability and paramilitary violence in Poland. Strictly speaking, the commission sent to Poland was more a crisis management commission than a territorial commission. The council wanted more information about the prospect of a popular uprising in successor Poland among ethnic Germans.[100] Ultimately, of course, all Polish questions would become territorial questions.

At the January 30 meeting of the council, Wilson suggested supplementing personal appearances by nationalists with inter-allied commissions of experts.[101] For example, a commission on Romania would submit its "conclusions to the Roumanians for their opinion. By this means they [the members of the committee] would eliminate from the discussion everything with which they were in agreement." The Council could thereby streamline its discussion through bracketing uncontroversial issues. Internationalizing expertise through such commissions could make political geography essentially a technical enterprise. "Experts" could decide facts impartially, and thereby lay the groundwork for just political decisions.

As we will see in Chapter 5, Brătianu's bombastic appearances before the Council of Ten on January 31 and February 1 heralded a sustained and surprisingly effective challenge to the sovereignty of the Supreme Council. Brătianu's territorial demands exceeded even those of the secret Treaty of Bucharest of 1916, and further heightened the concern on the Council as to how they could receive accurate information on

---

[100] "Draft of Instructions for the Delegates of the Allied Governments in Poland," published as appendix to "Secretary's Notes of a Conversation Held in M. Pichon's Room at the Quai d'Orsay, Paris, on Wednesday, 29 January 1919, at 11 a.m.," *FRUS: PPC*, 3: 779.

[101] "Secretary's Notes, January 30, 1919," *FRUS: PPC*, 3: 814–15.

territorial issues.[102] Lloyd George supported Wilson's proposal for an inter-allied committee on Romania, which would "reduce the questions for decisions within the narrowest possible limits, and to make recommendations for a just settlement" (852). The five powers represented on the Council of Ten would each name two members to the committee.

But to Vittorio Orlando of the Italian delegation, the establishment of such a committee would raise as many questions as it would answer. He did not consider "specialist" a self-evident category: "Should they be geographical, historical, strategical or ethnographical specialists?" (853). Orlando, a distinguished jurist before entering politics, argued that doing so would make the experts examining magistrates. Essentially, he believed, "the experts would constitute the Court of First Instance and the delegates of the Great Powers, the Final Court of Appeal" (854). As the main proprietors of relevant knowledge, the committee would exercise considerable power over decisions made. The Council agreed to set up a commission on Romanian affairs. The power to decide, of course, would lie with the Council of Ten, self-represented as the guarantor of political neutrality.

The exact total number of expert bodies established by the Paris Peace Conference will remain a matter of opinion. Tardieu counted 58 technical committees in all, which held a combined total of 1,646 meetings. He counted some twenty-six additional commissions sent into the field further to advise the Council.[103] Poland alone had three separate committees, each staffed by different experts.[104] Many of the other committees established by the conference handled issues of territoriality in one way or another. A complex diagram by F.S. Marston showing the General Organization of the conference pointed to at least twenty committees and commissions dealing with territorial matters in Europe and beyond.[105] Like any executive body, the Supreme Council would on occasion find it desirable to postpone difficult decisions by establishing subordinate bodies to study the issues. This way of proceeding and the intrinsic complexity of the decisions to be made did not foster celerity in the drawing of borders.

Harold Nicolson, one of the many frustrated professional diplomats who served in Paris, disdained the way in which the conference decided territorial settlements, which he saw as wholly lacking in "guidance, precision, co-ordination, principle, and scope."[106] He lambasted the incompetence of the Supreme Council, which failed to leave things to people such as himself. Such, after all, had been the order of things under the Vienna System. But real change had taken place in the international system. Whether they liked it or not, the Great Powers had agreed

---

[102] "Secretary's Notes of a Conversation held in M. Pichon's Room at the Quai d'Orsay, Paris, on Saturday, 1 February 1919, at 3 p.m.," *FRUS: PPC*, 3: 852–55.

[103] Tardieu, *La Paix*, 103.

[104] The Interallied Mission to Poland (established January 29, 1919); the Permanent Interallied Teschen Commission (established January 31, 1919); and the Commission on Polish Affairs (established February 12 and 26, 1919). "Directories of the Peace Conference," *FRUS: PPC*, 3: 82.

[105] F.S. Marston, *The Peace Conference of 1919: Organization and Procedure* (London: Oxford University Press, 1944), xii.

[106] Harold Nicolson, *Peacemaking 1919* (London: Constable, 1919), 126.

simultaneously to write treaties and to redesign the international system according to Wilsonian principles. "Unmixing" lands and peoples could never be left wholly to professionals.

As winter gave way to spring in 1919, the scope of the day-to-day demands of peacemaking in its two senses had plainly exceeded the capacities of the Council of Ten. As we saw in Chapter 1, in late March 1919 the council divided into the Council of Four (eventually known as the Supreme Council and comprising Clemenceau, Lloyd George, Wilson, and Orlando) and the Council of Five, comprising the five foreign ministers.[107] The Supreme Council would concentrate on completing the treaty with Germany. It would also supervise writing the treaty with Austria. Focusing on Germany and on Austria nevertheless brought only the most volatile territorial issues before the Supreme Council—such as the disposition of the Saar and of the exterritorial rights in Shandong, the boundaries of Poland, and the status of Danzig and Fiume.

Other territorial matters came before the Council of Five, which included the Japanese.[108] This Council received the reports of the territorial committees. As the instrument of the Supreme Council, the Council of Five could only make recommendations. After the signing of the Treaty of Versailles on June 28, the Council of Five became de facto the Supreme Council, adopting on occasion the new name of the Council of the Heads of Delegations. Clive Day of the American delegation wryly observed: "If the Five did nothing definitive, at least they did it very well."[109] Clemenceau was the only head of government who attended the meetings, and he with decreasing regularity. At one such appearance on July 5, the Council agreed to admit outside experts only at the request of the chairman.[110] This seemingly minor procedural change, already in place for some time de facto, meant that sovereignty on territorial matters devolved to the territorial committees. Nicolson commented that the trees came to obscure the forest: "The main task of the [territorial] Committees was not, therefore, to recommend a *general* territorial settlement, but to pronounce on the particular claims of certain States."[111] After the signing of the Treaty of Versailles, the Council of the Heads of Delegations mostly ratified decisions made elsewhere.

Day to day, the conference proceeded in much the same manner as before. Paper flooded to the various organizational units, from time to time supplemented by personal appearances from nationalist spokesmen. Territorial subcommittees made recommendations to committees, which in turn made recommendations to the

---

[107] Marston, *Organization and Procedure*, 165–76; and Lord Hankey, *The Supreme Control at the Paris Peace Conference, 1919: A Commentary* (London: George Allen & Unwin, 1963), 97–119.

[108] On the delicate politics of Japanese inclusion and exclusion, see Naoko Shimazu, *Japan, Race and Equality: The Racial Equality Proposal of 1919* (London and New York: Routledge, 1998), esp. 137–63; and Thomas W. Burkman, *Japan and the League of Nations: Empire and World Order, 1914–1938* (Honolulu: University of Hawai'i Press, 2008), 81–86.

[109] Day, "Atmosphere and Organization," 32.

[110] "Notes of a Meeting of the Heads of Delegations of the Five Powers Held in M. Pichon's Office at the Quai d'Orsay, Paris, on Saturday, July 5, 1919, at 3 p.m.," *FRUS: PPC*, 7: 20.

[111] Nicolson, *Peacemaking 1919*, 127. Italics and capitalization in original.

Council, often with draft articles for treaties.[112] As had been the case with the Council of Four, the Council of the Heads of Delegations would at times discuss seemingly minor territorial adjustments in considerable detail. Most commonly, it would accept some version of the committees' recommendations, and their language would be sent more or less intact to the drafting committee. This had the effect, to paraphrase James T. Shotwell of the American delegation, of turning experts into negotiators.[113]

The embittered Nicolson was not the only participant to express frustration with this way of proceeding. Clive Day observed: "Dispersed and secluded, these [territorial] commissions attracted in general little attention." But their invisibility concealed "immense influence."[114] Harold Temperley of the British delegation criticized the refusal at the highest levels of the conference to admit "that the whole settlement was one, and that each decision depended in a sense on all the rest."[115] Even Tardieu, generally an arch-defender of the conference, expressed frustration beneath the circumspection of the career functionary: "Technical preparation, political unanimity—the two poles between which activity of the conference developed. Between one and the other, hesitations developed."[116] If geography was theater in Paris, the play began as a courtroom drama and evolved into the saga of a dispersed, squabbling family.

The patriarch holding the family together remained the Supreme Council as provisional world sovereign, tenaciously holding on to the idea that it alone could decide what there was to decide in the "unmixing" of lands, whatever the material realities. Wilson reminded his colleagues on May 8, 1919:

> The important thing is to preserve our authority; without that we will never be able to settle the still more delicate question of the boundaries of Russia. Let us remember that we will have to determine, for example, the boundaries between Poland and the Ukraine.[117]

By May 1919, the idea that the Supreme Council could somehow on its own engineer definitive territorial outcomes in a revolutionary Russia, volatile Poland, and lawless Ukraine must have seemed hopeful even at the time.

THE MIXED CRITERIA FOR "UNMIXING" LANDS

Of course, the Supreme Council still mattered a great deal. Throughout Eastern Europe and the Middle East, it approved many national boundaries still recognizable today. Acting as one, the Council could even thwart the territorial ambitions of

[112] Territorial committee and subcommittee documents appear in Albert Gouffre de LaPradelle, *La Paix de Versailles*, 12 vols. (Paris: Les Éditions internationals, 1929–39), esp. vol. 9, tomes 1 and 2, *Questions Territoriales*; and Conférence de la Paix, 1919–1920, *Recueil des Actes de la Conférence*, 6 vols. (Paris: Imprimerie Nationale, 1922–34).

[113] James T. Shotwell, *At the Paris Peace Conference* (New York: Macmillan, 1937), 153.

[114] Day, "Atmosphere and Organization," 26.

[115] Temperley, *Peace Conference*, 1: 258.   [116] Tardieu, *La Paix*, 107.

[117] "Conversation between President Wilson and MM. Clemenceau, Lloyd George, Orlando, and Baron Sonnino, May 8, 1919, 11 a.m.," in Mantoux, *Deliberations*, 2: 5.

a Great Power. French geographers could not persuade the conference to detach the Rhineland from Germany, any more than could French military commanders.[118] Even in the Saar, the French had to content themselves with ownership of the mines and shared governance with an international commission under the auspices of the League of Nations, to be followed by a plebiscite fifteen years later.[119] In many places, the Supreme Council could indeed decide. But it could not do so according to consistent criteria.

While Curzon evidently coined the term "unmixing" to apply to Europeans in the Balkans, the concept proved no less applicable to the former German and Ottoman imperial domains in Africa, the South Pacific, and the Middle East.[120] During the conference, imperial powers made familiar arguments for expansion through annexation. Such arguments ran up against the Wilsonian tenet of "no annexations" and the always peculiar Point V of the Fourteen Points, which required that "the interests of the populations concerned must have equal weight with the equitable government whose title is to be determined." As a territorial matter, the Supreme Council distributed mandates with less conflict, on balance, than many territorial decisions in Europe. But as we will see in Chapter 4, it would do so through a highly idiosyncratic "unmixing" of peoples through racial categorization.

British Empire, French, Belgian, and Japanese forces had overrun the German colonies in Africa and the Pacific during the war. South African troops invaded German South West Africa in September 1914, and the German colonial authorities yielded control by July 1915. Japan occupied the German islands in the Pacific north of the equator, Australia and New Zealand the islands to the south, along with German New Guinea. As Susan Pedersen reminded us, the occupiers brought with them the imperial doctrine of "What we have we hold."[121] The conference would need to construct a discourse that would either affirm or deny the present occupations, and define the nature of the occupying authority.

The British Dominions based claims for direct annexation primarily on the right of conquest. At the invitation of Clemenceau, Jan Smuts of South Africa, William Morris (Billy) Hughes of Australia, and William F. Massey of New Zealand presented their cases before the council of Great Powers on January 24.[122] At issue were German South West Africa, former German New Guinea, and the former German islands south of the equator, including Samoa. All three Dominion leaders reminded the Council of their considerable contributions to winning the European war, and the bare facts of their present occupations. Australia alone had lost some 60,000 men (722). In addition to its substantial contribution in Europe,

[118] Prott, *Politics of Self-Determination*, 78–80.

[119] Treaty of Versailles, Articles 48–50, with Annex.

[120] Article 119 of the Treaty of Versailles transferred sovereignty over the German colonies to the Principal Allied and Associated Powers. The Treaty of Sèvres created Syria and Mesopotamia as "independent states" receiving guidance by a mandatory power and Palestine as a formal mandate provisionally under the authority of Britain (Articles 94–97).

[121] Susan Pedersen, *The Guardians: The League of Nations and the Crisis of Empire* (New York: Oxford University Press, 2015), 20.

[122] "Secretary's Notes of a Conversation Held in M. Pichon's Room at the Quai d'Orsay on Friday, January 24, 1919, at 3 p.m.," *FRUS: PPC*, 3: 718–28.

the South African government had deployed some 40,000 troops to put down a German led-rebellion in the Union itself (722). New Zealand, with a population of some 1.2 million people, had sent more than 100,000 soldiers, more than 16,000 of whom never returned (727). Massey spoke for them all: "The men went out to fight for the great cause of civilization" (727). Having fought so bravely, the world owed the Dominions formal title to the occupied lands.

In the tradition of British political geography, Dominion claimants argued lands over peoples. The ebullient Hughes saw annexation as a matter of national security.[123] With a population of barely 5 million souls and a coastline stretching the distance from Australia to England, Australia needed the Pacific Islands to remain safe: "If they [the former German Pacific Islands] were in the hands of a superior power there would be no peace for Australia" (721). The unnamed enemy was Japan, whose delegates sat in the room at that very moment as members of the Council of Ten. The huge island of New Guinea was only 85 miles from the Australian mainland, Hughes continued, amidst a string of islands to the southeast ideally suited as bases for naval assault. Reminding the Council yet again of the sacrifices made by his country in the war, "Australia did not wish to be left to stagger under this load and not to feel safe" (722).

Moreover, Australian sovereignty over its new protecting territories could brook no compromise. "Control by the League of Nations," he continued, "would lead to confusion of authority, which could only be harmful" (722). Hughes further maintained that "the Mandatory" would be nothing less than the League itself, an intrusive and threatening super-state. As he argued with a peculiar bit of imagery, allowing the League in would close Australia out: "The Mandatory, as it were, would be living in a mansion and Australia in a cottage" (721).

General Smuts became his own political geographer. Annexing German South West Africa constituted a natural expansion of the Union of South Africa itself. Smuts produced a map proving "that the two countries [South Africa and German South West Africa] were geographically one" (722). Indeed, in the late nineteenth century, only the "dilatoriness of the Imperial [British] Government" (722) had prevented the joining of the two territories in the first place, leaving an opening for the wily Otto von Bismarck to annex South West Africa in 1884. Once there, the Germans "had done little else than exterminate the natives" (722). In contrast to his views as to the value of this territory later, Smuts painted a bleak portrait of "a desert country without any product of great value and only suitable for pastoralists" (722). Who could begrudge South Africa such a wasteland?

Nevertheless, Smuts's argument went, heroic Boer and Anglo-Boer settlers would once more step into the breach of civilization. Already, in contrast to the genocidal Germans, the forebears of Smuts "had established a white civilization in a savage continent and had become a great cultural agency over South Africa." Their descendants "were always looking for uninhabited country in which to settle" (723). Smuts deemed the indigenous peoples of South West Africa to be

---

[123] William Roger Louis, "Australia and the German Colonies in the Pacific, 1914–1919," *Journal of Modern History* 38.4 (1966): 407–21.

few and impressionable. Over more than two centuries of rule, the white community "had done its best to give a form of self-government to three million natives, and its policy had been tested and found good" (723). Annexation could thus accomplish the "liberal" goal of appropriate institutions for appropriate peoples.

Massey of New Zealand made a highly unusual assimilationist argument in support of annexing Samoa.[124] "There was a genuine impression," he contended, "that the natives of Samoa were, or had been not many years ago, savages. That impression was not correct" (724). As far back as the 1870s, Samoans concerned about German aggression had requested protection from Queen Victoria. The establishment of a condominium joining Britain, the United States, and Germany did little to stop the German advance. Only the outbreak of war in 1914 provided New Zealand the chance to provide the Samoans the protection they had long desired.

New Zealand, for its part, had carried on a successful racial experiment that justified annexation. Its total population of 1.2 million included "50,000 natives, who were treated exactly like all other citizens" (725). The New Zealand Parliament boasted six "native" members: "It could not be said that the native race was going out of existence; it was merging into the European population" (725). Samoa had a strategic significance for New Zealand comparable to the other Pacific islands for Australia. Moreover, encouraging the fusion of European and South Pacific Island civilizations in Samoa would keep this key piece of the Pacific firmly in British imperial hands. Massey, "on behalf of his fellow citizens, and on behalf of the people in the Islands of the South Pacific," requested that the conference endorse annexation "for the sake of the native races, and for the sake of humanity" (727).

By early May 1919, with only sporadic discussion since late January, the Supreme Council "unmixed" the former German possessions in Africa and the Pacific.[125] The Supreme Council acceded to British and Dominion requests, while the French received part of Cameroon and Togoland. No territorial commission informed these decisions, rather a personal agreement between British Colonial Secretary Albert Milner and French Colonial Secretary Henry Simon. Under separate arrangements, Japan would receive the German Pacific Islands north of the equator, one of its war aims since 1914.[126]

For all the drama of the Anglo-French Declaration and the personal appearance of Emir Faisal in Paris, the territorial settlement in the Arabic-speaking Ottoman domains followed the broad outlines of the Sykes–Picot agreement, and so would divide Roman and Ottoman Syria. The Council did make some changes, mostly to reflect geopolitical compromises. Palestine became a British mandate rather than an international zone. Eventually, the Council would allocate oil-rich Mosul

---

[124] James Watson, *W.F. Massey: New Zealand* (New York: Haus Publishing, 2011), esp. 65–83.

[125] "Notes of a Meeting Held in M. Pichon's Room at the Quai d'Orsay, Paris, on Tuesday, May 6, 1919, at 5:30 p.m.," *FRUS: PPC*, 5: 491–94; and "Conversation between President Wilson and MM. Clemenceau and Lloyd George, May 6, 1919, 5 P.M.," Mantoux, *Deliberations*, 1: 496–99.

[126] See Mark R. Peatie, *Nan'yo: The Rise and Fall of the Japanese in Micronesia, 1885–1945* (Honolulu: University of Hawai'i Press, 1988), 56.

to Iraq rather than Syria.[127] The French would receive mandates in Lebanon and northern Syria. The British would receive Palestine, Trans-Jordan, and Iraq.[128] The San Remo Conference of April 1920 ratified the partition, with the boundaries demarcated by a convention between the British and the French in December 1920, followed by the publication of formal mandates by the League of Nations in August 1922.[129] But this relatively swift territorial "unmixing" simply displaced the matter of annexation to "unmixing" peoples, as we will see in Chapter 4.

In Europe, all the criteria for the successful creation of a new state appeared to converge in Czechoslovakia. Talented émigré nationalists had told a compelling story in allied capitals throughout the war. At the conference, experts agreed across various fields of knowledge on a maximal territorial solution. In recognizing "Czechoslovakia" as an exemplary liberal democracy, the conference could establish itself as the arbiter of a new and progressive international system. Like no other successor state, Czechoslovakia combined ethnic and historic boundaries. The support of a maximal territorial settlement in Czechoslovakia by the Paris Peace Conference would prove a blessing in 1919, a curse later.

By the end of the war, a distinguished triad of expatriates—Tomáš Garrigue Masaryk, Edvard Beneš, and Milan Štefánik—had largely naturalized the idea of "Czechoslovakia" in allied capitals. Their political and linguistic skills gave them access to public intellectuals in the Anglophone world such as R.W. Seton-Watson and the New Europe Group.[130] Masaryk had married an American, and had spoken eloquently and often to Czech and Slovak immigrant communities in the United States. Beneš had studied extensively in France, and had excellent connections there. Štefánik, the glamorous face of Slovak nationalism, had achieved fame in France as an astronomer and as a pilot in the French army.[131]

According to the national narrative, foreign oppressors had deprived a timeless "Czechoslovakia" of its proper sovereignty.[132] The tragedy began in 907 CE, when Hungarian tribes tore Slovakia from the deteriorating Great Moravian Empire and attached it to the lands of the Crown of St. Stephen. Even more catastrophically, the defeat of Czech-speaking Protestants at the Battle of White Mountain of 1620 inaugurated nearly three centuries of Habsburg (that is, German/Catholic) colonial domination. Generations of Habsburg rule, as both emperors of Austria and kings of Hungary, alienated Czechs and Slovaks from their very identity as a people, and

---

[127] See Nevin Coşar and Sevtap Demirci, "The Mosul Question and the Turkish Republic: Before and after the Frontier Treaty of 1926," *Middle Eastern Studies* 42.1 (2006): 123–32.

[128] As to whether Iraq was ever legally a mandate at all, see Susan Pedersen, "Getting out of Iraq—in 1932: The League of Nations and the Road to Normative Statehood," *American Historical Review* 115.4 (2010): 978–79.

[129] "Franco-British Convention on Certain Points Connected with the Mandates for Syria and the Lebanon, Palestine and Mesopotamia," December 23, 1920, in *AJIL* 16, No. 3, Supplement (1922) 122–26; "Mandate for Palestine" and "Mandate for Syria and the Lebanon," August 1922, in *AJIL* 17, No. 3, Supplement (1923): 164–71; 177–82.

[130] See the account of two loyal sons, Hugh and Christopher Seton-Watson, *R.W. Seton-Watson and the Last Years of Austria Hungary* (Seattle: University of Washington Press, 1981).

[131] The death of Štefánik in a plane crash in Italy on May 5, 1919 only enhanced his reputation.

[132] See Andrea Orzoff, *Battle for the Castle: The Myth of Czechoslovakia in Europe, 1914–1918* (Oxford: Oxford University Press, 2009).

thus from one another. But over the nineteenth century, "Czechoslovaks" had embarked on the long process of self-realization beginning in language, literature, and music. The Paris Peace Conference, the argument went, could now complete the work of "national self-determination" by "reuniting" the lands of the Crown of Saint Wenceslaus (Bohemia, Moravia, and Silesia), and Slovakia. Inconveniently, all the Czech and Slovak lands had been enemy territory during the war. Thousands of Czechs and Slovaks had taken up arms against the Allied and Associated Powers.

Reinforcing "Czecho-Slovaks" as a "subject people" solved this problem. The heavy hand of the Habsburgs could still impress unwilling "Czechoslovak" soldiers into its service in 1914. But in their collective hearts, "Czechoslovaks" had never been at war with the allies. Indeed, calamity had created opportunity by creating an international forum for Czechoslovak claims. The Pittsburgh Agreement signed by exiles in May 1918 proclaimed the unity of the Czech and Slovak lands, and promised linguistic and political autonomy to the Slovaks.[133] A Declaration of Independence issued from Paris on October 18, 1918 proclaimed the historic unity of the subject peoples of Bohemia, Moravia, Slovakia, and Teschen.

At the conference, veteran French diplomat Jules Cambon chaired the Commission on Czechoslovak affairs, which included Harold Nicolson from Britain, as well as Charles Seymour and Allen Dulles from the United States. Like the other territorial commissions, it created, received, and debated briefing papers. The various *"Mémoires"* on Czechoslovakia confirmed a nationalist program well known on both sides of the Atlantic by that time.[134] The experts admitted that even allowing for suspect Habsburg census data and excluding Silesian Teschen, a good third of any "Czechoslovak" population would be neither Czech nor Slovak.[135]

But history could help place those figures in their proper perspective. One *mémoire* counseled the peacemakers to remember that the German majority in Western Bohemia comprised only "colonists, or the descendants of colonists,"[136] curiously unconcerned that the same could be said of virtually the entire American elite of the day. Ferocious Habsburg policies of "Magyarization" had left Slovakia poor and isolated. The document noted that even Oszkár Jászi, minister for minorities in a short-lived liberal government in Hungary, admitted to the systemic undercounting of non-Magyars in the Hungarian lands.[137]

---

[133] Josef Kalvoda, *The Genesis of Czechoslovakia* (New York: Columbia University Press, East European Monographs, 1986), 283–85.

[134] Some *mémoires* were written by the Commission itself, such as "Mémoire No. 1: Les Tchécoslovaques." Others were documents apparently submitted to plead the Czechoslovak case, such as. "Mémoire No. 10, Problèmes des Rectifications des frontières Tchécoslovaques et Germano-Autrichiennes." Both in LaPradelle, ed., *Paix de Versailles*, 9-1: 17–29; 118–25. Subsequent *mémoires* are identified by title and page numbers.

[135] The *mémoire* provided figures supplied by the new government: Czechoslovaks (2,160,000); Ruthenes (155,000); Magyars (860,000); Germans (approximately 240,000). "Mémoire No. 5, La Slovaquie," 86. All of the *mémoires* remained silent on the Jewish population of the Czech and Slovak lands.

[136] "Mémoire No. 3, Le problème des Allemands de Bohème," 53.

[137] "Mémoire No. 2, Les Revendications teritoriales de la République Tchécoslovaque," 35.

Yet the program for successor Czechoslovakia looked forward as well as back. The Germans of Bohemia would quickly see the advantages of belonging to a victorious Czechoslovakia rather than a defeated Germany. In any event, one *mémoire* asserted, the postwar state would prove "absolutely democratic," willing and even eager to go beyond the legal protection of minorities: "The regime will resemble that of Switzerland."[138] "Magyarized" residents of Slovakia could return to their "real" Slovak identities, live as Magyar-Slovaks in a liberal republic that promised equality, or leave Czechoslovakia altogether. One *mémoire* went so far as to hope for ethnographic rebalance through the return of some 700,000 emigrant Slovaks, many from the United States.[139] Once the conference properly "unmixed" the Czech and Slovak lands, peoples would follow.

The commission report, submitted to the Supreme Council on March 12, 1919, supported the foregone conclusion that Czechoslovakia had to combine the Czech and Slovak lands along historic borders. The commission claimed "it had been guided above all by ethnic considerations," though it recognized the recommended borders would leave "a considerable number of Czechs and Slovaks in neighboring countries."[140] The commissioners also considered economic and strategic viability: "It is essential to put the new state in a position to take care of its own economic necessities." The conference hardly granted such consideration to Austria, Hungary, Bulgaria, or post-Ottoman Turkey. The exceptional successor state of Czechoslovakia needed exceptional consideration.

French geography sought to do for Romania what "history" had done for Czechoslovakia. As with Czechoslovakia, the conference instrumentalized expert knowledge in support of a more circumstantially determined settlement. The Supreme Council needed the strongest possible Czechoslovakia more than it needed consistency or even fairness in drawing the new borders. Likewise, the Supreme Council was always going to agree to a greatly expanded Romania. The problem became limiting Romanian claims. Few populations in Europe proved less subject to clear ethnographic demarcation than those of Transylvania and the Banat (both previously under Hungarian rule), Bukovina (an Austrian crownland), or Bessarabia (long contested between Romania and Imperial Russia and its successors). Yet successor Romania claimed them all.

At his appearance before the Council on February 1, 1919, Ion I.C. Brătianu argued that the lands promised Romania in the 1916 Treaty of Bucharest constituted simply a starting point. At the end of the war, the peoples of Transylvania, the Banat, and Bukovina, he alleged, had spontaneously clamored to rejoin their Romanian brethren. All Romania required from the Supreme Council was "the recognition of the union of these provinces with Roumania, for that union had already been proclaimed and the latter [Transylvania, the Banat, and Bukovina] had already sent three Ministers to the Roumanian Cabinet." Moreover, the people of Bessarabia had declared that "the incorporation of Bessarabia with Russia was an

---

[138] Mémoire No. 3, 55.   [139] Mémoire No. 2, 36.
[140] "Rapport présenté au Conseil Suprême des Alliés par le Comité des Affaires Tchécoslovaques (12 mars 1919)," in LaPradelle, ed., *Paix de Versailles*, 9-1: 142, 153.

anachronism which could no longer be allowed to exist."[141] Claiming Bessarabia
went beyond the 1916 Bucharest Treaty.

While the Council viewed Romanian claims skeptically, it lacked good alternatives. None of the ethnically diverse territories in play had effective independence
movements of their own, even assuming that it would have been a good idea to create
yet more potentially fissile successor states. The Council was hardly going to allocate
Transylvania to criminalized successor Hungary, particularly after Béla Kun came to
power in March 1919. Moreover, even the disdained 1910 Hungarian census
identified Romanians as the single largest ethnic group in Transylvania.[142] The
rival claimants for Bessarabia and Bukovina were respectively revolutionary Russia
and chaotic Ukraine. Only in the Banat did a difficult territorial decision seem
necessary, between Romania and the emerging South Slav successor state.

Emmanuel de Martonne had directed the study of Romania for the Comité
d'Études, and served on the peace conference commission for Romanian and Yugoslav
affairs.[143] He had worked alongside Tardieu as part of the French delegation in
Washington, D.C., during the war, and had developed close relations with American
geographers. Isaiah Bowman perhaps had his French friend and colleague in mind
when he wrote: "A new instrument was discovered—the map language. A map was
as good as a brilliant poster, and just being a map made it respectable, authentic.
A perverted map was a lifebelt to many a foundering argument."[144]

Whether perverted or not, de Martonne's map, originally created for the Comité
d'Études, was probably his masterpiece. A highly schematic version appears as Map 3.
Even its title suggests the political possibilities of French geography—*Répartition
des Nationalités dans les pays ou dominent les roumains* (Division of Nationalities
in the Lands Where the Romanians Predominate). The map did show substantial
linguistic minorities, color-coded, which is impossible adequately to reproduce in
black and white. The linguistic and ethnic diversity represented on the map never
undermined its essential reality, the representation of Greater Romania including
the Banat, Transylvania, Bukovina, and Bessarabia. Ethnic Romanians, represented
in a vivid red, dominated the center, around which revolved other groups in less

[141] "Secretary's Notes," February 1, 1919, 849, 848. Spoken Romanian and Moldavian are essentially
the same language, though Moldavian may also be written in Cyrillic. Opinions differ as to whether
Romanians and Moldavians are the same ethnic group. Charles King, "The Ambivalence of
Authenticity, or How the Moldovan Language Was Made," *Slavic Review* 58.1 (1999): 117–42.

[142] Cited in "La Roumanie devant le Congrès de Paix: La Transylvanie et les Territoires Roumains
de Hongrie," LaPradelle, *Paix de Versailles*, 9-1: 290. The census reported a population 48.3%
Romanian, 31.8% Magyars, and 10.3% Székelers (a culturally distinct group of Magyar speakers
prominent in the mountainous regions of Habsburg Hungary).

[143] See Gavin Bowd, *Géographe français et la Roumanie: Emmanuel de Martonne, 1873–1955* (Paris:
Hartmann, 2012); Jacques Bariéty, "Le Comité d'Études du Quai d'Orsay et les frontières de la
Grande Roumanie," *Revue Roumaine d'histoire* 35 (1996): 43–51; Emmanuelle Boulineau, "Un
Géographe traceur de frontières: Emmanuel de Martonne et la Roumanie," *L'Espace géographique*
30 (2001): 358–69. On the influence of de Martonne into World War II, see Gavin Bowd and Daniel
Clayton, "Emannuel de Martonne and the Wartime Defense of Greater Romania: Circle, Set Square
and Spine," *Journal of Historical Geography* 47 (2015): 50–63.

[144] Isaiah Bowman, "Constantinople and the Balkans," in House and Seymour, eds., *What Really
Happened*, 142.

striking colors.[145] De Martonne grouped together Poles, Serbs, and Ruthenes/ Ukrainians, simply as "Slavs." Bulgarians were identified separately, though they too were Slavs. The substantial urban Jewish population remained barely visible as such anywhere. As was common in mapmaking traditions of French geography, the countryside dominated the city, independent of population densities. Even Bucharest is barely visible on the original map.

Taline Ter Minassian has written of "the quasi-hypnotic effect of the maps [from the Comité d'Études] and their splashes (*taches*) of color, doubtless giving the negotiators the illusion of appreciating the situation immediately."[146] In a 1920 article, de Martonne described just what his ethnographic map of Romania could demarcate:

> Let us note from the outset that so-called ethnographic maps of Europe cannot claim to represent which *races* live where [*l'extension des races*]. We are interested only in *nationalities*, that is to say the groups of very mixed ethnic populations, united by an ensemble of practices of a material or ethical order.[147]

His underlying premise rested on an intriguing if unexplained distinction between race (*race*) and nationality (*nationalité*). "Race" appears to mean an irreducible ethnic reality. As such, it appears to be unknowable, or at least beyond representation. "Nationality," on the other hand, becomes largely a function of language, and thus of the politics of education and taking censuses. Cartographers could map nationality, but not race, at least not with scientific accuracy. Maps could not "unmix" races, but they could "unmix" nationalities and thus lands.

De Martonne's overall views on Greater Romania certainly prevailed in the report of the commission on Romanian and Yugoslav affairs, submitted on April 6, 1919.[148] The report endorsed a maximal "Greater Romania," including Bukovina, undivided Banat and Transylvania, and Bessarabia. The commission counseled explicit protections for the inevitably large communities of minorities. In Transylvania, the Magyar, Székeler,[149] and German populations deserved "complete autonomy in local administration, education, and religion" (359). The commission advised the Supreme Council to "confirm officially" guarantees of autonomy made by the Romanian government. Jews likewise merited special mention, both Jews already in Romania and in the new territories. All of these minorities, the report concluded, "will find the necessary protection in the provisions being made by the League of Nations" (362).

Determining the boundaries of successor Romania left considerable unfinished business. Because of ongoing claims of Bolshevik Russia, the legal status of

---

[145] Palsky, "Emmanuel de Martonne."

[146] Taline Ter Minassian, "Les Géographes français et la delimitation des frontières balkaniques en 1919," *Revue d'histoire modern et contemporaine* 44 (1997): 254–55.

[147] Emmanuel de Martonne, "Essai de carte ethnographiques pays roumains," *Annales de Géographie*, No. 158 (1920): 81–82. Italics in original.

[148] "Rapport présenté au conseil suprême des allies par la commission pour l'étude des questions territoriales relative à la Roumanie et à la Yougoslavie," April 6, 1919, in LaPradelle, *Paix de Versailles*, 9-1: 355–83. See also the analysis in Prott, *Politics of Self-Determination*, 119–31.

[149] The Székelers speak a dialect of Magyar, but are often considered a distinct ethnicity.

Bessarabia remained unresolved, despite the Treaty of Paris of October 28, 1920 granting it to Romania.[150] Ethnic tensions particularly between Romanians and Ukrainians in Romanian Bukovina continued throughout the interwar period.[151]

No school of political geography supported by any combination of Great Powers could master the task of deciding borders in Poland. The Supreme Council had decisive control over some borders, partial control over others, and virtually none over still others. None of the armistices of 1918 had effectively ended fighting in the disputed lands of Poland. Norman Davies counted no fewer than six wars over Polish borders between 1918 and 1921.[152] Paramilitary violence and violence between successor states became essentially indistinguishable. Poles fought Ukrainians over Eastern Galicia, Germans over Posen (or Poznan), Germans (mostly) over three uprisings in Upper Silesia, Lithuanians over Vilna (Wilno to Poles), and Czechoslovaks over Teschen (to Germans—it was Cieszyn to Poles or Těšín to Czechs and Slovaks). Most seriously, nascent Poland fought Bolshevik Russia over Poland's eastern border, and ultimately over the existence of successor Poland itself. Through it all, in Davies's words, the efforts of the allies "to arbitrate by distant preaching were despised by all the parties concerned."[153]

Article 87 of the Treaty of Versailles accorded the Principal Allied and Associated Powers unrestricted sovereignty over deciding all borders for Poland not explicitly covered by the treaty. But the geographic problems in doing so ran to all four points of the compass.[154] To the north, Polish access to the sea had to involve either incorporating or bisecting historically and ethnically German East Prussia. To the east and south, borders ipso facto articulated a certain relationship to the other successor states. To the south and west, successor Poland would have to compete with criminalized Germany and favored Czechoslovakia. At the heart of conflict along these borders lay Silesia (including Teschen), an ethnically mixed Bohemian crown land mostly but not entirely conquered by Prussia in the eighteenth century. Germany, Poland, and Czechoslovakia all made claims to this resource-rich and industrialized area.

The utilitarian approach to political geography of Isaiah Bowman perhaps best expressed itself in the resolution of the "Polish Corridor" along the western border with Germany.[155] The Black Book had proposed the corridor as a way around the internal contradiction of Point XIII. As was his practice, Bowman drew a clear

[150] See Malborne W. Graham, "The Legal Status of Bukovina and Bessarabia," *AJIL* 38.4 (1944): 667–73.

[151] See Irina Livezeanu, *Cultural Politics in Greater Romania: Regionalism, Nation Building, and Ethnic Struggle, 1918–1930* (Ithaca, NY: Cornell University Press, 2000), 49–87.

[152] Norman Davies, *God's Playground: A History of Poland,* 2 vols. (New York: Columbia University Press, 1979), 2: 292.

[153] Davies, *God's Playground,* 297.

[154] Piotr S. Wandycz, "The Polish Question," in Manfred F. Boemeke, Gerland D. Feldman, and Elisabeth Glaser, eds., *The Treaty of Versailles: A Reassessment after 75 Years* (Cambridge: Cambridge University Press, 1998), 313–35; and Kay Lundgreen-Nielson, *The Polish Problem at the Paris Peace Conference: A Study of the Policies of the Great Powers and the Poles, 1918–1919*, Alison Borch-Johansen, trans. (Odense: Odense University Press, 1979).

[155] Smith, *American Empire,* 149–56, provides a succinct explanation more focused on Bowman's personal role.

border that, to him, reflected a clear ethnography: "The line of separation of Eastern Prussia from Poland is a very sharply defined linguistic line, and leaves relatively small Polish populations subject to Germany and small German populations to Poland."[156] More subtle demographers pointed out that by the early twentieth century, these lands contained a mixed population comprising Germans, Poles, and Kashubs, who spoke their own Slavic dialect and espoused either Protestantism or Catholicism. Counting the Kashubs as "Germans" or "Poles" yielded either a substantial or a tiny German majority in the lands of the Corridor.[157] Bowman further proposed that the Baltic port city of Danzig at the mouth of the Vistula River be ceded to Poland. Bowman understood that Danzig had an overwhelmingly German population of some 200,000 people. But here too, the matter seemed straightforward. Two hundred thousand Germans could not deprive more than 20 million Poles of access to the sea.

In its report to the Council delivered on March 19, 1919, the Commission on Polish Affairs proposed a generous corridor, and ceded Danzig to Poland.[158] However, by this time, Lloyd George had become concerned about the overall settlement with Germany becoming so harsh that no government there could sign it. Less than a week later, he would write his "Fontainebleau Memo," in which he fretted about a Germany subject to Bolshevism and chaos should it be given too harsh a treaty. No one disputed the "German" demography of Danzig. He persuaded the Council that giving the city to Poland would constitute an avoidable provocation. In a rare example of the Supreme Council overturning a recommendation by a territorial committee, the Council decreed a smaller corridor, and the establishment of Danzig and its immediate hinterland as a Free City. Danzig would have a unique status, neither its own sovereign state, nor a mandate, nor part of any national territory.

As created under Article 102 of the Treaty of Versailles, Danzig would live "under the protection of the League of Nations." The League would appoint a high commissioner who in association with "duly appointed representatives of the Free City" would draw up a constitution. The high commissioner would also handle disputes present and future between the Free City and the new state of Poland (Article 103). But the treaty created the Free City primarily to guarantee Polish access to the port. Under Article 104, "the Principal Associated Powers [will] undertake to negotiate a Treaty between the Polish Government and the Free City of Danzig." This future treaty would place the Free City in the Polish customs union, would guarantee Polish access to all port facilities, and would protect ethnic

---

[156] *Black Book*, 226–27.

[157] The Kashubs, some 200,000 in 1919, were predominantly Protestant in the north, Catholic in the south. Roger Moorhouse, "'The Sore that Would Never Heal': The Genesis of the Polish Corridor," in Conan Fischer and Alan Sharp, eds., *After the Versailles Treaty: Enforcement, Compliance, Contested Identities* (London: Routledge, 2008), 186–87.

[158] Anna M. Cienciala, "Danzig and the Polish Corridor at the Paris Peace Conference," in Paul Latawski, ed., *The Reconstruction of Poland, 1914–1923* (New York: St. Martin's Press, 1992), 71–94; and Prott, *Politics of Self-Determination*, 131–42.

Poles and others from discrimination within ethnically German Danzig. Poland would conduct the foreign relations of the Free City.

While the stated purpose of the Free City was specific and economic, it had important political implications. Danzig would become neither German nor Polish. Establishing the Free City linked the economic future of Poland to a port not on Polish national territory. As per Article 106, residents of the Free City could opt for German nationality, but within a year such individuals would have to move to Germany. The Free City would exist for the benefit of Poland, but its citizens would not be Poles. By definition, the treaty linked the viability of the Free City to the viability of the League of Nations. The hybrid sovereignty created in Danzig would in theory exist forever.[159]

As T.K. Wilson has noted, even the term "Upper Silesia," a neologism at the time, constituted an example of "unmixing" lands by creating a distinction with less-contested "Lower Silesia."[160] All parties understood the stakes in Upper Silesia from the outset.[161] With a territory of some 4,150 square miles containing substantial coal and iron ore deposits and with a population of some 2,280,000 people, Upper Silesia ranked second only to the Ruhr as a center of German industrial power.[162] Germany could not have waged the Great War as ferociously as it did without it. Rapid industrialization had led to substantial migration across ethnographic categories, particularly in the cities of what became known as the "Industrial Triangle" in the southeast. There remained a substantial rural population.

The territorial commission on Poland, like the commission on Czechoslovakia chaired by Jules Cambon and greatly influenced by Isaiah Bowman, embraced clarity and simplicity. It assigned all Upper Silesia to Poland without a plebiscite.[163] Indeed, the report never mentioned "Upper Silesia" by name. It likewise avoided not just the term "Industrial Triangle," but even the material facts of rapid industrial growth and the demographic shifts that had come with it. In the statistical appendix, according to the borders recommended in the report, the former Oppeln District would have a population of 1,112,800 Poles and 574,000 Germans (366). Even these figures drew from the 1905 German census, described in the report as "strongly biased." With at least a 2:1 Polish majority, there seemed little need for a plebiscite. The Supreme Council accepted the territorial commission's recommendation on the matter, and incorporated it into the draft treaty.

As we saw in Chapter 2, in their counterproposals to the draft treaty of May 29, the German delegation bitterly protested the separation of Upper Silesia from

---

[159] Hurst Hannum, *Autonomy, Sovereignty, and Self-Determination: The Accommodation of Conflicting Rights*, 2nd ed. (Philadelphia: University of Pennsylvania Press, 1990), 375–79.

[160] T.K. Wilson, *Frontiers of Violence: Conflict and Identity in Ulster and Upper Silesia, 1918–1922* (Oxford: Oxford University Press, 2010), 19. The Kaiserreich term for the approximate lands of "Upper Silesia" had been *Regierungsbezirk Oppeln* (Oppeln District).

[161] Peter Polak-Springer, *Recovered Territory: A German-Polish Conflict over Land and Culture, 1919–1989* (New York: Berghahn Books, 2014), 21–54.

[162] Sarah Wambaugh, *Plebiscites since the World War*, 2 vols. (Washington, D.C.: Carnegie Endowment for International Peace, 1933), 1: 206.

[163] "Report No. 1 of the Commission on Polish Affairs: Frontier between Poland and Germany, 12 March 1919," *Miller Diary*, 6: 350–66.

Germany. They demanded it remain German unconditionally.[164] Lloyd George sought to revisit the matter by proposing a plebiscite. At a contentious meeting of the Supreme Council on June 3,[165] Lloyd George fretted: "I am afraid of finding another Moscow in Berlin, that is, of not having anyone before us with whom we can sign the peace" (282). A plebiscite would constitute more than the allies had first offered, less than the Germans had demanded. He reminded his colleagues that with at least a 2:1 Polish majority, according to the experts, the outcome seemed a foregone conclusion. Partition was not seriously discussed at that juncture.

Though he would eventually agree to a plebiscite, Clemenceau remarked: "I very much fear that in order to avoid certain difficulties, we are jumping from the frying pan into the fire" (283). But the most strident opposition came from Wilson. The president maintained that the German elites would fix the outcome through voter intimidation and suppression: "The main point is that all of Upper Silesia is in the hands of fifteen or twenty German capitalists; it is from this quarter that all the protests we hear are coming" (280). But in the end, it proved impossible for Wilson to resist so Wilsonian a solution as asking Upper Silesians to self-determine. Unable to "unmix" lands in Upper Silesia, the Council agreed to "unmix" peoples through a plebiscite held by a League of Nations commission. Wilson did ask how they could compel the Germans to comply with the results. Clemenceau responded with atypical tact: "They will make promises to you, and, if that is enough for you, you will be content" (282). Indeed, as we will see, holding a plebiscite in Upper Silesia would raise more questions than it would answer.

No matter in Paris took up more time per square kilometer than Teschen.[166] The Habsburgs had inherited the Duchy of Teschen through the Bohemian crown in 1653, and ruled it as part of Austrian Silesia. At the Paris Peace Conference, Teschen perhaps remains best known through a heedless comment at one point made by an exasperated Lloyd George before the House of Commons: "How many members have ever heard of Teschen? I do not mind saying that I have never heard of it."[167]

Teschen in fact counted among the smaller disputed territories, though it had a high population density. It comprised some 880 square miles with a population in 1910 of 426,370 people. But location mattered. Teschen had mineral wealth, industry, and the best railroad link joining the Czech lands of Bohemia and Moravia to Slovakia. The new Czechoslovak Republic considered control over that link crucial to weaning Slovakia away from its historic economic integration with Hungary. Teschen had a multilingual population hitherto of fluid ethnic identity. According to the 1910 Habsburg census, a reasonably clear line of demarcation

---

[164] Pytor S. Wandycz, *France and Her Eastern Allies, 1919–1925: French-Czechoslovak-Polish Relations from the Paris Peace Conference to Locarno* (Minneapolis: University of Minnesota Press, 1962), 29–48.

[165] "Conversation between President Wilson and MM. Clemenceau, Lloyd George, and Orlando, June 3, 1919, 4 p.m.," in Mantoux, *Deliberations*, 2: 279–86.

[166] See Félix Buttin, "The Polish-Czechoslovak Conflict over Teschen Silesia (1918–1920): A Case Study," *Perspectives* 25 (2006): 63–78; and Wandycz, *France and Her Eastern Allies*, Ch. 3, 5–6.

[167] Quoted in Margaret MacMillan, *Paris 1919: Six Months That Changed the World* (New York: Random House, 2002), 239.

suggested itself between a Polish-speaking majority eastern section and a Czech-speaking majority western section. Indeed, local Polish and Czech authorities had come to a provisional understanding on that basis as early as November 5, 1918. Yet neither successor government would accept these arrangements. The Poles particularly resisted any settlement before their government stabilized.[168]

Both the Czechoslovak and Polish governments sent troops to Teschen, inaugurating more than a year of military and paramilitary violence. Czech claims based on the historic unity of the lands of the Crown of St. Wenceslaus clashed with Polish claims based on ethnicity. In February 1919, the Council sent an Interallied Commission of Control to Teschen, to enforce the provisional border and to ensure continued industrial production, particularly the mining of coal crucial to both Prague and Warsaw. As in Upper Silesia, the inability of the Supreme Council to decide borders in Teschen led it on September 27, 1919 to change from a policy of "unmixing" lands to "unmixing" peoples through a plebiscite.

Another difficult "unmixing" exposing the limits of Supreme Council sovereignty involved the boundary between Poland and Lithuania. The problem lay in dividing the Vilna Governorate of Imperial Russia between the two successor states, particularly in the area southeast of Vilna (Vilnius in Lithuanian, Wilno in Polish).[169] Most of the former governorate had been part of a Polish–Lithuanian monarchy in the early modern period. Centuries of migration had produced a mixed, multilingual population of Poles, Lithuanians, Belarusians, Germans, and Jews. Religion, notably Roman Catholicism, cut across ethnic categories based on language. For statistical ammunition, nationalists used conflicting data, from a Russian census of 1897, a German census of 1916, and a Polish census of 1919.[170] History further complicated "unmixing" the two states. Polish heroes such as Tadeusz Kościuszko and Adam Mickiewicz had been born in Vilna, not to mention Józef Piłsudski, head of the new Polish state. Some nationalists considered the former Vilna Governorate the moral equivalent of Virginia or Massachusetts to Americans.

During the war, the occupying Germans recognized an "independent" Lithuania, though the Paris Peace Conference never followed. Marshal Piłsudski occupied Vilna in April 1919, and the Polish delegation in Paris proposed a plebiscite for the former governorate. Augustinas Voldemaras, prime minister of German-recognized Lithuania, opposed any plebiscite held under Polish occupation. The Commission on Polish Affairs declined to award the area to anyone, as one of the "districts in which doubt arises as to the ethnographical character or wishes of the population [that as a result] cannot be awarded to the Polish State."[171] The Vilna area thus fell under Article 87 of the Treaty of Versailles, which gave the Council the authority

[168] Jules Laroche, "La Question de Teschen devant la Conférence de la Paix en 1919–1920," *Revue d'Histoire diplomatique* 62 (1948): 8–27; and the informative Coolidge commission reports, *FRUS: PPC*, 12: 312–65.

[169] Robert H. Lord, "Lithuania and Poland," *Foreign Affairs* 1.4 (1923): 38–58; and Alfred Erich Senn, *The Great Powers: Lithuania and the Vilna Question, 1920–1928* (Leiden: E.J. Brill, 1966).

[170] Sarah Wambaugh, *Plebiscites since the World War*, 2 vols. (Washington, D.C.: Carnegie Endowment for International Peace, 1933), 1: 301–03.

[171] "Report No. 2 of the Commission on Polish Affairs: Eastern Frontier of Poland," April 22, 1919, *Miller Diary*, 9: 15–16.

to decide the final border. In December 1919, the Supreme Council affirmed provisional borders that excluded the Vilna area from Poland.[172]

Yet the views of the Supreme Council became increasingly irrelevant as the war between Poland and Bolshevik Russia intensified in 1920. The advancing Red Army in that summer largely supported Lithuanian claims. Although the Battle of Warsaw in August 1920 had restored Polish fortunes, the situation remained unstable. In September 1920, the Polish government appealed to the League of Nations for help in settling the boundary dispute with Lithuania. As we will see in Chapter 6, the League would make a good-faith effort to discover the views of "the people" of the Vilna area through a plebiscite.

On the other borders of Poland, the Paris Peace Conference toiled on. The eastern borders of Poland would depend in part on whether former Imperial Russia would permanently divide into successor states. The territorial commissions debated, among other things, whether Ukraine even existed or not. One *mémoire* contended that the very notion of a Ukraine distinct from Russia or Poland was part of a German–Austrian conspiracy of *Mitteleuropa*, the keystone of "their conception of Eastern Europe under their influence." This conspiracy continued even after the armistice, and "has sought to win over opinion within the Entente."[173] The stronger and more numerous the successor states, the argument went, the weaker Bolshevik Russia.

Most of the time, the Supreme Council took a cautious approach to the southeastern borders of Poland, clinging to the increasingly forlorn hope that the Bolshevik regime might give way to one or more regimes more acceptable to the allies. In Habsburg Galicia (predominantly Polish, Ukrainian, and Jewish), the Council advocated without great controversy allocating the western portion to Poland. But a territorial sub-commission chaired by General Henri Le Rond approached despair of ever knowing "whether Poland in Eastern Galicia will border upon the Ukraine or upon Russia, and if upon Russia—then ruled by whom."[174]

This chapter has examined how the Paris Peace Conference sought to invent a new territoriality "unmixing" the lands and peoples of the defeated multinational empires. The intellectual infrastructure for doing so drew from planning for peace. Once the Paris Peace Conference began, the council of Great Powers became a sovereign court hearing competing claims all based in the discursive structure of Wilsonianism. Inevitably, doing so complicated territorial settlements. In some situations, the conference would accept a specific framework as decisive. "History" justified giving Bohemia, Moravia, and Slovakia to Czechoslovakia. French geography helped justify Greater Romania. Bowman's pragmatic interpretation of Wilsonianism helped the Supreme Council decide on a Polish Corridor. Everywhere, categorizing

---

[172] Piotr Eberhardt, "The Curzon Line as the Eastern Boundary of Poland: The Origins and the Political Background," *Geographia Polonica* 85.1 (2012): 11–12.

[173] "Les Relations entre la Pologne et les Terres Lithuaniennes et Ruthènes avant les Partages: Mémoire présenté à la Conférence des préliminaires de Pais par la Commission Polonaisse (Paris, Mai 1919)," LaPradelle, *Paix de Versailles*, 9-1: 183.

[174] Quoted in Eberhardt, "Curzon Line," 9.

territories ultimately meant categorizing peoples. As we will see, the Great Powers would develop a whole system of racial classification in the mandates, paradoxically for territorial rather than for racial reasons. In some places, such as the borders of Poland, no decisive discourse could be found to "unmix" lands, at least not all of them. In such places, the Paris Peace Conference would contrive population policies that are the subject of Chapter 4.

4

The "Unmixing" of Peoples

Implicating "the people" in their own identification had vastly complicated territoriality at the Paris Peace Conference. The Supreme Council's claim of sovereignty over borders in the lands of the defeated multinational empires rested, at least in part, on its claim to be building a more democratic world. Preserving that sovereignty remained a preoccupation of the Council. Someone, after all, still needed to figure out who "the people" actually were. The conference had two broad choices—adjusting boundaries to suit peoples, or adjusting peoples to suit boundaries. In a nutshell, the Council turned to the latter when and where it could not accomplish the former.

This chapter examines four varieties of population policies—plebiscites, minority treaties, racial classification of mandate populations, and "population exchanges." All these policies sought to identify peoples. Under plebiscites, peoples could supposedly "self-determine." But every decision on where to hold a plebiscite also constituted a territorial decision, which demarcated borders within which voters would be presented with a choice. Plebiscites also provided only preselected categories of identity. Minority treaties bracketed certain aspects of identity, notably religion and ethnicity, and placed them under supranational protection through the League of Nations. But this meant politically significant differentiations among citizens within successor states. For this reason, all of the successor states ferociously opposed the minority treaties. These treaties also produced a hierarchy of states, in which some states had their national sovereignty circumscribed by international protections, and others not.

The sovereignty of the conference over "unmixing" peoples had two particularly blunt manifestations. The system of "A-," "B-," and "C-" class mandates created a racial categorization of peoples pure and simple. But these identities followed the requirements of imperial politics. Peoples were either more or less "civilized" and either more or less suitable for eventual independence depending on how vigorously the mandatory power had sought direct annexation. Population exchanges were the most brutal of population policies. They imposed "national" identities with no input from the affected populations, and were carried out by physical force or the threat thereof. Indeed, for that reason, the conference went to some trouble to keep population exchanges at arm's length. But in the end, population exchanges simply amounted to "national self-determination" carried to one logical conclusion. The "self" by that point had little to do with choices made by the peoples in question.

"NATIONAL SELF-DETERMINATION"
IN THE PLEBISCITES

Believers in democracy have hailed plebiscites since the French Revolution. They had paved the way to Italian unification in the previous century.[1] On the face of it, plebiscites seemed the most liberal of population policies. What could be more democratic than simply asking "the people" to identify the state to which they wished to belong? From the point of view of the Supreme Council, plebiscites also offered a way out of the conundrums of conflicting expert advice, as well as the conflicting claims of nationalists. Now freed from their ethnic captors, "the people" could decide for themselves. The plebiscite seemed to promise the Holy Grail of politically neutral knowledge.

Yet the territorial commissions had generally eschewed plebiscites, as instruments likely to raise more questions than they answered. By definition, each plebiscite had already framed what there was to decide. The locus of the sovereignty behind that framing lay well beyond the voters. The Supreme Council never seriously considered plebiscites in many contested borderlands, such as Alsace-Lorraine, the German-speaking areas of Bohemia and Moravia, the Banat, Transylvania, Fiume, most of Anatolia, and the Arabic-speaking former Ottoman domains. Rather, the Council sought plebiscites where there seemed genuine ethnic uncertainty and where none of the Great Powers had an obvious direct territorial interest.

All plebiscites comprised territorial choices already made. For example, individuals could vote to join Germany or Poland, but not "Silesia." Still less could millions of Eastern European Jews vote for a Jewish homeland. Where plebiscites did take place, they often fostered the very ethnic conflict they sought to resolve. Suspicions abounded of ethnic gerrymandering. For example, in Upper Silesia, the plebiscite territories excluded several areas within prewar regional boundaries comprising uncontested German majorities. Excluding these areas served to reduce the overall German vote in Upper Silesia.

Plebiscites also brought with them pre-made decisions about peoples. Most of the contested lands had seen substantial shifts in population even before the upheavals of the war years, because of economic migration. Someone had to decide voter eligibility. Apparently simple criteria such as "birth" and "residence" led to endless disputes. Should birth suffice as a qualification, even if the prospective voter had not lived thereafter in the territory in question? Did "residents" include wartime immigrants, and if so or if not, how long a residency would suffice? How would voters' choices remain "free," meaning free of local pressure from notables such as landowners, capitalists, or functionaries?

Plebiscite commissions operating in the name of either the peace conference or the League of Nations were responsible for the provisional administration of the territories and for carrying out the plebiscites. These commissions had administrative and in some cases military resources toward that end. Contending states were

---

[1] Sarah Wambaugh, *A Monograph on Plebiscites, with a Collection of Official Documents* (New York: Oxford University Press, 1920).

supposed to withdraw troops from the plebiscite areas, sometimes to be replaced by small contingents of allied troops. The commissions had the responsibility for keeping order in places where ethnic tensions ran high, and for guaranteeing the fairness of political campaigning. Commissions inevitably received blame from voters unhappy with the results.

By definition, plebiscites took place in areas of contested state authority. This lack of clarity fostered paramilitary violence, in some places so severe as to defeat the plebiscites themselves.[2] Paramilitary violence stood as a structural affront to the Weberian sovereignty provisionally possessed by the commissions. Commissions could maintain order only through local police (widely perceived as ethnically partisan) or through foreign troops. The global needs of empire and accelerating demobilization kept allied contingents of peacekeepers small. Moreover, so as not further to enflame tensions, allied troops typically had strict orders not to fire except in cases of imminent danger. Paramilitary violence fed on itself, guaranteeing instability before, during, and after the plebiscites.

A given plebiscite in itself simply recorded preferences. Some external authority would have to interpret the results, likely to be mixed and controversial, and recommend boundaries accordingly. Inevitably, and like other population policies, plebiscites did not so much "unmix" peoples as "remix" them. In some places, plebiscites produced decisive results, and borders that held throughout the interwar period. But this does not mean that all went smoothly. In looking at the plebiscites from least controversial to most controversial, we can see an apparent centralization of sovereignty in the peace conference and its instruments. Yet paradoxically, in deciding what there was to decide in areas of failed plebiscites, the Supreme Council revealed that the real locus of decision lay elsewhere.

The plebiscite held in Schleswig in February and March 1920 involved Denmark, a country that had not even fought the Great War. After their victory against the Danes in 1866, the Prussians had promised a plebiscite fixing the German border with northern Schleswig, but had never carried it out.[3] In February 1919, the Danish government asked the Council of Ten for a plebiscite. A Commission on Danish Affairs took up the matter. Articles 109–17 of the Treaty of Versailles specified the conditions of the plebiscite. It demarcated the plebiscite territories, who would be eligible to vote, and established an international commission to oversee the plebiscite. The commission essentially accepted the recommendation of the Danish government to divide the area in question into two zones—a northern zone virtually certain to vote for Denmark, and a southern zone likely to vote for Germany. The German delegation protested holding a peace conference-mandated plebiscite to determine a boundary with a country with which Germany had not been at war, and against the transparent gerrymandering of the two zones. Nevertheless, this least controversial of plebiscites went ahead, and produced the expected results.

---

[2] Robert Gerwarth and John Horne, eds., *War in Peace: Paramilitary Violence in Europe after the Great War* (Oxford: Oxford University Press, 2012).

[3] Sarah Wambaugh, *Plebiscites since the World War: With a Collection of Official Documents*, 2 vols. (Washington, D.C.: Carnegie Endowment for International Peace, 1933), 1: 46–98.

A plebiscite might have been avoided in Klangenfurt entirely, had the matter not gotten caught up in the drama between Italians and Yugoslavs over Fiume.[4] As it was, most parties considered the October 1920 plebiscite a success. The Klangenfurt basin constituted a small, predominantly Slovene enclave economically integrated into its German-speaking surroundings, former Habsburg Carinthia. A mountain range separated the Slovenes from Slovenia proper. The emerging South Slav state had sent troops into Klangenfurt around the time of the armistice, leaving German speakers to mobilize their own home guard or Landwehr. The local Germans appealed to the new regime in Vienna and to the allied powers for help in arranging a plebiscite. The two paramilitary forces agreed to lay down their arms, and to refer the matter to the peace conference.

The Council of Ten discussed the matter at length beginning on February 18, 1919. South Slav representatives questioned the Habsburg census, and proposed use of confessional records that they claimed to be more accurate.[5] Articles 49–51 of the Treaty of Saint-Germain would lay out provisions for the plebiscite. The Klangenfurt basin would be divided into two zones. A southern Zone A, believed to be the more ethnically ambiguous, would hold a plebiscite. Only if that zone voted in favor of Yugoslavia would a plebiscite be held in Zone B (directly adjacent to Austria). The treaty also delineated the criteria for eligibility—men and women twenty years of age; "habitual residence" in the plebiscite zone as of January 1, 1919; or birth or "rights of citizenship" prior to January 1, 1912. An inter-allied commission supplemented with members from Austria and the South Slav state would govern the area provisionally.

The vote on October 10, 1920 mostly but not completely followed predicted ethnicity. Of some 37,000 votes counted, slightly over 59 percent of the residents of Zone A voted to join Austria, just under 40 percent voting to join Slovenia. This meant the cancellation of the vote in Zone B. Even the distrusted 1910 Habsburg census determined that 68.6 percent of the Zone A population recorded Slovene as their *Umgangssprache*, or common language.[6] This meant that at least 10,000 "Slovenes" voted to remain with Austria, well over a third of the entire pro-Austria vote. An enraged South Slav government sent in two battalions to occupy two allegedly pro-Yugoslav towns, but withdrew them immediately upon the demand of the plebiscite commission. The South Slavs protested to the allies pro forma, but did not otherwise contest the result.

The construed success of the referendum in Sapron between Austria and Hungary concealed a more ominous story. Paramilitary violence there set in motion a plebiscite that reversed a provision of the Treaty of Trianon.[7] Sapron had

---

[4] The Italian delegation opposed any solution anywhere that provided for the extension of Yugoslav territory. Wambaugh, *Plebiscites*, 1: 163–205.

[5] "Secretary's Notes of a Conversation Held in M. Pichon's Room at the Quai d'Orsay, Paris, on Tuesday, 18th February, 1919, at 3 p.m.," *FRUS: PPC*, 4: 48.

[6] Statistics come from Wambaugh, *Plebiscites*, 1: 198.

[7] John C. Swanson, "The Sopron Plebiscite of 1921: A Success Story," *East European Quarterly*, 34.1 (2000): 81–94; and Mari Vares, *The Question of Western Hungary/Burgenland, 1918–23: A Territorial Question in the Context of National and International Policy* (Jyväskylä, Finland: Jyväskylä Studies in Humanities, No. 90, 2008).

been a mostly rural, German-speaking enclave within a larger strip of Western Hungary.[8] This had caused little trouble under the Habsburgs, as subjects could simply consider themselves loyal to the king of Hungary, the same person as the emperor of Austria. The Coolidge Mission recommended ceding all of Western Hungary to Austria without a plebiscite, partly because of an assumed German majority and partly because of the practical difficulties of holding a fair plebiscite.[9] Continued instability in successor Hungary in 1919 and 1920 encouraged the conference to agree. Article 27 in both the Treaty of Saint-Germain and the Treaty of Trianon awarded the lands to Austria.

From the outset, paramilitary violence afflicted the transfer of these lands. Hungarian irregulars, probably a combination of demobilized soldiers and armed students, effectively blocked the advance of Austrian authority.[10] The Hungarian government disavowed all knowledge of the irregulars, a claim not widely believed at the time or subsequently.[11] The allies, eager to disengage from what was after all a minor dispute between two defeated successor states, worked to limit their involvement. Only in August 1921 did the Council of Ambassadors send in a commission of three allied generals to oversee the actual transfer of territory. They were to be assisted by Austrian gendarmes, but no Austrian troops. Almost immediately, Hungarian irregulars halted the transfer. The stalemate continued.

Ultimately, the Italians, ever eager to increase their influence in the region, stepped in to mediate, with the approval of the Council of Ambassadors.[12] The result recognized de facto the success of the paramilitaries. According to the Protocol of Venice on October 13, 1921, the Hungarian government agreed to stop insurgent activities in exchange for an internationally supervised plebiscite.[13] The plebiscite would occur six days after the commission of generals pronounced the plebiscite area calm. Local officials from the Hungarian administration would authenticate the voter rolls, under allied supervision.

The Protocol of Venice did not in itself resolve the situation. On the same day as the signing of the protocol, ex-King Charles appeared in Hungary to reclaim the crown of St. Stephen. This brought consternation not just to the Austrians, but to the still-stabilizing regime in Hungary of Admiral Miklós Horthy. The Austrians claimed that internal disorder provided an excuse for the Horthy government to look the other way from Magyar intimidation in Sapron. Only on December 8 did the allies send 450 soldiers from Upper Silesia to calm the situation. On December 12,

[8] The Sapron plebiscite area comprised some 80 square miles, inhabited by some 48,000 people. Wambaugh, *Plebiscites*, 1: 271.

[9] See "Major Lawrence to Professor A.C. Coolidge," March 3, 1919; and Memorandum by Professor A.C. Coolidge, "The New Frontiers in Former Austria-Hungary," March 10, 1919, in *FRUS: PPC*, 12: 264–71; 276–77.

[10] Bela Bodo, "The White Terror in Hungary, 1919–1921: The Social Worlds of Paramilitary Groups," *Austrian History Yearbook* 42 (2011): 133–63.

[11] Wambaugh, *Plebiscites*, 1: 278–79. Vares argues for differing opinions on the irregulars within the Hungarian government. *Western Hungary*, 228–32.

[12] Allesandro Vagnini, "A Disputed Land: Italy, the Military Inter-allied Commission and the Plebiscite of Sapron," *Nationality Papers* 42.1 (2014): 126–44.

[13] "Protocol and Additional Article Regarding the Settlement of the Question of Western Hungary. Signed at Venice, October 13, 1921," in Wambaugh, *Plebiscites*, 2: 261–65.

the commission declared the Sapron plebiscite area "pacified," and ordered voting to begin on December 14. The Austrian authorities refused to endorse the voter rolls, and essentially ceased official participation in the plebiscite.

The results of the plebiscite reflected a familiar disparity between the ethnography of the towns and the ethnography of the hinterlands. The towns voted heavily for Hungary, the countryside more narrowly for Austria. The protocol precluded division of the (already small) plebiscite area. Some 63.7 percent of slightly more than 24,000 votes went to Hungary, as opposed to 34.1 percent for Austria.[14] This result "overstated" by nearly a third the percentage expected to vote for Hungary. Clearly, quite a few people counted by the Habsburgs as "ethnically" German or Croat voted to join Hungary.

Initially, the Austrians roundly condemned the outcome, based on intimidation and voter irregularities. The Hungarians responded that the people of Sapron had made their own decision as to their ethnicity, whatever the Habsburg assessment of their native language. In the end, the stakes in Sapron were small enough for both successor states to accept the results and set the matter aside.[15] This mutual acceptance of the outcome made possible understanding the plebiscite as a "success." Doing so meant setting aside the role of paramilitary violence in bringing about the plebiscite in the first place.

Trying to use plebiscites to "unmix" peoples in Poland laid bare all their potential agonies. Former East Prussia constituted the least controversial case. The allies considered "East Prussia" indisputably "Germany," notwithstanding the requirement of a Polish Corridor. Plebiscites could help discern ethnographic boundaries separating a "German" East Prussia from a "Polish" Poland. Articles 94–98 of the Treaty of Versailles established the boundaries and conditions for plebiscites in Allenstein (Olsztyn) and Marienwerder (Kwidzyn). The Polish government stridently opposed plebiscites in either place, arguing that powerful Junkers and their lackeys would artificially suppress the Polish vote among a largely dependent rural population. The Poles worried especially about the Masurians, Polish speakers who had lived under German sovereignty since before the partitions, and who had long ago converted to Lutheranism.[16]

The Commission on Polish Affairs, whose membership included the always-certain Isaiah Bowman, recommended that "primary consideration be given to the line of ethnic separation in such a way as to secure the fairest possible settlement between the two peoples concerned" (352).[17] In deciding the plebiscite area, the peace conference should recognize "that due weight be attached to lines of religious cleavage, as for example, in Mazuria, where a Protestant population exists which is Polish in speech and race" (352). A plebiscite would give Masurian Protestants and their immediate Catholic neighbors a choice denied to Polish Catholics who lived close to Germany.

[14] Calculated from figures in Wambaugh, *Plebiscites*, 1: 292.
[15] Vares, *Western Hungary*, 276–89.   [16] Wambaugh, *Plebiscites*, 1: 99–141.
[17] "Report No. 1 of the Commission on Polish Affairs," March 12, 1919, in Miller, *Diary*, 6: 352–57.

Plebiscite commissions for Marienwerder and Allenstein included members from Italy, France, Britain, and Japan. The local police and judiciary were not displaced, but served at the pleasure of the plebiscite commissions. Article 95 of the Treaty of Versailles guaranteed the vote to any adult born in the plebiscite areas, both residents and non-residents (known as "out-voters"), and those resident in the areas since a date to be determined by the commission. Despite widespread allegations on both sides of voter intimidation, little actual violence took place on the day of the plebiscite, July 11, 1920. In Marienwerder, only about 8 percent of the voters chose Poland, in Allenstein only slightly over 2 percent. The "Polish" populations were estimated at 15 percent.[18]

Allowing any accuracy at all to these estimates of ethnicity, many Masurian "Poles" had voted to remain German.[19] Richard Blanke has explained this outcome by a long process of self-categorization, "culminating in the transformation of the Masurians into ethnic as well as political Germans."[20] Yet the Polish government complained bitterly to the plebiscite commission. The commission had disqualified "excessive" numbers of Poles and registered "excessive" numbers of Germans. Moreover, corrupt practices for "out-voters" had heavily favored Germany. Poles had been systematically intimidated into not voting, because not enough time had elapsed for the plebiscite commission to wrest local authority from the German elite. Further, the Polish government asserted that the dire state of the war between Poland and Bolshevik Russia during the referendum period gave the Germans an unfair advantage. Yet the decisive results in Allenstein and Marienwerder made them the least controversial plebiscites in successor Poland.[21]

Paramilitary violence played a formative role in demarcating the other Polish borderlands.[22] That violence always took many forms—from armed individual vigilantes, to gangs with mixed and often sordid motivations, to semi-regular units led by senior officers with murky connections to state authorities. Violence deepened rather than clarified ethnic confusion. Certainly, paramilitary violence demonstrated that any borders "unmixing" peoples would in fact only "remix" them. In Teschen (including Spisz and Orava) and Vilna, paramilitary violence forced the cancellation of the plebiscite. In Upper Silesia, persistent violence further clouded an already ambiguous outcome at the polls. Yet paradoxically, the chaos toward which paramilitary violence pointed provided an opening for the peace conference and its instruments. Successor states still needed the international recognition only the peace conference could provide. Recognition could support the legitimacy of

[18] Complete figures appear in Wambaugh, *Plebiscites*, 1: 132–34.

[19] Stefan Berger, "Border Regions, Hybridity, and National Identity: The Cases of Alsace and Masuria," in Q. Edward Wang and Franz L. Fillafer, eds., *The Many Faces of Clio: Cross-Cultural Approaches to Historiography* (New York: Berghahn Books, 2006), 366–81.

[20] Richard Blanke, *Polish-Speaking Germans?: Language and National Identity among the Masurians since 1871* (Cologne: Böhlau, 2001), 196.

[21] Ethnic hybridity among Masurians would exact its price later. After 1945, the Red Army expelled most of the small number of Masurians who had avoided Nazi persecution as "Poles" to West Germany as "Germans."

[22] Robert Gerwarth, *The Vanquished: Why the First World War Failed to End* (New York: Farrar, Straus and Giroux, 2016), 190–94.

the successor regimes, which could then work to establish Weberian sovereignty, which could in turn bring paramilitary violence to an end, at any rate for the time being. Paramilitary violence, successor states, the peace conference, and the League of Nations became unwitting partners in the "remixing" of peoples.

As we saw in Chapter 3, the dispute over Teschen in Silesia involved competing claims of two allied successor states: Czechoslovak claims based on "history" and Polish claims based on "ethnicity." But any plebiscite would encounter formidable practical challenges. Teschen occupied a strategic location at the intersection of Poland, the Bohemian crown lands, and Slovakia. Divisions of ethnicity criss-crossed divisions of class. Many industrialists and landowners self-identified as German, skilled laborers as Czech, industrial workers and miners as Polish.[23] Capitalists sometimes sided with the Czechs, in hopes of preserving the economic unity of Teschen. Substantial migration driven by rapid industrialization drove resentments all around as to just who "belonged" in Teschen. Further complicating the matter, of a total population of a bit over 425,000 people according to the 1910 Habsburg census, some 200,000 people spoke a hybrid dialect of Polish and Czech, known as Slonzak. According to the Czechs, the Habsburg census had classified the Slonzaks as Poles, even though politically they tended to side with the Czechs.[24] The Poles, in contrast, claimed that Czech local officials under Habsburg rule had systematically undercounted the Polish population.

Paramilitary violence had immediately followed the disintegration of Habsburg and Hohenzollern imperial authority beginning in October 1918. The provisional border agreed on by the Polish and Czechoslovak national councils on November 5 became contested from the outset. Czechs and Poles on both sides of the border complained that they could not protect "their" people on the other side. Words swiftly passed to deeds. The line demarcating "military" from "paramilitary" forces remained vague. Labor unrest in a chaotic economic situation added to the instability, and to mutual recriminations of opening the doors of Teschen to Bolshevism.

As we saw, the Supreme Council had decided on a plebiscite in late September 1919. Since neither the League Council nor the League Assembly had begun to meet, the Supreme Council would have to create its own body to supervise the plebiscite. The new commission would comprise representatives of the principal Allied and Associated Powers, as well as Poland and Czechoslovakia. The Council granted the plebiscite commission "all the powers necessary to enable it to ensure the maintenance of public order and the proper administration of the country." The commission could determine its own relationship to local authorities. It would have at its disposal "troops of occupation" and could recruit its own police force.[25] But the commission was not actually established until January 30, 1920, and did not have any allied troops until the following May. Even then, the number of

[23] See Wambaugh, *Plebiscites*, 1: 144–45.

[24] At least as reported in [No author], "Situation in Teschen," *The Czechoslovak Review* 3 (1919): 184–85.

[25] "Decision of the Supreme Council of the Principal Allied and Associated Powers, Dated September 27th 1919, with Regard to the Territory of Teschen," in Wambaugh, *Plebiscites*, 2: 108–09.

soldiers, mostly French with some Italians, never exceeded 1,200. Furthermore, the soldiers had strict orders from the commission and from Paris not to fire on the populace.

Teschen miners alone could organize ten times the number of allied troops in place.[26] Labor action and paramilitary violence became increasingly difficult to disentangle. Moreover, disorder within Poland because of the war with Bolshevik Russia made the situation in Teschen increasingly intractable. It became impossible for the commission to establish reliable voter rolls, and the prospect of actual voting promised extended violence. Nationalist demonstrations over Teschen spread to Prague and Warsaw. The plebiscite commission asked without success for more troops. Recurrent strikes ground industry to a halt. The Poles threatened to break off diplomatic relations with the Czechoslovaks, a development of great concern to the French, who saw building a "Little Entente" of successor states as a vital guarantee against a revived Germany.

Eventually, the increasingly dire nature of the war with Bolshevik Russia convinced the Polish government that it needed to make peace with its allies.[27] The Supreme Council, resurrected for the Spa Conference of July 1920, took care to perform allied unity. At Spa, Władysław Grabski of Poland and Edvard Beneš of Czechoslovakia signed an agreement admitting that conflict between their two nations precluded a plebiscite deciding the matter of the border: "This struggle, though animated by patriotic sentiments on both sides has often been carried on with regrettable methods. Acts of violence have taken place, accusations have been made and threats have been uttered." Both successor states deferred to the sovereignty of the allies, "convinced that the Supreme Council, guided by sentiments of justice and equity, will have due regard to the true interests of the two nations."[28] The Council, for its part, considered the matter "too grave to permit of any further prolongation of a dispute which reacts upon the general situation, affects injuriously the interests of Europe and endangers the peace of the world."[29] This reconciliation claimed the plebiscite as a casualty, with the border to be drawn by the Supreme Council.

The resulting Solomonic solution gave much of the mines and industry to Czechoslovakia and the city of Teschen to Poland. This division shattered the local economy, an outcome that pleased no one. Enflamed by political passions, "the people" in Teschen had proved unable or unwilling to "unmix" themselves.[30] We will never know the outcome of a plebiscite in Teschen, because of the paramilitary violence that overwhelmed the whole process. But it is far from clear that

[26] Wambaugh, *Plebiscites*, 1: 152.

[27] Gerhard P. Pink, *The Conference of Ambassadors: Paris, 1920–1931* (Geneva: Geneva Research Centre, 1942), 87–104; and Piort Wandycz, *France and Her Eastern Allies, 1919–1925: French-Czechoslovak-Polish Relations from the Paris Peace Conference to Locarno* (Minneapolis: University of Minnesota Press, 1962), 158–59.

[28] "Declaration of the Polish and Czechoslovak Delegates to the Conference of Spa with Regard to the Question of Teschen in Silesia," July 10, 1920, in Wambaugh, *Plebiscites*, 2: 122.

[29] "Resolution of the Spa Conference on July 11th, 1920," in Wambaugh, *Plebiscites*, 2: 122.

[30] On the persistence of ethnic conflict, see Ellen Paul, "Czech Teschen Silesia and the Controversial Czechoslovak Census of 1921," *The Polish Review* 43.2 (1998): 161–71.

a majority existed for any territorial decision. This enabled the Supreme Council to decide the matter, for the time being.[31]

The Treaty of Versailles laid out in some detail the conditions for the plebiscite in Upper Silesia.[32] It specified boundaries for the plebiscite, which did not exactly coincide with the boundaries of the Regierungsbezirk Oppeln. The Germans resented these boundaries as favoring the Polish population. The treaty required Germany to cede practical sovereignty in the plebiscite area to an International Commission comprising members of four Great Powers (France, Britain, Italy, and the United States). Like the Teschen commission, the Upper Silesia commission could hire and fire local officials at will. It could also expel from Upper Silesia "any person who may in any way have attempted to distort the result of the plebiscite by methods of corruption or intimidation" (Annex, Section 3). Allied troops would be sent to the area to guarantee freedom of voting. The treaty also sought to define the vexed question of "out-voters" (Annex, Section 4). After the plebiscite, "Germans" and "Poles" in territories ceded to the other country would lose their "ethnic" nationality. These ethnic "foreigners" could recognize their new nationality, continue to reside where they did as foreign nationals, or relocate.

Any attempt to hold a plebiscite in industrialized Upper Silesia would face some of the same challenges as in Teschen, but on a much larger scale. Ethnic, class, and religious fault lines all crossed throughout the region. The anti-Catholic *Kulturkampf* of the Bismarck era had guaranteed decades of overt discrimination against Polish-speaking Catholics. Industrialists and landowners generally considered themselves German, some Protestant, others Catholic. Rapid industrialization brought oppor-tunities for Polish speakers, some of whom had sought assimilation into the German-speaking bourgeoisie. Industrial workers, in contrast, tended to become more "Polish" as they increased in numbers, though many continued to vote for the German Social Democratic Party rather than the Polish Party in Reichstag elections before the war.[33] Further complicating the matter, most Upper Silesians spoke one version or another of a Western Slavic, Silesian dialect. Germans, Poles, and Czechs all claimed versions of this dialect as their own.[34] Imposing clear ethnic categories over "Silesians" was never going to be easy.[35]

---

[31] Poland would annex the Czechoslovak portion of Teschen after the Munich Pact of 1938, only to have it revert to Nazi Germany in 1939. The Soviets restored the 1920 borders after 1945.

[32] Articles 87–93, with the accompanying annexes.

[33] T. Hunt Tooley, *National Identity and Weimar Germany: Upper Silesia and the Eastern Border, 1918–1922* (Lincoln: University of Nebraska Press, 1997), 12–20.

[34] T.K. Wilson uses the term *Wasserpolnich* (literally Water Polish), originally a derogatory German term adopted by some speakers of the dialect. *Frontiers of Violence: Conflict and Identity in Ulster and Upper Silesia, 1918–1922* (Oxford: Oxford University Press, 2010), 70–71. Other names for the Silesian dialect include *Język śląski* which highlights connections to Polish, and *Slezština*, which refers to a sub-dialect drawing more from Czech. Kevin Hannan, *Borders of Language and Identity in Teschen Silesia* (New York: Peter Lang, 1996); Tomasz Kamusella, "Silesian in the Nineteenth and Twentieth Centuries: A Language Caught in the Net of Conflicting Nationalisms, Politics, and Identities," *Nationalities Papers* 39.5 (2011): 769–89.

[35] Tomasz Kamusella, "Upper Silesia, 1870–1920: Between Region, Religion, Nation and Ethnicity," *East European Quarterly* 38.4 (2005): 443–62; and Peter Polak-Springer, *Recovered Territory: A German-Polish Conflict over Land and Culture, 1919–1989* (New York: Berghahn Books, 2014), 21–54.

Preparations for the plebiscite began in January 1920, as soon as the Treaty of Versailles came into effect.[36] On February 11, the plebiscite commission assumed administrative authority. One month later, it established a Special Court of Justice to adjudicate any criminal activity connected to the plebiscite. The commission placed an allied military officer in command of each *Kreis* (county). In response to chronic complaints from the Poles about the continued power of German local officials, the commission established "technical" advisers on May 6 specifically to safeguard the Polish population. The French sent 11,000 soldiers to Upper Silesia, and the Italians 2,000, to help keep order. In January 1921 (less than three months before the voting) the British would send two battalions (a total of some 2,000 men).

Germans and Poles could each establish plebiscite commissariats to organize political campaigning. The head of the German Commissariat, Kurt Urbanek (a family name of Czech/Slovak origin), mobilized support from landowners, industrialists, middle-class professionals, and skilled industrial workers. Wojiech Korfanty, a former Polish Party member of the Reichstag, led the Polish Commissariat. Germans and Poles alike considered him the mastermind of Polish paramilitary activity.

By good measure, Upper Silesia suffered more paramilitary violence on both sides than any other plebiscite area. T.K. Wilson arrived at a figure of 2,824 violent fatalities between the armistice and the end of June 1922.[37] Wilson concluded that rape, torture, mutilation, and simple massacre were more common in Upper Silesia than in Ulster during the deadliest periods of the partition of Ireland. Sordid exploits of Freikorps units in Upper Silesia became the stuff of legend, inspiring paramilitary violence that continued in Weimar Germany throughout the interwar period.[38]

On three separate occasions, paramilitary violence became so widespread that they became known as "Silesian Uprisings." Two took place before the plebiscite. The first, in August 1919, constituted an attempt to secure Upper Silesia for Poland before the plebiscite could take place. Demobilized German soldiers known as *Grenzschutz* (border guards) put down the uprising in a few days. A second, in August 1920, followed an untrue rumor that the Red Army had taken Warsaw. Fearing a German paramilitary offensive, Korfanty launched a pre-emptive operation of his own. As in Teschen, paramilitary violence and strikes overlapped. Given the reluctance, not to say more, of the French troops to intervene on behalf of the German side, the Poles as a result of the uprising controlled much of the Industrial Triangle by the time the plebiscite took place.

The actual vote on March 20, 1921 proved rather calmer than its violent preliminaries might have suggested. As shown in Figure 4.1, some voters went to considerable trouble to cast their ballots. While it took more than a month for the plebiscite commission to certify the results, it was known early that nearly 60 percent

---

[36] Wambaugh, *Plebiscites*, 1: 206–60; and F. Gregory Campbell, "The Struggle for Upper Silesia, 1919–1922," *Journal of Modern History* 42.3 (1970): 361–85.

[37] Wilson, *Frontiers of Violence*, 5.   [38] Tooley, *National Identity*, 229–34.

Figure 4.1. Assisting a voter in the Upper Silesia plebiscite, March 20, 1921.
gallica.bnf.fr/Bibliothèque nationale de France.

of the total vote had been for Germany. Heavy voting for Germany in the cities had outweighed voting for Poland in the industrial suburbs and the countryside. In the densely populated Industrial Triangle, 54.4 percent had voted for Germany.[39]

---

[39] Of 1,186,342 votes cast (a 79 percent turnout rate), 59.6 percent voted for Germany, 40.4 percent for Poland. See Tooley, *National Identity*, 236–37.

Non-resident "out-voters," presumed to be overwhelmingly German in sympathy, accounted for some 13 percent of the overall vote. In aggregate, the plebiscite results reversed predictive results from the prewar German census figures, which identified 58.6 percent of Upper Silesians as having Polish as their mother tongue.[40] "Poles" voted in substantial numbers for Germany. Assumptions that had made their way to the Supreme Council of a resounding vote for Poland proved inaccurate.

The allies would never permit Germany to reclaim so rich a prize as all of Upper Silesia, whatever the outcome of the plebiscite. Article 88 of the Treaty of Versailles required the plebiscite commission to make a recommendation as to the actual border and had not explicitly called for the partition of Upper Silesia., However, given the ambiguous and contested plebiscite results, partition seemed a likely outcome. Yet how to divide Upper Silesia? As Georges Kaeckenbeeck put it, "the communes with a German majority could not, by any contrivance, be separated from those with a Polish majority by a continuous frontier line. Important islands, both German and Polish, would remain in any case."[41] A Solomonic solution similar to the one in Teschen proved both controversial and deadly.

The plebiscite commission proved unable to submit a unanimous final report. The British and French delegations proposed different borders. The commission president, General Henri Le Rond of France, recommended ceding the entire Industrial Triangle to Poland. His British and Italian colleagues submitted a majority report giving a sizeable portion of the Triangle to Germany, while leaving most of the mines in Poland. Through mysterious means, the majority report became public, leading Korfanty to proclaim that the Great Powers had abandoned Poland. A third Silesian uprising ensued—by far the most deadly of the three. Korfanty at first carefully dissociated himself from the troubles. But by May 3, he assumed formal leadership of the uprising. While opinions differ as to whether the Polish government instigated the third uprising, few doubt that the government sought to capitalize on it.[42] Both sides clearly received material support from their respective states. The third Silesian uprising raised the prospect of an open war between Germany and Poland.

In response, the peace conference commissioned yet another expert report, submitted to the Council of Ambassadors on August 6.[43] While the report itself proved a model of diplomatic tact, it could not conceal the obvious. The plebiscite and the paramilitary violence surrounding it had muddied rather than clarified the situation in Upper Silesia. The plebiscite results precluded any solution that kept the economy of the Industrial Triangle intact. The expert committee agreed

[40] The 1910 census figures come from Tooley, *National Identity*, 240. Any aggregated figures homogenize substantial differences by *Kreis*.

[41] Georges Kaeckenbeeck, *The International Experiment of Upper Silesia: A Study in the Working of the Upper Silesian Settlement, 1922–1937* (London: Oxford University Press, 1942), 6. Kaeckenbeeck served for an extended period on the arbitration court for Upper Silesia.

[42] See Tooley, *National Identity*, 255–56.

[43] "Report of the Committee of Experts Appointed to Study the Frontier to be Laid Down between Germany and Poland in Upper Silesia as the Result of the Plebiscite," August 6, 1921, in Kaeckenbeeck, *International Experiment*, Appendix 1, 552–57.

unanimously on principles that would lead to partition—the practical impossibility of allocating all of Upper Silesia to one party or the other, and the stated priority in the treaty of ethnicity over economic concerns. "If for political reasons it became necessary to consider the division of the triangle" (557), the report concluded, the two parts of bisected Upper Silesia would need to develop separately, doubtless to the detriment of both. The conference thus would need to create some sort of supranational or international "technical organization" to oversee an inevitably painful economic divorce (557).

The third Silesian uprising continued unabated, and the French and the British still disagreed as to a German role in Upper Silesia. As a result, the Supreme Council on August 12 decided to appeal the matter to the League of Nations on the basis of Article 11 of the Covenant. Upper Silesia had become a matter threatening "to disturb international peace or the good understanding between nations upon which peace depends." This had the effect of linking the "unmixing" of lands and peoples in Upper Silesia to the early history of the League, as we will see in Chapter 6.

In common usage, we often distinguish between the "nation" as an affective community and the "state" as a formally constituted agent in international relations. In his famous speech at the Sorbonne in 1882, Ernest Renan described the nation as "a daily plebiscite [*une plebiscite de tous les jours*]. As the existence of the individual perpetually affirms life itself, so too does daily consent affirm the life of the nation."[44] The Paris Peace Conference construed the organized plebiscite as a foundational act in turning nations into states. "The people" would self-define through a one-time choice that naturally would evolve into Renan's daily plebiscite. In the best of worlds, this would make possible the drawing of borders to suit peoples. James Bjork, among others, has contested this teleology for Upper Silesia in favor of a persistent regional identity.[45] The *événement* of the plebiscite obscured a *longue durée* of "Silesian-ness" rooted particularly in trans-ethnic and transnational Roman Catholicism. Real people could resist as well as embrace ethnic categorizations. Peoples could make their own daily choices, beyond the states that ruled them.

Plebiscites sought to resolve the identities of populations left open by expert inquiries. Yet plebiscites, from their least controversial to their most controversial, faced similar limitations and critiques. Plebiscite results brought forth endless accusations of political manipulation and outright cheating. Plebiscites both responded to and exacerbated paramilitary violence that cost thousands of lives. And to hundreds of thousands of Europeans dissatisfied with the results, they raised more questions than they ever answered. Furthermore, no plebiscite, by definition, could create the ethnic homogeneity the logic of "national self-determination" seemed to require.

[44] Ernest Renan, *Qu'est-ce qu'une nation?* (Paris: Calmann Levy, 1882), 27.
[45] James E. Bjork, *Neither German nor Pole: Catholicism and National Indifference in a Central European Borderland* (Ann Arbor: University of Michigan Press, 2008), 215. See also Brendan Karch, "Nationalism on the Margins: Silesians Between Germany and Poland, 1848–1945," *Bulletin of the German Historical Institute*, Issue 50 (Spring 2012): 39–55; and James Bjork, Tomasz Kamusella, Tim Wilson, and Anna Novikov, eds., *Creating Nationality in Central Europe: Modernity, Violence and Belonging in Upper Silesia* (London: Routledge, 2016).

PROTECTING PEOPLES, CREATING STATES:
THE MINORITY TREATIES

Any territorial settlement was always going to leave ethnic and religious minorities strewn across Central and Eastern Europe and beyond. Too numerous to ignore and too dispersed to concentrate in distinct states, minorities precluded drawing neat boundaries of ethno-national states. If boundaries could not be drawn to suit peoples, peoples would have to be tailored to suit boundaries. As a population policy, the minority treaties sought to provide a politically acceptable form of ethnographic heterogeneity in the new and newly transformed states. Legitimizing and managing this heterogeneity, as Jennifer Jackson Preece has reminded us, could help disarm irredentism.[46] In other words, if Magyars could remain Magyars in Romania, they and their compatriots might feel themselves less inclined to insist that Transylvania revert to Hungary. If peoples could or would not "unmix" themselves, the treaties could help them live together peacefully in "remixed" national states.

But the minority treaties exposed a paradox in the liberal values ostensibly underpinning the new states. Liberalism is about commensurability among citizens within the political community. By definition, minority treaties identified distinct communities and provided for their protection beyond the national state. As a result, they created differentiated citizenries within states, and differentiated states within the international system—all in the name of fostering a system of Wilsonian liberal democracies. Some communities received protection, others did not; some states were subject to minority treaties, others were not.

Minority treaties exemplified the sovereignty of the Paris Peace Conference as deciding what there was to decide. New and augmented states would assume their postwar identities though signing the minority treaties. As we will see in Chapter 5, according to the constitutive theory of international law, a state can become a state through recognition, by signing just such an international agreement. In fact, none of the minority treaties actually bore the name. Rather, the documents refer simply to a "treaty of peace" or simply a "treaty" between the Principal Allied and Associated Powers and the state in question. According to the constitutive theory, for example, Poland became Poland through accepting the treaty, and the other signatories recognizing that Poland had done so. After ferocious resistance, the Polish government signed the treaty because the Great Powers would not recognize it otherwise.

In seeking to forge and transform states in this way, the Supreme Council raised a host of foundational questions for the international system itself. What makes a minority a minority? Were religious minorities ipso facto also ethnic minorities? Was language a sufficient condition to establish a minority? What forms of difference deserved protection? Would protection be offered to individuals, or to groups? As Carole Fink has shown, by 1919 minority protection had been a matter of

---

[46] Jennifer Jackson Preece, *Minority Rights* (Malden, MA: Polity Press, 2005), 13.

international relations for more than four decades.[47] But no previous arrangements had established institutional means of enforcement. And no previous set of minority protections had been part of a larger scheme to remake the international system itself.

For different reasons, the Americans and the Japanese raised the issue of minority rights in February 1919, in the commission writing the Covenant of the League of Nations. Wilson on February 8 introduced a draft article according to which League members "will make no law prohibiting or interfering with the free exercise of religion," and banning discrimination "in law or in fact," on that basis.[48] His likely motivations included a genuine concern for the plight of religious minorities, pressure from Jewish groups in the United States, and a simple desire to make the Covenant resemble the Bill of Rights as closely as possible. Just five days later, Baron Makino Nobuaki proposed what became known as the "racial equality clause." This amendment would guarantee to "all alien nationals of states members of the League equal and just treatment in every respect making no distinction, either or in law or in fact, on account of their race or nationality."[49] As Makino was said to remark elsewhere: "It seems that matters of religion and race could go well together."[50] Naoko Shimazu has argued that Makino cared most about racial equality for the Japanese, as the people of a Great Power.[51]

Certainly, the two amendments laid bare the racial politics of the Paris Peace Conference. Roman Catholics in the United Kingdom, and for that matter the United States, might have questioned the commitment of their respective states to banning discrimination based on religion. And no Great Power, including Japan, pretended to ban domestic discrimination based on race. Wilson would never support minority protection based in "race" as a matter of color. Nor was Wilson alone in seeing religious and racial equality as very different things. At one League commission meeting, according to David Hunter Miller, Arthur James Balfour opined that the American contention in the Declaration of Independence that all men are created equal "was an eighteenth century proposition which he did not believe was true." He might believe that all men might be equal within a given nation, "but not that a man in Central Africa was equal to a European."[52]

The most ferocious opposition to the Japanese proposal came from the Australians, who feared it would compel them to open their doors to unlimited non-white immigration. Resistance from the Dominions, more than anything else,

[47] See Carole Fink, *Defending the Rights of Others: The Great Powers, the Jews, and International Minority Protection, 1878–1938* (Cambridge: Cambridge University Press, 2004), 6–65.

[48] Quoted in Fink, *Defending the Rights*, 152–53.

[49] Quoted in Naoko Shimazu, *Japan, Race and Equality: The Racial Equality Proposal of 1919* (London: Routledge, 1998), 20.

[50] Quoted by David Hunter Miller, *The Drafting of the Covenant*, 2 vols. (New York: G.P. Putnam's Sons, 1928), 1: 269.

[51] For a more nuanced view, see Xu Guoqi, *Asia in the Great War: A Shared History* (New York: Oxford University Press, 2016), 185–210.

[52] Miller quoting from his own diary recounting the Fifth Meeting of the Commission on the League of Nations (February 7, 1919), *Drafting of the Covenant*, 2: 183.

persuaded the British to oppose the amendment.[53] But hesitations went beyond Anglo-Americans. Eleftherios Venizelos, mindful of the large Muslim populations in lands Greece expected to annex, argued that the League surely would handle matters of "race and religion" once established, but "that it would be better for the moment not to allude to them."[54] Even Wellington Koo of China, who presumably had a direct interest in the matter, remained distinctly non-committal on racial equality. He wanted further instructions from his government, presumably on the linkage between the racial equality issue and Shandong. Neither Wilson's amendment on religion nor the Japanese amendment on race would pass the League commission.

In April 1919, the commission by majority vote voted on a much-diluted Japanese proposal supporting "the principle of the equality of nations and the just treatment of their nationals."[55] Even though the measure passed by a vote of eleven to four, Wilson, as chair of the committee, invoked a dubious unanimity rule, which led to the defeat of the amendment. Even here, however, Wilson never spoke against racial equality per se. Rather, he sought delay based on the importance of avoiding open conflict between Japan and Australia. Such a position was wholly in keeping with his contentment at the glacial pace of progress in race relations in the United States. But in not accepting the Japanese amendments, the commission also rejected a universal approach to protecting minorities. Specific protections directed toward specific minorities would replace that approach.

At a meeting of the Supreme Council on May 1, Wilson observed: "One of the things that troubles the peace of the world is the persecution of the Jews.... You know that they are especially badly treated in Poland, and that they are deprived of civic rights in Romania."[56] He proposed adding two articles on Poland to the German treaty, one guaranteeing "the same treatment in law and in fact" to "all racial and national minorities." A short but revealing discussion ensued that would shape the framework for the minority treaties. Lloyd George largely agreed with Wilson, but argued against "autonomy" for Jews, notably in Poland. Lloyd George alleged that Polish Jews "wish to form a kind of state within the state. Nothing could be more dangerous." Wilson countered that well-treated Jews made for good national citizens, with which Lloyd George and Clemenceau heartily agreed. At the May 1 meeting, Wilson proposed forming what would become the New States Committee. This committee effectively wrote the minority treaties.

As Carole Fink has shown, external events, particularly the persecution of Jews, also encouraged the conference to take up minority protection. Throughout the former multinational empires, mutually antagonistic groups united to act out a shared hatred of Jews. For example, serious anti-Jewish violence occurred in contested Eastern Galicia, along the still-undetermined eastern border of Poland, and

[53] Shimazu, *Japan, Race and Equality*, 117–36.

[54] "Minutes of the Ninth Meeting, February 13, 1919, at 10:30 AM," in Miller, *Drafting of the Covenant*, 2: 325.

[55] Shimazu, *Japan, Race and Equality*, 27–30.

[56] "Conversation between President Wilson and MM. Clemenceau and Lloyd George, May 1, 1919," Mantoux, *Deliberations*, 1: 439–41.

elsewhere as the war came to an end.[57] Influential Jewish leaders, such as Lucien Wolf from Britain, and Julian Mack and Louis Marshall from the United States, pleaded for allied action.

Their success at bringing the plight of Jews to the attention of the Supreme Council highlighted that Jews were a unique minority in the successor states. In Europe, only the Germans were so dispersed. Only the Jews had so many trans-national political connections, or, except for the Armenians, so much need of them. Centuries of diaspora had heightened the diversity of European Jews, and led to diverse desiderata. Many Jewish leaders in Eastern Europe sought a kind of ethno-religious federalism within the new states. Others, particularly from Western Europe, sought civil equality and assimilation. Still others prioritized the Balfour Declaration of November 1917, which, however vaguely, had raised the prospect of a "homeland" for Jews in the Middle East.

Protecting Jews exemplified the definitional problems that beset the minority treaties as a population policy. Who would get to be a people, and what would be the relationship among peoples, the nation, and the state? Just who, in fact, were "the Jews"? In a May 16 report, the New States Committee stated a common view that "the Jews are both a religious and a racial minority." As such, they argued, Jews merited two levels of protection, for their religious practices as well as their persons and property.[58] As we will see, having rejected a universal approach, the Paris Peace Conference would take up the messy business of defining minorities differently in different places.

The details of defining minorities led to some remarkably detailed discussions within the Supreme Council. On June 23, 1919, just five days before the treaty with Poland was to be signed, the Council met with James Headlam-Morley, chair of the New States Committee.[59] Lloyd George expressed his continued concern that "our desire to protect the Jews doesn't have to go so far as to make them into a state within a state." This led to an involved discussion not just of the status of Yiddish, which Lloyd George called "only corrupt German," but of the proper languages of instruction in Polish primary and secondary schools. Lloyd George disputed the wisdom of state-supported primary education in Yiddish. Wilson and Headlam-Morley argued in response that young children could only properly assimilate if taught in a language they could understand.[60] It seems unlikely that Lloyd George knew much more about Yiddish than he claimed he knew about Teschen. But those present clearly understood that to define language was to define peoples, and to define peoples was to define states.

Nationalist leaders understood this axiom as well, and ferociously contested minority treaties on that basis. States required to sign minority treaties or treaties that included minority provisions included defeated states (Austria, Hungary,

[57] Fink, *Defending the Rights*, 101–30, 171–208.

[58] Annex (B), Second Report to the Eighth Meeting, May 16, 1919, in Miller, *Diary*, 13: 55.

[59] "Conversation between President Wilson, MM. Clemenceau and Lloyd George, Barons Sonnino and Makino, and Mr. Balfour," in Mantoux, *Deliberations*, 2: 524–27.

[60] "Notes of a Meeting at President Wilson's House in the Place des États-Unis, Paris, on Monday, June 23, 1919, at 12:10 p.m.," *FRUS: PPC*, 6: 626.

Bulgaria, and Turkey), new states (Czechoslovakia, Poland, and Yugoslavia), and existing allied states (Romania and Greece). Leaders in all these states had sworn for months to embrace religious and ethnic tolerance as a matter of domestic policy. But to a man, they objected to the treaties on the bases of state sovereignty and equality of states under international law. The very existence of external protection weakened state sovereignty. Truly independent states defined their own peoples as part of governing them. States with conditional sovereignty over defining their peoples could not consider themselves the equals of those with the absolute power of definition. Nationalists found it particularly galling that the Treaty of Versailles did not contain protections for minorities in Germany.[61]

On May 21, the New States Committee wrote to the Romanian delegation in Paris to enquire as to its plans for minority protection. Ion I. C. Brătianu responded that his government "assured complete equality of rights and liberties, religious and political, to all her citizens, without distinction of race or religion." However, Romania would accept only provisions for minority protection applicable to all League members: "Under any other conditions Roumania could not admit the intervention of foreign Governments in the application of her domestic laws."[62] Czechoslovakia, its delegates proclaimed to the New States Committee, "will be an extremely liberal regime, which will resemble that of Switzerland," thereby making a formal treaty unnecessary.[63]

Successor states pressed such critiques in a stormy meeting of the plenary on May 31. Brătianu reiterated his claim that as a victorious ally and fully sovereign state, Romania could accept only obligations that all League members, above all the Great Powers, applied to themselves.[64] Ante Trumbić of the Serb-Croat-Slovene State added similarly that no minority provisions could be applied to his country, because like Romania, Serbia had been fully sovereign before the war. This meant asserting that "Yugoslavia" was actually Greater Serbia, and forgetting that Croatia and Slovenia had been part of Austria-Hungary. Even the usually docile Czechoslovak delegation protested that a minority treaty would be "superfluous and even rather wounding to our feeling of independence" (402).

Strong debating points do not always win the argument. The Supreme Council affirmed its authority to decide what there was to decide on minority protection. As president of the conference, Clemenceau reminded the assembled company that "in the matter of minorities, everyone's history is not quite the same" (399). Wilson asserted the sovereignty of the Supreme Council more bluntly. He reminded the plenary that "had it not been for the Great Powers," specifically, "their military action, we would not be here to settle these questions."

[61] Carole Fink suggests that the allies did not consider Germany subject to minority protections because they considered it a once-and-future Great Power. *Defending the Rights*, 215.

[62] "M. Brătianu to M. Berthelot" [Philippe Berthelot, chairman of the New States Committee], May 27, 1919, in Miller, *Diary*, 13: 89–90.

[63] Czecho-Slovak Delegation, "Note on the Régime of Nationalities in the Czecho-Slovak Republic," May 20, 1919, in Miller, *Diary*, 13: 70.

[64] "Preliminary Peace Conference, Protocol No. 8, Plenary Session of May 31, 1919," *FRUS: PPC*, 3: 394–410.

Moreover, right would continue to need might in the postwar era: "in the last analysis the military and naval strength of the Great Powers will be the final guarantee of the peace of the world." Romania and Serbia would emerge from the peace conference with vast territorial gains, made possible because of the allied victory. They sought recognition of these gains from the Great Powers, which the Great Powers could grant or deny. On that basis, Wilson argued:

> ... if this Conference is going to recognize these various Powers as new sovereignties within definite territories, the chief guarantors are entitled to be satisfied that the territorial settlements are of a character to be permanent and that the guarantees given are of a character to ensure the peace of the world. (406–07)

This public confrontation between the Supreme Council and the successor states did not resolve the matter. As we will see in Chapter 5, Brătianu would employ opposition to the minority treaties as part of a general assault on the sovereignty of the Supreme Council. A June 15 memorandum from Ignacy Paderewski of Poland to the Council[65] continued to insist on "the nefarious consequences which may result from the protection exercised by foreign Powers of ethnical and religious minorities" (487). After all, he contended, the partitions of Poland in the eighteenth century had justified themselves partly in the name of protecting religious minorities. He reiterated the injustice of giving guarantees to Germans in Poland but not to Poles in Germany. The minority provisions amounted to "regarding the Polish nation as a nation of an inferior standard of civilization, incapable of ensuring to all its citizens the rights and civic liberties and ignorant of the conception of the duties of a modern state" (489). Any recourse to League of Nations institutions on minority matters "must be struck out as being prejudicial to the sovereignty of Poland" (489).

Just four days before the signing of the treaty with Germany, Clemenceau as president of the conference sent a public letter to Paderewski explaining again the need for the minority treaty.[66] Politely but firmly, he asserted the sovereignty of the Council over the matter. Clemenceau reminded Paderewski that "it is to the endeavors and sacrifices of the Powers in whose name I am addressing you that the Polish nation owes its independence" (418). In signing the minority treaty, Poland "also receives in its most explicit and binding form the confirmation of her restoration to the family of independent nations" in the form of recognition by the signatory powers.

Clemenceau stressed the historical continuity of the Polish treaty. The Congress of Berlin of 1878 had required newly recognized Serbia, Montenegro, and Romania to recognize religious liberty. The present treaty indeed broke new ground, by providing for international enforcement. By turning minority protection over to the League of Nations, "differences which might arise will be removed from the political sphere," and as a result "any danger of political interference by the Powers

[65] "Memorandum by M. Paderewski," June 15, 1919, in Mantoux, *Deliberations*, 2: 487–93.
[66] "Letter Addressed to M. Paderewski by the President of the Conference Transmitting to Him the Treaty to be Signed by Poland under Article 93 of the Treaty of Peace with Germany," June 23, 1919, *AJIL* 13, Supplement: Official Documents (1919): 416–24.

in the internal affairs of Poland will be avoided" (419). He argued that minority protections, paradoxically, would actually foster national unity in Poland: "The very knowledge that these guarantees exist will, it is hoped, materially help the reconciliation which all desire, and will indeed do much to prevent the necessity of its enforcement" (420).

The five Great Powers formally recognized independent Poland through what became known as the "Little Versailles" treaty, signed just after its namesake on June 28, 1919.[67] The treaty established a Poland in which religious and ethnic difference were recognized and protected beyond the Polish state. Article 3 accorded Polish nationality to all residents of territorial Poland who had not chosen otherwise. This provision applied to a highly diverse population, in as yet unsettled borders, comprising ethnic Poles, Byelorussians, Ukrainians, Jews, Germans, and, if the Polish government got its way, quite a few Lithuanians. Article 2 guaranteed freedom of religion for all Poles, while Articles 7 and 8 guaranteed equality under the law for all "Polish nationals who belong to racial, religious or linguistic minorities."

Of the nineteen articles in the treaty, only two mentioned Jews by name. Article 10 provided for educational committees "appointed locally by the Jewish communities" but under "the general control of the state," to ensure linguistic equality for primary education (that is, ensuring the availability of primary education in Yiddish). For all minorities, the state could compel parallel language instruction in Polish. Article 11 protected the Jewish Sabbath. Jews could not be compelled to transact matters of law on the Sabbath, nor could Poland hold elections on Saturdays. Jews, like all other Poles, would be subject to military service.

Article 12 placed enforcement of the treaty "under the guarantee of the League of Nations," thus institutionalizing what the Polish government saw as the greatest affront to its national sovereignty. The protection of minorities became a matter of Polish domestic law, and could not be changed without the permission of a majority of the League Council. Poland agreed to defer to decisions on minority affairs by the Permanent Court of International Justice once established. As written, the Polish treaty defined Polish minorities and "Poland," reciprocally. Minorities were simply those people who did not share the language, religion, or "race" of the majority. But the treaty, and the other treaties like it, constructed successor states that the international system could not trust to treat their minorities according to the liberal values expounded almost obsessively by their leaders.

Four other treaties recognized "new" or substantially augmented states—Czechoslovakia, Romania, the Serb, Croat, and Slovene State, and Greece.[68] All four treaties contained the same basic guarantees of nationality, freedom of religion,

[67] "Treaty of Peace between the United States of America, the British Empire, France, Italy, and Japan and Poland," *AJIL* 13, Supplement, Official Documents (1919): 423–40.

[68] The *AJIL* published all of the minority treaties: "Treaty of Peace between the Principal Allied and Associated Powers and Czechoslovakia," 14, No. 4, Supplement: Official Documents (1920): 311–23; "Treaty of Peace between the Principal Allied and Associated Powers and the Serb, Croat, and Slovene State," 14, No. 4, Supplement: Official Documents (1920): 333–43; "Treaty of Peace between the Principal Allied and Associated Powers and Romania," 14, No. 4, Supplement: Official Documents (1920): 324–32; "Treaty of Peace between the Principal Allied and Associated Powers and Greece," 15, No. 2, Supplement: Official Documents (1921): 161–69.

equality before the law, non-discrimination based in religion, ethnicity, or language, linguistic equality in private and commercial matters, state-sponsored primary education instruction in minority languages, and deference to the League in domestic law on minority protection. The treaties of Saint-Germain, Neuilly, and Trianon had minority protections written into them.[69]

Different minorities received different manners of protection in different places. Only the Romanian and Greek treaties specifically mentioned Jews at all. Article 7 of the Romanian treaty specifically guaranteed nationality to resident Jews, provided they did not already possess some other nationality, a direct response to the systematic legal exclusion of Jews in Romania after the Congress of Berlin. Article 10 of the treaty with Greece provided protection "where there is resident a considerable proportion of Greek nationals of the Jewish religion." The treaty with Czechoslovakia provided for an autonomous region for Ruthenes, but contained no specific mention of Jews, Germans, or Magyars. This was perhaps a silence that tried to speak. As the exemplary liberal successor state, and certainly the one with the most generous territorial settlement, Czechoslovakia could be trusted, relatively speaking, to treat its minorities fairly.[70]

The minority provisions in the short-lived Treat of Sèvres with Turkey emphasized external tutelage in the treatment of minorities. In addition to the protections offered in the other treaties, Article 142 asserted that "the terrorist regime which has existed in Turkey since November 1, 1914" distorted the number of true converts to Islam. Persons before that date certified as holding to other faiths had to "voluntarily perform the necessary formality for embracing the Islamic faith" if they wished to remain Muslim. No other treaty required a positive act of religious affiliation. Two articles clearly referring to Armenians without naming them required the Turkish government to locate survivors of "the massacres perpetrated in Turkey during the war" and to restore their property (Articles 142 and 144). Article 150 guaranteed the Jewish as well as the Christian Sabbath.

On July 31, 1919, Eleftherios Venizelos of Greece wrote what might have seemed a very formulaic letter of resistance to Philippe Berthelot of France, then chair of the New States Committee. He argued that external interference in Greek affairs would actually hinder national unity among "Greeks" of various ethnicities and faiths who had lived together for centuries. Yet Venizelos also looked ahead: "The peace of the world seems to require that, while leaving to each ethnic minority within the frame of the Constitution and local laws the privilege, if it [the state] wishes, to cultivate its own language and religion, to close the door firmly to foreign influences and propaganda."[71] Politely, and in somewhat tangled syntax, Venizelos

---

[69] Treaty of Saint-Germain (Articles 62–69); Treaty of Neuilly (Articles 49–57); Treaty of Trianon (Articles 54–60).

[70] A report from the New States Committee admitted that "the prosperity and perhaps almost the existence" of Czechoslovakia would depend on good relations with the wealthy and powerful German minority. Yet "the very magnitude of this task" argued for the conference simply walking away from it, on the basis that "the solution of it is probably best left to the Czechs themselves." "Report No. 3; Czecho-Slovakia," Annex (B) to the Eleventh Meeting, May 21, 1919, in Miller, *Diary*, 13: 79.

[71] Venizelos to Berthelot, July 31, 1919, "Annex (A) to Forty-second Meeting," in Miller, *Diary*, 13: 366.

maintained that the national state, sooner or later, would rule in its own house on who belonged and who did not.

Minority treaties as a population policy externally defined peoples, and bent some of the contours of state sovereignty in order to accommodate them. The treaties sought to shift states to suit peoples in situations in which shifting borders could not do so. The whole question of minorities, to the way of thinking outlined by Venizelos, was really a question of borders. "Foreigners" belonged on the other side of national borders, or had to accept separate and unequal status as resident foreigners. In the end, states would assert the sovereign right to discern just who foreigners were. Successor states doing so would largely explain the dismal results of the minority treaties between the wars.[72] For his part, not long after signing a minority treaty, Venizelos would endorse population exchanges, a far more brutal policy for identifying and "unmixing" lands and peoples.

THE MANDATES: A TERRITORIAL POLICY BECOMES A POPULATION POLICY

As we saw, the "unmixing" of lands in the German overseas empire and Arabic-speaking Ottoman domains gave rise to relatively little controversy at the Paris Peace Conference. But just what rule over these lands constituted gave rise to a great deal of controversy. Australia, New Zealand, and South Africa pressed for direct annexation, which would have given them full and exclusive sovereignty over peoples as well as lands. Yet President Wilson had brought with him to Paris no principle dearer than "no annexations," which specifically precluded colonial aggrandizement reminiscent of the last century. The racial classification of the mandates emerged to resolve the resulting impasse, and invented a population policy to solve a territorial problem.

On January 27, Wilson offered before the Council of Ten his understanding of mandates as an alternative to annexation, using the example of former German South West Africa. Defining mandate territories meant defining mandate peoples. "If any nation could annex territory which was previously a Germany Colony,"[73] he stated flatly, "it would be challenging the whole idea of the League of Nations" (742). Rather than "to exercise arbitrary sovereignty over any people," mandates sought "to serve the people in undeveloped parts, to safeguard them against abuses such as had occurred under German administration and such as might be found under other administrations." South Africa indeed could "administer it [South West Africa] as an annex to the Union so far as consistent with the interest of the inhabitants." But the white rulers of South Africa would govern these inhabitants in such a way that "when the time came, their own interests, as they saw them,

---

[72] See Fink, *Defending the Rights of Others*, 267–365.
[73] "Secretary's Notes of a Conversation Held in M. Pichon's Room at the Quai d'Orsay, Paris, on Monday, January 27, 1919, at 10hrs. 30," *FRUS: PPC*, 3: 740–42.

might qualify them to express a wish as to their ultimate relations—perhaps lead them to desire their union with the mandatory power."

Remarkably, given his retrograde views on race at home, Wilson made no explicit distinction between the indigenous and settler populations: "It was up to the Union of South Africa to make it so attractive that South West Africans would come into the Union of their own free will" (741–42). In the meantime, the not-yet-born League of Nations would hold sovereignty in the mandates: "The fundamental idea would be that the world was acting as a trustee through a mandatory, and would be in charge of the whole administration until the day when the true wishes of the inhabitants could be ascertained." Either Wilson considered the indigenous population wholly invisible, or he considered all inhabitants of South West Africa as, if not equals, parts of some kind of whole. As we will see in Chapter 5, his early views on the League suggested the latter.

Wilson encountered predictable opposition from representatives from the Dominions. General Louis Botha of South Africa predicted ruin should the conference deny direct annexation. Animal diseases from North Africa would arrive unchecked (through unexplained means), and the tiny German settler population would form a rebel republic. The peace between Boers and British creating the Union of South Africa in 1910 might itself become undone (744). Hughes of Australia emphasized the "natural" character of his country's rule over New Guinea, which he compared, less than coherently, to that of Britain over Ireland, France over Alsace-Lorraine, and the United States over Mexico (746). The Dominions, a powerful voice in the British Empire delegation, would not acquiesce easily.

The French, who ruled the world's second largest overseas empire, remained remarkably quiet. Clemenceau, who seldom lacked an opinion on anything, appointed Minister for Colonies Henry Simon to address the Council on January 28.[74] Simon made a succinct, logical presentation in opposition to applying the mandatory principle to the former German colonies. "Every mandatory was revocable," he contended, "and there would therefore be no guarantee for its continuance" (761). Because of this uncertainty, he argued, mandates would draw neither the capital nor the settlers necessary for the modernization of the territories in question. Only colonial government that called itself such, Simon concluded, could guarantee "the development of the country and the effective protection of the natives during the period required for their development toward a higher plane of civilization" (761). As with Smuts and Hughes, proximity played a role. The Cameroons and Togoland were adjacent to French Equatorial Africa, a federation of French colonies established in 1910.

Simon sought to dress old-fashioned colonial acquisition in Wilsonian clothing. Old colonial ideologies "were part of a theory which was today quite obsolete and condemned by all" (761). Now, in the age of Wilson, he argued, "all the great Powers worthy of the name considered their colonies as wards entrusted to them

---

[74] "Secretary's Notes of a Conversation Held in M. Pichon's Room at the Quai d'Orsay, Paris, on Tuesday, 28 January, 1919, at 4:00 p.m.," *FRUS: PPC*, 3: 758–63.

by the world" (761). Guided by the Wilsonian moral compass, nations such as France could govern the former German colonies even more justly in the future than in the past.

Moreover, Simon reminded his listeners of Point V of the Fourteen Points, which awkwardly had called for equal concern for the interests of colonizers and colonized. Simon used Point V to make an assimilationist argument. The French had already absorbed some of their colonies into the national territory. Simon referred presumably to the Ancien Régime colonies in the Caribbean, Réunion, the Four Communes of Sénégal, and Algeria, which had been directly annexed. There, he argued less than truthfully, "the inhabitants had equal rights, they had their representatives in the French Chamber [of Deputies], their system of local government was exactly the same as that of the French, and the natives enjoyed the same rights as French citizens" (762). Yet, Simon concluded, France asked nothing more but nothing less than "to be allowed to continue her work of civilization in tropical Africa" (763) through annexing the former German colonies.

With uncomfortable frankness, Vittorio Orlando of Italy pointed the way to a compromise that preserved the mandate principle, but drew mandates closer to the familiar hierarchical contracting of empire:

> The attributes of the mandatory might well be camouflaged by hypocrisy. Therefore he [Orlando] thought that the powers of the mandatory should be properly graduated to meet the requirements of each case, and in his opinion it was necessary from the very commencement to define the powers to be attributed to the mandatories. (769)

The Mandate System could thus "unmix" lands by "unmixing" peoples. The criteria for doing so would lie not in those peoples themselves, but in imperial designs on their lands.

On January 30, Lloyd George brought forward a proposal from the British Empire delegation that outlined the Mandate System, almost verbatim as it would appear as Article 22 of the Covenant of the League of Nations. The conference would "accept the doctrine of a mandatory for all conquests."[75] However, that doctrine would apply differently in different places, through what became known as the A-, B-, and C-class mandates. Lloyd George described the proposal in broad strokes (785–86), and not always delicately. A-class mandates "must be different from that which would have to be applied to cannibal countries, where people were eating each other." B-class applied to "territories which did not form an integral part of any particular mandatory country." Typically, this class would apply to territories "situated a long way from the country of the possible mandatory," though confusingly, he referred specifically to New Guinea, whose proximity to Australia was the point, at any rate to the Australians. But in this class, "the full

---

[75] "Draft Resolution in Reference to Mandatories," Appendix, "Secretary's Notes of a Conversation Held at Mr. Pichon's Room at the Quai d'Orsay, Paris, on Thursday, January 30, 1919, at 11 a.m.," *FRUS: PPC*, 3: 795–96. The text left for subsequent decision possible mandates in Anatolia, including Armenian or Kurdish lands.

principle of a mandatory would be applied, including the 'open door.'"[76] "C-class" mandates comprised lands "which formed almost a part of the organization of an adjoining power, who would have to be appointed by the mandatory."

To be sure, the formal proposal avoided reference to cannibals. But it reflected a compromise that enabled Wilson as well as his opponents to see what they wanted to see in it. The Mandate Principle would apply throughout the former imperial domains. The defeat of the German and Ottoman empires afforded a historic opportunity: "to apply to those territories the principle that the well-being and development of such peoples form a sacred trust of civilization and that securities for the performance of this trust should be embodied in the constitution of the League of Nations" (795). German and Ottoman rule had created lands "inhabited by peoples not yet able to stand by themselves in the strenuous conditions of the modern world" (795). These malevolent population policies required remedial population policies through the differentiated forms of mandatory rule. The situation authorized the rhetorical shift from ruling lands to ruling peoples. As the proposal put it, "the character of the mandate must differ according to the stage of development of the people, the geographic situation of the territory, its economic conditions and other similar circumstances" (796). In this way, differentiated geography—differentiated for political reasons pertaining to annexation—produced differentiated populations and differentiated mandatory rule.

No serious discussion ever took place, either within the Council of Ten or the commission writing the Covenant, of the actual capacities of any of the mandate peoples. Indeed, the Council never elicited the views of the League commission on the classification system at all. Still less did the Council ever consider consulting the peoples of the mandate territories. As we saw in Chapter 3, there was nothing especially novel about using political geography to categorize peoples. British geography had done so for strategic reasons, and French geography invariably found a "unity" of lands and peoples where French policy wished to find it. Even the King–Crane Commission found a Greater Syrian population suitable for democracy because Wilsonian liberalism required one. But making peoples purely a function of lands, and most notably the locations of those lands, would inevitably weaken the Mandate Principle.

The compromise of the classification system compromised everyone. As we will see in Chapter 5, applying the Mandate Principle in any form gave rise to a new confrontation between Wilson and the leaders of the Dominions. In the end, Article 22 of the Covenant opened the way for further conflation of mandatory and traditional colonial rule. As provisional world sovereign, the Paris Peace Conference had decided upon the Mandate Principle, its application, and had identified the mandatory powers. But at its own insistence, it would not and could not administer the Mandate System. That would be a matter for the League of Nations.

---

[76] Here meaning trade on equal terms between the mandate and all League members.

POPULATION EXCHANGES

The mass transfers of persons that came to be known as "population exchanges" proved a simple, brutal way to "unmix" peoples in order to "unmix" lands. As Eric Weitz has argued, contemporaries and historians long considered the exchanges an embarrassing exception to the liberal principles motivating the Paris Peace Conference. In fact, as he put it, population exchange as a policy was "an intrinsic element of the principles enunciated at Paris."[77] In an international system in which one nation inhabited one state, exchanges provided the simplest way to determine the "self" eligible for "self-determination." Individuals of a certain ethnicity, the logic went, would want to live in their own self-determined, ethnonational state. Those who did not could legitimately be coerced into moving anyway, in the name of peace and stability between such states.

Population exchanges had a unique relationship to the international system being built in Paris. Not all forced transfers acquired that name, notably the French expulsion of some 150,000 "Germans" from reconquered Alsace and Lorraine.[78] Successor states, not Great Powers or even the Supreme Council, initiated population exchanges after the Great War. But both accepted and legitimized exchanges as part of the international system. Population exchanges took place on the fringes of the effective authority of the conference, where neither plebiscites nor minority treaties proved feasible.

Certainly, the brutality of the exchanges gave rise to considerable embarrassment on the part of those who supported them. For precisely that reason, both the Paris Peace Conference and the Conference of Lausanne kept them at arm's length. Statesmen spoke of the exchanges surprisingly rarely, and then in oblique language. Both conferences maintained a largely artificial distinction between "voluntary" and "mandatory" exchanges. Written recognition and regulation of the exchanges occurred, not through the treaties, but through bilateral agreements between successor states. All exchanges identified as such after the Great War were bilateral, and left various anomalies in their wake.

Of course, conflict evoked the movement of people long before the Great War.[79] As Ottoman power in the Balkans waned late in the nineteenth century, Muslims in the new Balkan states migrated to the Ottoman Empire—estimated at over 1 million people in the twenty years following the Congress of Berlin of 1878.[80] Population movements accelerated and became more complicated following the

---

[77] Eric D. Weitz, "From the Vienna to the Paris System: International Politics, and the Entangled Histories of Human Rights, Forced Deportations, and Civilizing Missions," *American Historical Review* 113.5 (2008): 1334.

[78] Philipp Ther, *The Dark Side of Nation-States: Ethnic Cleansing in Modern Europe*, Charlotte Kreutzmüller, trans. (New York: Berghahn Books, 2014), 68–70.

[79] Donald Bloxham, "The Great Unweaving: The Removal of Peoples in Europe, 1875–1949," in Richard Bessel and Claudia B. Haake, eds., *Removing Peoples: Forced Removal in the Modern World* (Oxford: Oxford University Press, 2009), 167–207.

[80] Philipp Ther, *Ethnic Cleansing*, 49; André Wurfbain, *L'Échange Gréco-Bulgare des minorités ethniques* (Paris: Payot, 1930), 19–33; and Ryan Gingeras, *Sorrowful Shores: Violence, Ethnicity, and the End of the Ottoman Empire* (Oxford: Oxford University Press, 2009).

Balkan Wars of 1912 and 1913. The First Balkan War completed the near-removal of the Ottomans from Europe, leading to a new wave of Muslim emigration. The irredentist victors (Bulgaria, Serbia, and Greece) set upon each other in the Second Balkan War, producing considerable movements of peoples along ethnographic and religious lines. Christian communities throughout the Ottoman Empire also came to consider themselves threatened, and moved to "Christian" lands. Together, the two Balkan wars displaced some 700,000 people.[81] Within this population, no one could, or even tried to, distinguish among "voluntary" migrants, war refugees, and people expelled from transferred territories.

States sought to regularize this situation before the Great War. In 1913, Bulgaria and the Ottoman Empire signed the Treaty of Constantinople, which provided for population exchange along a strictly defined border zone, and minority protections beyond that zone.[82] Greece and the Ottoman Empire began extended negotiations for a "voluntary" population exchange. Mixed commissions would guarantee the "voluntary" nature of migrations, and the property rights of the relocated populations.[83] Only the outbreak of war brought the negotiations to an end. When Venizelos raised the issue of population exchange in the summer of 1919, he returned to the matter essentially where it had lain five years earlier.

Peacemaking after the Great War facilitated both the "voluntary" exchange between Greece and Bulgaria affirmed by the Treaty of Neuilly, and the "compulsory" exchange between Greece and Turkey affirmed by the Treaty of Lausanne. In theory, a "voluntary" resembled a personal plebiscite, an individual choice of ethnic identity that determined an individual's nationality. Hundreds of thousands of people had to make this "choice" literally in the heat of military or paramilitary battle. Successor states and the allies accepted or even supported migration under various levels of coercion. One way or another, peoples would shift to suit boundaries.

As we saw in Chapter 2, Bulgaria lost Western Thrace to Greece through the Treaty of Neuilly. But having "unmixed" the lands, how now to "unmix" the peoples? Many Christian and Muslims spoke both Greek and/or Bulgarian, as well as Turkish.[84] Religious division within Christian Orthodoxy further complicated matters. Greek speakers recognized the Greek Patriarchate based in Constantinople. Most but not all Christian speakers of Bulgarian recognized the Bulgarian Exarchate, also based in Constantinople but separated from the Greek Patriarchate since the mid nineteenth century. Bulgarian nationalists tended to make language the primary marker of Bulgarian ethnic identity. Greeks, on the

[81] Calculated from Stephen Ladas, *The Exchange of Minorities: Bulgaria, Greece and Turkey* (London: Macmillan, 1932), 15–16.

[82] Ther, *Ethnic Cleansing*, 62–63.

[83] Its anti-Turkish position notwithstanding, see Yannis G. Mourelos, "The 1914 Persecutions and the First Attempt at an Exchange of Minorities between Greece and Turkey," *Balkan Studies* 26.2 (1985): 389–413.

[84] A.A. Pallis endeavored to categorize the various populations of Western Thrace using prewar Ottoman and postwar censuses in "Racial Migrations in the Balkans during the Years 1912–1924," *Geographical Journal* 66.4 (1925): 326–27.

other hand, generally emphasized religious adherence to the Patriarchate, at least in Western Thrace.[85]

On July 25, 1919, the New States Committee received a proposal from the Greek delegation to establish a mixed commission "to superintend and facilitate emigration of Greeks resident in Bulgaria to Greece, and of Bulgarians resident in Greece to Bulgaria."[86] Three days later, the committee sent a favorable report on the Greek proposal on to the Supreme Council.[87] Indeed, the committee posited that facilitated migration "might with advantage be extended to all Balkan countries," and that such migration could "do much to help a permanent settlement of the troubles which have so long affected the Balkans, and might be a valuable supplement to the clauses dealing with the protection of minorities" (310). Certainly, the committee gave every indication of believing in genuinely "voluntary" migration, and annexed to its report a draft minority treaty with Bulgaria to protect those who did not wish to do so.

The Supreme Council still needed to articulate its precise relationship to any population exchange.[88] On November 19, Frank Polk of the American delegation raised the issue of whether signing the treaty meant endorsing the exchange.[89] With President Wilson seriously ill and with ratification prospects of the Treaty of Versailles withering in the Senate, Polk hesitated to agree to anything that might even hint at increased American involvement in European affairs should the exchange not go smoothly. Matsui Keishiro of Japan opined that all the Great Powers should sign, though he added that his government was unlikely to do so if the Americans declined.[90] Giocomo de Martino of the Italian delegation countered that signing the treaty with the exchange included constituted a "moral obligation" on the part of the Great Powers to take "an effective part in the execution of these clauses with Bulgaria by affixing their signatures thereto." Allen Dulles of the American delegation suggested that as the exchange and minority provisions would come into effect "under the aegis of the League of Nations," perhaps it was not necessary for all the Great Powers to sign.

On November 25, just two days before the signing of the Treaty of Neuilly, the Supreme Council formally established its distance from the population exchange.[91] The Council endorsed the conclusion of the Drafting Committee "that the Treaty between Bulgaria and Greece relative to reciprocal immigration was in no way dependent upon the signature of the Bulgarian Treaty by the Principal Allied and

[85] Theodora Dragostinova, "Speaking National: Nationalizing the Greeks of Bulgaria," *Slavic Review* 67.1 (2008): 162–64.

[86] Thirty-Seventh Meeting, New States Committee, July 25, 1919, Miller, *Diary,* 13: 306.

[87] "Letter to the Council of Five on the Special Clauses Proposed by M. Venizelos," Thirty-Eighth Meeting, New States Committee, July 28, 1919, Miller, *Diary*, 13: 309–21.

[88] Ladas, *Exchange of Minorities*, 31–48.

[89] "Notes of a Meeting of the Heads of Delegations of the Five Great Powers Held in M. Pichon's Room, Quai d'Orsay, Paris, on Wednesday, November 19, 1919, at 11:00 a.m.," *FRUS: PPC*, 9: 222.

[90] Neither the United States nor Japan had declared war on Bulgaria, though both would sign the Treaty of Neuilly.

[91] "Notes of a Meeting of the Heads of Delegations of the Five Great Powers Held in M. Pichon's Room, Quai d'Orsay, Paris, on Tuesday, November 29, 1919, at 10:30 a.m.," *FRUS: PPC*, 9: 332–33.

Associated Powers." De Martino renewed his protest, on the basis that "the decisions already taken by the Council relative to affairs in the Balkans seemed to him to have created many opportunities for trouble in the future. As a general matter, he felt that those Powers who were directly interested in maintaining peace in the Balkans should participate more actively in Balkan affairs." Nevertheless, given the pressing need to conclude peace with Bulgaria, de Martino left the matter there. The exchange would come into effect through a convention between Greece and Bulgaria alone, signed the same day as the treaty. This distancing of the Great Powers from the population exchange set the pattern for the later convention between Greece and Turkey.

As written, the Greece–Bulgaria convention presumed a strong desire on the part of minority populations to self-designate and migrate to their respective ethno-national states.[92] As written, it relied wholly on national self-identification. The convention held that members of "racial, religious or linguistic minorities" henceforth had a recognized right "to emigrate freely to their respective territories" (Article 1). Bulgaria and Greece agreed "not to place directly or indirectly any restriction on the right of emigration," to the point of annulling existing domestic law (Article 2). But the convention remained silent on Greece or Bulgaria facilitating emigration through encouragement, pressure, or outright coercion. The "voluntary" act would consist of a declaration of intent to emigrate before a mixed commission or its representative (Article 4). Adult men could declare on behalf of wives and minor children. The mixed commission would comprise a Greek member, a Bulgarian member, and two members of neither nationality, named by the Council of the League of Nations. The League Council would choose one of these two as president. In the case of a tie vote, the president could vote twice (Article 8).

In addition to certifying the "voluntary" nature of emigration, the mixed commission had the task of lowering financial barriers. Emigrants maintained unrestricted rights over moveable property (Article 10). Immoveable property (most commonly land and houses) would be assigned a value by the mixed commission, and that sum would be forwarded to the emigrant as an advance, "according to the funds available" (Articles 11–12). Title to the transferred property would revert to the relevant states (Article 10), which, in theory, would supply the funds to compensate the former owner. The mixed commission had broad if unspecified powers to facilitate the liquidation of properties belonging to churches, convents, schools, hospitals, etc. (Article 6). In short, the mixed commission would serve as an honest broker of persons and goods.

As Theorora Dragostinova has shown, "voluntary" emigration presented Greek-speaking Bulgarians and Bulgarian-speaking Greeks with an unappealing choice.[93] They could choose to self-identify as minorities in states that had expressed a public preference that they leave. Or they could become refugees, strangers in new

[92] "Convention Between Greece and Bulgaria Respecting Reciprocal Emigration," November 27, 1919, in *AJIL* 14, Supplement, Official Documents (1920): 356–60.
[93] Theodora Dragostinova, *Between Two Motherlands: Nationality and Emigration among the Greeks of Bulgaria, 1900–1949* (Ithaca, NY: Cornell University Press, 2011), 117–56.

lands, often with resentful neighbors with whom they happened to share a common language and/or religion. Moreover, Greeks and Bulgarians had asymmetrical responses to the convention. Greece generally encouraged the "return" of Greek Bulgarians, to bolster the Greek presence in newly acquired territories in Macedonia and Thrace. Bulgaria, on the other hand, generally wanted Bulgarians to remain in place as minorities, to support claims for border revision later.[94] As in the plebiscites, peoples did not always want to "unmix" according to state preferences. As late as the signing of the Treaty of Lausanne in June 1923, only 197 Greek families and 166 Bulgarian families had registered their desire to emigrate.[95]

Much more substantial population exchanges in Thrace occurred thereafter. Terrified Greeks fled Anatolia after the burning of Smyrna in September 1922. The Greek government, eager to settle them in Greece, forcibly removed large numbers of Bulgarians in Eastern Thrace to other parts of Greece to make room for the new arrivals.[96] Eventually, Bulgaria responded in kind toward its Greek minority. Many made declarations to the mixed commission to try to protect as much of their property as possible, calling into question the "voluntary" nature of such declarations. By the end of 1925, 154,691 people submitted declarations to the commission—101,800 Bulgarians and 52,891 Greeks.[97] About 80,000 others migrated without making use of the commission, many of them Bulgarians who hoped eventually to return. But substantial numbers of people resisted "unmixing"—indeed in roughly the same numbers as those who left. Some 140,000 Bulgarians chose to remain in Greece, and 12,000 Greeks chose to remain in Bulgaria.[98] Observers seemed to draw the lesson that a "voluntary" exchange was a confused exchange.

The Greek–Turkish population exchange of 1923 took place under very different circumstances. The Greek and Turkish successor states met on the field of battle, each intent on establishing or affirming an ethno-national polity. The population exchange followed from the outcome of that war. In the event, of the 1.3 million Greeks expelled from the borders of postwar Turkey, 1.1 million had already left, most in the wake of the defeated Greek army.[99] It seems reasonable to speculate that there would have been at least as extensive a population exchange had Greece won the war.

How did the international system of 1923 incorporate this outcome? As we saw in Chapter 1, the defeat of Greece in 1922 was also a proxy defeat of the European empires that had won the Great War. In treating successor Turkey as a negotiating

---

[94] Theodora Dragonistova, "Navigating Nationality in the Emigration of Minorities between Bulgaria and Greece, 1919–1941," *East European Politics and Societies* 23.2 (2009): 185–212.

[95] Dragostinova, "Navigating Nationality," 194.

[96] The population of Western Thrace previously classified as "Muslim" comprised mostly speakers of Bulgarian, Turkish, and Roma. Further precision remains at best problematic, as Greece stopped including religion in its census figures in 1913, and Bulgaria in 1912. Pallis, "Racial Migrations in the Balkans," 320.

[97] Dragostinova, "Navigating Nationality," 186.

[98] Dragostinova, "Navigating Nationality," 186.

[99] Christa Miendersma, "Population Exchanges: International Law and State Practice—Part 1," *International Journal of Refugee Law* 9.3 (1997): 346. These figures came from the mixed commission established by the convention. Those who fled were mostly Aegean Greeks. Expulsions concerned primarily Greeks living elsewhere in Anatolia.

partner rather than a defeated enemy, the Conference of Lausanne departed from the Paris Peace Conference rather than continued it. The Conference of Lausanne served to demarcate the limits of allied influence in Anatolia, and to incorporate Turkey into the new international system. As part of that settlement, the Greek and Turkish successor states, however asymmetrically, would decide what there was to decide on populations. As we will see in Chapter 6, the Conference of Lausanne would implicate the League of Nations in this brutal tailoring of populations to suit borders.

Until recently, the Conference of Lausanne and the Greek–Turkish population exchange maintained surprisingly distinct historiographies. Some of the most informative English accounts of the conference either scarcely mention the exchange, or leave it aside altogether.[100] Historiographical literature on the exchange has focused more on the human cost.[101] Onur Yildirim has provided a much-needed corrective that considers the exchange in the context of the Lausanne Conference.[102]

Yildirim's central claim—that both the Greek and Turkish delegations arrived at Lausanne preferring compulsory exchange—puts state interests at center stage. The Greeks saw compulsory exchange as a means of stabilizing domestic politics. Three kings reigned between 1920 and 1922, each with his own political friends and enemies. Venizelos had survived an assassination attempt, the ongoing threat of paramilitary violence, and electoral defeat in December 1920, only to return to lead the Greek delegation at Lausanne. Defeat against Turkey in 1922 exacerbated an existing, grave refugee crisis. Compulsory population exchange, according to Yildirim, provided a way to address this crisis and to lay the demographic foundation for a more "authentically" Greek ethno-nation state. The Turks, for their part, had broken with allied peacemaking and had waged war with Greece in the name of a more authentically "Turkish" post-Ottoman Turkey. Yet as we saw in Chapter 1, early republican Turkey still wanted recognition from an international system still led by the European imperial powers. Compulsory population exchange offered common ground to these parties.

As Yildirim has shown, Greeks, Turks, and the allies also generally agreed as to just who was to be exchanged. Apart from some important exceptions negotiated with some difficulty, ethnicity became a function of religion. Christians were "Greek" and Muslims were "Turks." No serious discussion of any other criteria took place, either within the Greek and Turkish delegations or at the conference

---

[100] Roderic H. Davison, "Turkish Diplomacy from Mudros to Lausanne," in Gordon A. Craig and Felix Gilbert, eds., *The Diplomats, 1919–1939* (Princeton, NJ: Princeton University Press, 1953), 172–209; Briton Cooper Busch, *Mudros to Lausanne: Britain's Frontier in West Asia, 1918–1923* (Albany: State University of New York Press, 1976), 359–92; and Erik Goldstein, "The British Official Mind and the Lausanne Conference, 1922–23," in Erik Goldstein and B.J.C. McKercher, eds., *Power and Stability: British Foreign Policy, 1865–1945* (London: Frank Cass, 2003), 185–206.

[101] See, for example, Renée Hirschon, ed., *Crossing the Aegean: An Appraisal of the 1923 Compulsory Population Exchange between Greece and Turkey* (New York: Berghahn Books, 2003); and Bruce Clark, *Twice a Stranger: The Mass Expulsions that Forged Modern Greece and Turkey* (Cambridge, MA: Harvard University Press, 2006).

[102] Onur Yildirim, *Diplomacy and Displacement: Reconsidering the Turko-Greek Exchange of Populations, 1922–1934* (New York: Routledge, 2006).

itself. To be sure, the Turkish delegation in late November 1922 proposed a plebiscite in Western Thrace.[103] But given the dismal record of the plebiscite in Upper Silesia, not to mention failed plebiscites in Teschen, Vilna, and elsewhere, there was no reason to expect the European Great Powers to accept the idea.

By 1922, the war between Greece and Turkey had effectively split the allies. The French, for their part, cared most about a stable border for their new mandate in Syria, and toward that end had ceded Cilicia to Turkey in the Treaty of Ankara of October 1921.[104] The French also held enormous amounts of Ottoman debt, the regularizing of which required an overall settlement with the new regime. As we saw in Chapter 1, the Chanak Affair of 1922 disrupted the identity of the British Empire itself. Erik Goldstein has shown that the British "official mind" at Lausanne had plenty of reasons to settle with the new regime in Turkey—the Straits, the disposition of Thrace and Mosul, capitulations, the future of the caliphate, and the Kurdish and Armenian lands. The imperial powers had powerful incentives to take population issues off the table.

Most of the drama at Lausanne about the compulsory population exchange thus revolved around avoiding responsibility for it. As we will see in Chapter 6, the definitive solution would lie in "internationalizing" the problem by fixating on the role of Fridjof Nansen as agent of the League of Nations. The Conference of Lausanne sought to distance itself from the exchange, much as the Paris Peace Conference had from the Greek–Bulgarian exchange. The public sessions, published with remarkable speed as the official record, recorded elaborate performances of evasion and self-contradiction toward that end.[105]

At Lausanne, a First Commission on Territorial and Military Questions considered refugees, minorities, and population exchange mostly as interchangeable topics. On December 1, 1922, the First Commission heard a report from Nansen that would normalize compulsory exchange as a policy. Unease as to the actual implications of a population exchange appeared immediately. Mustafa İsmet İnönü, commonly known as İsmet Paşa, spoke immediately after Nansen's report to try to change the subject. While he had listened "with interest" to the report, "he could only attach a personal character [to the report] as no official relations existed between Turkey and the League of Nations; he [İsmet Paşa] regarded it as emanating from a private person."[106] İsmet Paşa thus sought to make the issue not the exchange, but Turkey's relationship to the League. The discussion quickly

---

[103] See Busch, *Mudros to Lausanne*, 366.

[104] Yücel Güçlü, "The Struggle for Mastery in Cilicia: Turkey, France, and the Ankara Agreement of 1921," *International History Review* 23.3 (2001): 580–603.

[105] Ministère des Affaires Étrangers, Documents Diplomatiques, *Conférence de Lausanne*, 2 vols. (Paris: Imprimerie Nationale, 1923); and *Lausanne Conference on Near Eastern Affairs, 1922–1923: Records of Proceedings and Draft Terms of Peace* (London: His Majesty's Stationery Office, 1923). The French and British publications are essentially identical in content. French was the official language of the conference, though the British, American, and Japanese delegates spoke in English. The British version (quoted here) provides translations of the French texts. Hereafter referred to as *Lausanne Conference*.

[106] Territorial and Military Commission, "Minutes of the Eighth Meeting, December 1, 1922, at 3:30 p.m., under the Presidency of Lord Curzon," *Lausanne Conference*, 111–24.

evolved into a testy debate about other populations affected, notably prisoners of war, civilian prisoners, and residents of Thrace and Constantinople.

Lord Curzon opined that while all might prefer a voluntary exchange, "compulsion would very probably be found necessary for more reasons than one" (121). Should the conference decide on a "voluntary exchange" (a term without clarity given the chaotic refugee situation), "months might pass before it was carried out." Such a delay would only exacerbate the refugee crisis in Greece and could prevent the planting of crops the following spring, particularly in Thrace. Camille Barrère of France and Venizelos likewise asserted the need for celerity in carrying out the exchange (119). No one raised other options. The commission agreed to the appointment of a sub-commission specifically charged with handling the exchange of populations.

In the sessions that followed, speaker after speaker denounced the very idea of a population exchange, yet oh-so-reluctantly admitted its absolute necessity as a matter beyond their control. On December 13, İsmet Paşa lamented that "constant wars," first the Balkan Wars and then the Great War, "placed many Turkish subjects in the position of aggressors against their own country, and led to their forcible repatriation by the invading army" (207).[107] The Conference of Lausanne had simply to concede that "the idea of an exchange had forced itself on the attention of all," but that this "painful necessity" had become unavoidable. Seeing an opening, Venizelos made an argument he would repeat often, "that the idea of compulsory exchange of populations had not been put forward by the Greek delegation. On the contrary, such an exchange was repugnant to them" (210). Curzon also disowned any connection to a compulsory exchange, or British involvement in events leading to it. Curzon "deeply regretted" a compulsory exchange, famously referring to it as "a thoroughly bad and vicious solution, for which the world would pay a heavy penalty for a hundred years to come. He detested having anything to do with it" (212). Yet neither he nor his colleagues considered any other solution.

This sub-commission on population exchange, chaired by Giulio Montagna of Italy, made its report on January 8, 1923.[108] As we will see in Chapter 6, this report clearly laid the exchange at the feet of Nansen. The report recounted a rearguard (and perhaps not altogether sincere) effort on the part of the Greeks to make the exchange "voluntary," but treated a compulsory exchange as settled law, barring a decision otherwise on the part of the conference. The Montagna report put in writing the basis of a final agreement to mitigate the effects of the exchange by exempting the Greeks of Constantinople and the Muslims from Western Thrace from the exchange.[109] These exceptions, as well as the vexed question of whether the Greek

---

[107] Territorial and Military Commission, "Minutes of the Fourteenth Meeting, December 13, 1922, at 11 a.m., under the presidency of Lord Curzon," *Lausanne Conference*, 204–15.

[108] "Report addressed to Lord Curzon, President of the First Commission, by M. Montagna, President of the Sub-Commission on the Exchange of Populations," January 8, 1923, *Lausanne Conference*, 328–37.

[109] Much of the commercial elite of Constantinople was Greek, and the Muslims of Western Thrace comprised large numbers of Bulgarian- and Roma-speakers that Turkey wanted to protect, but not necessarily absorb. Stefanos Katsikas, "The Muslims of Greece (1923–41)," in Benjamin Fortna et al.,

Orthodox Patriarchate ought to be allowed to remain in Constantinople, caused far more dispute when Montagna presented the report than the matter of compulsory exchange as such.[110]

The convention on Greek and Turkish population exchange, signed like the Treaty of Lausanne on July 24, 1923, opened a new chapter in the history of international population policy.[111] Parallel to the Greek–Bulgarian exchange, only Greek and Turkish representatives signed the convention. But the convention constituted an inseparable part of peacemaking with the Turkish state that succeeded the Ottoman Empire. According to the Lausanne convention, the Greek and Turkish states became the exclusive identifiers of peoples within their borders. Article 1 called for:

> ...a compulsory exchange of Turkish nationals of the Greek Orthodox religion established in Turkish territory, and of Greek nationals of the Moslem religion established in Greek territory.

Gone was the inclusive reference to "racial, religious or linguistic minorities" in the Greek–Bulgarian convention. "Greek" and "Turk" had ceased to be a matter of national spirit, culture, language, or even political loyalty. Least of all could ethnic identity remain a matter of personal choice. Religion became the exclusive marker of ethnicity, by state decree. Even convicted criminals and prisoners were to be expelled to their country of religious origin (Article 6). Emigrants lost nationality upon departure, and acquired a new nationality upon arrival (Article 7). Sovereignty in the ethno-national state required ethnic clarity. Likewise, for reasons of state, Christians in Constantinople and Muslims in Western Thrace were excluded from the exchange.[112] Other Greeks, notably the substantial community of Pontic Greeks in Eastern Anatolia, were not.[113]

The mixed commission, the linchpin of the "voluntary" exchange between Greece and Bulgaria, became the instrument for classifying and dividing people and property between Greece and Turkey. The commission would comprise four members named by Greece, four by Turkey, and three named by the League, from countries that had not participated in the Great War (Article 11). As with Bulgaria and Greece, the commission would assess the value of fixed property, such as churches and mosques. But any financial transfers based on the liquidation of such

eds., *State-nationalisms in the Ottoman Empire: Greece and Turkey, Orthodox and Muslims, 1830–1945* (London: Routledge, 2013), 153–75, esp. 154–56.

[110] Territorial and Military Commission, "Minutes of the Twentieth Meeting, January 10, 1923, at 11 a.m., Lord Curzon in the Chair," *Lausanne Conference*, 113–20.

[111] "Convention Concerning the Exchange of Greek and Turkish Populations," January 30, 1923, in *AJIL* 18, Supplement, Official Documents (1924): 84–90.

[112] Ladas estimates some 300,000 Greeks in Constantinople and some 130,000 Muslims in Western Thrace. *Exchange of Minorities*, 400. Alexis Alexandris, on the other hand, estimates 110,000 Greeks in Constantinople and 100,000 Turks in Western Thrace. Alexis Alexandris, "Religion or Ethnicity: The Identity Issue of the Minorities in Greece and Turkey," in Hirschon, ed., *Crossing the Aegean*, 118, 122.

[113] Volker Prott, *The Politics of Self-Determination: Remaking Territories and National Identities in Europe, 1917–1923* (Oxford: Oxford University Press, 2016), 197–206.

properties would occur only between states (Article 14). Displaced individuals and communities could collect compensation only from their new states of residence.

The mixed commission also had the vast but vaguely defined power "to take the measures necessitated by the execution of the present convention and to decide all questions to which this convention may arise" (Article 12). This included the delicate issue of just who was subject to the exchange. Greek and Ottoman authorities had required a statement of religion in civil registers. But most Albanians in Greece were Muslim, and followers of the "Greek Orthodox" religion in Turkey could consider themselves Serbs, Romanians, Russians, or even Arabs.[114] "Greeks" in Turkey could likewise adhere to Protestant, Catholic, or Jewish faiths. No religious conversion that could not be demonstrated to have taken place before January 1, 1922 could exempt an individual from the exchange. Through the mixed commission, the very souls of the expelled population became points of articulation of successor state sovereignty.

As was the case between Greece and Bulgaria, the convention on population exchange between Greece and Turkey served largely to regularize mutual expulsions that had already taken place. The problem, both for the international system and for the states it comprised, was that regularizing forced migrations meant legitimizing them. In point of brute fact, compulsory exchange suited both state actors and the postwar international system. But legitimizing a population policy of forced removal of hundreds of thousands of people, and removing from them control not just of their property but of their persons, raised troubling issues as to the ethical character of the new international system. As we will see in Chapter 6, "internationalizing" the issue served to obscure responsibility for the compulsory exchange.

Everyone understood at the time that "unmixing" lands and peoples in the defeated empires would prove a messy business. This chapter has argued that population policies proved one logical consequence of "national self-determination." The very concept assumed a concurrence of individual and collective identities. "The people" would "unmix" themselves, or could be persuaded by various means to do so. The result would be a system of coherent ethno-nation states that could live alongside one another in peace. All the policies examined here, one way or another, shared this common goal.

In the event, the conference and its various components decided the identities of lands and peoples as acts of sovereignty. Plebiscites were surely the most democratic of population policies. But plebiscites, by definition, circumscribed choice, and often raised as many questions as they answered. Plebiscites did not always produce territorial coherence, and if strictly followed would exacerbate economic dislocations. In themselves, plebiscites could never resolve irredentist sentiments among people who happened to live outside states to which they believed they belonged. Moreover, substantial numbers of people voted for the very hybridity plebiscites were designed to eliminate. Managing hybridity lay at the heart of the minority treaties. They sought to tailor national identity so that, for example,

---

[114] See Ladas, *Exchange of Minorities*, 377–98.

Polish Jews could live as both Jews and Poles. All the successor states proclaimed their allegiance to the principles of the minority treaties, and all of them ferociously opposed them on the grounds of state sovereignty. No successor state wanted to cede even the slightest degree of minority protection to a site of sovereignty beyond itself. Considered as a population policy, the mandates categorized peoples for reasons beyond themselves. Yet as we will see in Chapter 5, even the B- and C-class mandates helped normalize the idea of peoples around the globe being on some theoretical trajectory to self-determination and independence. The significance of this norm would become clear decades later.

Violent conflict before, during, and after the Great War in the Balkans rendered problematic the "voluntary" nature of the population exchange between Greece and Bulgaria. The muddiness of that exchange contributed directly to the compulsory exchange called for by the Lausanne convention, which allowed the Greek and Turkish successor states to decide what there was to decide about ethnicity in Greece and Anatolia. At Lausanne, the "self" to be determined became a matter of state, radically reduced to religion for reasons of state. Peacemaking after the Great War produced no more harrowing affirmation of the ethno-national state as the locus of sovereignty.

Such an externalization of "self-determination" and its detachment from individual agency seem a far cry from what either Wilson or Lenin had in mind as they competed for the ideological high ground in early 1918. If the peace was supposed to produce a better world, compulsory exchange based solely on religion seemed even at the time a curious way to get there. The international system after the Great War, in short, had acquired quite a bit to hide. How much better then, to redirect blame for a policy endorsed by all. Participants could blame each other, and emphasize their own regret at the "necessary" outcome not of their making. Clemenceau had prophesized correctly that peace would be made for peoples. But that peace would be made more over them than by them.

5

Mastering Revolution

This chapter evokes the term "revolution" in a broad sense, as the overthrow of the existing order, national or international, through violent or non-violent means. Revolution had been endemic to the Great War. From the beginning, states had fomented revolution beyond their borders as an instrument of policy. As we saw in Chapter 1, the bidding war for Polish sovereignty began in 1914, as both sides sought to mobilize Poles against their Habsburg, Hohenzollern, or Romanov rulers. In November 1914, Ottoman religious and political rulers called on Muslims under British, French, and Russian rule to defend the faith by rebelling against the Entente powers.[1] The British paid both Hussein of Mecca and the House of Saud to resist Ottoman rule. Notoriously, the Germans subsidized the Bolsheviks, so as to foment revolution and thus remove Imperial Russia from the war.[2] The thankless Bolsheviks then encouraged revolution in Germany through proselytizing German soldiers on the Eastern Front.[3] All of the millenarian creeds emerging from the Great War had revolutionary potential. Certainly, no one more earnestly sought an overthrow of the prewar international system than Woodrow Wilson.

States could never be sure of controlling the revolutions they sought to unleash. The Germans had encouraged jihad, but remained anxious that Muslim religious fervor might threaten resident nationals from the Central Powers and the neutrals.[4] The British would likewise find it difficult to restrain the Arab nationalism they had stoked. Poles on both sides proved reluctant to rise against one imperial regime simply to join another as a quasi-independent state. German governments remained sporadically concerned about the Bolshevik program to turn Russian defeat into European revolution. Revolution in Germany, in fact, was crucial to early Bolshevik plans to change the world.

Nor, of course, could revolution remain in state hands. Grass-roots discontent exacerbated by the strains of war challenged state authority everywhere.[5] Soldiers

---

[1] Mustafa Aksakal, "'Holy War Made in Germany'?: Ottoman Origins of the 1914 Jihad," *War in History* 18.2 (2011): 184–99.

[2] P.W. Dyer, "German Support of Lenin during World War I," *Australian Journal of Politics and History* 30.1 (1984): 46–55.

[3] Arno Mayer, *Political Origins of the New Diplomacy, 1917–1918* (New Haven, CT: Yale University Press, 1959), 305.

[4] See Sean McMeekin, *The Berlin-Baghdad Express: The Ottoman Empire and Germany's Bid for World Power* (Cambridge, MA: Belknap Press, 2010), 123–37.

[5] Richard Bessell, "Revolution," in Jay Winter, ed., *The Cambridge History of the First World War*, 3 vols. (Cambridge: Cambridge University Press, 2014), 2: 126–44; Leonard V. Smith, "Mutiny," 2: 196–217; Antoine Prost, "Workers," 2: 325–57; and Benjamin Ziemann, "Agrarian Society," 2: 382–407.

and sailors proved especially dangerous and volatile. Mutiny could destroy the war-time state, as well as articulate it. Wartime industry had brought millions more Europeans to factories, and into well-established patterns of labor unrest. Strikes and the prospect of strikes troubled the sleep of bosses and politicians for the duration. Historians are still trying to understand the nuances behind the apparent stoicism of the rural populations. They had borne more than their share of wartime suffering, simply because they constituted the single largest group in the belliger-ent armies. In fact, the rural population seldom posed a threat to the waging of war until the state itself disintegrated, as in Imperial Russia. There, cities and the countryside taking opposing sides provided a recipe for civil war.

Behind its exquisitely polite appearance, the Pan-African Congress beginning in Paris in February 1919 posed in its way a revolutionary challenge to the new inter-national system.[6] It brought together luminaries of the African diaspora such as W.E.B. Dubois of the United States and Blaise Diagne, a member of the French Chamber of Deputies representing the Four Communes of Senegal. The congress asserted itself as its own locus of sovereignty, representing peoples of African roots seeking various forms of self-determination. The Pan-African Congress sought to transform colonialism by putting African peoples under the protection of the League of Nations.

As provisional world sovereign, the Paris Peace Conference sought not so much to oppose revolution as to master it. The stated commitment to Wilsonianism had real consequences, whatever the intentions of those who made it. I begin by showing how the conference endeavored to master two sources of transnational revolution—anti-colonialism and industrial worker discontent. The peacemakers planned to give colonized peoples and workers a stake, however subordinated, in the new international order. The Mandate Principle sought to transform empire and in so doing highlighted the problematic nature of empire itself. The conference addressed the specter of workers' revolution through a long-run, transnational approach by forming the International Labour Organization (I.L.O.).

The second part of the chapter considers how the conference sought to master revolution at the state level through recognition—collective decisions admitting new states to the international system. All the new states had come into being through the overthrow of their former imperial masters. The council of Great Powers developed a template for a revolutionary liberal democracy in Czechoslovakia. This template proved ill-suited elsewhere, notably in successor Hungary and successor Romania. Eventually, recognition became not an expression of the sovereignty of the conference, but the site of compromise in articulating the international system. In its haphazard and unsuccessful dealings with revolutionary Russia, the confer-ence tried to master revolution as both a transnational and a state phenomenon. Russia and Bolshevism, it turned out, could survive beyond the sovereignty of the Paris Peace Conference.

---

[6] See P. Olisanwuche Esedebe, *Pan Africanism: The Idea and Movement, 1776–1991* (Washington, D.C.: Howard University Press, 1994), 3–94; and David Levering Lewis, *W.E.B. Du Bois: Biography of a Race, 1868–1919* (New York: Henry Hold and Company, 1993), 561–80.

PRE-EMPTING ANTI-COLONIALISM:
THE MANDATES

Much of the historiography of the mandates considers them from the perspective of what Michael Callahan called a "'new' colonialism."[7] This approach emphasizes what the mandates became—rebranded colonies, part of a rearguard stratagem to protect the dying enterprise of Great Power formal empire.[8] The mandates thus constituted a step back in the teleological march forward to decolonization after World War II. Consequently, Susan Pedersen has argued, the Mandate System deepened rather than resolved what she called the "crisis of empire" by making empire a matter of transnational concern through the League of Nations.[9]

Here, however, I focus on the establishment of the mandates, and why and how they came to assume the forms that they did. The Mandate System tried to pre-empt anti-colonialism, and its potential destabilization of the international system, by applying differentiated self-determination, actual or potential, to the colonized territories of the defeated Central Powers. To be sure, the Supreme Council only rarely discussed the mandates in this context in so many words. Sir Robert Borden of Canada opined before the Council of Ten on January 30 that "the future destinies of the world depended largely on it [a Mandate System] because there were forces in Russia which would manifest themselves unless some proposal of that kind could be accepted."[10] But ever since there had been European empires, competition among colonizers and revolts among the colonized had threatened the peace. The mandates evolved in part to pre-empt both forms of instability.

Mandates as a discursive construct evolved gradually. In a famous speech on British war aims given on January 5, 1918, Lloyd George stated that the "wishes and interests of the native inhabitants" had to be of primary concern, and the very purpose of outside rule was "to prevent their exploitation for the benefit of European capitalists or governments."[11] Far more explicitly than Wilson ever did, Lloyd George extended self-determination to the German colonies in Africa and the South Pacific:

> The natives live in their various tribal organizations under chiefs and councils who are competent to consult and speak for their tribes and members and thus to represent their wishes and interests in regard to their disposal. The general principle of national self-determination is, therefore, as applicable in their cases as in those of occupied European territories.

---

[7] Michael D. Callahan, *Mandates and Empire: The League of Nations in Africa, 1914–1931* (Brighton: Sussex Academic Press, 1999), 30.

[8] Jane Burbank and Frederick Cooper, *Empires in World History: Power and the Politics of Difference* (Princeton, NJ: Princeton University Press, 2010), 380–93; and William Mulligan, *The Great War for Peace* (New Haven, CT: Yale University Press, 2014), 267–301.

[9] Susan Pedersen, *The Guardians: The League of Nations and the Crisis of Empire* (Oxford: Oxford University Press, 2015).

[10] "Secretary's Notes of a Conversation Held at Mr. Pichon's Room at the Quai d'Orsay, Paris, on Thursday, January 30, 1919, at 11 a.m.," *FRUS: PPC*, 3: 794.

[11] David R. Woodward, "The Origin and Intent of David Lloyd George's January 5 War Aims Speech," *The Historian* 34.1 (1971): 22–39.

In his Fourteen Points speech just three days later, Wilson would stake out his own clearly revolutionary position. Point V called for "a free, open-minded, and absolutely impartial adjustment of all colonial claims, based upon a strict observance of the principle that in determining all such questions of sovereignty the interests of the populations concerned must have equal weight with the equitable claims of the government whose title is to be determined." This swiftly morphed into the Wilsonian tenet of "no annexations," in the nineteenth-century sense of a colonial power directly appropriating the sovereignty of a foreign domain.

But such general statements raised as many questions as they had answered. Did "self-determination" really apply everywhere? Where would sovereignty lie in determining the "free, open-minded, and absolutely impartial" adjudication of colonial claims—the peace conference, the future League, or a consortium of colonial powers? How to determine the interests of the concerned populations? What if their interests conflicted with the "equitable claims" of the colonial states? How could conflicting claims be reconciled if conflicting claims of colonizers and colonized had equal weight?

No one had thought more deeply, if idiosyncratically, about empire in the postwar world than General Jan Smuts of South Africa, more so than any of the other principal authors of the Covenant, including Lord Robert Cecil, Sir Walter Phillimore, Léon Bourgeois, or for that matter Woodrow Wilson. To be sure, Smuts held retrograde if common views on race. The former German colonies, he wrote in a pamphlet on the future League of Nations published in December 1918, were "inhabited by barbarians, who not only cannot possibly govern themselves, but to whom it would be impractical to apply any ideas of political self-determination in the European sense."[12] At most, the victors might ask such peoples the specious question of whether they would like the Germans to return as their rulers. But they could not be part of any Mandate System that envisioned independence, ever.

Yet at the same time, Smuts posited radical views for the modernization of empire, and the role of a future League of Nations in that historic task. Through the Great War, the German Empire, the Habsburg Monarchy, Imperial Russia, and the Ottoman Empire had succumbed to old age and moral decrepitude. In defeat, these ex-empires had collectively fallen into receivership. "Europe is being liquidated," he wrote, "and the League of Nations must be the heir to this great estate" (111). In a claim that seems strange today, he argued that the League already had a model in the "British Commonwealth of Nations."[13] This commonwealth comprised the white-led regimes in the United Kingdom, the Dominions, and the white-ruled Government of India, not to be confused with the totality of hierarchical contracts that made up the "British Empire." This commonwealth provided a role model "because it is based on the true principles of national freedom

---

[12] J.C. Smuts, *The League of Nations: A Practical Suggestion* (London: Hodder and Stoughton, 1918), 15.

[13] Lloyd George, for his part, remarked in September 1918: "In fact the league of nations has already begun. The British Empire is a league of nations." Quoted in Mark Mazower, *Governing the World: The History of an Idea* (New York: Penguin Press, 2012), 128.

and political decentralization" (9). He envisaged this commonwealth, and a League modeled after it, as a community of political equals (29–30).[14]

A League of equals, Smuts argued, could make responsible use of its inheritance. The League would become the provisional imperial power. For example, he considered the Republic of Georgia in former Imperial Russia as eligible for mandatory status. No mandatory power would be placed over Georgia without the consent of the Georgians, and the Georgian government would be in a strong position to determine just what level of assistance it would need from the League. Georgia could press the League for a change of mandatory power should the tutelary regime prove unsatisfactory (19–20). Syria, presumably under Faisal, could probably enjoy similar arrangements (16). In other cases, such as Palestine, Armenia, the Balkans, and Mesopotamia, more involved supervision would be indicated, because of the diversity and historic antagonisms of peoples living in those lands. The League would inherit the peacekeeping function of the former empires. Smuts did admit one non-reproducible difference between his British commonwealth and a League of Nations—the "common allegiance" to the British crown. Somewhat vaguely, he concluded that the League itself would have to come up with something comparable by way of "special arrangements" (30). Whatever these arrangements, the League would become the imperator guiding certain new states to independence.

Certainly, Smuts's League rested on white supremacy. Rulers of European descent would continue to govern Black Africans and Pacific Islanders as colonial subjects, outside the Mandate System. Smuts's world view accorded Arabic-speaking peoples of the Middle East, and far-flung Europeans in the Balkans and Georgia, some sort of improvable racial status. This made them eligible, eventually, for independence. But the point here revolves around Smuts's willingness to see the League as the solution to the problem of empire, through founding a different kind of global empire. Hence the appeal of Smuts to liberals at the conference, themselves no strangers to white supremacy.

Wilson also came to see the League as imperator. Isaiah Bowman took notes on a meeting with officials of The Inquiry aboard the *George Washington* on December 10, 1918. Wilson indicated that the German colonies should become the common property of the League of Nations. "The poison of Bolshevism," Wilson argued, "was accepted readily by the world because 'it is a protest against the way in which the world has worked.'" A "just" settlement of colonial questions would help displace the global threat of Bolshevism: "It was to be our business at the Peace Conference to fight for a new order, 'agreeably if we can, disagreeably if necessary.'"[15]

Wilson's draft posited a sovereign, imperial League.[16] The League would decide what there was to decide in all the German colonies and all the former Habsburg

[14] Smuts too could not control his own revolutionary message. See Daniel Gorman, *Dominions in The Emergence of International Society in the 1920s* (Cambridge: Cambridge University Press, 2012).

[15] Bowman's redaction of Wilson's words in Bowman's report to David Hunter Miller dated December 18, 1920. David Hunter Miller, *The Drafting of the Covenant*, 2 vols. (New York: G.P. Putnam's Sons, 1928), 1: 43.

[16] "Wilson's First Draft" (undated), in Miller, *Drafting of the Covenant*, 2: 12–15. See also George Curry, "Woodrow Wilson, Jan Smuts, and the Versailles Settlement," *American Historical Review* 66.4 (1961): 968–86.

and Ottoman domains. The League would become "the residuary trustee with [the] sovereign right of ultimate disposal or of continued administration in accordance with certain fundamental principles hereinafter set forth."[17] The draft article expressly forbade the annexation of any territories by any state inside or outside the League. The inhabitants, whether Europeans, Africans, Arabic-speakers, Pacific Islanders, or anybody else, would come to live in lands where "the rule of self-determination, or consent of the governed to their form of government shall be fairly and reasonably applied" (87). Such views if applied in the United States would have come as a welcome surprise to W.E.B. Dubois.

Indeed, legal expert David Hunter Miller took issue with such a sweeping application of self-determination. "This rule [of government by consent of the governed] as last stated," he opined, "is an American principle, whereas the rule of self-determination is one of very limited application and of practically no application at all in such territories as Turkey and the German Colonies" (87). Moreover, a general application of self-determination would preclude other desiderata in the new world order, such as the establishment of a Jewish homeland in Palestine or an autonomous Armenia, so depleted of Armenians by 1919 (87–88).

Nevertheless, the vast reach of Wilson's Mandate System survived in his next draft, dated January 20, 1919.[18] The League would hold "any authority, control, or administration which may be necessary in respect of these peoples and territories other than their own self-determined and self-organized autonomy" (103). The concerned peoples would nominate and/or approve the mandatory authority "wherever possible or feasible" (104). As Smuts had previously suggested, mandatory authority would mean different things in different places. A written contract would establish each mandate, a "special Act or Charter" (104). The League would have full enforcement powers, particularly guaranteeing the open door in trade, and in preventing militarization. Most radically, all mandates would expire eventually, to be replaced by something that certainly looked like independent nation-states:

> The object of all such tutelary oversight and administration on the part of the League of Nations shall be to build up in as short a time as possible out of the people or territory under its guardianship a political unit which can take charge of its own affairs, determine its own connections, and choose its own policies. (104)

Although he soon dropped the idea of mandates in Europe, Wilson continued to insist on the universality of "self-determination." We saw in Chapter 4 how he envisioned mandatory rule as a means toward the end of self-determination in former German South West Africa. Extending self-determination to Black Africans, Pacific Islanders, and former Ottoman peoples would have revolutionary implications for empire everywhere, and surely would have complicated Wilson's political position in the United States. Yet Wilson considered anything less as "annexation,"

[17] "Wilson's Second or First Paris Draft, January 10, 1919 with Comments and Suggestions by D.H.M.," Miller, *Drafting of the Covenant*, 2: 87.

[18] "Wilson's Third Draft or Second Paris Draft, January 20, 1919," Supplementary Agreements I–III, in Miller, *Drafting the Covenant*, 2: 103–04.

and a return to prewar imperial realism. Through the mandates, the League would be "seeking to lay down a law which would rally the whole world against an outlaw, as it had rallied against Germany during the last war."[19] Doubting the efficacy of this structure demonstrated "a fundamental lack of faith in the League of Nations."

Where would sovereignty actually lie in the new mandates? If the future League held sovereignty, it would have held a key attribute of a world state—something even its most avid supporters would have been reluctant to admit. The logical conclusion drawn from the Wilsonian imaginary was that sovereignty lay with "the peoples" of the mandate territories, and would be administrated by someone else until they could rule themselves effectively and justly. This logic, of course, drew Wilson much closer than he would have cared to admit to the Pan-African Congress. The mandatory principle to Wilson implied eventual independence. As H. Duncan Hall, who worked for the League secretariat, would put it: "The assumption [of the Mandate System] was that it would come to an end when the various mandated territories were able to 'stand by themselves.'"[20] The Dominions resisted it as ferociously as they did for precisely that reason.

As written, the Mandate System would revolutionize the trajectory of imperial rule. The classification system discussed in Chapter 4 sought to control that revolution through a territorial policy that became a population policy. Wilson's continued unease at the hazy distinction particularly between the "B-" and "C-" class mandates and annexation provoked the most intense argument that ever took place between himself and the Dominion delegates, on the afternoon of January 30.[21] Wilson asked whether the Dominions were in fact presenting an ultimatum, and linking the founding of the League to the acceptance of the Lloyd George compromise establishing the classification system (799). In the most commonly accepted version of the story, Wilson then asked Hughes: "Am I to understand that if the whole civilized world asks Australia to agree to a mandate for these islands [in the South Pacific], Australia is prepared to defy the opinion of the whole civilized world?" Hughes fiddled with his hearing aid, and asked him to repeat the question. When Wilson did so, he responded: "That's about the size of it, Mr. President."[22]

The French, representing the world's second most extensive empire, remained remarkably quiet through it all. Clemenceau had a personal contempt for empire, tempered by his appreciation of Great Power realism and his political dependence on the Colonial Lobby at home. He preferred direct annexation of the Cameroons and Togoland, though as he put it, "since Mr. Lloyd George was prepared to accept the mandate of a League of Nations he would not dissent from the general

---

[19] "Secretary's Notes of a Conversation Held in M. Pichon's Room at the Quai d'Orsay, Paris, on Monday, January 27, 1919, at 10hrs. 30," *FRUS: PPC*, 3: 742.

[20] H. Duncan Hall, *Mandates, Dependencies and Trusteeship* (Washington, D.C.: Carnegie Endowment for International Peace, 1948), 31.

[21] "Secretary's Notes of a Conversation Held in M. Pichon's Room at the Quai d'Orsay, Paris, on Thursday, January 30, 1919, at 15 Hours 30," *FRUS: PPC*, 3: 797–817.

[22] Quoted in Carl Bridge, *William Hughes: Australia* (London: Haus Publishing, 2011), 81–82. Bridge counted at least eight different (if similar) versions of this confrontation in the documentary and memoir record.

agreement, merely for the sake of the Cameroons and Togoland."[23] Clemenceau's more immediate concern involved protecting the French tradition of raising troops from Black Africa. In a notorious turn of phrase generally taken as indicating what Lloyd George actually thought of Black Africans, he assured his colleague: "so long as M. Clemenceau did not intend to train big nigger armies for the purposes of aggression, that was all this clause [against militarizing the mandates] was intended to guard against."[24]

The Supreme Council agreed on January 20 to return to its discussion of the mandates, but did not actually do so until May 7.[25] The discussion formalized the "unmixing" of mandatory lands, and avoided discussion of mandatory peoples.[26] Yet the revolutionary potential of the mandates would not disappear so easily. As a logic of political rule, the mandates, even in the compromised form in which they emerged in 1919, struck at the heart of empire. We can read the Mandates System as both revolutionary and counter-revolutionary. In accepting the mandates as written, the Great Powers agreed to a trajectory of history in which empire would never quite be the same. Even if one agreed that in 1919 Arabic-speaking peoples lived farther down the road to "civilization" than Black Africans, why should Black Africans in former German colonies be theoretically eligible at some indefinite point in the future for self-determination, and not Black Africans already under British, French, Belgian, or Portuguese rule? Conceding even theoretically the extension of self-determination beyond persons of European descent opened Pandora's Box, precisely why the Dominions had fought so hard to close it.

For all its flaws, the Mandate System made race a matter of international relations in new ways. It did so in combination with the rejection of the Japanese "racial equality clause" to be added to the League Covenant. A private note Colonel Edward House slipped to Wilson at a crucial point of the League commission discussions showed that House for one understood the real significance of the mandates: "The trouble is that if this Commission passes it [the racial equality clause], it would surely raise the race issue throughout the world."[27] The racial equality clause, certainly its first version, simply carried "self-determination" implicit in the Mandate Principle to a logical conclusion. An uncomfortable realization perhaps explains Wilson's dubious parliamentary maneuver to quash the clause in the commission, and the willingness of Imperial Japan to relinquish the clause upon recognition of its assumption of German rights in Shandong. Neither Wilson, nor the Japanese, nor their colleagues, could face the revolution of real racial equality around the world.

---

[23] "Secretary's Notes of a Conversation Held in M. Pichon's Room at the Quai d'Orsay, Paris, on Tuesday, 28 January, 1919, at 4:00 p.m.," *FRUS: PPC*, 3: 769.

[24] "Secretary's Notes," January 30, 1919, 15h30, *FRUS: PPC*, 3: 804.

[25] "Notes of a Meeting Held in the Conference Room of the Supreme War Council at the Grand Hotel Trianon, Versailles, on Wednesday, May 7, 1919, at 4:15 p.m.," *FRUS: PPC*, 5: 506–09.

[26] See also "Conversation between President Wilson, and MM. Clemenceau, Lloyd George, Orlando, Balfour, Baron Sonnino, and Henry Simon," May 7, 1919, 4:20 P.M., in Mantoux, *Deliberations*, 2: 507–09.

[27] House to Wilson, April 11, 1919, quoted in L.F. Fitzhardinge, "W.M. Hughes and the Treaty of Versailles, 1919," *Journal of Commonwealth Studies* 5.2 (1967): 139.

For its part, the Pan-African Congress did not forget the applicability implicit in the Mandate Principle of self-determination to all peoples. The next meeting of the congress took place in August and September 1921, and brought together persons of African descent from British-, French-, Belgian-, and Portuguese-ruled Africa, the Caribbean, the United States, and Europe. It welcomed "fraternal visitors" from India, Morocco, the Philippines, and French Indochina.[28] The congress addressed the League of Nations directly, believing, as DuBois put it, that "the greatest international body in the world must sooner or later turn its attention to the great racial problem as it today affects persons of Negro descent." The congress called on the League to make African labor across the diaspora a central concern. Further, "a man of Negro descent, properly fitted in character and training," should become a member of the Permanent Mandates Commission as soon as a vacancy occurred. The Pan-African Congress, surely comprising some of the most persistent believers in full-measure Wilsonian sovereignty, sought to revolutionize the new international system by joining it.

PRE-EMPTING WORKER UNREST:
THE INTERNATIONAL LABOUR ORGANIZATION

The Paris Peace Conference sought to integrate workers of the world into the international system through establishing the International Labour Organization (I.L.O.). The I.L.O. had a different relationship to Wilsonianism than the other international organization established by the conference, the League of Nations. The Fourteen Points had said nothing about labor. Neither did the Covenant of the League of Nations have much to say, as Patricia Clavin put it, "beyond a lofty pronouncement endorsing free trade,"[29] and the interdiction of any form of slavery in the mandates.[30] Rather, the conference itself sought to intervene in restructuring and co-opting an international labor movement torn apart by the war. The conference designed the I.L.O. to give workers an international forum, and to adjudicate their concerns within a system of global capitalism. The peacemakers thus sought to render the specter of Bolshevism irrelevant.

The conference took up the issue of labor against the backdrop of a complicated wartime record of collaboration, co-optation, and confrontation among labor, capital, and the state.[31] When war came in August 1914, patriotic workers on both sides abandoned the transnational unity of the Second International. When the

[28] W.E. Burghardt Dubois, "Manifesto to the League of Nations," *The Crisis*, 23 (November 1921): 18.

[29] Patricia Clavin, *Securing the World Economy: The Reinvention of the League of Nations, 1920–1946* (Oxford: Oxford University Press, 2013), 11.

[30] Amalia Ribi, "'The Breath of a New Life'?: British Anti-Slavery Activism and the League of Nations," in Daniel Laqua, ed., *Internationalism Reconfigured: Transnational Ideas and Movements between the World Wars* (London: I.B. Tauris, 2011), 93–113.

[31] John Horne, "Labor and Labor Movements in World War I," in Jay Winter, Geoffrey Parker, and Mary R. Habeck, eds., *The Great War and the Twentieth Century* (New Haven, CT: Yale University Press, 2000), 187–227.

stalemated war called for unprecedented industrial mobilization, workers, bosses, and politicians had to strike new kinds of bargains. But the strains of war would fray wartime collaboration. Wage increases stoked the inflation to which they constituted a response. Labor unrest increased everywhere in the last two years of the war, most of all in Britain and Germany, the two countries with the strongest union movements. As much as anyone, workers wanted a new and more just world after the Great War.

Given the international prominence of German labor unions before 1914, the war created a serious split in the international labor movement.[32] British, French, Belgian, and North American unions convened in Leeds in June 1916 to consider a plan from Léon Jouhaux of the French Confédération Générale du Travail (C.G.T.) to incorporate workers' interests into any peace treaty. In an attempt to repair unity among organized labor, the German president of the International Federation of Trade Unions (I.F.T.U.), Carl Legien, called an international conference in Berne, Switzerland in June 1917. Entente unions boycotted the event. French and Italian unions tried to attend a second conference in Berne the following October, only to be denied passports by their national governments.

The rupture continued after the armistice. The I.F.T.U. held another conference in Berne in February 1919. While the French sent delegates (including future I.L.O. Director General Albert Thomas), the Belgians declined because of German participation. Out of deference to the Belgians, British unions previously affiliated with the I.F.T.U. did not send representatives, though a British delegation from the Independent Labour Party included Ramsay MacDonald and Arthur Henderson.[33] The Americans declined to attend, because Samuel Gompers of the American Federation of Labor (A.F.L.) considered the occasion too "political" because of its proximity to the peace conference.

The manifesto from the February 1919 Berne conference tried to pick up where matters had left off with the Second International. It began with the flat assertion: "The emancipation of the workers cannot be completely realized except by the abolition of the capitalist system itself."[34] It maintained silence on the Bolshevik challenge to capitalism then unfolding in Russia. Specific demands were practical and immediate—such as a ban on industrial employment for children under the age of 15, assured maternity leave and maternity insurance, and an eight-hour workday and a forty-eight-hour workweek. Workers would acquire guaranteed rights of combination. Foreign workers would be treated equally to their domestic counterparts. "Emigration shall generally be free" (339), though states could limit immigration in difficult economic times, and stop it entirely for a time "in the interest of public health" (339).

---

[32] Reiner Tosstoroff, "The International Trade-Union Movement and the Founding of the International Labour Organization," *International Review of Social History* 50.3 (2005): 399–433.

[33] *International Socialism and World Peace: Resolutions of the Berne Conference, February, 1919*, I.L.P. Pamphlets, New Series, No. 1 (London: Independent Labour Party, 1919).

[34] "Manifesto of the International Trade Union Conference at Berne, February 10, 1919, on International Labor Legislation," in James Shotwell, *The Origins of the International Labor Organization*, 2 vols. (New York: Columbia University Press, 1934), 2: 336–40.

The manifesto called for a Labor Charter as part of any treaty of peace, which would also set up a permanent commission on labor. The states making up the membership of the League of Nations would name half the members of the commission, the I.F.T.U. the other half. The commission would draw up international legislation on labor, to be submitted to a yearly international conference. The contracting states would send half the delegates to this conference, the other half comprising "representatives of the organized workers in each country" (340). This body would constitute the locus of sovereignty on labor: "The resolutions of the Conference shall have legal force internationally" (340).

The Paris Peace Conference would co-opt several of these ideas in forming the I.L.O. Labor quickly found its way to the agenda of the conference. As early as January 5, a background document prepared for Clemenceau by André Tardieu referred to "international legislation on labor" as one of the main questions to be addressed by the conference.[35] At a meeting on January 17, the council of Great Powers affirmed international labor legislation as a subject "requiring immediate consideration," on which all states invited to the conference would be invited to present their views in writing to the conference secretariat.[36] On January 23, the Council approved a proposal according to which the conference would establish a commission on labor, with two members named by each of the Great Powers, and five more by the conference at large.[37] The plenary approved the establishment of the proposal on January 25.[38] The commission was to consider "the conditions of employment from the international aspect," as well as "the international means necessary to ensure common action" on labor questions. The commission would also make a recommendation on "the form of a permanent agency to continue such inquiry and consideration in co-operation with, and under the direction of the League of Nations" (Annex 4, 202–03).

By that time, the Council of Ten was already discussing a draft proposal from the British delegation. The British delegation saw the value of seizing the high ground simply by having a concrete proposal in hand well before anyone else. At the same time, British labor activists were already collaborating with their American and French colleagues.[39] Through these efforts, the three most powerful delegations had largely agreed on the framework of the British proposals before the Council ever saw them.[40]

---

[35] "Plan of the Preliminary Conversations between the Allied Ministers," January 5, 1919, *FRUS: PPC*, 1: 390.

[36] "Secretary's Notes of a Conversation held in M. Pichon's Room at the Quai d'Orsay, on Friday, January 17, 1919, at 15 O'clock (3 p.m.)," *FRUS: PPC*, 3: 609.

[37] "Secretary's Notes of a Conversation Held in M. Pichon's Room at the Quai d'Orsay on Thursday, January 23, 1919, at 10:30 O'clock a.m.," *FRUS: PPC*, 3: 697–98.

[38] "Preliminary Peace Conference, Protocol No. 2, Plenary Session of January 25, 1919," *FRUS: PPC*, 3: 176–207.

[39] Markku Ruotsila, "'The Great Charter for the Liberty of the Workingman': Labour, Liberals and the Creation of the ILO," *Labour History Review* 67.1 (2005): 29–47.

[40] See three accounts in Shotwell, *Origins*: Edward J. Phelan, "British Preparations" (1: 105–26); Charles Piquenard, "French Preparations" (1: 83–97); and Leifur Magnusson, "American Preparations" (1: 97–105).

In contrast to the manifesto from the Berne conference, the British proposals focused on organization rather than worker protection.[41] The organization would mirror the League of Nations in structure, and would be lodged alongside it. The organization would comprise an annual conference of delegates from the contracting states, each of which would send three delegates—one from the government, and one each from capital and labor. However, government delegates would receive two votes, to ensure that the interests of the states could not be outvoted.

A permanent International Bureau would handle the administrative functions of the new organization, "under the authority and protection of the Chancellor of the League" (139). The exact duties of the bureau, and indeed of the organization itself, would be determined by the first labor conference. But these were presumed to include gathering information on work conditions around the world, distributing that information to all governments, and carrying out such special investigations as the annual conference might require. The proposal did not say whether the organization could propose international agreements on labor, let alone issue its own rules protecting workers. The organization as outlined would not revolutionize the relationship between labor and capital around the world, but it would have much to do.

In Paris, the commission on labor debated issues that would frame the role of labor in the new international system. By definition, a new labor organization would constitute an international organization representing a transnational constituency. No state would surrender national representation in the new body. But how to represent the interests of labor, capital, and state within each national delegation? Moreover, what would be the status of the outcomes produced by the new organization? If its dictates had the status of international law, sovereignty over the workers of the world would in effect have passed to an issue-specific international parliament. If sovereignty over labor remained with the individual states, what actually would have changed in the new international system?

The commission in Paris debated these issues in February 1919. The British delegation wanted to create a labor conference that could pass binding conventions on labor.[42] Once passed by a two-thirds majority, conventions would become subject to ratification by national bodies. National governments would have the final say. But under a Wilsonian discursive structure, individual states would find it difficult to resist measures passed by a large majority in the interest of the transnational community of workers.

On February 17, George Barnes of Britain raised the issues of representation and what the labor conference would actually do.[43] He affirmed the importance of

[41] "Draft Convention Creating a Permanent Organisation for the Promotion of International Regulation of Labour Conditions, Prepared by the British Delegation, January 21, 1919," Shotwell, *Origins*, 2: 137–40.

[42] "Memorandum by the British Delegation on the Question of Voting Power at the Conference, February 10, 1919," Shotwell, *Origins*, 2: 330–35. This memo was a response to criticism of standing British proposals.

[43] Barnes emphasized limited and reformist objectives in *History of the International Labour Office* (London: Williams and Norgate, Ltd., 1926).

enabling the labor conference to pass binding conventions. Referring to the British proposal to give two votes to each state delegate (and one vote each for labor and capital), he observed that if the conference "were to concern itself simply with the expression of aspirations and to put forward the claims of the workers, there would evidently be no need to give two votes, or, indeed, any vote to the Governments."[44] An amendment proposed by Émile Vandervelde of Belgium and eventually accepted by the commission proposed essentially the same result, but with two government representatives rather than one with two votes. Significantly, delegates would not be required to vote by country. As Jouhaux would write later: "Still modest in its practical applications, this affirmation [of voting by member rather than by country] overthrew many juridical fictions hitherto sovereign."[45]

Differences over the role of national states revolved around whether the state itself was the friend or the foe of labor. The British reasoned that the state "represents the whole population, a greater voice than the representation of a particular section only of the population [that is, labor], however important."[46] Moreover states would have final say in ratifying whatever the labor conference did. The French and Italians also supported strong state representation in the labor conference, confident of the role of labor in shaping postwar national politics. Oka Minoru of Japan went so far as to assert that "the government was more concerned with the progress of labor legislation than were the working class themselves. To give strong representation to the Government was therefore to secure the success of this legislation."[47] In contrast, Samuel Gompers of the United States argued for direct worker representation in the new body.[48]

Of related concern was representing workers in the imperial domains. The matter seemed straightforward for the white-led Dominions, where according to Gompers, labor was "constructive, democratic, uncontaminated by any of the philosophies that are cousin to Bolshevism."[49] But some delegates advocated representing workers under other forms of colonial rule through the colonial power. No one advocated equal labor protection around the globe. Even Jouhaux contended: "There was no question of applying international labor legislation in its entirety to the Colonies, for there were differences which had to be taken into account." But he hastened to add that the future organization would concern itself with colonial labor, "not simply [as] a question of sentiment, but [as] one of the

[44] "Minutes of Proceedings No. 9—February 17, 1919," in Shotwell, *Origins*, 2: 175. Subsequent references will cite meeting number and date. LaPradelle, *Paix de Versailles,* Vol. 5, *Commission de la Législation Internationale du Travail* includes full French versions of the stenographic minutes as well as the official minutes (Procès-Verbal) for each meeting, which add nuance to the abridged versions in Shotwell.

[45] Léon Jouhaux, *L'Organisation internationale du travail* (Paris: Les Sirènes, 1921), 41.

[46] "British Memorandum on Voting," 2: 335.

[47] "Minutes of Proceedings No. 8—February 13, 1919," 2: 177.

[48] Wilson appointed Gompers to the labor commission, and apparently saw to his election as commission president. Elizabeth McKillen, *Making the World Safe for Workers: Labor, the Left, and Wilsonian Internationalism* (Urbana: University of Illinois Press, 2013), 181–207.

[49] Samuel Gompers, "The Labor Clauses of the Treaty," in Edward Mandell House and Charles Seymour, eds., *What Really Happened at Paris: The Story of the Peace Conference of 1918–1919 by American Delegates* (New York: Charles Scribner's Sons, 1921), 334.

development of civilization."[50] The labor commission cast aside organized representation of female labor altogether, though as we will see, the treaty would take a less retrograde position.[51]

The status of the outcomes produced by the new international labor organization proved the most controversial issue. The French and the Italians supported a capacity to legislate conventions with the legal status of treaties. Baron Edmondo Mayor des Planches of Italy proposed obligating all states participating in the annual labor conference to implement any convention approved by a two-thirds majority. States would have only the right to appeal to the League Council, which if it declined to review the matter, would leave the convention to stand. Émile Vandervelde of Belgium warned that this "amounted to the creation of a super-Parliament."[52] The American delegation, upon consultation with American legal experts, stated flatly that the United States Constitution could not accommodate labor legislation passed abroad.

Weeks of discussion revealed a nearly intractable problem—creating a new organization serving the transnational constituency that would be acceptable to national legal systems, such as that of the United States. Finally, James Shotwell, called in to consult with the American delegation, crafted a somewhat tortured compromise that appeared in the treaty.[53] Measures passed by the new labor conference could constitute either conventions for adoption by states or recommendations for domestic legislation. The language invited federal states (such as the United States or Canada) to take all measures passed by the labor conference as recommendations. Shotwell's proposal had its critics. Arthur Fontaine of France, perhaps condescendingly, explained the American resistance in terms of inexperience in the international politics of labor. Baron Mayor des Planches lamented that "the American counter-proposal weakens even further the posers of the [labor] Conference" (267–68). Gompers, on the other hand, proclaimed a triumph for Wilsonian sovereignty, in creating an organization that would emerge as "a moral force which has the power to bring truth into the light and give reason and justice an opportunity to be heard."[54]

The conference formally established the I.L.O. through Part XIII (a preamble and Articles 387–427) of the Treaty of Versailles.[55] The preamble laid out the stakes, asserting that the universal peace sought by the League of Nations "can be established only if it is based on social justice." Continuing that current sources of

---

[50] "Minutes of Proceedings No. 21—March 13, 1919," 2: 236.

[51] Following an audience given to a women's delegation that advocated the establishment of a consultative commission of women, Arthur Fontaine of France observed to general approval: "the proposal was of too exclusive a character and that there was no reason why a similar commission should not be set up as regards men." "Minutes of Proceedings No. 34—March 22, 1919," 2: 319.

[52] "Minutes of Proceedings No. 9—February 17, 1919," 2: 179–80.

[53] McKillen, *Making the World Safe for Workers*, 195–96; and Harold Josephson, *James T. Shotwell and the Rise of Internationalism in America* (Rutherford, NJ: Fairleigh Dickinson University Press, 1975). For the lively debate around the compromise, see "Minutes of the Proceedings No. 25—March 17, 1919," and "Minutes of the Proceedings No. 26—March 17, 1919," 2: 255–73.

[54] Gompers, "The Labor Clauses," 325.

[55] The other four treaties repeated these provisions verbatim, like the Covenant of the League of Nations.

injustice afflicting labor "produce unrest so great that the peace and harmony of the world are imperiled," the preamble went on to list specifics such as working hours, unemployment, wages, child and female labor, immigrant labor, and freedom of association. Section II, Article 427, commonly known as the "Labor Charter," reemphasized these specifics and added to them, as guiding principles for the new organization. In recognition of labor in colonies and in the mandates, and in newly industrializing countries such as Japan, the High Contracting Parties would "recognize that differences of climate, habits, and customs, and of economic opportunity and industrial tradition" would not for the time being make possible common labor standards across the globe. This kept faith with what Glenda Sluga called "the imperial spirit of the peace."[56]

But the charter set forth an ambitious agenda that encapsulated much of what the Berne conference of 1919 had advocated. Above all, "labor should not be regarded merely as a commodity or article of commerce," arguably the most anti-capitalist sentiment expressed in the entire treaty. The organization would aspire to achieving for workers "a wage adequate to maintain a reasonable standard of life as this is understood in their time and country." It would also pursue an eight-hour workday and a forty-eight-hour workweek, as well as full rights of association for employees and employers. The I.L.O. would include women in making some kinds of decisions,[57] and would commit itself to "the principle that men and women should receive equal remuneration for work of equal value."

The I.L.O. would comprise an International Labor Office and a General Conference of Representatives that would meet at least annually. The office would organize the conference and would produce and disseminate information on labor worldwide. Each contracting state would send four delegates: two representing the government, and one each representing capital and labor (Article 389). All delegates would be named by the state in question, but the General Conference would review the credentials of all delegates to ensure proper representation. As per the Shotwell compromise, the General Conference could pass either recommendations or draft conventions, with the assumption that federal states would interpret all measures passed as recommendations (Article 405). However, should a member state violate a convention it had ratified, other member states could raise a complaint with the International Labor Office (Article 411). A Commission of Enquiry would make a report to the secretary general of the League of Nations. Should negotiations facilitated by the League not resolve the matter, it could be referred to the (not yet established) Permanent Court of International Justice, whose judgment of the facts and remedies would be final (Articles 415–18).

---

[56] Glenda Sluga, *Internationalism in the Age of Nationalism* (Philadelphia: University of Pennsylvania Press, 2013), 50.

[57] Article 389 stipulated that delegates could bring up to two technical advisers to the annual conference: "When questions specifically affecting women are to be considered by the Conference, one at least of the advisers should be a woman." Article 426 placed women's employment on the agenda for the first General Conference.

An April 11 plenary session of the Paris Peace Conference accepted these articles with much comment but little controversy.[58] Barnes of Britain presented the recommendations of the commission, adding: "I need scarcely remind you [the plenary] of the urgency of this work of labor amelioration because it is known to all of us that new thoughts are surging up all around and among us, and as a result the world is at present in a ferment" (247). In other words, the role of labor in the world was changing, and the Paris Peace Conference could embrace that change, or reject it at its peril. Vandervelde of Belgium saw a vast "transition between the absolutism of the employers, which was the rule of yesterday, and the sovereignty of labor, which I am ardently convinced will be the rule of tomorrow" (253). In effect, he continued, a revolution was afoot that the new I.L.O. would seek to master:

> If I dared to express my thoughts in a tangible way, I should feel that there are two methods of making the revolution which we feel is happening throughout the world, the Russian and the British method. It is the British method which has triumphed in the Labor commission.... (253)[59]

The French and Italians wistfully regretted that the commission had not been able to agree on a labor organization with more of a legislative capacity. Yet they recognized the timeless adage that politics is the art of the possible. French Minister for Labor Pierre Colliard concluded generously: "We regret none of these sacrifices, certain as we are that the future will bring with it the settlement most favorable to a progressive and continuous improvement in Labor legislation" (248).

President Wilson, for his part, endorsed the recommendations with "the greatest heartiness" (247), as well he might have. As much as the Covenant of the League of Nations, the I.L.O. both affirmed state sovereignty and provided an institutional moral compass, formed to guide state behavior in the new international system.[60] The transnational community of labor would find representation through national delegations. States would nominate all delegates, and half of all delegates would directly represent state interests. Yet to believers in Wilsonian sovereignty, the new organization would hold real power. What capitalist liberal democracy could resist the reformist will of the mobilized workers of the world, whether that reformism expressed itself as draft conventions or as recommendations? Drawing in part from the early history of the I.L.O., political scientist Ernst B. Haas in the 1960s would develop a functionalist theory, according to which international organizations could gradually displace state authority itself.[61] Certainly, the first

---

[58] "Preliminary Peace Conference, Protocol No. 4, Plenary Session of April 11, 1919," *FRUS: PPC*, 3: 240–60.

[59] James Shotwell, "The International Labor Organization as an Alternative to Violent Revolution," *Annals of the American Academy of Political and Social Science* 166 (1933): 18–25.

[60] Eventually, the contracting states would conclude that the I.L.O. and the League of Nations were legally distinct. See Jean Morellet, "Legal Competence of the International Labor Organization," *Annals of the American Academy of Political and Social Science* 166 (1933): 46–52.

[61] Ernst B. Haas, *Beyond the Nation-State: Functionalism and International Organization* (Stanford, CA: Stanford University Press, 1964).

director of the I.L.O., French reformist socialist Albert Thomas, saw his duty along these lines.[62]

The historiography of the I.L.O. has been tinged with regret that the transnational community of labor found expression in an international rather than supranational organization with binding legislative power. Reiner Tosstoroff, for example, explained this outcome by the fact that socialist politicians and diplomats seized the initiative from trade unionists. As a result, he argued: "Rather than 'content', the I.L.O. offered only 'form'." By this, he meant that the I.L.O. assumed the all-too-familiar form of an international talking shop, "just a public platform for trade-union demands, not the decisive *lever* by which they could be realized."[63] I would argue, however, that for the I.L.O. as it emerged from the Paris Peace Conference, the content *was* the form. The conference established an international organization to serve a transnational constituency. It would become one thing if Wilsonian sovereignty existed, another if it did not.

In very different ways, the conference designed the mandates and the I.L.O. in part to master revolution by incorporating potential revolutionary constituencies into the international system. Yet each created a logic that would resist mastery. The Mandate Principle pointed to a historical trajectory beyond colonialism toward national independence. Was it ever reasonable to think that the League of Nations, or the imperial powers themselves, could forever limit this trajectory to the former German and Ottoman imperial domains? The I.L.O. sought to accommodate labor within global capitalism. But it faced a powerful competitor in Bolshevism, which provided its own logic, and its own imagined transnational community for labor. That alternative would bitterly divide both labor and socialists across Europe and beyond.

RECOGNIZING REVOLUTION IN THE SUCCESSOR STATES

Contemporaries, particularly in the successor states, saw the end of the multi-national empires as its own form of revolution. "Ending" the revolution in the successor states depended in part on achieving recognition in the international system. From the point of view of the allies and later the Supreme Council, granting and refusing recognition was thus central to mastering revolution, and in doing so affirming their sovereignty over the new international system. What would qualify a given new state for admission to the system? Sovereignty in a Weberian sense, in any event a rare commodity in Central and Eastern Europe after the armistices, would not in itself satisfy the logic of Wilsonianism. The international system itself, that logic went, had changed, and had placed liberal democracies at its core. Internal legitimacy externally confirmed and coded as "self-determination" would underpin

---

[62] Albert Thomas, "The International Labour Organisation: Its Origins, Development and Future," *International Labour Review* 136 (1996 [originally published 1921]): 261–76.

[63] Tosstoroff, "International Trade-Union Movement," 432–33. Emphasis in the original.

recognition. Democratic Great Powers would recognize emerging democracies, and in doing so would create and enforce new norms for the system.

By the early twentieth century, diplomatic recognition under international law had acquired clear forms, contents, and meanings. Traditionally, recognition would occur bilaterally. As Hans Agné put it: "International recognition takes place most visibly when an existing government announces that another political entity has become a sovereign state."[64] Two states exchange diplomats, and engage in the ceremonial trappings and policy intrigues of regular diplomacy. As the Great War began to end, recognition became more collective. Bilateral recognition had the effect of nudging other Allied and Associated Powers toward a collective decision. As the conference became established, recognition and non-recognition became the main, and in the end the only, form of power it held in the vast swaths of Europe in which it had little to no military force.

Scholars of international law have debated exactly what recognition does. According to the constitutive theory of recognition, the international system actually creates new states by recognizing them as members of the international system. A state, in other words, is not fully sovereign until other states recognize it as such. A critical aspect of statehood thus remains external to the state in question. Correspondingly, the withdrawal of recognition would mean that in some sense a state would cease to exist, or would exist only as an outcast to the system. In contrast, under the declaratory theory, the international system reacts rather than creates. It simply recognizes the self-declared state sovereignty that already exists. States thus create themselves. Revolutionaries would stress the declaratory theory, as a successful revolution ipso facto creates or recreates a state. A peace conference, on the other hand, would stress the constitutive theory.

Eva Erman has argued for considering both theories in combination to understand how recognition actually operates.[65] Such an approach seems particularly important historically. States do not simply exist because they say so, and recognition, while necessary, seems insufficient to create them. The Paris Peace Conference applied inconsistent criteria to the recognition of different successor states, all of them created through some form of revolution. Stephen Krasner has argued that such inconsistencies are not aberrations, but rather intrinsic to any international system as "organized hypocrisy."[66] Recognition after the Great War proved more a process of organized hypocrisy than an event. It comprised a variety of gestures—from recognizing aspects of statehood as a prelude to recognizing statehood, to sending fact-finding missions to states that theoretically did not exist, to threatening to de-recognize a recognized allied state.

Constitutive and declarative theories worked in tandem in the recognition of Czechoslovakia. During the war and immediately after, nationalist leaders bit by

---

[64] Hans Agné, "The Politics of International Recognition: Symposium Introduction," *International Theory* 5.1 (2013): 95. Subsequently referred to as *Recognition Symposium*.

[65] Eva Erman, "The Recognitive Practices of Declaring and Constituting Statehood," *Recognition Symposium*, 129–50.

[66] Stephen D. Krasner, "Recognition: Organized Hypocrisy Once Again," *Recognition Symposium*, 170–76.

bit declared a Czechoslovak state. Along the way, the allies recognized aspects of that state, and ultimately the Czechoslovak state itself. By the time the Paris Peace Conference opened, "Czechoslovakia" had attained full membership as a recognized liberal democracy. In that state, nationalists and allies alike appeared to have mastered the inherently destabilizing phenomenon of revolution. The conference sought with ever-increasing difficulty to apply the template of Czechoslovakia elsewhere.

Erik Ringmar has characterized "self-recognition" as a crucial first stage of recognition.[67] New states learn to recognize themselves through creating autobiographical narratives. "Czechoslovak" national narratives had blended characteristics of an urbane, Protestant-led Bohemia with those of an agrarian, Catholic, and far more traditional Slovakia.[68] The Czech lands led, Slovakia followed. Tomáš Masaryk explained the recognition of Czechoslovakia as material reality catching up with discursive reality.[69] In the sixteenth century, a timeless "Czech nation" allied with Austria and Hungary to protect Europe by driving off "the Turkish danger." Once that alliance had served its purpose, Habsburg rule became essentially coercive. Through the nineteenth century, the Czech and (rarely mentioned) Slovak nations resisted through a continuing cultural revolution to assert their language and culture. By igniting the Great War, the Habsburgs shattered whatever remained of royal and imperial legitimacy. "Our revolution," Masaryk wrote in 1918, "is fully justified by the democratic effort for the restitution of our rights and independence" (386).

This narrative in hand, exiled Czech leaders, such as Masaryk, Edvard Beneš, and later Slovak nationalist Milan Štefánik, spent the war years lobbying allied governments. "I was a revolutionary instrument," Masaryk would write of himself some years later.[70] Czechs and Slovaks in uniform never embraced the Habsburg cause, a wartime mythology explained, and deserted to the Russians at the earliest opportunity.[71] The military arm of the new state would emerge from this population. Czecho-Slovak military units composed of exiles and former prisoners of war would fight in France, Italy, and most importantly, in Russia. "An independent army," Masaryk would remind his readers, "is always considered one of the chief attributes of sovereignty."[72] Eventually, exiles would establish a proto-state, the Czecho-Slovak National Council. "The National Council became a *de facto* Government," Masaryk wrote, "which, like our army, was progressively recognized

[67] Erik Ringmar, "The International Politics of Recognition," in Thomas Lindemann and Erik Ringmar, eds., *The International Politics of Recognition* (Boulder, CO: Paradigm Publishers, 2012), 6.

[68] Nadya Nedelsky, *Defining the Sovereign Community: The Czech and Slovak Republics* (Philadelphia: University of Pennsylvania Press, 2009).

[69] Thomas G. Masaryk, "The Czechoslovak Nation," *The Nation* 107, No. 2779, October 5, 1918, 386–88.

[70] Thomas Garrigue Masaryk, *The Making of a State: Memories and Observations, 1914–1918* (New York: Frederick A. Stokes Company, 1927), 377.

[71] More recent research has questioned the trope of "disloyal" Czechs. Richard Lein, "The Military Conduct of the Austro-Hungarian Czechs in the First World War," *The Historian* 26.3 (2014): 518–49; and Alon (Iris) Rachamimov, *POWs and the Great War: Captivity on the Eastern Front* (Oxford: Berg, 2002), 133–39.

[72] Masaryk, "Czechoslovak Nation."

by the Allied Governments."[73] All that remained was for the allies formally to recognize the new state as a partner in making peace.

The problem was that both the Czech and Slovak forces and the National Council remained far from Bohemia, Moravia, and Slovakia. Before the revolutionaries could exercise Weberian sovereignty, what exactly would recognition recognize? Allied recognition did not so much respond to the Czech and Slovak revolution as seek to foster it. In so doing, the allies also sought to create norms under the new international system. In recognizing "Czechoslovakia" the Great Powers could legitimize certain kinds of revolutions and delegitimize others. Recognized Czechoslovakia eventually became an idealized, liberal, self-determined, ethno-national state.

The Allied and Associated Powers recognized different attributes of "Czechoslovakia" for different reasons at different times.[74] As early as December 1917, the French recognized a Czecho-Slovak Legion, to be recruited from Czechs and Slovaks living outside the Habsburg Monarchy.[75] Soldiers of the Legion would serve under a Czechoslovak flag, but under the command of the French army. The whole matter of the Legion would become much more fraught after the signing of the Treaty of Brest-Litovsk on March 3, 1918. Article 8 of the treaty called for the repatriation of all prisoners of war. The French, daily more desperate for manpower, advocated an idiosyncratic form of "repatriation" by way of service on the Western Front. A complicated plan to "repatriate" some 70,000 Czech and Slovak prisoners through Siberia swiftly turned the Legion into a belligerent on the side of the Whites in the Russian Civil War.[76] "Rescuing" the Czecho-Slovak Legion provided the British, French, Italians, and Americans with a rationale for sending troops to Siberia, alongside the Japanese, who had their own agenda.[77]

Few today regard this intervention as anything but unwise. But at the time, it gave the allied powers an additional reason to recognize Czech and Slovak belligerency, and a political authority behind that belligerency. Yet the uncertain state of the war on the Western Front in the spring of 1918 made the Allied and Associated Powers cautious as to just what they would recognize. On April 21, Italy joined France in recognizing the belligerency of the Czecho-Slovak Legion, and of the Czecho-Slovak National Council in Paris.[78] The British followed on June 3,

---

[73] Masaryk, *Making of a State*, 378.

[74] Josef Kalvoda, *The Genesis of Czechoslovakia* (Boulder, CO: East European Monographs, 1986), 377–416.

[75] "Decree on Formation of Czechoslovak Legion," December 16, 1917, in Cestmir Jesina, ed., *The Birth of Czechoslovakia* (Washington, D.C.: Czechoslovak National Council of America, 1968), 19–20. This volume conveniently brings together reprints and translations of the central primary texts.

[76] According to estimates at the time, the Czecho-Slovak Legion comprised some 8,000 Slovaks, or under 12% of the total. Jozef Lettrich, *History of Modern Slovakia* (New York: Frederick A. Praeger, 1955), 51.

[77] Popular history has long been drawn to the Czech Legion. See, for example, Kevin J. McNamara, *Dreams of a Great Small Nation: The Mutinous Army that Threatened a Revolution, Destroyed an Empire, Founded a Republic, and Remade the Map of Europe* (New York: PublicAffairs, 2016).

[78] Memo from the Italian Ambassador to Secretary of State Lansing, May 7, 1918, in Jesina, ed., *Birth of Czechoslovakia*, 28–29.

recognizing "the Czechoslovak Army as an organized unit operating in the Allied cause" and the "Czechoslovak National Council as the supreme organ of the Czechoslovak movement in the Allied countries."[79] None of this amounted to recognizing a territorial "Czechoslovakia," every hectare of which remained under Habsburg rule. The American government proved even more cautious, limiting itself through the summer of 1918 to vague gestures of support of Masaryk and the Czech and Slovak cause.[80] The Fourteen Points, after all, had not explicitly called for the breakup of the Habsburg Monarchy.

Public statements from Czech and Slovak nationalists had long proclaimed an ongoing liberal revolution. Crucially, and in conspicuous contrast to the bitter internal rivalries in Poland and future Yugoslavia, unified voices proclaimed "Czechoslovakia" in the allied public sphere. As early as the Cleveland Agreement of October 22, 1915, expatriate Czechs and Slovaks agreed to work for a future federal-style state. The Epiphany Declaration of January 6, 1918, made by Czech deputies in the Vienna Reichrat, called for a "sovereign, equal, democratic and socially just state of its own, built upon the equality of all its citizens within the historic boundaries of the Bohemian Lands and of Slovakia, guaranteeing full and equal rights to all minorities."[81] The Pittsburg Agreement of May 31, 1918, signed by representatives of Czech and Slovak groups in the United States in the presence of Masaryk, affirmed that "the Czechoslovak State shall be a republic, and its constitution a democratic one."[82]

As the tide of battle turned over the summer of 1918 on the Western Front, in the Balkans, and in the Middle East, the pace of recognition quickened. On June 29, 1918, a letter from French Foreign Minister Stephen Pichon proclaimed the intent of the French government "to recognize publicly and officially the National Council as the supreme organ of the general interests and policy of the future Czechoslovak Government."[83] By definition, however, a "future" government was not an actual one. On August 9, the British Foreign Office echoed this recognition by promissory note through recognizing "the right of the Czecho-Slovak National Council, as the supreme organ of the Czecho-Slovak National interests, and as the present trustee of the future Czecho-Slovak Government, to exercise supreme authority over this Allied and belligerent Army [the Czech and Slovak Legion]."[84] The Japanese, with the most direct interest in Czech and Slovak belligerency in Siberia, would recognize the Czecho-Slovak National Council as the supreme political authority over the Legion on September 9.[85]

[79] Arthur James Balfour to Edvard Beneš, June 3, 1918, in Jesina, ed., *Birth of Czechoslovakia*, 38.

[80] Victory S. Mamatey, "The United States Recognition of the Czechoslovak National Council of Paris (September 3, 1918)," *Journal of Central European History* 13 (1953): 47–60.

[81] "The Epiphany Declaration," January 6, 1918, in Jesina, ed., *Birth of Czechoslovakia*, 22.

[82] "Czecho-Slovak Agreement," May 31, 1918, in Jesina, ed., *Birth of Czechoslovakia*, 35.

[83] Stephen Pichon to Edvard Beneš, June 29, 1918, in Jesina, ed., *Birth of Czechoslovakia*, 48.

[84] Foreign Minister Arthur James Balfour to Edvard Beneš, August 9, 1918, in Jesina, ed., *Birth of Czechoslovakia*, 63.

[85] "Japan Recognizes the Czechoslovak National Council," September 9, 1918, in Jesina, ed., *Birth of Czechoslovakia*, 78.

On September 3, after extensive discussions within the State Department, the United States offered a highly specific de facto recognition to the Czecho-Slovak National Council.[86] First and foremost, as Victor Mamatey noted, the United States based its recognition not in the already contentious principle of "national self-determination," but on the material fact of Czech and Slovak belligerency.[87] Czecho-Slovak sovereignty, to the Americans, took shape from below. "The Czecho-Slovak peoples, having taken up arms against the German and Austro-Hungarian Empires," the statement asserted, "had placed organized armies in the field which are waging war against those Empires under officers of their own nationality and in accordance with the rules and practices of civilized nations." Of course, reasonable people could differ as to whether a Czech and Slovak Legion fighting Bolsheviks in Siberia actually constituted a national uprising against Habsburg rule. Yet furthermore, to those who supported recognition, the "Czecho-Slovaks" had "confided supreme political authority to the [Paris-based] Czecho-Slovak National Council." This convergence of the military and the political provided a means of entering "formally into relations with the de facto government thus constituted for prosecuting the war against the common enemy," identified not as the Bolsheviks, but as Germany and Austria-Hungary.

As the crumbling of Austria-Hungary and Imperial Germany continued, the Czechs and Slovaks refined the public presentation of their liberal, democratic revolution. On September 28, a joint resolution from the Czecho-Slovak National Committee in Prague and the Union of Czech Deputies in the Reichrat pointedly rejected any reformist schemes from the House of Habsburg: "Our nation has nothing in common with those who are responsible for the horrors of this war."[88] On October 14, the National Council in Paris declared itself the Provisional Government of a Czecho-Slovak Republic, with Masaryk as president, Beneš as foreign minister, and Štefanik as minister of war. This Provisional Government would seek to enter into formal diplomatic relations with allied governments.[89] The same day, the Czech Social Democrats and the Czech National Socials in Prague declared themselves "representatives of a new State, as citizens of a free Czechoslovak Republic."[90]

Four days later, on October 18, 1918, the National Council in Paris issued its Declaration of Independence, which bore a non-coincidental resemblance to its American counterpart. Like the American colonists, Czech and Slovak nationalists

---

[86] Statement by Secretary of State Robert Lansing, September 3, 1918, in Jesina, ed., *Birth of Czechoslovakia*, 74. On October 3, the Italian government would declare retroactively that its recognition of Czecho-Slovak belligerency on April 21 had amounted to recognition of a de facto government. Declaration of Vittorio Orlando, October 3, 1918, in Jesina, ed., *Birth of Czechoslovakia*, 83–84.

[87] Mamatey, "United States Recognition," 58.

[88] "A Resolution Adopted by the National Committee in Prague and the Union of Czech Deputies on September 29, 1918," in Jesina, ed., *Birth of Czechoslovakia*, 83.

[89] Edvard Beneš to the heads of the allied governments, October 14, 1918, in Vladimir Nosek, *Independent Bohemia* (London: J.M. Dent & Sons, 1918), 176–78.

[90] "Czechoslovak Socialists Proclaim a Free Republic," October 14, 1918, in Jesina, ed., *Birth of Czechoslovakia*, 85.

emphasized the Lockean nature of their revolution.[91] Czecho-Slovaks in 1918, like Americans in 1776, had reverted to a state of nature, and had a historic opportunity to create something new. The new Czecho-Slovak republic would rest on universal suffrage (male and female), freedom of religion and assembly, and on the separation of church and state. The republic would not discriminate among citizens: "The rights of the minority shall be safeguarded by proportional representation; national minorities shall enjoy equal rights." "Czechoslovakia," if not yet quite sovereign in Prague, was ready to take its recognized place among the victorious liberal democracies.

It remained only to unite the revolutionaries in exile with the revolutionaries at home. This occurred on October 28, with the declaration from the National Committee in Prague: "Today the Czechoslovak State has entered into the ranks of the independent States of the World."[92] The proclamation named Masaryk and Wilson as joint liberators. On October 20, a Slovak National Council proclaimed: "The Slovak Nation is part of the Czecho-Slovak Nation, united in language and in the history of its culture, in all the cultural struggles which the Czech Nation has fought and which have made it known throughout the world, the Slovak branch has also participated."[93] Even the normally skeptical historian Andrea Orzoff affirmed the harmonious knitting together of expatriates and officials who only days before had drawn pay from the Habsburg Monarchy.[94] "Czechoslovakia" completed its self-recognizing by proclaiming its democratic credentials.

The Paris Peace Conference would seek to instrumentalize the Czechoslovak revolution fostered by the allies by inviting the new republic to participate in the international system. Czechoslovakia declared, and the conference constituted. Beneš duly would take his seat at the first plenary meeting on January 18, 1919. "The Czecho-Slovaks won their right to independence," President Raymond Poincaré of France would proclaim, "in Siberia, in France, and in Italy."[95] In recognizing "Czechoslovakia" as part of an international system just then beginning to redesign itself in Paris, the new state would participate in the construction of an idealized successor state identity—nationalist as well as democratic. "Czechoslovakia" had also ended the war on the winning side, in geopolitical and Wilsonian terms.

A parallel and equally democratic revolution was occurring in Germany at the same time. International law had long assumed a continuity of state personhood,

---

[91] "Declaration of Independence of the Czechoslovak Nation by Its Provisional Government," October 18, 1918, in Jesina, ed., *Birth of Czechoslovakia*, 93–99.

[92] "The Birth of Czechoslovakia," October 28, 1918, in Jesina, ed., *Birth of Czechoslovakia*, 105–06.

[93] "The Slovak Declaration," October 30, 1918, in Jesina, ed., *Birth of Czechoslovakia*, 107–08. See also Natalia Krajčovičová, "Slovakia in Czechoslovakia, 1918–1938," in Mikulas Teich, Dusan Kovac, and Martin D. Brown, eds., *Slovakia in History* (Cambridge: Cambridge University Press, 2011), 137–55.

[94] Andrea Orzoff, *Battle for the Castle: The Myth of Czechoslovakia in Europe, 1900–1948* (New York: Oxford University Press, 2009), 50.

[95] "Preliminary Peace Conference, Protocol No. 1, Session of January 18, 1919," *FRUS: PPC*, 3: 162.

independent of the regime in charge.[96] "France" remained "France" when the Bourbons replaced Napoleon in 1815, and when the Third Republic replaced the Second Empire in 1871. As we saw in Chapter 2, even Brockdorff-Rantzau's challenge to the draft treaty of Versailles rested more on the presumed Wilsonian contract made at the armistice than on a "Germany" that had become something else through revolution. International recognition of Germany thus would be continuous, and a peace treaty would simply restore normal diplomatic relations. The problem from the point of view of the conference was whether the Germans could master their own revolution, and support a government willing to sign a treaty constructing a criminalized Great Power.

Discussion in the Supreme Council of the risk of Bolshevism spreading to Germany remained surprisingly sporadic. The Spartacist revolt was coming to its bloody conclusion just as the Paris Peace Conference was getting underway in January 1919.[97] In his "Fontainebleau Memo" of March 25, Lloyd George expressed his concern that "Germany may throw her lot with Bolshevism and place her resources, her brains, her vast organizing power at the disposal of the revolutionary fanatics whose dream is to conquer the world for Bolshevism by force of arms."[98] But he wrote this memo as part of the protracted struggle over reparations, which Lloyd George had done as much as anyone to enflame. His anxiety about Bolshevism struck some of his colleagues as situational. The ill-fated Bavarian Soviet Republic of April–May 1919 merited scant mention. On April 8, Lloyd George spoke of events in Munich, but only in the context of whether there would be a unitary Germany able to sign the treaty.[99] Well aware of the conservative Catholic hinterland surrounding Munich, the Supreme Council on April 12 discussed a proposal of Marshal Foch to establish contact with representatives of the Peasants' League in Bavaria.[100]

Clearly, Foch already had in mind plans to invade the principalities of southern Germany. When the Supreme Council turned to a serious discussion of Foch's plans in the tense last weeks before the signing of the treaty, the peacemakers neglected even to mention the threat of Bolshevism reviving in Germany. By that time, a German "revolution" would arrive externally through the dismemberment of Germany by the allied armies. The allies would cross the bridge of recognizing multiple German states when and if they arrived at it.

For the states designated by the conference as criminalized residuals of the former empires—Austria, post-Ottoman Turkey, and Hungary—recognition

---

[96] For example, Lassa Oppenheim wrote: "A State remains one and the same international person in spite of changes in its headship, in its dynasty, in its form, in its rank and title, and in its territory." *International Law: A Treatise* (New York: Longmans, Green, and Co., 1905), 115.

[97] Eric Weitz, *Creating German Communism, 1890–1990* (Princeton, NJ: Princeton University Press, 1997), 62–99.

[98] "A Memorandum by David Lloyd George," March 25, 1919, *PWW*, 56: 261.

[99] "Conversation between MM. Clemenceau, Lloyd George, Orlando, and Colonel House," April 8, 1919, in Mantoux, *Deliberations*, 1: 183. See also Allan Mitchell, *Revolution in Bavaria, 1918–1919: The Eisner Regime and the Soviet Republic* (Princeton, NJ: Princeton University Press, 1965).

[100] "Conversation between President Wilson and MM. Clemenceau, Lloyd George, and Orlando," April 12, 1919, in Mantoux, *Deliberations*, 1: 234–35.

posed distinctly different issues. In each case, recognition by the conference implied both continuity and the creation of a new state. For Austria and post-Ottoman Turkey, the storyline of recognition proved straightforward, for reasons explored in Chapter 2. A republic of Austria was born through an exceedingly polite "revolution" on October 21, 1918 by sitting members of the Imperial Reichrat.[101] Thereafter, Austria proved generally a pliant successor state, which the allies cautiously began to rehabilitate as the "Other" of the recalcitrant German successor state taking shape in Weimar. In Turkey, as we saw in Chapters 1 and 2, the regime of the semi-captive sultan basically did what it was told, including signing the Treaty of Sèvres. All the time, however, a "revolution" was taking place under a new regime led by Mustafa Kemal. This regime would reverse the outcome of the war in Anatolia. It would achieve de facto and then formal recognition as an equal through the Conference of Lausanne. Bulgaria, its own state before the war, simply changed tsars, and somewhat curtailed his powers. The continuity of the Bulgarian state was never in question. In all the cases discussed up to this point— Czechoslovakia, Germany, Austria, the sultan's Turkey, and Bulgaria—recognition proceeded in one direction. The principal Allied and Associated Powers made a unilateral decision to recognize these states which, however reluctantly, accepted recognition on the conditions offered.

The eventual recognition of successor Hungary calls for a more involved explanation. Recognizing revolution in Hungary cannot be disentangled from what the IR scholar Erik Ringmar has called the "recognition game," played not so much for gain or loss in realist terms as for mutual definition.[102] Such a game, as he put it, is not about "what we can win, but instead who or what we can be" (120). "Self-recognition" eventually requires some form of external recognition. Three entities played the "recognition game" in and around Hungary. The Supreme Council recognized itself as the sovereign authority over recognition, and at least in theory, required all parties to the peace to do the same. Revolutionary Hungary tried to achieve internal instability through self-recognition, and ultimately external recognition, as a wronged successor state. Romania recognized itself as a victorious ally, as a justly irredentist successor state, and as a bulwark against Bolshevism. In asserting these aspects of its self-recognition, it would seriously challenge the recognition of the Paris Peace Conference. In the end, the Supreme Council, Hungary, and Romania would all define one another.

As we saw, no fewer than three arguably "revolutionary" regimes tried to rule in Hungary in the immediate aftermath of the Great War—a liberal democracy under Count Mihály Károlyi, a Soviet republic under Béla Kun, and a counterrevolutionary regency led by Admiral Miklós Horthy. One thing united these mutually antagonistic regimes: the identity of Hungary as a wronged successor state, subject to mutilation by the conference thanks to the lackeys of the allies,

[101] Barbara Jelavich, *Modern Austria: Empire and Republic, 1815–1986* (Cambridge: Cambridge University Press, 1987), 151–52.

[102] Erik Ringmar, "The Recognition Game: Soviet Russia against the West," *Cooperation and Conflict* 37.2 (2002): 115–36.

Czechoslovakia and Romania. As we saw in Chapter 1, the ambiguity of the Hungarian armistice meant that allied armies could occupy strategic positions of their choosing, but that "Hungary" would remain under Magyar administration pending a final settlement. Hungarians would take "Hungary" to mean all the lands of the Crown of St. Stephen, and would see attempts by Czechs, Serbs, and Romanians to claim lands promised to them or believed to be promised to them as violations of the armistice.

The emergence of the self-declared Soviet republic under the direction of Béla Kun on March 21, 1919 raised the stakes in the recognition game. The next day, the new regime declared "its complete theoretical and spiritual union with the Russian Soviet government and welcomes an armed alliance with the proletariat of Russia."[103] It called on workers throughout Central and Eastern Europe to rise against their masters. If workers succeeded emperors as sovereign, the theory went, successor states ruled by them would have no fraught territorial issues to resolve.[104] Specifically, no one would find the borders of historic Hungary problematic. What was the Paris Peace Conference to do with a revolutionary successor state it had neither created nor sanctioned and that had ideologically aligned itself with outcast Bolshevik Russia?

Romania self-recognized as a legitimately irredentist successor state and a victorious ally, its problematic wartime record notwithstanding. At the conference, Ion I.C. Brătianu time and again painted a portrait of continuous resistance to the Central Powers by a liberal constitutional monarchy. The proclamation of the Soviet republic, Brătianu argued, made Romania the last best hope in southeastern Europe against Bolshevism. Such an exemplar of Wilsonian values, his argument went, required a maximal territorial settlement, and of course could not accept the humiliation of a minority treaty. For Romania, territorial demands and resistance to any minority treaty reflected two sides of the same coin of self-recognition. Internally or externally, Romania could not be Romania without massive territorial acquisition and unquestioned sovereignty over all of its resident peoples.

As early as January 24, 1919, the Supreme Council fretted about successor states taking territorial matters into their own hands. "If they expect justice," according to a warning drafted by Wilson and passed by the Council, "they must refrain from force and place their claims in unclouded good faith in the hands of the Conference of Peace."[105] Yet armed Romanian incursions into Transylvania continued, as did

---

[103] "Mndenkihez," *Vörös Ujság*, March 22, 1919, quoted in Zsuzsa L. Nagy, "Problems of Foreign Policy before the Revolutionary Governing Council," in Iván Völgyes, ed., *Hungary in Revolution, 1918–1919: Nine Essays* (Lincoln: University of Nebraska Press, 1971), 123.

[104] There is a substantial Cold War-era literature debating the "Bolshevik" character of the Kun regime. See the essays in Völgyes, ed., *Hungary in Revolution*, as well as Rudolf L. Tőkés, *Béla Kun and the Hungarian Soviet Republic: The Origins and Role of the Communist Party in Hungary in the Revolutions of 1918–1919* (New York: Praeger [for the Hoover Institution on War, Revolution and Peace], 1967); and Peter Kenez, "Coalition Politics in the Hungarian Soviet Republic," in Andrew J. Janos and William B. Slottman, eds., *Revolution in Perspective: Essays on the Hungarian Soviet Republic of 1919* (Berkeley: University of California Press, 1971), 61–84.

[105] "Secretary's Notes of a Conversation Held in M. Pichon's Room at the Quai d'Orsay on Friday, January 24, 1919, at 12:15 O'clock p.m.," *FRUS: PPC*, 3: 715.

corresponding Hungarian incursions into Slovakia, which the Magyars claimed the right to administer pending a final peace settlement.[106]

An allied military mission under the command of Lieutenant Colonel Ferdinand Vix of the French army struggled to maintain the military provisions of the Belgrade armistice.[107] By late February, the Council had begun to discuss establishing a disarmed neutral zone to prevent armed conflict between Hungarians and Romanians. What became known as the "Vix Ultimatum" of March 19, 1919 established such a zone, within what had been territory formally under Hungarian military command since the Belgrade armistice. Civilian administration would remain in Hungarian hands for the time being.[108] The Károlyi government declared itself "not in a position to bear responsibility for the execution of this decision" of the conference, and promptly resigned.[109] The coalition government of Bolsheviks and socialists under Béla Kun would inherit this situation, alongside continuing labor unrest and desperate cries for land reform in the countryside.

Emissaries sent by the Supreme Council had trouble deciding which they detested more in the new regime: its claimed affinities with Bolshevism, or the Jewish origins of Kun. Harold Nicolson famously wrote in his diary of an "oily little Jew—fur-coat rather moth-eaten—string greet tie—dirty collar."[110] Not to be outdone, the private secretary to General Jan Smuts wrote of "a Jew of most unprepossessing looks, and his Jewish companions were no more attractive than their leader."[111] At the very least, anti-Semitism complicated the task of dealing with the Soviet republic.[112]

On March 24, 1919, only three days after coming to power and only two days after the statement of fraternity with Bolshevik Russia, Kun as commissar of foreign affairs sent a secret memo to the Supreme Council through Vittorio Orlando practically pleading for recognition.[113] Kun did not renounce the domestic goals of the new regime, "the peaceful social re-organization" of Hungary. But he stressed that the proposed alliance with Bolshevik Russia did not imply "the desire to break all diplomatic intercourse with the Powers of the Entente," rather

[106] Antoine Marès, "Mission militaire et relations internationals: l'exemple franco-tchécoslovaque, 1918-1925," *Revue d'histoire moderne et contemporaine* 30 (1983): 559–86.

[107] See two articles by Peter Pastor, "The Vix Mission in Hungary, 1918–1919: A Re-Examination," *Slavic Review* 29.3 (1970): 481–98; and "Franco-Rumanian Intervention in Russia and the *Vix Ultimatum*: Background to Hungary's Loss of Transylvania," *Canadian-American Review of Hungarian Studies* 1.1–2 (1974): 12–27.

[108] "Communication of General Lobit, Provisional Commander of the Allied Armies in Hungary, to Count Károlyi, President of Hungary, March 19, 1919," in Francis Deák, *Hungary at the Paris Peace Conference: The Diplomatic History of the Treaty of Trianon* (New York: Columbia University Press, 1942), 407–09.

[109] "Communication of Count Károlyi, President of Hungary, to Lt. Col. Vyx, Chief of the Allied Military Mission to Hungary, March 21, 1919," in Deak, *Hungary at the Paris Peace Conference*, 409.

[110] Harold Nicolson, *Peacemaking 1919* (London: Constable, 1919), 298.

[111] E.F.C. Lane, "General Smuts's Mission to Austria-Hungary," April 15, 1919, in W.K. Hancock and Jean Van der Poel, eds., *Selections from the Smuts Papers*, 7 vols. (Cambridge: Cambridge University Press, 1966–74), 4: 109.

[112] Eliza Ablovatski, "The 1919 Central European Revolutions and the Judeo-Bolshevik Myth," *European Review of History* 17.3 (2010): 473–89.

[113] "Memorandum by Béla Kun," March 24, 1919, *PWW*, 56: 242–43.

"a natural friendship justified by the identical construction of their respective constitutions." Soviet Hungary declared its eagerness "to negotiate territorial questions on the basis of the principle of self-determination of the People, and they [the new government] view territorial integrity solely as in conformity with that principle." Hungary would welcome a diplomatic mission from the Council to work out the particulars.

On March 29 and 31, the Supreme Council discussed whether responding positively to Kun's note of March 24 would constitute de facto recognition of the regime. Wilson and Lloyd George favored sending representatives to investigate, while making clear that doing so did not indicate any form of recognition. On March 29, Wilson asked rhetorically, "haven't we sent missions of inquiry far and wide?"[114] Lloyd George added that declining to deal with Hungary on ideological grounds could enflame the very Bolshevik menace they sought to control: "Let's not deal with Hungary as with Russia. One Russia is enough for us." Clemenceau took a more skeptical position. As French Foreign Minister Stephen Pichon put it on March 31, to yield to Kun even by talking to him meant yielding to Bolshevism: "Are we to enter, against our allies, into relations with a government of soviets? Would that be the preface to negotiations with Russia?" (94). Ultimately, the Council on March 31 agreed to send not "diplomatic agents," but what Wilson called "a confidential agent" (96), specified as "a soldier of high rank...who also has the qualities of a diplomat" (98). The Council found this figure in the ever-reliable General Smuts.

Certainly, the arrival of the Smuts mission created a frisson among the Hungarians. Shortly after crossing the Hungarian frontier on April 3, the allied delegation dispatched Nicolson to "Bolshevik headquarters" to establish contact.[115] A Hungarian functionary asked: "This means...that you recognize the Government of Bela Kun?" Crisply informed by Nicolson that it meant nothing of the sort, the official proceeded to alert his superiors in Budapest. Upon arrival on April 4, Nicolson found "red guards all along the platform with fixed bayonets and scarlet brassards." Yet Smuts refused to leave his railroad car, and required Kun to visit him there. After four such meetings, the train left again the night of April 5.

These meetings simply clarified the impasse.[116] Kun rejected the neutral zone as established under the Vix Ultimatum as inconsistent with the Padua armistice. Moreover, he claimed to lack command authority over the Székler troops from Transylvania occupying territory to be given up there. Any additional territorial concessions, he warned, would capsize his or any other government in Budapest. Should this happen, the victors should expect to "occupy the capital and other

---

[114] "Conversation between President Wilson and MM. Clemenceau, Lloyd George, and Orlando," 29 March 29, 1919, in Mantoux, *Deliberations*, 1: 73–76.

[115] The following draws from Nicolson, *Peacemaking 1919*, 292–308.

[116] "Telegram from General Smuts, Buda Pesth, to Mr. Balfour, April 4, 1919," *FRUS: PPC*, 5: 41–43; and Smuts's handwritten version, "Report," April 4, 1919, in Hancock and Van Der Poel, eds., *Smuts Papers*, 4: 103–05. For a largely consistent account using Hungarian sources, see Zs. L. Nagy, "The Mission of General Smuts to Budapest, April 1919," *Acta Historica Academiae Scientiarum Hungaricae* 11.1/4 (1965): 163–85.

districts as well as the neutral zone" as the only way to preserve order. Instead, Kun proposed a regional peace conference, perhaps chaired by Smuts himself. Representatives of successor state governments meeting together would decide borders. Hungary would bring to the meeting "an accommodating spirit and willingness to make concessions from the territorial point of view." Of course, such a proposal would have removed sovereignty over borders from the proceedings in Paris, and thus remained a dead letter. Smuts left Budapest with matters unresolved.

A stalemate of mutual non-recognition followed. The Kun regime proclaimed that Hungary could not be Hungary if it accepted the neutral zone as demarcated by the conference. The conference declined to recognize any Hungarian regime, particularly a Soviet one, that would not do so. "A situation of mutual non-recognition," Ringmar wrote, "is always unstable."[117] Mutual non-recognition created a vacuum in former Habsburg Hungary that encouraged Romania to assert its successor state identity by taking matters into its own hands.

Romania also had the only viable standing national army in the region. On April 4, 1919, Supreme Allied Commander in the Balkans General Louis Franchet d'Esperey reminded Clemenceau that in March he had requested reinforcements of fourteen allied divisions to keep the peace in the Balkans pending a final settlement.[118] The unrealistic nature of the request highlighted the material weakness of the allies in the Balkans. As Romanian forces continued to advance into former and present Hungarian territory, the Supreme Council returned to the situation sporadically and indecisively. On April 26, President Wilson suggested, almost plaintively:

> ...Roumania should be asked to cease their aggressive action towards Hungary. Roumania has had considerable assistance from the Allies and was pressing her advantage of numbers and equipment. Her action was distinctly aggressive and might constitute a danger to the Peace.[119]

Lloyd George suggested inviting Brătianu to appear before the Council and to be asked directly to stop the incursions. Wilson, perhaps remembering Brătianu's tendency to harangue, proposed sending a letter instead.

In the coming weeks, Brătianu began a full-fledged revolt against the sovereignty of the Supreme Council, materially against Hungary and discursively against the minority treaties. On May 19, Wilson presented an alarming report from his delegation on deteriorating conditions in Hungary.[120] Romanian incursions were proving counterproductive to ridding Hungary of the Soviet regime, by casting it in the role of national defender. Wilson endorsed the conclusion that "the only

[117] Ringmar, "Recognition Game," 121.
[118] Franchet d'Esperey to Clemenceau, April 4, 1919, in Miller, *Diary*, 17: 518–19.
[119] "Notes of a Meeting Held at President Wilson's Residence, Place des Etats-Unis, on Saturday, April 26, 1919, at 12:15 p.m.," *FRUS: PPC*, 5: 291. No record of this meeting appears in Mantoux, *Deliberations*.
[120] Wilson summarized a memo from Philip Marshall Brown, "The Hungarian Situation" (n.d., received by Wilson on May 17), *PWW*, 59: 239–40.

way to settle the Hungarian question is by military intervention. There would be no resistance; Béla Kun himself is ready to obey the orders of the Entente if they are imposed on him."[121] Clemenceau, well aware that France had the only significant allied force anywhere in the Balkans, remained skeptical.

At the plenary sessions of May 29 and 31, the Romanian challenge to the sovereignty of the Supreme Council came into the open. On May 29, the Council presented the plenary with the draft version of the Austrian treaty.[122] Brătianu, speaking not just for Romania but also for the governments of Greece, Poland, Yugoslavia, and Czechoslovakia, began what H.W.V. Temperley would call "a revolt of the Small Powers against the dictation of the Great."[123] Brătianu sought to exploit contradictions within the entire discursive structure of the conference. The Covenant of the League of Nations called for "the firm establishment of the understandings of international law as the actual rule of conduct among Governments." What were the minority treaties if not a blatant violation of the doctrine of equality of states under international law?

At the May 31 plenary, Wilson explicitly connected the sovereignty of the Supreme Council to recognition.[124] The Great Powers, after all, had won the war, and "had it not been for their action, their military action, we would not be here to settle these questions" (406). Further, they had assumed responsibility for winning the peace, as "in the last analysis the military and naval strength of the Great Powers will be the final guarantee of the peace of the world" (406). The equality of nations under international law, this point implied, did not necessitate equality in the making of international law. The history of international law certainly bore this out. Wilson predicted that nothing would be "more likely to disturb the peace of the world than the treatment which might in certain circumstances be meted out to minorities" (406). To take responsibility for enforcing the peace implied sovereignty over determining the peace. Wilson continued: "Where the great force lies, there must be the sanction of peace" (408). He urged the Romanian and Serbian delegates "to remember that while Roumania and Serbia are ancient sovereignties the settlements of this Conference are greatly adding to their territories" (406). The Paris Peace Conference would create modern Poland and Czechoslovakia. In the end, Wilson concluded: "If we agree to these additions of territory we have the right to insist on certain guarantees of peace" (407).

The entire situation carried implied threats of mutual non-recognition. Romania, and more timidly the other small states, threatened not to recognize the identities prepared for them by the minority treaties. Should new or augmented states claim new territories anyway, the Great Powers had no material means of stopping them

---

[121] "Conversation between President Wilson and MM. Clemenceau and Lloyd George," May 19, 1919, in Mantoux, *Deliberations*, 2: 105.

[122] "Preliminary Peace Conference, Protocol No. 7, Plenary Session of May 29, 1919," *FRUS: PPC*, 3: 391–93.

[123] H.W.V. Temperley, *A History of the Peace Conference of Paris*, 6 vols. (London: Henry Frowde, Hodder and Stoughton, 1920), 1: 272.

[124] "Preliminary Peace Conference, Protocol No. 8, Plenary Session of May 31, 1919," *FRUS: PPC*, 3: 394–410.

short of war. But the discursive power of recognition could not be treated lightly by the new states. According to a constitutive theory, Poland, Czechoslovakia, and the Serb-Croat-Slovene State would not legally exist in the absence of the treaties creating them, treaties linked to minority protection. Nor would the conference recognize the substantial territorial gains of Romania and the predicted gains for Greece. Mutual non-recognition if pushed too far could not just create instability, but wreck the entire peace settlement in eastern and southeastern Europe.

By the late spring of 1919, Romanian incursions into lands under Hungarian administration came increasingly to look like an invasion. Even before the "revolt of the Small Powers," the Supreme Council expressly denied a Romanian proposal to march on Budapest.[125] Appearing before the Council on June 10, Brătianu casually dismissed its concerns as based on erroneous or false information.[126] The original armistice line drawn by Franchet d'Esperey had been "absolutely arbitrary" (376). "I remind you that we are still in a state of war with Hungary," Brătianu concluded, "and that it is necessary for us to keep our positions as long as the state of war lasts" (381). Karel Kramář and Edvard Beneš of Czechoslovakia, also present at the meeting, supported an image of an aggressive Hungary, then continuing its own incursions into Slovakia.[127]

On June 26, just two days before the signing of the Treaty of Versailles, the Supreme Council considered a strategy of recognizing the Soviet regime in Hungary, thereby affording it some measure of protection from Romania.[128] Clemenceau presented a telegraph from Kun on June 16.[129] Kun made no apologies for the Soviet regime, but repeated the request made to Smuts "to summon together the Governments of the Peoples of the former Monarchy to a Conference where they will be able to discuss the liquidation of the former Monarchy as parties equally interested" (519). Of course, doing so meant recognizing de facto the Soviet regime. In exchange, Hungary would renounce the "territorial integrity" of the lands of the Crown of St. Stephen. Soviet Hungary would trade territory for recognition. But discussion of the Kun telegram did not lead to resolution. Unable to resolve the matter, the heads of government dispersed after the signing of the Treaty of Versailles. The Supreme Council decided neither to recognize the revolutionary regime in Hungary, nor to dispatch its own forces to depose it, nor to authorize the forces of its nominal Romanian ally to do so on its behalf.

Within Hungary, the situation became more chaotic in the summer of 1919. A counter-revolutionary regime founded in Szeged in May 1919 gathered strength

[125] "Council of the Principal Allied and Associated Powers: *Acta*," *FRUS: PPC*, 6: 133.

[126] "Conversation among President Wilson, and MM. Clemenceau, Lloyd George, Orlando, Brătianu, Misu, Kramar, and Beneš," June 10, 1919, in Mantoux, *Deliberations*, 2: 375–84.

[127] Peter A. Toma, "The Slovak Soviet Republic of 1919," *American Slavic and East European Review* 17.2 (1958): 203–15.

[128] "Notice of a Meeting Held at President Wilson's House in the Place des Etats-Unis, Paris, on Thursday, June 26, 1919, at 11 a.m.," *FRUS: PPC*, 6: 697–709; and "Conversation between President Wilson, MM. Clemenceau and Lloyd George, and Barons Sonnino and Makino," June 26, 1919, in Mantoux, *Discussions*, 2: 557–64.

[129] "Telegram from Bela Kun to M. Clemenceau," June 16, 1919, *FRUS: PPC*, 6: 518–20.

by the day.[130] On July 20, the besieged Kun regime launched an ill-conceived attack on the Romanian positions toward the Tisza River. The Romanian counter-offensive, completely unauthorized by the Supreme Council, began on July 24. The Kun government fell on August 1, and by August 4, the Romanians occupied Budapest.

Practically speaking, between the fall of Kun in August and the arrival of Admiral Miklós Horthy in Budapest as head of the counter-revolutionary forces from Szeged on November 16, 1919, there was no viable "Hungary" for the Supreme Council to recognize even if it wanted to.[131] A short-lived center-right regime led by István Friedrich did not help matters by accepting Archduke Joseph, a distant cousin of former Emperor-King Charles, as regent.[132] The Supreme Council, and particularly the other successor states, would never recognize another Habsburg on the Hungarian throne. It seems safe to assert that there was not a majority for anything in Hungary by the late summer of 1919.

By that time, the Supreme Council had lost control over both the diplomatic and the military situations. On August 4, 1919, Frank L. Polk, head of the American delegation after the departures of Wilson and Lansing, delivered reports of widespread looting by the Romanians in the suburbs of Budapest. Fearing worse, the Hungarians requested the sending of an inter-allied police force. According to Foch, the French had 15,000 soldiers, the Italians one battalion (1,000 soldiers at most), and the British 40 through the entire Balkan theater, which included the Bulgarian front as well.[133] The minutes recorded the Council's predicament:

> MR. BALFOUR asked what the Council could do to enforce good behavior on the Romanians.
> MARSHAL FOCH said that he did not know.[134]

Three days later, the Supreme Council debated measures to be taken against Romania. Balfour proposed blockading Romania by sea, a peculiar measure if the problem was Romanian requisitions from Hungary.[135] By late August, the Council seemed reduced to vague threats. A telegram from Clemenceau dated August 25 warned that "if the conduct of the Roumanian authorities in Hungary does not undergo a complete and immediate change, such an attitude will entail the most serious consequences for Romania."[136]

---

[130] Thomas Sakmyster, *Hungary's Admiral on Horseback: Miklós Horthy, 1918–1944* (New York: Columbia University Press, 1994), 18–28.

[131] Ferenc Pölöskei, *Hungary after Two Revolutions (1919–1922)* (Budapest: Akadémiai Kaidó, 1980).

[132] Eva S. Balogh, "István Friedrich and the Hungarian Coup d'État of 1919: A Reevaluation," *Slavic Review* 35.2 (1976): 269–86.

[133] Telegram, Polk to Wilson and Lansing, August 5, 1919, Miller, *Diary*, 20: 378–79.

[134] "Notes of a Meeting of the Heads of Delegations of the Five Great Powers held in M. Pichon's Room at the Quai d'Orsay, Paris, on Monday, August 4, 1919, at 3:30 p.m.," *FRUS: PPC*, 7: 507.

[135] "Notes of a Meeting of the Heads of Delegations of the Five Great Powers Held in M. Pichon's Room at the Quai d'Orsay, Paris, on Thursday, August 7, 1919, at 3:30 p.m.," *FRUS: PPC*, 7: 606.

[136] "Telegram from the Supreme Council of the Allies to the Roumanian Government," August 25, 1919, Appendix C to HD-38, "Notes of a Meeting of the Heads of Delegations of the Principal Allied and Associated Powers Held in M. Pichon's Room at the Quai d'Orsay, Paris, on Monday, August 25, 1919, at 3:30 p.m.," *FRUS: PPC,* 7: 857.

The limited options for carrying out such threats illustrated that the one-directional approach to recognition taken by the conference up to that time would no longer suffice. The French, the British, and the Americans had already stopped shipments of all military and non-military supplies to Romania.[137] An actual rupture of diplomatic relations would be a gesture toward a war that the Great Powers had clearly shown they would not be willing to fight. To be sure, expelling Romania from the international system being created in Paris would certainly have brought consequences to Romania, in trade and diplomatic isolation. But the conference would have paid a price as well. Withdrawing recognition of Romania coupled with continued non-recognition of an unstable Hungary would have meant abdicating sovereignty over the territorial settlement in much of the Balkans. Why would the South Slav state accept the authority of the Supreme Council when it had simply walked out on the conflict between Romania and Hungary? Romania would have become master of peacemaking with Hungary, its revolt against the authority of the Council complete.

Romanian requisitions in occupied Hungary, Hungarian protests, and threats from the Supreme Council continued into the fall of 1919. The Supreme Council decided to send a personal emissary, Sir George Clerk of the British Foreign Office. Doing so meant that the recognition game had changed. Clerk arrived in October 1919 not as a messenger from the provisional world sovereign, but as a negotiator. He engaged in what today we might call "shuttle diplomacy" between Budapest and Bucharest.[138] An exit strategy emerged based on recognition—practically speaking, the only weapon the Supreme Council had at its disposal. The allies could facilitate the construction of a recognizable Hungary, then threaten Romania with making peace with it. Recognizing Hungary would make it possible to isolate Romania and, at least theoretically, carry through on the persistent threat to expel Romania from the international system.

According to an interview he gave to *Pester Lloyd*, an influential German-language Budapest newspaper, Clark came to Hungary to serve the Hungarian people, a proper successor to the Woodrow Wilson of November 1918:

> I would like to bring to your country interior and exterior peace, elections to the national assembly, and the conclusion of the treaty of peace. I hope to obtain this result, counting on the support of all Hungarian public opinion without distinction of party, class, or confession.[139]

Behind the scenes, Clark lent support to Admiral Horthy, who appeared able to unify the Szeged counter-revolutionaries and center-right factions in Budapest.[140]

---

[137] "Notes of a Meeting of the Heads of Delegations of the Principal Allied and Associated Powers Held in M. Pichon's Room at the Quai d'Orsay, Paris, on Monday, August 25, 1919, at 3:30 p.m.," *FRUS: PPC*, 7: 838.

[138] Gerald J. Protheroe, *Searching for Security in a New Europe: The Diplomatic Career of Sir George Russell Clerk* (London: Routledge, 2006), 43–73.

[139] "Enclosure to Dispatch, Sir G. Clerk (Budapest) to M. Clemenceau, 28 October 1919," *DBFP*, First Series, 6: 312. My translation of the French text.

[140] Protheroe, *Searching for Security*, 53–62; and Miklós Lojko, *Meddling in Middle Europe: Britain and the "Lands Between," 1919–1925* (Budapest: Central University Press, 2006), 18–23.

In a November 1 telegram to the Council, Clark described Horthy as a figure who "inspires confidence," notably on the delicate matter of reining in the "White Terror" (the paramilitary campaign against leftists and Jews) once the Romanians began their withdrawal.[141] Clerk requested the authority to grant provisional recognition to a coalition regime brought together under Horthy's auspices. In his ceremonial entry on a white horse into Budapest on November 16, Horthy carried with him the tacit support of the Supreme Council. The admiral proclaimed that he had come both to "arraign" but ultimately to "forgive" the errant capital for its revolutionary crimes.[142] Horthy's now-recognizable regime began the lengthy task of working out the details of the Treaty of Trianon, signed on June 4, 1920 (see Figure 5.1).[143]

At the same time, Romania tested the limits of its self-recognized identity. It had withheld its signature from both the Treaty of Saint-Germain with Austria (September 10, 1919) and the Treaty of Neuilly with Bulgaria (November 27, 1919), mostly over the matter of minority protection. A bizarre scheme for personal

Figure 5.1. The Hungarian delegation marched to (or from) signing the Treaty of Trianon, June 4, 1920.

gallica.bnf.fr/Bibliothèque nationale de France.

---

[141] "Telegram from Sir George Clerk, Budapest, to Sir Eyre Crowe, Astoria," November 1, 1919, Appendix B to HD-83, "Notes of a Meeting of the Heads of Delegations of the Five Great Powers Held in M. Pichon's Room, Quai d'Orsay, Paris, on Tuesday, November 4, 1919, at 10:30 a.m.," *FRUS: PPC*, 8: 947.

[142] Sakmyster, *Hungary's Admiral on Horseback*, 37–45.

[143] Mária Ormos, *From Padua to the Trianon 1918–1920*, trans. Miklós Uszkay (Boulder, CO: Social Science Monographs, 1990), 366–82.

union of the Hungarian and Romanian crowns under Romanian King Ferdinand had met so much derision that even Brătianu had to retain plausible deniability on the matter.[144] If the Romanians did not intend to annex Hungary, sooner or later they would have to release it. The question then became the degree to which Romania would recognize the sovereignty of the Supreme Council over the peace settlement.

On November 15, the day before Horthy's entry into Budapest, the Supreme Council sent a "final" ultimatum to the Romanian government that made recognition the central issue.[145] The Council decreed that Romania "cannot with impunity disregard the principles and the reciprocal agreements of the Allies," and correspondingly, disregard the sovereignty of the Council. The ultimatum made three demands: the evacuation of Romanian forces to boundaries determined by the conference; the acceptance of an inter-allied commission on reparations (including material already requisitioned); and signature of both the Treaty of Saint-Germain and the Romanian minorities treaty. The Council would allow the Romanian government eight days to answer yes or no, without further discussion or reservations. In the event of a negative answer, Romania would "deprive herself of all title to the support of the Powers, as well as to the recognition of her rights by the Conference." Romania would be required to recall its delegates to the conference, and the five Great Powers would withdraw their diplomatic missions in Bucharest.

Romania's final play in the recognition game had a particularly theatrical quality.[146] King Ferdinand sent a letter dated November 24 to three heads of state—President Raymond Poincaré of France, King George V of Great Britain, and King Vittorio Emanuele III of Italy. Inexplicably, he had not sent the same letter either to President Wilson or to Emperor Yoshihito of Japan, which Clemenceau described as a "most serious act of discourtesy."[147] The Romanian king, hitherto not heard from and barely spoken of at the conference, complained that "from the beginning of the operations of the Conference, the Council of Four alone made all the decisions." He pleaded with Poincaré (and presumably the two kings, neither of whom played a direct role in foreign policy either) "to bring the Government of the Republic to a more friendly and just attitude toward us." In turn, the Supreme Council responded through a note published in the *Times* of London on December 4, in which it revealed its decision "to make a final

---

[144] "Mr. Rattigan (Bucharest) to Earl Curzon (Received August 28) No. 143 [12199/392/19]," August 19, 1919, *DBFP*, First Series, 6: 173.

[145] "Note from the Supreme Council to the Rumanian Government," Appendix A to HD-93, November 15, 1919, "Notes of a Meeting of the Heads of Delegations of the Five Great Powers Held in M. Pichon's Room, Quai d'Orsay, Paris, on Saturday, November 15, 1919, at 10:30 a.m.," *FRUS: PPC*, 9: 182–84.

[146] On Romanian domestic politics during this period, see Sherman David Spector, *Rumania at the Paris Peace Conference: A Study of the Diplomacy of Ioan I.C. Brătianu* (New York: Bookman Associates, 1962), 197–225; and Keith Hitchins, *Ion I.C. Brătianu: Romania* (London: Haus, 2011), 126–32.

[147] "Notes of a Meeting of the Heads of Delegations of the Five Great Powers Held in M. Pichon's Room, Quai d'Orsay, Paris, on Saturday, November 29, 1919, at 10:30 a.m.," *FRUS: PPC*, 9: 370. The text of the letter to Poincaré is published as Appendix D to HD-102, 9: 376–77.

appeal to the wisdom of the Rumanian government and people, leaving to them the responsibility of the grave consequence which would result from a refusal or from an evasive reply."[148] With considerable ill will, the Romanian government on December 9 signed the Treaty of Saint-Germain, the Treaty of Neuilly, and the minority treaty.[149]

Eventually, the Supreme Council, successor Romania, and successor Hungary all found ways to recognize one another. Recognition at the Paris Peace Conference had changed a good bit in the interim, and had shown itself a process rather than an event. Declarative and constitutive approaches needed each other. Further, recognition proved an uncertain tool for mastering revolution. The limits of one-directional recognition from the conference as sovereign, created for Czechoslovakia, certainly became clear in Hungary and Romania. After months of struggle among the Supreme Council and two successor states (three including Czechoslovakia over Hungarian claims to Slovakia), the only weapons at the disposal of the Supreme Council were discursive. It could recognize the evolving Horthy regime and openly threaten to withdraw recognition from Romania. The recognition game in this part of the former Habsburg lands proved to be about negotiating identities and saving face.

EPILOGUE: STATE AND REVOLUTION IN RUSSIA

In the tumultuous period between the February and October revolutions of 1917, V.I. Lenin wrote his famous essay *The State and Revolution*. Among other things, the author declared war on the existing state system itself. The state had risen and would fall as the instrument of class oppression:

> The state is a product and a manifestation of the *irreconcilability* of class antagonisms. The state arises where, when and insofar as class antagonism objectively *cannot* be reconciled. And, conversely, the existence of the state proves that the class antagonisms are irreconcilable.[150]

After the completion of the proletarian revolution, there would be no "international system," nor any need for one. The workers of the world would rule by and for themselves, without states. Of course, Lenin found it easy enough to write all this when Bolshevism did not hold power in Moscow or Petrograd, let alone around the world. As the Russian Revolution became the Bolshevik Revolution, the Bolsheviks had to confront actual rule over actual lands and peoples.

---

[148] "Text of Note from the Supreme Council to the Rumanian Government," December 3, 1919, in Temperley, *History of the Paris Peace Conference*, 4: 518.

[149] Spector, *Rumania at the Paris Peace Conference*, 215–18.

[150] V.I. Lenin, *The State and Revolution: The Marxist Theory of the State and the Tasks of the Proletarian Revolution*, in Stepan Apresyan and Jim Riordon, eds. and trans., *V.I. Lenin: Collected Works*, 35 vols. (Moscow: Progress Publishers, 1974 [originally published in 1918]), 25: 392. Emphasis in the original.

The Bolsheviks ruled territory, indeed the central heartland of European Russia, throughout the civil wars.[151] They fought for Weberian sovereignty across the domains of the former tsar—from Ukraine, to the Caucasus, to Central Asia, to Siberia. Yet the Bolshevik Revolution did not plan to stop at the Romanov borders. "The Government of the victorious revolution," went a Bolshevik appeal of November 27, 1917, "does not require recognition from the professional representatives of capitalist diplomacy, but we do ask the people: 'Does reactionary diplomacy express your ideas and aspirations?'"[152] The Bolsheviks self-recognized as the vanguard of a world revolution that would annihilate and replace the international system.

For its part, the Supreme Council wanted to deal with the Russia they had hoped was taking shape between the February and October revolutions—a liberal democracy. Yet the Council could not constitute a liberal Russia by decree, nor could it bring itself to recognize a Bolshevik Russia that slowly was coming to win the civil wars. The latter Russia had declared war on everything happening in Paris. In deciding how to deal with the Bolshevik regime, the Paris Peace Conference faced revolution as a world phenomenon and geographic locus of sovereignty almost wholly beyond its control.

The Supreme Council found itself caught between theories of recognition. The declarative theory implied doing business with the Bolsheviks. The constitutive theory implied supporting the Whites and hoping for the best. The conference pursued at intervals policies based on both theories. During the conference and long after, the Bolshevik regime played its own version of the recognition game. It participated in various diplomatic initiatives, all the while doing what it could through the Comintern to foment world revolution.[153] Bolshevik Russia could survive without international recognition from the conference, leaving recognition up to individual states. As the Union of Soviet Socialist Republics, the Bolshevik regime eventually would accept socialization into the international system.

While Herbert Hoover's famous description of Bolshevik Russia as "Banquo's ghost sitting at every Council table" seems overdrawn, discussion did turn early and often to the erstwhile ally.[154] Lloyd George exemplified the confusion at the first two meetings of the council of Great Powers on January 12, 1919. In the morning meeting, he referred to the 1.2 million Russian prisoners of war still in German hands as a possible force to mobilize against Bolshevism.[155] But by that afternoon, he called the Bolshevik regime the "*de facto* Government." He lamented:

---

[151] Jonthan D. Smele has argued that given the diversity of peoples and fronts, the very term "Russian Civil War" is something of a misnomer. *The "Russian" Civil Wars, 1916–1926: Ten Years that Shook the World* (New York: Oxford University Press, 2015).

[152] "Appeal to Belligerents on Peace," November 14 (27), 1917, in Rex Wade, ed., *Documents of Soviet History*, 8 vols. (Gulf Breeze, FL: Academic International Press, 1991–2008), 1: 50.

[153] See Ringmar, "Recognition Game," 123–25; and Zara Steiner, *The Lights that Failed: European International History, 1919–1933* (Oxford: Oxford University Press, 2005), 131–81.

[154] Herbert Hoover, *The Memoirs of Herbert Hoover, Volume 1: Years of Adventure, 1874–1920* (New York: Macmillan, 1951), 411.

[155] "Procès-verbal of the Meeting of the Supreme War Council Held in M. Pichon's Room at the Quai d'Orsay, on Sunday, January 12, at 2:30 p.m.," *FRUS: PPC*, 3: 472.

"We had formally recognized the Czar's Government, although at the time we knew it to be absolutely rotten. Our reason had been that it was the *de facto* government." To choose which among the bickering counter-revolutionary factions was the legitimate government, without hearing from the Russian people, "was contrary to every principle for which we had fought."[156] But how to discern just what the Russian peoples wanted?

American leadership on the matter seemed crucial. Point VI of the Fourteen Points had promised Russia "unhampered and unembarrassed opportunity for the independent determination of her own political development," and all of this "under institutions of her own choosing." Yet only seven months later, in July 1918, the United States sent some 5,500 soldiers to northern Russia, and another 8,500 to Siberia, supposedly to head off German advances in northern Russia and to protect the evacuation of the Czecho-Slovak Legion through Siberia.[157] By January 1919, some 180,000 allied troops operated within the boundaries of former Imperial Russia—enough to antagonize all factions, but not enough to intervene anywhere decisively.[158] As months passed, the allies looked more and more like co-belligerents on the side of the Whites. Wilson and the allies needed an exit strategy that would enable them to withdraw their troops, and to bring a recognizable Russia to the negotiating table.

On January 21, Wilson drafted a proposal to hold an inter-allied conference with all the interested parties on the Prinkipo Islands in the Sea of Marmara near Constantinople.[159] The following day, the Council publicly declared: "They [the members of the Council] recognize the revolution without reservation, and will in no way, and in no circumstance, aid or give countenance to any attempt at a counter-revolution."[160] The demonstrable untruth of this statement notwithstanding, the members of the Council promised "to do what they can to bring Russia peace and an opportunity to find her way out of her present troubles." They extended the invitation to "every organized group that is now exercising, or attempting to exercise, political authority or military control," anywhere in Russia. All "aggressive military action" by all parties would cease, though the de facto armistice could be enforced only by good faith. The conference would begin on February 15.

The Pinkipo invitation represented the Paris Peace Conference at its most Wilsonian. It sought to bring the civil wars in former Imperial Russia into the international public sphere. Once this happened, "the peoples" could make their wills felt, and in doing so restore unity (or amicable disunity) to the fractured

[156] "Secretary's Notes of a Conversation Held in M. Pichon's Room at the Quai d'Orsay on Sunday, January 12, at 4 p.m.," *FRUS: PPC*, 3: 491.

[157] Carl J. Richard, *When the United States Invaded Russia: Woodrow Wilson's Siberian Disaster* (Lanham, MD: Rowman & Littlefield, 2013), x.

[158] Ian C.D. Moffat, *The Allied Intervention in Russia, 1918–1920: The Diplomacy of Chaos* (New York: Palgrave Macmillan, 2015), 165.

[159] John M. Thompson, *Russia, Bolshevism, and the Versailles Peace* (Princeton, NJ: Princeton University Press, 1966), 82–130; and David W. McFadden, *Alternative Paths: Soviets and Americans, 1917–1920* (New York: Oxford University Press, 1993), 191–217.

[160] See the entire document in "Secretary's Notes of a Conversation Held in M. Pichon's Room at the Quai d'Orsay, January 22, 1919, at 15 Hours 15," *FRUS: PPC*, 3: 676–77.

polity. No one on the Council claimed to believe that, if asked, the peoples of former Imperial Russia would actually choose the Bolsheviks. The failure of the Prinkipo invitation was over-caused, in that it papered over considerable national differences within the Supreme Council. Interventionists such as Marshal Foch, Winston Churchill (then secretary of state for war), and probably Clemenceau wished it to fail.[161] The Bolsheviks initially responded warmly, suspicions of bad allied faith notwithstanding. Most White factions seethed at the possibility of facing Bolsheviks across the table, and did not respond.

An ambitious young American diplomat, William Bullitt, picked up the initiative when the Pinkipo effort failed. Only twenty-eight years old in 1919, Bullitt had been serving as gatekeeper of information for the American delegation. He had attended the February 1919 labor conference in Berne as an observer and was considered one of the more left-leaning members of the American delegation.[162] Bullitt led a small, secret mission to Russia in February and March 1919.[163] He met personally with Lenin, Maxim Litvinov (diplomat at large), and Georgi Chicherin (commissar for foreign affairs). Unlike the seasoned Smuts in Budapest, the relatively inexperienced Bullitt conceived his mission in Moscow as not just finding facts, but making peace.

On March 16, Bullitt telegraphed a proposal endorsed by the Soviet authorities that amounted to a declaratory recognition of Bolshevik Russia.[164] Like the Pinkipo proposal, the Bullitt proposal called for an armistice to be set in place, until such time as "the peoples inhabiting the territories controlled by these *de facto* Governments shall themselves determine to change their Governments." The allies would withdraw all troops and assistance to anti-Bolshevik factions. All understood that the White cause could not long survive without foreign aid. The substantial imperial foreign debt, recognized in principle, would be on the table for future negotiations. Foreign nationals could circulate in Russia and Soviet nationals elsewhere, provided they "do not interfere in domestic politics." Combatants on all sides would receive a blanket amnesty.

Like the Pinkipo initiative, the failure of the Bullitt initiative was overdetermined. The French had never been consulted, and the Bullitt mission coincided with Marshal Foch's quixotic efforts to persuade the Supreme Council to approve an international military crusade to defeat Bolshevism.[165] The Bullitt proposals ran against allied hopes, however increasingly forlorn, that the White cause would somehow prevail. They were never formally brought before the Council of Ten.

---

[161] J. Kim Munholland, "The French Army and Intervention in Southern Russia, 1918–1919," *Cahiers du monde russe et soviétique* 11 (1981): 43–66; and McFadden, *Alternative Paths*.

[162] Michael Cassella-Blackburn, *The Donkey, the Carrot, and the Club: William C. Bullitt and Soviet–American Relations, 1917–1948* (Westport, CT: Praeger, 2004); and Will Brownell and Richard N. Billings, *So Close to Greatness: A Biography of William C. Bullitt* (New York: Macmillan, 1987).

[163] Thompson, *Russia, Bolshevism, and the Versailles Peace*, 131–77; and McFadden, *Alternative Paths*, 218–43.

[164] Telegram, William C. Bullitt to the Commission to Negotiate Peace, March 16, 1919, *Papers Relating to the Foreign Relations of the United States, 1919: Russia* (Washington, D.C.: Government Printing Office, 1937), 77–80. Subsequently referred to as *FRUS 1919: Russia*.

[165] See Thompson, *Russia, Bolshevism, and the Versailles Peace*, 178–221.

Bitterly disappointed, Bullitt would resign from the American delegation and shortly thereafter would turn on the Wilson administration itself.[166]

International policies of food aid to Russia combined partial de facto recognition and continued hope for regime change.[167] Aiding civilians in Bolshevik-ruled areas meant dealing with Bolshevik officials. But many allied officials continued to believe that only mass starvation kept the Bolsheviks in power. As Secretary Lansing put it, "full stomachs mean no Bolsheviks."[168] Dealing with local Bolsheviks could thus serve as a preliminary move in a longer strategy of deposing them. The American and British delegations developed what became known as the Hoover–Nansen Plan, after renowned humanitarians Herbert Hoover and Fridjof Nansen. Modeled on Hoover's wartime relief program in Belgium, the plan would distribute food through neutral parties, facilitated by some sort of truce in the relevant areas. Hoover himself did not separate humanitarianism and politics in Russia. "We cannot even remotely recognize this murderous tyranny," he wrote to Wilson on March 28, "without stimulating actionist radicalism in every country in Europe and without transgressing on every National ideal of our own."[169] Rather, aid to suffering Russians could provide a pause, in which the allies could do well by doing good. "Time can thus be taken," Hoover continued, "to determine whether or not this whole system is a world danger, and whether the Russian people will themselves swing back to moderation and themselves bankrupt these ideas."

The Bolsheviks received the plan in the spirit Hoover intended it—humanitarianism as a prelude to counter-revolution. In a blistering telegram to Nansen denouncing the allied blockade and assistance to the Whites as the problem, Chicherin scolded: "your sincerely charitable intentions have been misused by others in order to cover such purposes which are obviously political with the semblance of an action originally humanitarian only."[170] This oblique humanitarian approach to creating a recognizable Russia failed as well.

The Whites never cohered into a viable partner in mastering revolution in Russia. Throughout the conference, the Supreme Council struggled to locate accurate information about their prospects and even their objectives. Émigrés provided invariably hopeful perspectives, most of the time seriously overstating the strength and liberal credentials of the various factions.[171] For example, on May 10, 1919 the Supreme Council received Nicolai Tchaikovsky, who claimed to represent

[166] In September 1919, Bullitt testified before the Senate Foreign Relations Committee denouncing the Treaty of Versailles. *The Bullitt Mission to Russia: Testimony before the Committee on Foreign Relations, United States Senate of William C. Bullitt* (New York: B.W. Huebsch, 1919).

[167] Thompson, *Russia, Bolshevism, and the Versailles Peace*, 222–67; and McFadden, *Alternative Paths*, 244–46.

[168] Quoted in Thompson, *Russia, Bolshevism, and the Versailles Peace*, 222.

[169] "The Director General of Relief, Supreme Economic Council (Hoover), to President Wilson," March 28, 1919, *FRUS 1919: Russia*, 101.

[170] Telegram, Chicherin to Nansen, May 7, 1919, *FRUS 1919: Russia*, 111–15. See also Bruno Cabanes, *The Great War and the Origins of Humanitarianism, 1918–1924* (Cambridge: Cambridge University Press, 2014), 189–247.

[171] Peter Kenez, "The Ideology of the White Movement," *Soviet Studies* 32.1 (1980): 58–83; and N.G.O. Periera, "White Power during the Civil War in Siberia (1918–1920): Dilemmas of Kolchak's 'War Anti-Communism,'" *Canadian Slavonic Papers/Revue Canadienne des Slavistes* 29 (1987): 45–62.

a united anti-Bolshevik front. Wilson informed Tchaikovsky almost plaintively: "We wish to give our support only to a government which will commit itself to maintaining in Russia a truly democratic political system and a land policy which leaves the land in the hands of the peasants."[172] Tchaikovsky provided a rosy if inaccurate account of the good relations between General Anton Denikin in the south and Admiral Alexander Kolchak in Siberia, and of the democratic bona fides of both.[173] He acknowledged some differences of opinion, but assured his listeners that even if the Whites established a constitutional monarchy, "it would end in a republic, and a federal republic at that."[174]

Shortly thereafter, the Council tried to constitute an alternative Russia by recognizing a de facto regime under Kolchak.[175] On May 24, the Council asked Viscount Chinda Sutemi to seek the necessary approval from his government, which had the greatest number of allied troops on the ground.[176] On May 26, the Council wrote to Admiral Kolchak outlining their policy.[177] The document did not actually promise recognition, rather it extended a promise to continue aiding the Kolchak government, "provided they [the allies] are satisfied that it will really help the Russian people to liberty, self-government, and peace." This condition seemed at odds with the additional claim: "It has always been a cardinal axiom of the Allied and Associated Powers to avoid interference with the internal affairs of Russia."

The message went on to describe a recognizable, liberal Russia. The Council insisted on "a freely elected Constituent Assembly," provided that those elected "stand for the civil and religious liberty of all Russian citizens and will make no attempt to reintroduce the régime [presumably of land ownership] which the revolution has destroyed." In its external relations, the new Russia would recognize the imperial foreign debt, and the independence of Poland and Finland. Other borders would be resolved bilaterally, or "through the peaceful arbitration of the League of Nations." The present de facto recognition would become official upon the formation of "a single government and army command as soon as the military situation makes it possible."

Kolchak responded on June 4, agreeing to the internal democratization of Russia, but maintaining that disposition of all border issues belonged to the future Constituent Assembly.[178] By this time, however, the military situation had taken a decided turn against the Whites, particularly in Siberia. With the drama over whether the Germans would sign the Versailles Treaty coming to a head, the Supreme Council had more pressing matters to consider. The allies, and particularly

[172] "Conversation between President Wilson and MM. Clemenceau, Lloyd George, and Orlando," May 10, 1919, in Mantoux, *Deliberations*, 2: 25.

[173] Peter Kenez, *Civil War in South Russia, 1919–1920: The Defeat of the Whites* (Berkeley: University of California Press, 1977).

[174] "Conversation," May 10, 1919, in Mantoux, *Deliberations*, 2: 29.

[175] See Thompson, *Russia, Bolshevism, and the Versailles Peace*, 268–308.

[176] "Notes of a Meeting Held at President Wilson's House in the Place des Etats-Unis, Paris, on Saturday, May 24, 1919, at 4 p.m.," *FRUS: PPC*, 6: 18–19.

[177] "Dispatch to Admiral Kolchak," May 26, 1919, *FRUS 1919: Russia*, 367–70.

[178] Telegram from Kolchak to Clemenceau, in "The French Chargé (De Martel) to the French Ministry of Foreign Affairs," June 4, 1919, *FRUS 1919: Russia*, 375–78.

Wilson, became increasingly reluctant to grant de facto recognition to an increasingly lost cause.

The Supreme Council could not create through constitutive recognition a liberal Russia that could not create itself. Nor did it believe it could recognize a Bolshevik Russia that had never renounced its mission of overthrowing the international system. Nor could the espoused anti-Bolshevism of the Supreme Council support the sort of fanciful and probably disastrous crusade envisaged by Marshal Foch. Even Clemenceau, the most consistently anti-Bolshevik of the Big Four, never took such schemes seriously.

The "recognition game" played itself out with Bolshevik Russia much as it had with Hungary and Romania. In time, the state identities in play learned to recognize one another. The Paris Peace Conference would never master the Bolshevik Revolution. Bolshevik Russia did not need recognition from the Paris Peace Conference to survive, and Russia's place at the table of the victors of the Great War would remain unoccupied. But de facto recognition of the Bolshevik regime would begin with the invitation to Chicherin to attend the Genoa Conference of April–May 1922.[179] Bolshevik Russia, by participating, recognized the proceedings at Genoa as the successor to the Paris Peace Conference. Chicherin, born to the Russian nobility, wore formal diplomatic attire rather than Bolshevik garb, and insisted on conservative diplomatic etiquette. His colleagues understood the meaning of such gestures.[180] Bolshevik Russia would also participate in the Conference of Lausanne. But formal recognition of the regime would occur bilaterally. France, Britain, and Italy would recognize the Soviet Union in 1924, and Japan in 1925. The United States would wait until 1933, when Franklin Roosevelt would send William C. Bullitt as its first ambassador. Communism and liberalism, each in its way, would continue to try to revolutionize the world.

[179] Carole Fink, *The Genoa Conference: European Diplomacy, 1921–22* (Chapel Hill: University of North Carolina Press, 1984).

[180] Theodore H. von Laue, "Soviet Diplomacy: G.V. Chicherin, People's Commissar for Foreign Affairs, 1918–1930," in Gordon Craig and Felix Gilbert, eds., *The Diplomats* (Princeton, NJ: Princeton University Press, 1953), 240.

6

Sovereignty and the League of Nations, 1920–23

Article 5 of the Covenant of the League of Nations called upon the president of the United States to summon the first meetings of the League Council. An ailing President Wilson performed this duty through written invitations to the member states. The League Council met for the first time on January 16, 1920, in the Salle de l'Horloge at the Quai d'Orsay in Paris. It immediately elected Léon Bourgeois of France as chair, an expected honor for the head of the delegation from the host country. Bourgeois (see Figure 6.1), who had served on the commission drawing up the Covenant, spoke first. Lord Curzon, British foreign minister, spoke second. The League would wrestle with the issues laid out in these speeches for the entirety of its existence.

Bourgeois had stressed the call in the preamble to the Covenant for the "firm establishment of the understandings of International Law as the actual rule of conduct among Governments."[1] He took this to mean making the League the lawgiver, particularly on the all-important matter of security. The League as Bourgeois saw it had two functions. The first, "of urgent necessity," consisted of "the practical execution of the clauses of the Treaty of Peace" (19). Once it achieved this task, the League could complete the transformation of the international system, through "the definite foundation of international justice, the organization of the security of peace-loving peoples by the general limitation of armaments, [and] the protection of races not yet able to stand by themselves" (19). Such goals implied greatly changed state identities. Toward that end, Bourgeois drew attention to Article 10, which obligated members "to respect and maintain the territorial integrity and the political independence of the Associated States against all aggression" (19). Long committed to transnational reconciliation between capitalism and socialism, Bourgeois also highlighted the early work of the International Labour Organization (I.L.O.), which would see to "the international regulation of the conditions of labour, in order to secure the welfare of the workers, [and assures] at the same time social peace" (19).

Bourgeois's lofty conclusion posed the difficult question of what the League actually was: "With eyes fixed on the distant future, but with our feet on the solid ground of political and social realities, we will create a world in which the League

---

[1] "Procès-Verbal of the first Meeting of the Council of the League of Nations," January 16, 1920, *Société des Nations: Journal Officiel/League of Nations: Official Journal* (February 1920), 18. Subsequently referred to as *League Council: JO*. Citations refer to the English version, though the French version appears alongside, with the same page number.

Figure 6.1. Léon Bourgeois at the first meeting of the League of Nations Council, January 16, 1920.

gallica.bnf.fr/Bibliothèque nationale de France.

can develop in the spirit of justice and the will for peace" (20). The Covenant had bound states to one another, and committed them to addressing issues as fundamental as labor and colonialism in and through international organizations. The peace of the world would depend on such commitments changing state identities.

Lord Curzon pronounced himself "in entire agreement with what Monsieur Bourgeois has said" (22). Yet his League placed state sovereignty at its center:

> It has sometimes been said that the League of Nations implies the establishment of a Super-State, or a Super-Sovereignty. The very title "League of Nations" should be sufficient to dispel this misconception. The League does not interfere with nationality. It is upon the fact of nationhood that it rests.
>
> The League is an association of sovereign States whose purpose is to reconcile divergent interests and to promote international co-operation in questions which affect—or may affect—the world at large. (21)

Curzon too paid warm tribute to the nascent I.L.O., as a "good augury" for the future League, particularly concerning "the use and the power of public debate in one field of international action" (21). He admitted that the Treaty of Versailles and the other treaties would obligate the League "to perform certain duties" (22). But he hastened to add: "in no case, however, will these obligations be inconsistent with the high conceptions which animated the founders of the League" (22). The League would channel these aspirations through states. The League would become what states made of it.

The absent presence in all this was President Wilson, or indeed any representative of the American government. Afflicted by several strokes during his western tour of the fall of 1919, Wilson was no longer in immediate physical danger by January 1920. His long and partial recovery had begun. But the confrontation between the president and the Senate over the League was coming to a head, with his opponents continuing to gain ground.[2] Wilson had become the figure represented in *Tōkyō Puck*, published the following September—infirm, hovering in frustration over events he could not control. The Senate had declined to ratify the Versailles Treaty for the first time on November 19, 1919. Bourgeois and Curzon both expressed fervent hopes that, as Bourgeois put it, "these last difficulties will be overcome" (18) and that the North American colossus would take its statutory place on the League Council. Such hopes would die with the second Senate rejection of the treaty on March 19, 1920.

Certainly, the abandonment of the League by the United States was a serious setback to its prospects. Financially, the League would not be able to draw support from the world's wealthiest nation. Everyone understood that any stable world peace would depend on the participation of the United States in some fashion.[3] But the failure to ratify the Treaty of Versailles was not so mortal a blow to the League as Americans have long preferred to believe. Europe was still the world's wealthiest continent, and its power, for better or worse, still spanned the globe. It had not yet fallen into the receivership of superpowers, as it would after 1945.

The salient question was not whether the League could function without the United States, but what the League actually was. Contemporaries debated this issue throughout the interwar period. State identity lay at the heart of the matter. P.E. Cobbett wrote in 1924: "Is the term 'League of Nations' merely an abridged way of saying 'Members of the League of Nations,' or does it correspond to a unit of an independent existence?"[4] In other words, did the League exist as a locus of sovereignty beyond the states it comprised? The peacemakers had created the League to change the international system. This implied changes in the agents that system comprised. As late as 1936, Alfred Zimmern could still ask: Are the "states members of the League" states in the same sense as in 1914?[5]

This chapter argues that, as we see in the *Tōkyō Puck* image, if Wilson and Wilsonian sovereignty were not controlling the scene, nor were they absent. Bourgeois and Curzon each in his way claimed aspects of the Wilsonian mantle. Bourgeois's vision emphasized a League that would decide through collective intentionality whether, when, where, and how the world would ever again go to war. This function give the League as a sovereign body the authority to decide what there was to decide in the international system. Curzon's vision emphasized state

[2] John Milton Cooper, *Breaking the Heart of the World: Woodrow Wilson and the Fight for the League of Nations* (Cambridge: Cambridge University Press, 2001), 297–314.

[3] Discreet contacts with the League continued through the interwar period. See Ludovic Tournès, *Les États-Unis et la Société des Nations (1914–1936)* (Bern: Peter Lang, 2016).

[4] P.E. Corbett, "What is the League of Nations?," *British Year Book of International Law: 1924* (London: Oxford University Press, 1924), 143.

[5] Alfred Zimmern, *The League of Nations and the Rule of Law, 1918–1935* (London: Macmillan and Co., 1936), 278.

sovereignty. But his vision did not necessarily rest on realism as the governing discourse. Nothing Curzon said inherently conflicted with the idea of a global liberal community providing a moral compass for state behavior. The devil, as always, would lie in the details of just what Wilsonianism meant.

As I argued in Chapter 1, the League had been written to function according to Wilsonian sovereignty—with states accountable to a transnational community of liberal citizens. That sovereignty would exist or it would not. If it would not, the League would have to find other ways in which to function.[6] The League in its early years functioned through the creation of possibilities, and in this way continued the laboratory of sovereignty established at the conference itself. Focusing on possibilities helps us get beyond what Susan Pedersen called the "decline and fall" narrative of the League of Nations. In this narrative, the end of the story—the descent into World War II—is implicit in the beginning. As she put it, historians' attention to the League today belongs to "the more properly historical question of what it did and meant over its twenty-five-year existence."[7]

In combination, the experiments coming out of the League of Nations did much to demarcate the international system between the wars. I begin by articulating the precise relationship of the League of Nations to the Paris Peace Conference, a relationship less than self-evident even at the time. I then return to themes and approaches of preceding chapters. Agents and structures met in new ways as the League sought to redefine international security. The early League became involved in the "unmixing" of lands through lingering and new border disputes. Inevitably, this drew the League into the "unmixing of peoples" through plebiscites, the Mandate System, and population exchanges.

THE LEAGUE OF NATIONS AND THE PARIS PEACE CONFERENCE

As we saw in Chapter 1, just when the "Paris Peace Conference" began and ended, and even exactly what it constituted were not always self-evident. After January 1920, when the League Council met for the first time, a Council of Ambassadors operating out of Paris would handle questions of detail stemming from the treaties. Periodic Great Power summits such as the Conference of San Remo in April 1920 and the Conference of Genoa of April–May 1922 continued the work of the Paris Peace Conference at a macro level.[8] What role was there for the newborn League of Nations in such a system?

---

[6] For a discussion of the early League in the context of competing aspirations for international law, see Stephen Wertheim, "The League of Nations: A Retreat from International Law?," *Journal of Global History* 7.2 (2012): 210–32. For broad context see also Mark Mazower, *Governing the World: The History of an Idea* (New York: Penguin Press, 2012), 116–53.

[7] Susan Pedersen, "Review Essay: Back to the League of Nations," *American Historical Review* 112.4 (2007): 1091–92.

[8] Resolution B, "Secretary's Notes of a Conference Held at 10, Downing Street, London, S.W.1, on Saturday, December 13, 1919, at 4:30 p.m.," *FRUS: PPC*, 9: 858.

The Treaty of Versailles, the Covenant of the League of Nations, and the new state (or minority) treaties had given the League a full agenda. Article 8 of the Covenant gave the League Council a leading role in arms reduction, including a provision that the League Council should advise League members on how to take the manufacture of weaponry out of private hands. Article 14 called on the League Council to design a Permanent Court of International Justice to handle disputes not solvable through regular diplomacy.[9] Perhaps most importantly, Article 22 gave the League Council charge over the Mandate System. Mandatory powers would administer sovereignty over mandatory lands and peoples on behalf of the League.

Moreover, the League would directly govern some territories. Articles 100–08 of the Treaty of Versailles established the Free City of Danzig, "under the protection of the League" (Article 102). Under Articles 16–40, the League would administer the Saar basin, seeing to the extraction of reparations from the mines to France and to holding an eventual plebiscite there. The League also would be drawn into fraught plebiscite struggles in Eupen and Malmédy (eventually annexed to Belgium), Upper Silesia, and Vilna. By definition, the minority treaties involved the League in the domestic politics of the successor states. All these tasks suggested that "the League" would eventually adopt an autonomous identity. John Eugene Harley was not alone at the time in believing that the conference had created a non-state actor with specified state-like functions, "an international person voluntarily created by the organized, sovereign states which form its membership."[10]

The Supreme Council had worked hard to downplay any understanding of the League of Nations as its own locus of sovereignty. Early discussions had given serious consideration to calling the head post "chancellor," along with granting the office wide powers to bring issues before the League.[11] Lord Robert Cecil of the British delegation had approached both Eleftherios Venizelos and Tomáš Masaryk about serving as chancellor. Both declined to have their names put forward on the grounds that they were needed at home. The authors of the Covenant ultimately decided on the more administrative title of "secretary-general."

The Supreme Council appointed as the first secretary-general Sir Eric Drummond, a career civil servant who previously had served as private secretary to Herbert Asquith, Sir Edward Grey, and Arthur Balfour. Such an appointment sent a signal that the secretary general should serve the League Council. But as a career functionary, Drummond always saw his charge as building the organization he led. While Drummond maintained close ties with the British Foreign Office, he never served as its minion.[12]

---

[9] The Permanent Court of International Justice did not render its first decision until August 1923, and its work lies mostly outside of the time frame here. See Manley O. Hudson, *The World Court, 1921–1931: A Handbook of the Permanent Court of International Justice* (Boston, MA: World Peace Foundation, 1931).

[10] John Eugene Harley, *The League of Nations and the New International Law* (New York: Oxford University Press, 1921), 55.

[11] James Barros, *Office without Power: Secretary-General Sir Eric Drummond, 1919–1933* (Oxford: Clarendon Press, 1979), 1–19.

[12] Klass Dykmann, "How International was the Secretariat of the League of Nations?," *International History Review* 37.4 (2015): 721–44.

The Supreme Council maintained a lively interest in the League prior to the first meeting of the League Council, to the point of setting the agenda for its first meeting. As the prospects for the Treaty of Versailles faded in the Senate, the central role of the American president in summoning the first meeting of the League Council seemed increasingly problematic. Moreover, as Henri Fromageot of the Drafting Committee reminded the Supreme Council on October 17, 1919, the League could not exist in a legal sense until the Treaty of Versailles came into effect.[13] But if the League did not legally exist, it could not administer the territories entrusted to it. Any serious delay thus would mean no formal sovereignty at all over the Saar basin and the city of Danzig. Time therefore became of the essence. On January 10, 1920, less than a week before the League Council met for the first time, the Council of Foreign Ministers decided the time and place of the first meeting and that following ceremonial introductions, the agenda would be limited to nominating members to the commission on the Saar.[14]

The fact that the Covenant of the League of Nations appeared as a preamble to all five treaties produced by the Paris Peace Conference supported the impression that the League existed to enforce the treaties. But the Great Powers never surrendered their sovereignty over the victory. The League played no role in writing the two treaties (Trianon and Sèvres) signed after it came into existence. The League administered the mandates, but the Supreme Council allocated them. Greece did not consult the League before extending its invasion of Anatolia in June 1920. Still less did France and Belgium do so before invading the Ruhr in 1923 to collect reparations.[15] None of these states considered themselves in violation of the Covenant.

The Treaty of Versailles established an array of inter-allied commissions to provide for the enforcement of the treaty. These commissions would report not to the League, but to the Allied and Associated Powers. The most important of these, the Reparations Commission (Article 233), would establish a final figure, and oversee the planned massive transfer of resources. Inter-allied commissions would assist the allies in drawing final boundaries of Poland (Article 87), and oversee plebiscites in Allenstein (Article 95) and Schleswig (Article 109). An inter-allied Commission of Control (Article 203) would enforce the military provisions of the treaty. Similar commissions would oversee the free navigation of German rivers—the Elbe (Article 340), the Oder (Article 341), and the Rhine (Article 355).

The claims of Bourgeois notwithstanding, the most important task of the League involved not enforcing the treaties, but building an infrastructure for permanent peace in the postwar world. Though few dared say so in 1920, the former Central Powers and the successor states that bore their names could not remain outcasts

---

[13] Henri Fromageot, "Note from the Drafting Committee," October 17, 1919, Appendix E to HD-72, "Notes of a Meeting of the Heads of Delegations of the Five Great Powers Held in M. Pichon's Room at the Quai d'Orsay, Paris, on Saturday, October 18, 1919, at 10:30 a.m.," *FRUS: PPC*, 9: 702–04.

[14] "Notes of a Meeting of Ministers of Foreign Affairs, Held at the Quai d'Orsay, Paris, on Saturday, January 10, 1920, at Noon," *FRUS: PPC*, 9: 958.

[15] See Conan Fischer, *The Ruhr Crisis, 1923–24* (Oxford: Oxford University Press, 2003), 84–85.

forever. Agents and structures had produced the League. In turn, the League as a formal structure would seek to articulate agents in the international system after the Great War.

AGENTS, STRUCTURES, AND THE SEARCH FOR SECURITY

The League of Nations corresponded to a certain configuration of agents and structures emerging from the Paris Peace Conference. As we saw, Wilsonianism had brought the Great Powers and then "the world" together to make peace and to redesign the international system. But "security" in the system as a whole would remain a Great Power issue. Wilsonianism had never argued otherwise. The League, then, had the task of permanently changing Great Power politics by permanently changing Great Power identities. The League began seeking to do so at an inauspicious time, when the formal authority of the Paris Peace Conference was crumbling in Anatolia. Nevertheless, the League took seriously its role as successor to the conference, and sought to build a formal structure toward that end. By 1923, it would produce a Draft Treaty of Mutual Assistance, a radical document worthy of the most dramatic flights of the Wilsonian imaginary. In rejecting the treaty, the Great Powers would reassert themselves as realist agents in the new international system. The "failure" of the League to guarantee security in the late 1930s proceeded from this early refusal to accord it much authority over the matter in 1923. On this issue, realism would successfully resist Wilsonian sovereignty.

Lord Robert Cecil told the League Assembly in November 1920: "The one danger that threatens the League is that it may gradually sink down into a position of respectable mediocrity and useless complication with the diplomatic machinery of the world. We must not be afraid of our power. We must be ready to take a bold line in the great work of reconciliation and pacification that lies before us."[16] The Covenant had created two institutions to carry out that work: the League Council and the League Assembly. Both had been written into the Covenant as though they would operate under Wilsonian sovereignty. The liberal citizenry of the world would keep the peace, needing only formal instruments such as these two bodies through which to do so. But how would they function in the absence of Wilsonian sovereignty?

During the drafting of the Covenant, the undefined relationship between the League Council and the Assembly gave rise to less controversy than might have been expected. In a memo of March 21, 1919, W.M. ("Billy") Hughes of Australia criticized the "slight and fragmentary" provisions for coordinating the two bodies. He further criticized a "false analogy" between the League and an actual governing body, and any assumption that either the League Council or the Assembly could

---

[16] Fifth Plenary Meeting, November 17, 1920, *League of Nations: The Records of the First Assembly, Plenary Meetings* (Geneva: League of Nations, 1921), 99. Hereafter referred to by session number, date, and page number.

make actual decisions: "Regarding both as consultative bodies, this is as it should be; but it is important that this should be made clear."[17] At a meeting of the League commission the next day, Paul Hymans of Belgium (later the first president of the League Assembly) added that whatever the sovereign properties of the League, "it would be useful to distinguish between the competence of the Executive Council and that of the Assembly of Delegates."[18]

At the same meeting, both Cecil and Wilson argued for positive imprecision. Cecil contended that "the spirit of the Covenant is to avoid excessively precise distinctions," and that it would be preferable to give both bodies "the ability subsequently to establish rules they believe appropriate." Wilson added: "Direction of the League will reside in the Executive Council, but freedom of discussion will belong to the Assembly of Delegates."[19] The final Covenant referred simply to the "Council (*Conseil*)," rather than "Executive Council," thus eliminating any overt reference to an executive function. Believers in Wilsonian sovereignty did not need precise definition, because the same moral compass would guide state behavior through both bodies. Non-believers could trust the Burkean teleology expressed by Cecil. The League would evolve as it ought to.[20]

The League Assembly met for the first time some eleven months after the first meeting of the League Council, on November 15, 1920.[21] Part of the reason for the long delay was simply logistical—transporting delegations from forty-one states to Geneva, and lodging them in a hitherto sleepy city before the era of mass tourism. But the League Council at the very least did not force the pace of bringing together the League Assembly, so as to affirm itself as the senior body. At its second plenary meeting, the League Assembly formed the First Committee, charged with articulating the relationship between the two bodies.[22] "The Truth is," its report submitted in December 1920 admitted, "that the League of Nations has no analogy in ordinary constitutional law."[23] Article 2 of the Covenant, the report continued, "provides that the action of the League shall be effected through the instrumentality of an Assembly and a Council" (282). Therefore, the report concluded, the world needed to consider the League of Nations as "a single organism that has at its disposal two organs" (282). It was impossible to consider the League Council an upper chamber and the League Assembly a lower chamber because each had specific areas of competence mentioned in the League Covenant. Article 8 had

[17] W.M. Hughes, "Notes on the Draft Covenant," March 21, 1919, in David Hunter Miller, *The Drafting of the Covenant*, 2 vols. (New York: G.P. Putnam's Sons, 1928), 1: 364.

[18] "Procès Verbal No. 11, Séance du 22 mars 1919," in Miller, *Drafting*, 2: 503–04.

[19] According to Miller, this discussion "was much better reported in the French minutes than elsewhere." Miller, *Drafting*, 1: 315. The translation back into English is my own.

[20] Milenko Militch, *Les Attributions Communes et les rapport du Conseil et de l'Assemblée: une etude de la Société des Nations* (Paris: A. Pedone, 1929).

[21] On the early work of the League Assembly, see Frances Kellor and Antonia Hatvany, *Security against War*, 2 vols. (New York: Macmillan Company, 1924), 1: 37–60; F.P. Walters, *A History of the League of Nations*, 2 vols. (London: Oxford University Press, 1952), 1: 98–112; and Margaret E. Burton, *The Assembly of the League of Nations* (Chicago, IL: University of Chicago Press, 1941), 61–93.

[22] Second Plenary Meeting, November 15, 1920, 48.

[23] "Report Presented to the Assembly by Committee No. 1," Fourteenth Plenary Meeting, December 6, 1920, 282–85, followed by a debate, 285–96.

called on the League Council to make proposals for the reduction of armaments, to be approved not by the Assembly, but by national governments. The League Council would also provide advice for the enforcement as required of Article 10, and would specify the conditions of the mandates (282–83).

The First Committee of the League Assembly endorsed the concept of Burkean, organic growth: "the less we attempt to formulate in explicit language the precise functions which the Council and the Assembly are respectively expected to perform, the better for the future of the League" (283). In time, debating reports sent by the League Council became the foundation of the yearly sessions of the League Assembly. The League Assembly questioned the acts of the League Council, and raised issues of its own. Public speech on any subject affecting the peace of the world thus found a forum, much as Wilson has envisaged. This said, the committee made clear that all speech in League bodies came from states: "Representatives on the Council and the Assembly are responsible to their own Governments and to those Governments alone."[24]

As we saw in Chapter 1, only Wilsonian sovereignty made sense of the "unanimity rule" under Article 5 of the Covenant. This rule required the agreement of all members present to any decision (*décision*) made at a given meeting of either the League Council or the League Assembly, except where the Covenant explicitly stipulated otherwise. Article 5 seemingly doomed the League to the "respectable mediocrity" of a talking shop, as Cecil had warned, in the absence of Wilsonian sovereignty. Yet the League invented a means of fulfilling the letter of Article 5 while altering its content. As written, the unanimity rule had never been absolute.[25] Particularly in the League Assembly, it became tempting simply to brand a matter "procedural," and thus not subject to the unanimity rule.[26]

The League Assembly also used a linguistic device to adapt the unanimity rule. The League Assembly formed its own committee covering disarmament, known as the Sixth Committee, which first reported on December 13, 1920.[27] Resolution 3(e) proposed the freezing of military expenditures for all League members.[28] Bourgeois (now an Assembly member for France), with the support of the British, objected. Given the need to protect their overseas empires, Britain and France could not guarantee that their military expenses would remain constant. Hymans, as president of the Assembly, recommended that the relevant resolution carry the following language (stated by him in French): "L'Assemblée émet le vœu que le Conseil soumette à l'examen des Gouvernements..." The juxtaposed English substitutes a single verb for "émet le vœu": "The Assembly recommends to the

---

[24] "Report Presented to the Assembly by Committee No. 1," Fourteenth Plenary Meeting, December 6, 1920, 284.

[25] Cromwell A. Riches, *The Unanimity Rule and the League of Nations* (Baltimore, MD: The Johns Hopkins Press, 1933), 37–38.

[26] Riches, *Unanimity Rule*, 61–62.

[27] On the operation of League Assembly committees, see Marcel-Henri Prévost, *Les Commissions de l'Assemblée de la Société des Nations* (Paris: Éditions E. Pedone, 1936).

[28] "Twenty-Second Plenary Meeting, Tuesday, December 14th, 1920, at Eleven o'clock" (Annex to the Twenty-Second Meeting: Armaments, Report of Committee No. VI), 520.

Council to submit to the consideration of the Governments…"[29] As international law scholar John Fischer Williams noted, "vœu" has many possible English translations. In addition to "recommendation" it can mean "wish," "view," "hope," indeed, any non-binding expression of the will. Williams himself considered the word "almost untranslatable."[30] Different listeners could hear different messages.

In the early years of the League, prominent figures such as Bourgeois, Cecil, and Paul Hymans circulated with ease between the two bodies. On February 25, 1921, Bourgeois brought before the League Council a proposal from the Assembly to establish a Temporary Mixed Commission on Disarmament.[31] Its uninformative name notwithstanding, the charge given the commission included "submitting to the Council in the near future all evidence and proposals connected with the question of the reduction of armaments contemplated by Article 8 of the Covenant" (148).

The commission would recognize what later generations would call the military-industrial complex, and would include military experts, specialists in economics and finance, and members of the governing body of the International Labour Office (148–49). Andrew Webster has argued that the proposal responded to frustration in the League Assembly that any progress on disarmament was being thwarted by military officers from the Great Powers. Toward that end, as Webster put it, "members were specifically appointed as *private individuals*, unrestrained by formal instructions from governments."[32] The League Council accepted the report immediately, and the Temporary Mixed Commission began its work in July 1921.

The work of the Temporary Mixed Commission would reflect a specifically French fixation on security highlighted by Bourgeois at the first meeting of the League Council. The chair, René Viviani, had led the French government in August 1914. He would insist on "disarmament" applying first and foremost to Germany, as would his influential compatriot Lieutenant-Colonel Edouard Réquin.[33] "Disarmament" to them could only be an effect of "security," not a cause. Yet to focus on the French appropriation of the new commission would be to miss part of the point. The League as a formal structure, like the Paris Peace Conference, never claimed to set aside Great Power preoccupations. The point is more how these preoccupations found new means of expression through the League.

In response to continued pressure from the League Assembly, and to suspicion of French motives, the Temporary Mixed Commission expanded its membership in July 1922. It now included Lord Robert Cecil, probably the most important

---

[29] Twenty-Third Plenary Meeting, Tuesday, December 14th, 1920, 529.

[30] Sir John Fisher Williams, "The League of Nations and Unanimity," *AJIL* 19 (1925): 479–80.

[31] "The Resolutions of the Assembly with Regard to Armaments," February 25, 1921, *League Council: JO* (March–April 1921), 143–51.

[32] Andrew Webster, "'Absolutely Irresponsible Amateurs': The Temporary Mixed Commission on Armaments, 1921–1924," *Australian Journal of Politics and History* 54.3 (2008): 373, italics in original.

[33] Peter Jackson, *Beyond the Balance of Power: France and the Politics of National Security in the Era of the First World War* (Cambridge: Cambridge University Press, 2013), 374–77; and Marie-Renée Mouton, *La Société des Nations et les intérêts de la France (1920–1924)* (Bern: Peter Lang, 1995), 297–312.

keeper of the Wilsonian flame in Europe by this time.[34] Then sitting in the League Assembly for South Africa, Cecil had more freedom of maneuver than most senior politicians. As one of the authors of the Covenant, Cecil had the prestige to counter Viviani and Réquin.[35] Largely through Cecil's influence, the Temporary Mixed Commission began work on a Draft Treaty of Mutual Assistance. The commission approved the draft treaty in August 1923, and sent it on to the League Assembly for discussion.[36]

Edvard Beneš of Czechoslovakia presented the Draft Treaty of Mutual Assistance to the Fourth Assembly on September 27, 1923.[37] He began with a specific understanding of collective security provided under Article 10 of the Covenant: "*The guarantee and disarmament are interdependent*" (3, italics in original). States could not disarm without security, which only disarmament could provide. The treaty provided an alternative to self-help realism by giving the League law-giving authority on making war and peace. Article 1 criminalized aberrant state behavior in the international system. The signatories "solemnly declare that aggressive war is an international crime and severally undertake that none of them will be guilty of its commission." "Aggressive war" mean a resort to violence under specified conditions: the refusal of a unanimous recommendation from the League Council; the refusal of a verdict of the Permanent Court of International Justice; or the refusal in practically all cases of an arbitral award.

The League Council would serve as a sovereign court, before or after the outbreak of violence. Aggrieved parties would take their cases to the League Council (Article 3), which would render a decision with the force of law (Article 4). Article 2 obligated all the signatories to assist a member besieged by aggressive war. The League Council could use all means necessary to enforce its decisions—from sanctions to establishing a military command over which it would have authority (Article 5). Article 10 extended to any future war the constructed meaning of Article 231 of the Treaty of Versailles. Henceforth, "the whole cost of any military, naval or air operations," as well as "all material damage caused by operations of war, shall be borne by the aggressor State up to the extreme limit of its financial capacity."

Under the treaty, disarmament would become a truly global issue, only partly under the control of the Great Powers.[38] The League Council would collect disarmament plans from the signatories, and would coordinate their implementation (Article 11). It would then form a plan for world disarmament, which it would send to the states for their approval (Article 11). As per Article 18, this plan would

[34] Peter Raffo, "The League of Nations Philosophy of Lord Robert Cecil," *Australian Journal of Politics and History* 20.2 (1974): 186–96, esp. 188–89.

[35] Webster, "Irresponsible Amateurs," 83.

[36] By this time, Cecil had joined the government of Stanley Baldwin, and sat quietly in the League Assembly. Webster, "Irresponsible Amateurs," 385.

[37] League of Nations: Reduction of Armaments, *Report of the Third Committee to the Fourth Assembly*, September 27, 1923, 7–10.

[38] In 1923, the League Council comprised eight members: four permanent (France, the British Empire, Italy, and Japan); and four members elected on a rotating basis from the Assembly.

come into effect when ratified by: five European states (including the three permanent League Council members), two Asian states (including Japan), four South American states, the United States (a bold prognostic under the circumstances), and various others. Article 19 raised the stakes on the issue of unanimity among signatories, by stipulating that if any of the signatories referred to in Article 18 denounced it, the entire treaty would cease to exist. Deviation would mean a return to pure realism. Only collective intentionality, underpinned by Wilsonian sovereignty, could make such a disarmament regime work. In ratifying the treaty, states would give a very Wilsonian League Council sovereign authority over war and peace.

By September 1923, such a treaty was going to draw detractors. Beneš's report admitted as much, if obliquely: "the difficulties inherent in such a complicated undertaking, and the pre-occupations of the moment are reflected in the document that has been drawn up" (6). While the Third Committee considered the document "a step forward on the difficult path to armament reduction," the committee found it "impossible to recommend to the Governments the immediate adoption of this text" (6). Rather, it recommended simply submitting the document to states for comment. The demise of the Draft Treaty could not have surprised many contemporaries. Practically all of Cecil's colleagues in the government disdained it. The first Labour government quietly rejected the document in July 1924.[39] Even in France, a countercurrent of opinion to the views of Bourgeois and Réquin, held by War Minister André Maginot and Prime Minister Raymond Poincaré, rejected any external constraints whatsoever on French defense policy.[40] Support elsewhere, particularly among the smaller European powers, mattered little if the two greatest powers on the League Council stood opposed.

By 1923, the Great Powers had appropriated disarmament as an issue, largely outside the League of Nations. The United States, which had so pointedly rejected the League, led the way. It is simply inaccurate to see the Americans as "isolationist" in the early 1920s. Globalized trade and the massive wartime debt to the United States meant that the Americans would have difficulty turning their back on Europe, even if they wanted to.[41] Moreover, disarmament in the early 1920s did not require pacifism. Fiscal conservatism among all the Great Powers made them eager to reduce military expenditures.

Within a year of taking office, Wilson's successor Warren G. Harding undertook a major effort to limit the arms race in the Pacific.[42] Led by Secretary of State Charles Evans Hughes, the Washington Naval Conference met from November 1921–February 1922. "Our hundred millions," proclaimed the president at the

[39] See Carolyn J. Kitching, *Britain and the Problem of International Disarmament, 1919–1934* (London: Routledge, 1999), 72–75.

[40] Jackson, *Beyond the Balance of Power*, 423–24.

[41] On the economic background, see Robert H. Van Meter, Jr., "The Washington Conference of 1921–22: A New Look," *Pacific Historical Review* 46.4 (1977): 603–24.

[42] Thomas A. Buckley, *The United States and the Washington Naval Conference, 1921–22* (Knoxville: University of Tennessee Press, 1970).

opening session, "want less of armament and none of war."[43] The United States, Britain, Japan, France, and Italy all agreed to substantially limit the size of their fleets. Whatever their shortcomings as revealed by the 1930s, the Washington agreements put in place the only noteworthy arms limitation regime of the inter-war period.[44] Moreover, the Washington Conference accomplished something the Paris Peace Conference could not, a framework for the partial disengagement of Japan from Shandong.

President Harding described the treaties resulting from the conference in surprisingly Wilsonian terms as "covenants of harmony" when he sent them to the Senate, which ratified them with little of the drama of the League fight. The League of Nations had played no role. This state-based approach to redefining security would later extend beyond arms control, culminating in the Kellogg–Briand Pact of 1928. The Great Powers (by then including the Soviet Union and Germany) and a host of other states renounced war itself as an instrument for solving international disputes.[45] State-based security in the interwar period reached its zenith on the eve of the Great Depression.

The League had produced an experiment in sovereignty that was intellectually interesting and morally defensible. But the League had not changed Great Power identities by 1923, nor was there much reason to have expected it to. The Great Powers largely excluded it from international security, through their non-reception of the Draft Treaty of Mutual Assistance. If we must understand the history of the League according to a "decline and fall" narrative, its fall began early. Yet from its origins Wilsonianism never wholly abandoned the preoccupations of realism. Perhaps for that reason, President Harding, who had risen to the presidency by not being Woodrow Wilson, could speak the word "covenant." But the League itself would need to find other issues for practical influence.

THE "UNMIXING" OF LANDS

The League never had sovereignty over borders, which remained the domain of the Paris Peace Conference. However, various entities would turn to the League for help with border disputes. In Persia, a state would seek its help to ward off imperial encroachments by Bolshevik Russia. Advocates for a mandate in Armenia would seek to involve the League far beyond its statutory role. In both cases, the League demurred, affirming Curzon's contention that the League would not seek to

[43] Quoted in Quincy Wright, "The Washington Conference," *American Political Science Review* 16.2 (1922): 287. On Hughes, see Robert Kaufman, *Arms Control during the Pre-Nuclear Era: The United States and Naval Limitation between the Two World Wars* (New York: Columbia University Press, 1990), 43–72.

[44] Erik Goldstein and John Maurer, eds., *The Washington Conference, 1921–22: Naval Rivalry, East Asian Stability, and the Road to Pearl Harbor* (Ilford: F. Cass, 1994).

[45] Harold Josephson, "Outlawing War: Internationalism and the Pact of Paris," *Diplomatic History* 3.4 (1979): 377–90. On Kellogg-Briand and the Wilsonian legacy, see Oona A. Hathaway and Scott J. Shapiro, *The Internationalists: How a Radical Plan to Outlaw War Remade the World* (New York: Simon and Schuster, 2017).

displace Great Power politics. In one case, the Åland Islands dispute between Sweden and Finland, the League provided a highly inventive solution for "unmixing lands." Yet here, the very success of the League showed its limits as a locus of sovereignty in the international system.

On May 19, 1920, Persia appealed to the League of Nations under Article 11 of the Covenant, according to which any member could request assistance to head off "any war or threat of war." The matter involved the integrity of an existing border. Since the nineteenth century, Persia had been a semi-independent monarchy divided between Russian and British spheres of influence.[46] Revolution in Russia had destabilized these arrangements. The British sought to benefit through the Anglo-Persian agreement of August 1919, which guaranteed British access to oil fields and solidified British economic and political influence throughout Persia.[47] The Bolsheviks, for their part, sought to extend the revolution to the outermost borders of the tsars and beyond. The Red Army defeated General Anton Denikin's White forces in Baku, Azerbaijan, in late April 1920. A small fleet bearing Denikin escaped to Anzali, Persia, where the British disarmed and interned the personnel and the fleet in accordance with international law. Nevertheless, the Bolsheviks bombarded Anzali and occupied it in May 1920. On June 5, 1920, Bolsheviks in the Gilan province proclaimed the Persian Socialist Soviet Republic.[48]

As Oliver Bast has argued, the Persians appealed to the League of Nations to assert national sovereignty.[49] The timing had a certain advantage, after the first meeting of the League Council but before the first meeting of the League Assembly. Persia could impress itself on an institution still taking shape. Prince Firuz Mirza Nosret-ed-Dowleh, Persian foreign minister, wrote to Secretary-General Drummond: "I beg to call the attention of the Council to the very serious situation in which Persia is placed by these events which threaten to disturb the peace of the Middle East."[50]

While Drummond convened the League Council, he hesitated to involve the League too deeply in a Great Power competition that dated to the previous century.[51] The British, accurately as it turned out, believed the incursion more a matter of entrepreneurial Bolsheviks than state-driven aggression. Moreover, the British hardly wanted to encourage an international appeal on the part of their Persian client. The British and the French also understood that dealing with the Bolsheviks on Persia, even through the League, would constitute de facto recognition. After pondering the matter for more than a month, the League

---

[46] Oliver Bast, "Les « Buts de guerre » de la Perse neutre pendant la première guerre mondiale," *Relations internationals*, No. 160 (2015): 95–110.

[47] Michael Axworthy, *A History of Iran: Empire of the Mind* (New York: Basic Books, 2008), 211–20.

[48] Guive Mirfenderski, *A Diplomatic History of the Caspian Sea: Treaties, Diaries, and other Stories* (New York: Palgrave, 2001), 103–05.

[49] Oliver Bast, "Duping the British and Outwitting the Russians?: Iran's Foreign Policy, the 'Bolshevik Threat', and the Genesis of the Soviet–Iranian Treaty of 1921," in Stephanie Cronin, ed., *Iranian–Russian Encounters: Empires and Revolutions since 1800* (London: Routledge, 2013), 261–97.

[50] Prince Firuz to Secretary-General Drummond, May 19, 1920, Annex 61, *League Council: JO* (July–August 1920), 215–16.

[51] See Barros, *Office without Power*, 117–21.

Council declined to intervene, citing the stated Bolshevik intent to withdraw from Anzali.[52] The resolution praised the Persian government for having "acted in the best interest of peace," and advised it to keep the Council "informed of the march of events." The new regime in Persia following a February 1921 coup would make a treaty with Bolshevik Russia just five days after coming to power. The "Great Game" over influence in Central Asia would continue in its new configuration.

A quixotic effort to involve the League in creating a territorial Armenia demonstrated that it had no intention to become a super-state. In March 1920, Viscount James Bryce of Britain began to lobby the League for a mandate in Armenia.[53] Drummond was personally sympathetic, and attempted to mobilize French support through his deputy Jean Monnet. On March 12, Lord Curzon, on behalf of the Supreme Council of the peace conference, asked the League Council to assume a mandate in Armenia.

Surely Curzon knew better at the time. Article 22 of the League Covenant made matters clear; mandates were exercised "on behalf of the League," not by the League itself.[54] The League Council response of April 11 stated the obvious: "It [the League Council] realizes that it is not a state; that it has as yet no army and no finances, and that its action upon public opinion would be fainter in Asia Minor than in the more civilized regions of Europe."[55] Moreover, establishing an Armenian mandate would require massive resources—to provide for the return of surviving Armenians, to establish a working economy, and to provide the military force necessary to protect Armenians from the successor state taking shape under Mustafa Kemal in Angora. The League Council concluded that if the Supreme Council provided it with "adequate assurance" as to just how all this was supposed to happen, the League Council would seek an appropriate state to serve as mandatory power. It could do no more.

If the legal status of the League foredoomed any request for a mandate, what was the entire affair really about? The problems of protecting Armenians in a territorial Armenia were in fact intractable, barring a formidable and open-ended commitment from war-weary allies. At precisely this time, the spring and summer of 1920, the Greek incursions in Anatolia, the surreal Treaty of Sèvres, and the consolidating new regime in Angora all threatened to explode peacemaking in Asia Minor. From a Great Power realist point of view, subcontracting Armenia to the League, even in contravention to the Covenant, could shift blame for at least one potential disaster.

Putting an unfeasible request before the League also served to demarcate its limits in the international system. The League Assembly took up Armenia in a vigorous debate held on November 22, 1920.[56] Mr. Spalaikovitch of the South

---

[52] "Resolution Adopted by the Council of the League of Nations, Meeting in London on 16th June, 1920," *League Council: JO* (July–August 1920), 217–18.

[53] Barros, *Office without Power*, 106–10.

[54] Quincy Wright, *Mandates of the League of Nations* (Chicago, IL: University of Chicago Press, 1930), 438–44.

[55] "Future Status of Armenia," Annex, April 11, 1920, *League Council: JO* (April–May 1920), 85–87.

[56] Ninth Plenary Meeting, Monday, November 22nd, 1920, 184–202.

Slav state castigated the "cold and cynical method of exterminating Christian people" (185), invented by the Ottomans and continued under the Kemalists. Hjalmar Branting of Sweden called on the Assembly to pass a unanimous vote for action, coupled with his hope that doing so "will exercise sufficient influence on the Great Powers to induce them to pass from words to acts and to take at last efficacious steps to save the martyred people of Armenia" (187). René Viviani described the predicament of the League Assembly with uncomfortable accuracy: "If the truth must be told we are a powerless Assembly, because we have been trusted with a responsibility without having been given any real authority" (190).

The Assembly debate illustrated what many surely knew. "The world" claimed to care a great deal more about post-genocide Armenia than it actually did. In the end, a motion carried to establish a committee of six persons to "consider and report to the Assembly during this Session what steps, if any, could be taken to put an end to the hostilities between Armenia and the Kemalists" (202). The Supreme Council would not intervene, nor would it consider giving the League Council the means of doing so. On issues such as Armenia, the League Assembly was on its way to becoming precisely the kind of "talking shop" Wilson had feared.

On the other hand, the territorial dispute between Sweden and Finland over the Åland Islands proved arguably the highpoint of League of Nations diplomacy during the whole interwar period, and is even today a case known to scholars of international law.[57] The matter showed what the League could do in the absence of Wilsonian sovereignty if member states sought to make use of it. Along the way, the League claimed a juridical role for itself in resolving certain kinds of international disputes, and even articulated a much-needed limiting concept to "self-determination."

The Åland Islands made up some 300 islands in the Gulf of Bothnia. It had a total population in 1920 of some 25,000 people, some 16,000 of whom lived on one main island.[58] An American observer reported the general conviction that some 97 percent of the population considered itself "Swedish in blood, language, culture, and national feeling."[59] The Treaty of Paris of 1856 recognized the islands as belonging to the Duchy of Finland under the Russian imperial crown. However, given their strategic position, the islands remained "demilitarized," meaning without fortifications. Russia held to this agreement until the Great War. In 1917, revolution in Russia spread to Finland, including a civil war between Finnish Bolsheviks and "Whites."[60] Sweden, Bolshevik Russia, and Germany all sent small

---

[57] See, for example, Oliver Diggelmannn, "The Aaland Case and the Sociological Approach to International Law," *European Journal of International Law* 18.1 (2007): 135–43.

[58] Philip Marshall Brown, "The Aaland Islands Question," *AJIL* 15.2 (1921): 268–72; Charles Noble Gregory, "The Neutralization of the Aaland Islands," *AJIL* 17.1 (1923): 63–76; James Barros, *The Aland Islands Question: Its Settlement by the League of Nations* (New Haven, CT: Yale University Press, 1968); and Tore Modeen, "The Åland Islands Question," in Paul Smith, ed., *Ethnic Groups in International Relations* (New York: New York University Press, 1991), 153–68.

[59] Gregory, "Neutralization," 66.

[60] Anthony F. Upton, *The Finnish Revolution, 1917–1918* (Minneapolis: University of Minnesota Press, 1980); and Risto Alapuro, *State and Revolution in Finland* (Berkeley: University of California Press, 1988).

contingents of troops, though all behaved with remarkable restraint. The situation remained in stalemate until the end of the war. A stabilized non-Bolshevik regime in a now-independent Finland declined to renounce its historic claim. The islanders appealed to the Supreme Council for "self-determination" and incorporation into Sweden.

British Foreign Secretary Lord Curzon duly wrote to the League Secretariat on June 19, 1920, referring to the dispute as a threat "to disturb the good understanding between nations upon which peace depends."[61] Since the League Assembly had not yet met and the Permanent Court of International Justice was some years away from functioning, the matter lay with the League Council. Finland, not yet a League member, considered the Åland Islands purely a domestic matter, and thus not under League jurisdiction. But neither Finland nor Sweden wanted war over the issue, and both saw Great Power dominance over the islands as the worst solution of all.

Consequently, neither Sweden nor Finland protested when on July 15, 1920 the League Council established an International Committee of Jurists to determine League competence in the matter.[62] Essentially, the jurists decided what there was to decide. Article 15 of the Covenant had given the League Council the authority to determine whether a matter brought to its attention was of domestic or international concern (4). Further, the jurists concluded that territorial sovereignty, like other "attributes of the sovereignty of a State, only applies to a nation which is definitively constituted as a sovereign State and an independent member of the international community" (5). Finland attained legal personality under international law only in May 1918, when the civil war ended and the foreign troops began to withdraw (9). The 1856 treaty assigning the islands to Finland had been made with an Imperial Russia that no longer existed. Consequently, they concluded, the League in fact had competence to decide the state to which the islands belonged.

Following the jurists' decision in September 1920, the League Council established a Commission of Rapporteurs, which presented its recommendations in April 1921.[63] In contrast to the jurists, the rapporteurs argued that the Grand Duchy of Finland had been sovereign enough to hold territory, and that on that basis the islands should remain Finnish. The rapporteurs recommended considerable autonomy for the islanders. They could preserve Swedish as the exclusive language of instruction in primary and technical schools. They could restrict the right of outsiders to acquire property and could even prohibit immigrants from the Finnish mainland from voting for the first five years of residence. To guarantee these arrangements, the islanders would have recourse to the Permanent Court of

---

[61] Curzon to Drummond, June 19, 1920, quoted in Gregory, "Neutralization," 63.

[62] "Report of the International Committee of Jurists Entrusted by the Council of the League of Nations with the Task of Giving an Advisory Opinion upon the Legal Aspects of the Aaland Islands Question," *League Council: JO*, Special Supplement No. 3, October 1920.

[63] *The Aaland Island Question: Report Submitted to the Council of the League of Nations by the Commission of Rapporteurs*, April 16, 1921, Council Document B7 (Geneva: League of Nations, 1921).

International Justice once established. In the event, protecting the "Swedish-ness" of the islanders never seemed a particularly controversial issue between Finland and Sweden. Finland readily recognized these protections in exchange for the affirmation of its territorial sovereignty. The 1856 provisions prohibiting fortification of the islands continued.

The jurists and the rapporteurs further agreed on the need to limit "self-determination" under international law. There was, the jurists pointed out, "no mention of it in the Covenant of the League of Nations" (5). No right to secede exists as a matter of international law, quite the contrary: "the right of disposing of national territory is essentially an attribute of the sovereignty of every state" (5). In other words, what mattered was not the wishes of the Åland Islanders, rather the status under international law of the former Duchy of Finland. The rapporteurs had found no evidence of the repression of "Swedish" ethnic identity among the islanders, quite the contrary. Therefore, they could put the matter bluntly:

> To concede to minorities, either of language or religion, or to any fractions of a population the right of separating itself from the community to which they belong, because it is their wish or their good pleasure, would be to destroy order and stability within States and to inaugurate anarchy in international life; it would be to uphold a theory incompatible with the very idea of the State as a territorial and political unity. (28)

At one level, in resolving the Åland Islands dispute, the League simply confirmed the status quo ante bellum, in a situation no one really wanted to disrupt. Everyone had far more pressing matters in 1920. Paradoxically, the League in this case asserted its capacity to rule on the subject of self-determination by affirming state sovereignty over self-determination. The League could help states work things out when they chose to do so.

The League would become marginally involved in various other territorial disputes between 1920 and 1923.[64] Typically, the League would decline involvement, or would see its views set aside by the Council of Ambassadors. Related disputes over the borders of Albania in 1923 and the Italian invasion of Corfu in 1923 largely sidelined League institutions. Unwillingness to antagonize a permanent member of the League Council also precluded serious League involvement in Fiume.[65] In chronic border disputes in successor Hungary, the Council of Ambassadors at intervals elicited the input of the League, only to set its views aside and resolve matters itself. "Unmixing" lands would remain primarily in the hands of the Great Powers.

[64] See Kellor and Hatvany, *Security against War*, 3: 181–97 (Albania); 198–235 (Corfu); 236–45 (Fiume); and 299–315 (Hungary); as well as James Barros, *The Corfu Incident of 1923: Mussolini and the League of Nations* (Princeton, NJ: Princeton University Press, 1965).

[65] With the reluctant assent of the Kingdom of the Serbs, Croats and Slovenes, Italy would annex Fiume formally in 1924. Alan Cassels, *Mussolini's Early Diplomacy* (Princeton, NJ: Princeton University Press, 1970), 127–45.

THE "UNMIXING" OF PEOPLES

Contemporaries well understood that the Paris Peace Conference would bequeath population policies to the League. This, after all, was why plebiscites, minority protections, mandates, and population exchanges found their way into the peace treaties and the new state treaties in the first place. The formal agreements were written in such a way that the Supreme Council jealously guarded its sovereignty over how and where it would apply population policies. It would turn to the League when it needed an outcome it could plausibly portray as "neutral" or apolitical. Under League auspices, peoples were not so much "unmixed" as "remixed" within new boundaries. Despite years of effort to create new solutions, the League in its first years became more a locus of blame than a locus of sovereignty.

Plebiscites

The League of Nations inherited two Polish border conflicts that involved plebiscites: Upper Silesia; and the former Vilna Governorate, contested between Poland and Lithuania. Both conflicts unfolded simultaneously, against the backdrop of the shifting fortunes of war between successor Poland and Bolshevik Russia. In Upper Silesia, the Great Powers asked the League to interpret the results of a contentious plebiscite. For the Poland–Lithuania border, the League Council tried to carry out a plebiscite, probably under foredoomed circumstances.

As we saw, the March 1921 plebiscite in Upper Silesia produced ambiguous results, bitter recriminations, and violence all around. An overall plurality for Germany of nearly 60 percent masked considerable differences among the various *Kreisen*. The Germans argued that the overall result required the return of Upper Silesia in its entirety to Germany, an outcome neither the Poles nor the French would consider accepting. British sympathy for the German position led to a rift between the two Great Powers within the inter-allied plebiscite commission. Polish suspicions that the outcome would tip Germany's way had provoked a Third Silesian Uprising, with paramilitary violence threatening to overwhelm public authority altogether.

In despair, hope, or most likely some combination of the two, the Supreme Council (distinguishing itself from the Council of Ambassadors) on August 12, 1921 appealed to the Council of the League of Nations under Article 2 of the League Covenant. Upper Silesia had become a matter "affecting international relations which threatens to disturb international peace or the good understanding between nations upon which peace depends." Writing on behalf of the Supreme Council, French Foreign Minister Aristide Briand requested recommendations "for the tracing of the frontier line which it is the business of the Principal Allied and Associated Powers to establish."[66] On August 24, Briand wrote to the League Council again, in effect requesting binding arbitration, since "each of the

---

[66] "Letter from the President of the Supreme Council to the Acting President of the Council of the League," August 12, 1921, *League Council: JO* (November 1921): 982.

Governments represented in the course of the discussion solemnly had undertaken to accept the solution recommended by the Council of the League of Nations."[67]

Involving the League meant involving non-Europeans in European affairs. According to the normal rotation, the presidency of the League Council had fallen to veteran Japanese diplomat Vicount Ishii Kikujiro.[68] Ishii convened an extraordinary session of the League Council in which he set up a special committee comprising members from countries with no previous involvement in Upper Silesia.[69] On September 2, the subcommittee elected as its chair Wellington Koo of China. The Upper Silesia affair set the stage for a rare episode of interwar cooperation between Japanese and Chinese diplomats. Sir Cecil Hurst of the British Foreign Office complained in an internal memo of something "almost grotesque in letting a Chinaman preside over a body which is to decide an issue of importance between France and Britain."[70] But even Hurst praised the ability of Koo, who held a Ph.D. from Columbia University, to "understand and talk English perfectly." Hurst, on balance, supported including Koo on the committee. Even in the heady days of November 1918, few would have foreseen Asians taking the lead in resolving a European border dispute.

The Koo committee studied Upper Silesia assiduously, but could only arrive at the obvious conclusion that drawing boundaries amounted to a zero-sum game. None of the protagonists would accept an autonomous Upper Silesia. Nor would the League Council or the Supreme Council award an undivided Upper Silesia to either Germany or Poland. Doing so would perpetuate paramilitary warfare on the part of the "losing" ethnicity. No outcome could please both successor Germany and successor Poland, and both a Britain that supported a stronger Germany and a France that supported a weaker one.

We saw in Chapter 4 that yet another expert report submitted to the Council of Ambassadors on August 6 proposed the Solomonic solution of dividing Upper Silesia, which even as a least bad solution would "remix" the very peoples the plebiscite had sought to "unmix." Given the divided vote between urban and rural areas, and even within urban areas, no border could be drawn without leaving large numbers of Germans in Poland, or large numbers of Poles in Germany. Any approximate ethnic division would also place resources in one angry country and workers in another.

Viscount Ishii as president of the League Council submitted the Koo committee report and recommendations on October 12, 1921. Ishii reminded the Supreme Council of the ambiguity of Article 88 of the Treaty of Versailles, and asked:

---

[67] Briand to Iishi, August 24, 1921, quoted by Viscount Iishi Kukijiro in "The Question of Upper Silesia: Report by Viscount Ishii on the Request Addressed by the Supreme Council of the Principal Allied Powers to the Council of the League of Nations to Find a Solution to the Question of Upper Silesia," *League Council: JO* (December 1921): 1221.

[68] Joseph F. Harrington, Jr., "The League of Nations and the Upper Silesian Boundary Dispute," *The Polish Review*, 23.3 (1978): 86–101.

[69] Takako Ueta, "The Role of Japan in Establishing the Frontiers in Europe after the First World War: The Upper Silesia Question and Japan," in Christian Baechler and Carole Fink, eds., *The Establishment of European Frontiers after the Two World Wars* (Bern: Peter Lang, 1996), 167–79.

[70] "Memorandum by Sir C. Hurst on Upper Silesia," August 16, 1921, *DBFP*, 16: 326–28.

"Should the results of the plebiscite determine by a single vote the fate of all the territory under consideration, or lead to the tracing of a frontier line which may or may not divide the territory?" The Koo committee concluded that the authors of the treaty envisaged "the determination of a frontier, no particular line being either prescribed or excluded in advance."[71] In other words, the Supreme Council had given the League Council the authority to interpret the treaty. The League Council saw "its duty above all to endeavor to find a solution in conformity with the wishes of the inhabitants" (1224). The results of the plebiscite and the preceding and subsequent unrest had, regrettably, left no alternative to partition.

The challenge, then, involved preserving the economic prosperity of Upper Silesia, for all Upper Silesians. Toward that end, the League Council proposed a fifteen-year transition period that involved shared sovereignty over the regional economy. The German Mark would remain the single currency. Railways, water, and electricity would continue as single systems. Workers could move across new national borders, though German workers would maintain their considerable social protections if their workplaces became part of Poland. Minorities, including the Poles in Germany, would receive explicit protection, the only minorities in Germany to do so (1225). A mixed commission comprising Poles and Germans, and presided over by someone from a neutral country, would manage the transition. The Council of Ambassadors accepted these recommendations, and directed Poland and Germany to begin negotiating the particulars.[72]

Nearly six months of agonized negotiations followed.[73] The final convention was longer than any of the treaties produced by the Paris Peace Conference, and comprised some 606 articles. At the end of the day, an estimated 30 percent of Upper Silesians in Poland would be German, with nearly half of Upper Silesians in Germany either Polish or bilingual. Germany received some three-quarters of the plebiscite territory, and a bit over half the population.[74] Poland received most of the Industrial Triangle, including some 75 percent of the coal mines and 97 percent of the iron ore. Tinkering by the League at the edges of national sovereignty in Upper Silesia ultimately led to a truce in the battle between the German and Polish successor states. Nazi Germany would reclaim all of Silesia in 1939, Poland almost the entirety of Upper and Lower Silesia in 1945.

In 1921, the League assumed responsibility for holding a plebiscite in the former Vilna Governorate, to help draw the border between Poland and Lithuania. Like Teschen and Upper Silesia, Vilna was beset by paramilitary violence. Like other troubled border regions, the Great Powers had virtually no military power anywhere in the vicinity. By 1920–21, the powers had even less leverage over

---

[71] Ishii, "The Upper Silesia Question," 1222.

[72] "Decision of the Conference of Ambassadors," October 20, 1921, *League Council: JO* (December 1921): 1226–32.

[73] Harrington, "League of Nations," 92–101.

[74] Summary figures here come from T. Hunt Tooley, *National Identity and Weimar Germany: Upper Silesia and the Eastern Border, 1918–1922* (Lincoln: University of Nebraska Press, 1997), 257–58; and T.K. Wilson, *Frontiers of Violence: Conflict and Identity in Ulster and Upper Silesia, 1918–1922* (Oxford: Oxford University Press, 2010), 30.

Poland than they had over Germany. The allies could cut off military aid to Poland only at great risk.

The shifting fortunes of war brought the disposition of the former Vilna Governorate before the League of Nations.[75] As the Red Army closed in on Warsaw, the Bolsheviks signed a treaty with the Lithuanian government on July 12 recognizing Lithuanian independence, and recognizing the governorate as Lithuanian. A secret clause authorized the Red Army to enter Vilna city, as well as other territories previously occupied by the Poles. After the Battle of Warsaw of August 12–15, the Poles advanced toward Vilna in pursuit of the Bolsheviks. This raised the prospect of a direct confrontation between Polish and Lithuanian forces. Rather than invade Vilna, at least for the time being, the Polish government appealed on September 6 to the League of Nations under Article 11 of the Covenant. As paraphrased by Secretary-General Drummond, the Polish government "requested the league to use every means to restrain the Lithuanian Government, and thereby avoid the necessity for Poland to fight Lithuania."[76]

Pending League action, Polish and Lithuanian representatives on October 7 signed the Suwalki Agreement, an armistice that provisionally partitioned the disputed territories.[77] The agreement left Vilna city in Lithuanian hands. But on October 9, "paramilitary" Polish forces led by General Lucjan Żeligowski invaded Vilna. The Polish government publicly disowned all knowledge of or responsibility for the Żeligowski adventure, a claim not widely believed at the time and not at all subsequently.[78] A native of the Vilna Governorate, Żeligowski supported a maximal, federally organized Greater Poland. By December, Żeligowski's forces in Vilna had expanded to some 50,000 men.[79] Everyone understood the old adage that possession is nine-tenths of the law.

The Polish invasion vastly complicated any League intervention. On October 14, 1920, Léon Bourgeois as president of the League Council wrote to Ignacy Paderewski, representing Poland pending the opening of the League Assembly, describing the invasion as "a violation of the undertakings given to the Council of the League of Nations."[80] On October 27, Szymon Askenazy appeared before the League Council on behalf of Poland. He contended that "for the moment, there were no Polish troops in the territory of Vilna," because the troops under the command of Żeligowski comprised "natives of the district." He also made the problematic argument that "the Polish Government considered that General Zeligowski

[75] Sarah Wambaugh, *Plebiscites since the World War*, 2 vols. (Washington, D.C.: Carnegie Endowment for International Peace, 1933), 1: 304–05.

[76] "The Dispute Between Lithuania and Poland: Memorandum by the Secretary General" (no date, sometime before September 9, 1920), *League of Nations Official Journal, Special Supplement No. 4., Documents Concerning the Dispute between Poland and Lithuania* (December 1920), 10. Hereafter referred to as *League JO: Poland and Lithuania*.

[77] Timothy Snyder, *The Reconstruction of Nations: Poland, Ukraine, Lithuania, Belarus, 1569–1999* (New Haven, CT: Yale University Press, 2003), 63–65.

[78] For example, see Norman Davies, *White Eagle, Red Star: The Polish-Soviet War, 1919–1920* (London: Macdonald, 1972), 237.

[79] Wambaugh, *Plebiscites*, 1: 307.

[80] Léon Bourgeois to Ignacy Paderewski, October 14, 1920, *League JO: Poland and Lithuania*, 140.

had acted as a rebel, but that the whole Polish nation regarded his *coup d'état* as legitimate."[81] This meant that the Polish government—which after all had brought the matter to the League in the first place—either was at odds with its own people, or argued one case at home and a contradictory one in Geneva. With some bitterness, Askenazy reproached the Lithuanians for seeking to profit from their understanding with the Bolsheviks, then still outcasts from the international system.

On October 28, the League Council passed a resolution calling for a "public expression of opinion" in the former Vilna Governorate. Drafted by Paul Hymans, the resolution reminded both Poland and Lithuania of their obligations under the Covenant.[82] The inhabitants of Vilna could choose between Lithuania (then governed from Kaunas [Kovno]) or Poland. The Council would set the boundaries of the plebiscite, as well as "the method of taking the public expression of opinion and its date, so as to ensure the freedom and genuine character of the vote." The Council also claimed the authority to order any measures necessary for a free vote, "whether for the withdrawal or for the disarmament of any troops of whatever nationality in occupation of the territories in which the public expression of opinion is taken." On November 7, Poland and Lithuania notified the League Council of their unconditional acceptance of the resolution.

No plebiscite in Vilna was going to be easy. Unsurprisingly, the prewar Russian census, the wartime German census, and the 1919 Polish census all had doubters. League representatives could never resolve the issue of voter eligibility. Continued war both dislocated populations and led to the destruction of massive amounts of civil records. This made it virtually impossible to determine either residents or "out-voters." The Polish government claimed that some 90 percent of Żeligowski's soldiers qualified as out-voters. Town/country and resulting class divisions inevitably appeared as well. Landowners tended to self-identify as Polish, peasants as Lithuanian or Byelorussian, and the commercial class as Jewish. In the 1897 Russian census, some peasants had described themselves simply as *tutejszych*, a Polish word for "local."[83] Jews comprised one-third to one-half of the residents of Vilna city, with similar percentages among other urban populations. Any way Jews voted would stoke anti-Semitism on the other side.

For the next five months, the League struggled to organize a plebiscite in the former Vilna Governorate. Żeligowski's occupying army of some 50,000 Polish soldiers hardly facilitated what the League called the "freedom and genuine character of the vote." The League Council made plans to assemble a multinational peacekeeping force comprising contingents from Britain, France, Greece, the Netherlands, Norway, and Sweden. The Lithuanians, beholden to Bolshevik Russian approval of territorial arrangements, passed on a flat refusal on the part of

[81] Extract from the Procès-Verbal of the Tenth Session of the League Council, October 26, 1920, *League JO: Poland and Lithuania*, 135.

[82] "Resolution of the Council of the League of Nations Calling for a Public Expression of Opinion under the Auspices and Supervision of the League. Adopted October 28, 1920," Wambaugh, *Plebiscites*, 2: 269–70. Poland was a founding member of the League, and Lithuania joined in September 1921.

[83] Wambaugh, *Plebiscites*, 1: 300.

Moscow to accept troops from Britain and France, as countries that had waged counter-revolutionary war against their regime. The Polish and Lithuanian governments quarreled bitterly and incessantly over the timing of the plebiscite, and over the plebiscite boundaries. Supposedly to expedite the proceedings and to reduce the expenditure of registering voters, the plebiscite commission put forward an unfortunate proposal allowing only men to vote. As both successor Poland and successor Lithuania provided for female suffrage, this earned the commission scorn from both sides. Finally, on March 3, 1921, the League Council cancelled the plebiscite, citing obstructions and prevarication on the Lithuanian side, reluctance on the Polish to reduce Żeligowski's forces, and bad faith on both sides. It called on Hymans to initiate direct negotiations between the Warsaw and Kaunas governments.[84]

In May and September 1921, Hymans presented his own, quite daring, proposals for shared sovereignty. The former Vilna Governorate would become part of a federated Lithuania. But the Vilna canton would recognize both Lithuanian and Polish as official languages, and would provide ample guarantees for all ethnic and religious minorities. All of Poland and Lithuania would constitute a free-trade area, with Poland having access to Lithuanian ports and roads, even for materiel of war. A joint council between Poland and Lithuania would handle foreign affairs, with defense regulated by a formal convention. However wise in the abstract, any such concept of pooled or shared sovereignty, whether in the economy, defense, or foreign affairs, defied the logic of the ethno-national successor state.

The League Assembly showered Hymans with praise, from which the conflicting parties conspicuously abstained. After explaining his plan on September 24, Hymans received "long and prolonged applause" followed by "many congratulations" for his efforts.[85] Yet speeches of bitter recrimination followed from the new Lithuanian representative, Oskaras Milašius,[86] and from Askenazy of Poland.[87] Each stressed the fraternal links between the two countries, and each blamed the other for a needlessly embittered family feud. Ultimately, the Assembly called "upon the two peoples to reach an agreement, which is as necessary for them as for the peace of the world" (399).

In the meantime, the forces of General Żeligowski remained in material possession of the former Vilna Governorate. He arranged his own "plebiscite" in January 1922, in the form of elections for a "constituent assembly of Central Lithuania." Possession had indeed constituted nine-tenths of the law. Amid widespread abstentions on the part of Jews, Byelorussians, and Lithuanians, 64 percent of those voting favored permanent incorporation into Poland.[88] The Polish Sejm duly approved direct annexation. For their part, the Lithuanians successfully achieved compensation in the Memel territory (previously part of Prussia), in an overt imitation of Żeligowski. Thereafter, the residual instruments of the Paris Peace

[84] W.J. Brockelbank, "The Vilna Dispute," *AJIL* 20.3 (1926): 483–501.
[85] Eighteenth Plenary Meeting, Saturday, September 24th, 1921, 385.
[86] Milašius was best known at the time as Oscar Milosz, and for his writings in French.
[87] Nineteenth Plenary Meeting, Saturday, September 24th, 1921, 388–94.
[88] Robert H. Lord, "Lithuania and Poland," *Foreign Affairs* 1.4 (1923): 54–57.

Conference simply capitulated. On March 15, 1923, the Council of Ambassadors fixed the borders more or less in accordance with the outcome determined in the field by General Żeligowski back in late 1920.[89] Żeligowski and his backers proved the real peacemakers in the former Vilna Governorate.

Nothing about involving the League of Nations could resolve the problems inherent to plebiscites in "unmixing" peoples. In the end, plebiscites could only demarcate the new "remix" of peoples in new boundaries. The League could do little but add "neutrality" or "objectivity" to territorial decisions bound to antagonize some party, or more commonly all parties. In Upper Silesia, the League could become the messenger delivering an unappealing message to Poles and Germans alike. In Vilna, it could try and fail to arrange a plebiscite where none of the protagonists wished to cooperate and where the Great Powers had feared to tread.

Minority Treaties

The minority treaties circumscribed national sovereignty by defining certain categories of nationals who would have a distinct relationship to the state guaranteed by an authority beyond that state. Successor states bitterly resented them on that basis. Enforcement of the treaties would lie principally with the League of Nations. Most of the dramas of enforcement and non-enforcement occurred after the time frame of this book. Attention here, then, turns to setting up the machinery of protection under the League. The League could establish norms, and wield a largely theoretical power of expulsion in its own ranks.[90] But it could not in itself re-engineer the identities of successor states in their treatment of minorities.

The treaty with Poland, the model for the other minority treaties, had provided little guidance on enforcement, apart from establishing the League Council as its locus. According to Article 12 of the treaty, any member of the League Council could bring a matter of "infraction or danger of infraction" before the whole Council, which would then take appropriate steps.[91] A committee charged with establishing a minority regime, chaired by Tommaso Tittoni of Italy, submitted its report on October 20, 1920.[92]

The Tittoni report established procedures for raising minority concerns. "Minorities themselves" or states not represented on the League Council could petition that body. Petitions had the Wilsonian advantage of granting public speech to peoples who considered themselves ill-used and to their advocates. However, the Tittoni report also made clear that petitions were not themselves part

---

[89] Gerhard V. Pink, *The Conference of Ambassadors: Paris (1920–1931)* (Geneva: Geneva Research Centre, 1942), 104–06.

[90] The only state ever actually expelled from the League was the Soviet Union, after the invasion of Finland in November 1939.

[91] Julius Stone, "Procedure under the Minorities Treaties," *AJIL* 26 (1932): 502.

[92] "Report Presented by M. Tittoni and Adopted by the Council of the League of Nations on October 22nd 1920," in Julius Stone, *International Guarantees of Minority Rights: Procedure of the Council of the League of Nations in Theory and Practice* (London: Oxford University Press, 1932), Appendix III, 273–75. These were interim arrangements pending the establishment of the Permanent Court of International Justice.

of a juridical process. Any petition had to "retain the nature of a report pure and simple; it cannot have the effect of putting the matter before the Council and calling upon it to intervene." The League Council alone could decide whether to initiate an investigation. The report proposed a procedure according to which the League Secretariat would receive petitions and pass them on to the League Council without comment. Pending the establishment of the Permanent Court, the League Council alone could decide whether and how to act.

The League Council shortly established the "Committee of Three." The League Council president and two additional colleagues would constitute an ad hoc committee to receive each petition, and to decide upon further action.[93] Eventually, a Minorities Questions Section of the League Secretariat would take on this role, determining whether a given petition was "receivable" and thus eligible to be passed on to the Committee of Three. Led by two of the most respected international civil servants of the interwar period, Erik Colban of Norway and Pablo de Azcárate of Spain, this section would serve as gatekeeper.[94] Colban would come to explain his task as pedagogical. Through ensuring the appropriate character of receivable petitions, his section would instruct minorities as to the rules of the minority regime, and thus play a certain role in transforming the 30 million members of religious and ethnic minorities into "loyal citizens."[95]

In December 1921, the League Council clarified the conditions for "receivable" petitions, which it would generalize in a resolution adopted in September 1923.[96] Petitioners had to restrict themselves to protections specifically provided for in the treaties. Petitions could not request for any kind of secession from the state in which the minority resided. Petitions could not be anonymous, nor could they come from "unauthenticated" sources. They were required to "abstain from violent language."[97] They could not repeat a petition recently submitted to the League Council.

Yet the League Council mechanism and standardized petitions could never overcome the internal contradiction on which the minority regime itself was based. As Carole Fink put it:

> The world's first international minorities system was based on two blatantly contradictory principles and practices. The petition procedure combined a relatively permissive sanction for minority complaints with an underlying denial of their legal status.[98]

---

[93] "Resolution Adopted by the Council on October 25th, 1920," in Stone, *International Guarantees*, 275.

[94] Pablo de Azcárate, *League of Nations and National Minorities: An Experiment*, Eileen E. Brooke, trans. (Washington, D.C.: Carnegie Endowment for International Peace, 1945).

[95] Erik Colban, "The League of Nations and the Minorities Problem," August 18, 1926, quoted in Carole Fink, *Defending the Rights of Others: The Great Powers, The Jews, and International Minority Protection, 1878–1938* (Cambridge: Cambridge University Press, 2004), 282–83. See also de Azcárate, *League of Nations and National Minorities*.

[96] "Resolution Adopted by the [League] Council on September 5th, 1923," in Stone, *International Guarantees*, 276–78.

[97] Jane K. Cowan, "Who's Afraid of Violent Language?: Honour, Sovereignty and Claims-making in the League of Nations," *Anthropological Theory* 3.3 (2003): 271–91.

[98] Fink, *Defending the Rights of Others*, 277.

To the extent that the minority regime created international law, its object would remain states rather than peoples. Moreover, the overall purpose of the League of Nations was to maintain peace, with minority protection as a means toward that end rather than the end itself. Ill-treated minorities could destabilize successor states, and destabilized successor states could go to war with one another. But both the Minorities Questions Section and the League Council would need to choose their battles carefully.

Bitter complaints from successor states never subsided. For example, a letter from Czechoslovak Foreign Minister Václav Girsa to Drummond in June 1920 (before the Tittoni report began to regularize procedures) protested a petition from an "Austrian Association for a League of Nations" to which the League Council had granted consideration. In the petition, as Girsa put it, "the Czechoslovak Republic and its president are attacked in the most violent manner by a private organization."[99] Such a petition, he argued, was "obviously inspired by a hatred of everything not German." Askenazy of Poland argued before the League Council in January 1923 for an even more state-centered approach, on the basis of inherently conflicted loyalties among minorities. He contended that "minorities do not live in complete isolation, but that on the contrary, they are, by the nature of things, in intimate intellectual and political contact with other countries in which they form a majority." Germans, Lithuanians, White Russians, Ruthenes had all implicated themselves with the irredentist politics of adjacent states. Himself Jewish, Askenazy added: "Even the Jews are under the influence of the Zionist organisations abroad, whose eyes turn toward Palestine."[100] He proposed reducing the role of the League Secretariat, by requiring a separate League Council resolution to accept any petition. In April 1923, Edvard Beneš of Czechoslovakia proposed the categorical rejection of petitions "only drawn up for propaganda purposes—that is to say, which are not really important and which do not make detailed statements or only contain information"—broad criteria for rejection, to say the least.[101] He further advocated rejecting out of hand any petition "incompatible with the dignity of a State."

The League Assembly would acquire an interest in the minorities regime, though its regular oversight of the work of the League Council. Gilbert Murray, Australian-born and since 1908 Regius Professor of Greek at Oxford University, sat in the League Assembly as a member for South Africa at the behest of his friend Jan Smuts.[102] At the League Assembly meeting of 1922, Murray put forward a variety of proposals for improving the minorities regime.[103] At the same

[99] Dr. V. Girsa to Sir James Eric Drummond, June 4, 1921, *League Council: JO* (September 1921), 796.

[100] "Proposals Submitted by the Polish Government Regarding the Procedure in Connection with Minority Petitions," January 16, 1923, *League Council: JO* (May 1923), 480–83.

[101] "Proposal Submitted by the Czechoslovak Government Regarding the Procedure in Connection with Minority Petitions," April 5, 1924, *League Council: JO* (July 1923), 717–18.

[102] See Peter Wilson, "Gilbert Murray and International Relations: Hellenism, Liberalism, and International Cooperation as a Path to Peace," *Review of International Studies* 37.2 (2011): 881–909.

[103] Lucy Philip Mair, *The Protection of Minorities: The Working and Scope of the Minorities Treaties under the League of Nations* (London: Christophers, 1928), 64–67.

time, he proposed that the Sixth Committee (handling Political Affairs as well as Disarmament) take a position exposing the internal contradictions underpinning the minorities regime:

> The [Sixth] Committee expresses the hope that those States which are not bound by any legal obligation to the League with respect to minorities will nevertheless observe in the treatment of their own minorities at least as high a standard as required by any of the treaties. (65)

Murray thus opened Pandora's Box by asking why minorities deserved League protection in some places and not in others. Murray and his colleagues would encounter difficulties in closing it.

The League Assembly debated the report from the Sixth Committee on September 21, 1922.[104] The Maharajah of Nawanagar, sitting for the British Government of India, rose to comment on the plight of the substantial Indian minority in South Africa. In complicated syntax that nevertheless conveyed the point, he called attention to "minority questions outside Europe, and the political order outside Europe, in other continents even, where distributions are of older standing [which], will not be happy, will not be contented, will not be completely stable as you would have them while any open sores remain unhealed" (174–75).

Nawanagar appealed directly to his colleagues from South Africa "to ask them to influence their Government, when they return home, in favor of satisfactory settlements of these particular minority questions, which are their very own" (175). To applause, he concluded by reminding all his colleagues that "outside this Assembly there have often been two justices, one for the West and one for the East. It is for the League of Nations to engraft its own conception, the far higher, the far better conception, upon the universal practice of mankind" (176). The maharaja abruptly returned to the radical potential of Wilsonianism, which the Paris Peace Conference and the League had worked so hard to contain.

Murray himself tried to contain the discursive explosion by reaffirming the exclusionary elements of Wilsonianism. He agreed that different standards of justice existed throughout the world, although, as he put it, "this is not the time to go into a detailed discussion of any particular case" (177). The real problem in South Africa, he continued, "is not so much a difficulty of dealing with minorities as a difficulty of dealing with a number of races at very different stages of civilization and development" (177). All minorities worthy of protection through a League of Nations regime, one could infer, were of European descent. Perceptive listeners might recall that in South Africa, the settlers themselves were a minority population.

Nevertheless, Murray continued that the British Empire had committed itself to "at least as high a standard of justice and toleration as is required by any of the Treaties" (177), a less than true assertion that seemed to avoid the maharaja's central concern. The fact that Nawanagar could speak at all testified that "the League of Nations is a reality and has already begun to exercise its power in the

---

[104] "Protection of Minorities: Report of the Sixth Committee, Resolutions," Thirteenth Plenary Meeting, Thursday, September 21, 1922, 170–86.

world" (178). Given the opportunity to respond, the maharaja backed down, stating: "It could never be my desire to wash, as we say, our dirty linen in public" (179). He simply asked his South African colleagues to influence their government on behalf of the Indian minority, and expressed confidence in their ability to do so.

As Carole Fink has shown, the minorities regime faced a generally grim future, as successor states asserted their national sovereignty by evading and simply ignoring minority protections.[105] Petitions brought to the League Secretariat would lead to investigations, mutual recriminations, and solutions or non-solutions that seldom pleased anyone. The later reputation of the League for endless and fruitless inquests without outcome had roots in the minority regime. Its attempt to smooth the "remixing" of peoples ended in failure, torn limb from limb by the resurgent nation-state. As designed at the time, the minorities regime had to rely on some form of Wilsonian sovereignty to become effective. Only transnational "public opinion" organized through the League could alter the identity of exclusionary successor states. The League and the international system, moreover, had never addressed the most glaring problem of the minorities regime in the first place—its highly selective applicability. After World War II, the international system would renounce minority protection in favor of what Mark Mazower called "the strange triumph of human rights."[106] The individual rather than the religious or ethnic minority group would become the locus of international protection.

Mandates

On May 17, 1922, Arthur Balfour spoke at a public meeting of the League Council on the still-unresolved British mandate for Palestine.[107] He put forward an explanation of what a mandate actually was that combined old and new: "A mandate was a self-imposed limitation by the conquerors on the sovereignty which they exercised over conquered territory."[108] The conquerors had chosen to limit the ancient right of conquest, "in the general interests of mankind," and would continue to do so through the League. The acts of the British Empire in mandatory Palestine, "at that moment, or in the future, would be done in the full light of day." A League of Nations Mandate represented an open covenant, openly arrived at: "The machinery of the Mandates Commission, of the Council and of the Assembly of the League was so contrived as to make it impossible for any transaction of general interest to take place except in the full glare of public opinion."

On the face of it, the Mandate Principle suggested that peoples belonged to themselves. It suggested, uncomfortably, that all the people of all religions in mandate Palestine were "Palestinians," who one day would become citizens of

[105] Fink, *Defending the Rights of Others*, Ch. 10–11.
[106] Mark Mazower, "The Strange Triumph of Human Rights, 1933–1950," *Historical Journal* 47.2 (2004): 379–98.
[107] Michael Joseph Cohen, *Britain's Moment in Palestine: Retrospect and Perspectives, 1917–1948* (London: Routledge, 2014).
[108] "Eleventh Meeting (Public) held at Geneva on Wednesday, May 17th, 1922, at 10:30 a.m.," *League Council: JO*, 548–49.

"Palestine." As we saw, the implied teleology toward independence had been ferociously contested at the conference, and papered over by the racial classification system of the mandates.[109] This system classified peoples according to the imperial designs on the lands they inhabited. But who exactly were these peoples, and what was their nationality?

The League had the duty to perpetuate the haphazard racial hierarchy established in the Covenant. As with the minority regime, the League would have to administer a Mandate System it had not created. The question of just who the peoples of the mandate territories were would not go away. As with the minority regime, the most serious dramas of the Mandate System would occur after the time frame of this book. Disputes among the Great Powers delayed the completion of most of the texts establishing the mandates until 1922 and 1923. These disputes included Japanese insistence on the application of the "Open Door" to class-C mandates, French insistence on military recruitment in its class-B mandates, and American insistence on influence in the Mandate System even as it withdrew from peacemaking after the defeat of the Treaty of Versailles.[110] The persistence of open warfare in Anatolia delayed the writing of mandates for the Middle East.

Susan Pedersen has shown how in the confusion of the early 1920s, the very idea of a Mandate System threatened to become "a shivering shadow of its Wilsonian self."[111] Entrepreneurial advocates of the League prevented this from happening. Secretary-General Drummond, his assistant Philip Noel-Baker, and William Rappard from the League Secretariat, together with prominent British politicians such as Balfour, Curzon, and Cecil, as well as other figures of international stature such as Paul Hymans of Belgium and Fridtjof Nansen of Norway, worked to make the Mandate System, for better or worse, a living reality.

Because the Covenant created the Mandate System well before the finalization of the mandate texts, the League would participate in crafting its own role. Article 22 of the Covenant gave the League vast if ill-defined responsibilities. A report from Hymans adopted by the League Council in August 1920 clarified the relationship between the Supreme Council and the League Council on the mandates.[112] Under international law, "there is no legal responsibility except in respect of another person" (339). As the League did not have its own legal personality, "whether the League of Nations is responsible in respect of the Mandatory Powers appears to be a moral rather than a legal question" (339). But any Wilsonian would believe that "moral" sovereignty was a form of "real" sovereignty. Hymans put the annual reports from the mandatory powers and League scrutiny of them at the center of the Mandate System. Each report "should include a statement as to

---

[109] Because of the attention to developing a Jewish homeland, the Palestinian mandate was *sui generis*, outside the classification system. "British Mandate for Palestine," *AJIL* 17, Supplement, Official Documents (1923): 164–71.

[110] Susan Pedersen, *The Guardians: The League of Nations and the Crisis of Empire* (New York: Oxford University Press, 2015), 33–44; and Walter Russell Batsell, "The United States and the System of Mandates," *International Conciliation*, No. 213 (October 1925): 269–315.

[111] Pedersen, *Guardians*, 45.

[112] "Obligations Falling upon the League of Nations under the Terms of Article 22 of the Covenant (Mandates)," *League Council: JO* (September 1920), 334–41.

the moral and material situation of the peoples under the Mandate" (340). International public opinion, as organized through the League, could become the guarantor of just rule in the mandates.

The League Council established the Permanent Mandates Commission called for in the Covenant on December 1, 1920.[113] The commission would receive the annual reports and "advise the Council on all matters relating to the obser- vance of the Mandates." It would comprise nine members, at least five from non- mandatory states, "selected for their personal merits and competence." None would hold government office. The International Labour Organization could send an observer. At meetings discussing the reports, a representative from the concerned mandatory power "shall participate with absolute freedom of discussion of this report." This representative would withdraw, however, when the commission discussed its own report to the League Council. The commission would hold yearly plenary meet- ings to discuss the reports as a whole. The Assembly would maintain additional scrutiny over the League Council on matters concerning the mandates.[114]

At the first meeting of the Permanent Mandates Commission on October 4, 1921, League Council President Wellington Koo prefigured the views of Balfour in 1922 by praising the willingness of the mandatory powers, "of their own free will," to share with the commission reports on the territories under their rule prepared for their own parliaments and colonial ministries. He emphasized, how- ever, that the commission would be developing its own set of criteria and questions for the mandatory powers in the future.[115]

The commission got to work right away examining these reports, beginning with a French report on the administration of Cameroon. Pending a formalization of the mandate in July 1922,[116] the report came from the French Ministry of Colonies. It detailed the transition from German to French rule, and concluded with ringing praise for how well the emerging Mandate System suited French republican imperialism. France, "faithful to its traditions and to its colonial doctrine, devotes itself to the sacred task of civilizing the populations over which it has tutelage."[117]

The Permanent Mandates Commission took care to maintain the racial hierarchy inherent to a B-class mandate such as Cameroon.[118] Rappard raised the question of native representation on the Administrative Council. Pierre Orts of Belgium observed that "the degree of civilization of these tribes would no doubt not allow" their representation, at least not by themselves. Paul Beau of France opined that it

[113] "Constitution of the Permanent Mandates Commission," December 1, 1920, in Wright, *Mandates*, 622–23.

[114] See Pedersen, *Guardians*, 50–52.

[115] *League of Nations Permanent Mandates Commission Minutes*, "Minutes of the First Session Held in Geneva, October 4th to 7th, 1921," October 4, 1921, 3. Subsequently referred to as *PMC Minutes*, followed by the date of the meeting.

[116] "French Mandate for the Cameroons," *AJIL* 17, Supplement: Official Documents (1923): 145–48.

[117] *Rapport au Ministre des Colonies sur l'administration des territoires occupés du Cameroun de la conquête au 1er juillet 1921* (Paris: Imprimerie des Journaux Officiels, 1921), 458.

[118] *PMC Minutes*, October 5, 1921, 12–13.

was certainly desirable for the indigenous people to have representation on an administrative Council, and that "no policy would be better calculated to retain their confidence." "But," he continued, "in the present condition of the mandated African Colonies, the natives could not, save in very exceptional cases, take part in a council which would have to deal with the territory as a whole. Nor could there be any question of having a white man elected by the natives." Alfredo Augusto Friere d'Andrade of Portugal suggested the appointment of indigenous individuals "in consideration of their knowledge of conditions in the country." The commission agreed to suspend discussion of the matter pending the actual establishment of the Administrative Council.[119]

Inevitably, representation raised the question of just who was being represented. Were the populations of the mandates nationals of the mandatory power, or did they hold some future nationality of their own? The issue mattered particularly in B- and C-class mandates, where mandatory status would be of uncertain but long duration. Contemporaries certainly understood the stakes in assigning a specific nationality to inhabitants of the mandate territories, and what a small step it would prove from annexing people to annexing lands.[120]

The Union of South Africa would force the issue of nationality in former German South West Africa, not over the indigenous people, but over some 20,000 white settlers.[121] On October 6, 1921, the commission discussed a report on the mandate.[122] Rappard observed with some concern that the introductory letter from General Smuts stressed "the principle laid down by the Treaty of Versailles, under which the Territory [of South West Africa] is to be governed as 'an integral part' of the Union of South Africa."[123] The report neglected to mention the Mandate System, or even the League of Nations. At the very least, the report encouraged the muddling of the thin line between a C-class mandate and annexation.

Rappard's suspicions did not lack foundation. South West Africa had been the only German colony to attract enough white settlers to populate a football stadium.[124] A May 1921 census conducted by the South African government recorded 19,432 men, women, and children of European descent.[125] This population comprised 10,673 of British Empire nationality (most migrants from South Africa) and 7,855 of prewar German nationality, along with 904 persons of some

---

[119] On continued French obfuscation, see *Rapport annuelle du Gouvernement français sur l'administration sous mandate des territoires du Cameroun pour l'année 1922* (Paris: Imprimerie Générale Lahure, 1923), 57–63.

[120] Andrew McNair, "Mandates," *Cambridge Law Journal* 3.2 (1928): 155–57.

[121] Strictly speaking, the British Empire held the mandate from the League, and the Union of South Africa from the British Empire. "Mandate for German South-West Africa," December 17, 1920, *AJIL* 18, Supplement: Official Documents (1923): 175–76.

[122] Union of South Africa, South-West Africa Territory, *Report of the Administrator for the Year 1920*, March 10, 1921 (Cape Town: Cape Times Limited, Government Printers, 1921), 1.

[123] *PMC Minutes,* October 6, 1921, 21. On the ensuing debate see Pedersen, *Guardians*, 71–73.

[124] Elsewhere in Africa and the South Pacific, the mandatory powers had simply deported the small numbers of German nationals.

[125] Union of South Africa, *Report of the Administrator of South-West Africa for the Year 1921* (Pretoria: The Government Printing and Stationery Office, 1922), 5, 12.

other European nationality. Naturalizing the white population as "South African" simultaneously made them subjects of the British Empire. This would permit their "self-determination" by joining the Union of South Africa, which could thus annex lands through annexing people. Almost in passing, the 1921 census also reported an indigenous and mixed-race population of 208,605.[126] This population would also become "South African," its subordinated position within that nationality to be determined exclusively by the Union of South Africa.

Rappard brought the issue of nationality to the Permanent Mandates Commission on October 7, 1921.[127] He reported that two views had emerged within the League Secretariat. A majority held "that the Mandatory Power could impose the status of British subjects upon the inhabitants of the mandated territory, unless they expressly protested against it." This point of view "appeared to strengthen the argument that a C Mandate amounted to disguised annexation." But a minority, on the other hand, "maintained that the status of British subject was a privilege, and that it was open to those who desired to acquire British nationality to become naturalised." A lively discussion followed. William Ormbsy-Gore of Britain observed that in the case of the New Zealand mandate in Samoa (like South West Africa a British mandate held through a Dominion and a C-class mandate), a council of jurists had concluded that naturalization not only was not automatic, but was impossible. Yanagita Kunio of Japan countered that inhabitants of the Pacific Islands north of the Equator "were, of right, Japanese subjects."

Pierre Orts of Belgium speculated that if the inhabitants of the mandate territories did not acquire the nationality of the mandatory power, were they not "homeless?" Alfredo Friere d'Andrade of Portugal wondered whether "the League of Nations might be considered as being the real sovereign of the mandated territories," as it could then issue passports in its own name. No one took the seemingly obvious position inherent to the Mandate Principle that the peoples of the territories belonged to themselves, and held their own nationalities. The commission also avoided the delicate matter of whether white settlers could live under mandatory rule at all.

The Permanent Mandates Commission returned to the matter in August 1922, following an exchange of letters between Rappard and General Smuts. The wily Smuts made the problem the German population (fewer than 8,000 people), and the assignation of South African nationality the solution.[128] Despite the "merciful attitude" shown by not expelling the stiff-necked Germans in the first place, they continued to "cling to the German Fatherland as if they were still a German Colony, and they long for the day when they will again be a German Colony."[129] Conferring South African nationality on the settlers would convince them that

[126] White settlers thus comprised some 8.5 percent of the entire population, in a territory of some 322,000 square miles, or about two-thirds the size of the Union of South Africa itself. E. Emmett, "The Mandate over South-West Africa," *Journal of Comparative Legislation and International Law* 9.1 (1927): 112.

[127] *PMC Minutes*, October 7, 1921, 40–41.

[128] Smuts to Rappard, July 4, 1922, in *PMC Minutes*, August 8, 1922, Annex 6, 91.

[129] Daniel Joseph Walther, *Creating Germans Abroad: Cultural Policies and National Identity in Namibia* (Athens: Ohio University Press, 2002).

Germany would never rule them again, and that their future lay in assimilating with their white South African compatriots. Smuts also showed a sudden and uncharacteristic concern with the nationality of the indigenous population. Would they, too, retain an imaginary German nationality forever? To permit this "would be most absurd, and yet it is difficult to draw any distinction in principle between born white German subjects and conquered black German subjects." Moreover, he believed, South Africa already had the authority on its own to naturalize and otherwise legally define all the peoples of South West Africa, because under Article 22, "the Union can administer the mandated territory under its law as an integral portion of the Union."

The nationality of peoples in the mandate territories reached the League Council in April 1923. The Permanent Mandates Commission argued that the inhabitants of a mandate territory did not ipso facto acquire the nationality of the mandatory power. The commission supported an "opt-in" solution, according to which "individual inhabitants should voluntarily accept naturalization from the Mandatory Power."[130] For example, German settlers could opt for South African nationality. Not having decided to date the nationality of the "native inhabitants," the commission urged the League to seek a specific legal term. Possible candidates included "administered persons under the Mandate [an adaptation of the French term *administés*]" or "protected persons under the Mandate."

The South African government had always favored an "opt-out" solution, in which settlers would become South African nationals unless they publicly chose otherwise. This they did in the name of "self-determination," that is, of a white-ruled expanded Union of South Africa. Speaking for South Africa on April 20, Sir Edgar Walton argued: "It was in accordance with the policy of South Africa to establish self-government in that territory, and to admit German settlers at the earliest possible moment to share in that self-government." To do otherwise would deny them representation, and place them "in a humiliating position" (569–70). Even asking them to take an oath, he argued, would foster their humiliation: "It would be difficult for any man, especially after the history of recent years if, in order to obtain political rights, he was compelled to approach the conquering Power in order to take the oath of allegiance to the British flag, and to renounce his previous nationality."

As we saw, Wilson in introducing the mandates in January 1919 had left surprisingly open the question of integrating indigenous peoples into the politics of the mandate territories. Walton resolved any ambiguity, and appropriated the Mandate Principle in the name of white rule. The point of mandatory rule in South West Africa was to prepare white settlers of South African nationality to join the Union of South Africa. Walton sought, in Pedersen's words, to create "a unified rights-bearing white citizenry" separate from the populations governed by the Mandate System.[131]

---

[130] Minutes, Sixth Public Meeting (Public), April 10, 1923, *League Council: JO*, 566. League Council President Edward Wood (later Lord Halifax) summarized the views of the commission.

[131] Pedersen, *Guardians*, 73.

The president of the League Council session of April 23 read a resolution in which it would concede "taking into consideration the special case presented to it" in the case of South West Africa.[132] The resolution gave South Africa the authority to naturalize the former German settlers, provided each settler "shall have the right to decline British nationality by a declaration made in such conditions as may be prescribed." Hjamar Branting of Sweden rose to recapitulate two years of arguments against such a move. He strongly opposed the idea that "the mandatory system only applies to the native population." Transparently, annexing former German settlers was a step toward annexing South West Africa. Doing so worked against the whole concept of unifying lands and peoples that had guided peacemaking since the Paris Peace Conference opened.

Nevertheless, at its April 23 meeting the League Council adopted a series of resolutions that obliquely affirmed the exception for South West Africa. The resolutions affirmed in somewhat tortured syntax that indigenous peoples did not ipso facto receive the nationality of the mandatory power. However, it was not inconsistent with this principle "that individual inhabitants of the mandated territory should voluntarily obtain naturalization from the Mandatory Power in accordance with arrangements which it is open to such power to make, with this object, under its own law." In other words, South Africa could nationalize former German settlers unless they chose otherwise. Some 90 percent accepted South African citizenship by 1925.[133]

Population Exchanges

As we saw in Chapter 4, population exchange pushed "national self-determination" to one of its logical conclusions. The careful political and legal distinction between "voluntary" and "compulsory" exchanges, on the ground, proved largely fictitious. Both the Paris Peace Conference and the Conference of Lausanne sought to keep the exchanges at arm's length, not least by consigning them to bilateral conventions not part of the actual treaties. The League of Nations had nothing directly to do with determining the exchanges. The issue of "blame" seemed less pressing for the Greek–Bulgarian exchange because of its ostensibly "voluntary" nature. The Greek–Turkish exchange was another matter. The Conference of Lausanne sought to implicate the League through perhaps its greatest luminary in its early years, Fridtjof Nansen. Historians of a juridical bent have helped keep the focus on the responsibility of the Great Man. Nansen, in fact, did little to shape the population exchange, but much to shape the image of the League of Nations in the international system through its relationship to the exchange.

---

[132] *League Council: JO*, April 23, 1923, 603–04. For the text see "Conditions Obtaining in the Mandated Territory of South-West Africa," Annex 497a, *League Council: JO* (June 1923), 659.

[133] Pedersen, *Guardians*, 73, 440–41, n. 78.

Nansen had been an international celebrity since his famed exploratory expeditions in the Arctic in the 1890s.[134] Indeed, Nansen seemed to consider his humanitarian and political values as the logical consequence of his encounter with nature. "True civilization," he wrote, "will not have been reached until all nations see that it is nobler to conquer nature than to conquer each other" (154). A true Renaissance Man, Nansen's scientific interests ranged from invertebrate zoology, to meteorology, to geology, to physics. As we saw, Nansen and Herbert Hoover worked with the Paris Peace Conference on food relief in revolutionary Russia. In April 1920, the League Council thus considered Nansen a logical choice for its first High Commissioner for Refugees. It was through his work with refugees from Russia that Nansen became embroiled in the population exchange.

What John F.L. Ross has described as "Nansen studies" reinforced a focus on the person of the Great Man.[135] As such, Nansen has long been part of historiographical judgments as to who was responsible for the exchange, and judgments of the exchange itself. Stephen Ladas, who wrote the first scholarly account, emphasized the culpability of Eleftherios Venizelos, and Nansen as his willing accomplice.[136] Others have emphasized Nansen as the figure who blunted the edges of the exchange, itself inevitable given the host of bad options available at the time. Some have gone so far as to make Nansen the hero of the piece.[137] But the matter could not end with inculpating, exonerating, or praising the Great Man. To judge Nansen was to judge the fledgling League of Nations.

The interpretation of Onur Yildirim adopted in Chapter 4 posits a wide if largely unspoken consensus at the Conference of Lausanne on the need for an involuntary exchange, and thus decenters the person of Nansen.[138] To be sure, Nansen proved a key interlocutor at the right/wrong places at the right/wrong times. Certainly, as Ross has shown, Nansen had reliable and immediate information on the refugee crisis emerging from the burning of Smyrna in September 1922 and the deterioration of the allied military position leading to the Mudanya armistice of October 11.[139] Nansen was himself in Constantinople by early October 1922, in his capacity as High Commissioner seeking aid for the many

---

[134] See Bruno Cabanes, *The Great War and the Origins of Humanitarianism, 1918–1924* (Cambridge: Cambridge University Press, 2014), Ch. 3, 133–88.

[135] John F.L. Ross incorporates the extensive literature in Norwegian in "Fridtjof Nansen and the Aegean Population Exchange," *Scandinavian Journal of History* 40.2 (2015): 134.

[136] Stephen P. Ladas, *The Exchange of Minorities: Bulgaria, Greece and Turkey* (New York: The Macmillan Company, 1932), 336–40. Bruce Clark largely echoed this view in *Twice a Stranger: How Mass Expulsion Forged Modern Greece and Turkey* (Cambridge, MA: Harvard University Press, 2006), 43–56.

[137] Roland Huntford, *Fridtjof Nansen and the Unmixing of Greeks and Turks in 1924* (Oslo: Det Norske Videnskaps-Akademi, 1999); Harry J. Psomiades, "Fridtjof Nansen and the Greek Refugee Problem (September-November 1922)," *Deltio Kentro Mikrasiatikon Spoudon* 18 (2009): 287–339; and Harry J. Psomiades, *The Eastern Question, The Last Phase: A Study in Greek-Turkish Diplomacy* (New York: Pella Publishing Company, 2000 [originally published in 1968]).

[138] Onur Yildirim, *Diplomacy and Displacement: Reconsidering the Turco-Greek Exchange of Populations, 1922–1934* (New York: Routledge, 2006), 40–43.

[139] Ross, "Fridtjof Nansen," 138–44.

refugees from revolutionary Russia then in the city. Within days, allied representatives approached him to begin discussions with Greek and Turkish authorities about a population exchange. Nansen, in turn, requested that Geneva extend his writ to helping refugees in all of Anatolia. Nansen's involvement in exchange and the involvement of the League thus became inextricable.[140]

But Yildirim's structural explanation of the exchange reveals perhaps a more important question. What has been at stake in blaming individuals in the first place, particularly Nansen? Yildirim's interpretation makes the role of Nansen largely performative, certainly by the time of the Conference of Lausanne. The state protagonists as well as the conference had all embraced the idea of an exchange. All understood the largely fictional distinction between a "voluntary" and a "compulsory" exchange. But no state wanted the opprobrium that would come with such a policy.

On December 1, 1922, Nansen made a report to the Territorial and Military Commission of the Lausanne Conference, which met under the presidency of Lord Curzon.[141] Nansen's report employed the circumspect language of the international civil servant, dispassionately laying out the issues handed to him by his political superiors. The League had asked Nansen "to bring some small relief with the funds placed at my disposal by the members of the League to the starving refugees of both nationalities" (113). The four Great Powers represented in Constantinople (Britain, France, Italy, and Japan) then charged him "to initiate negotiations between the Turkish and Greek Governments with a view to the conclusion of a treaty for the exchange of minority populations" (114). He thereby became simultaneously the representative of these Great Powers and the League. Nansen followed the direction he received: "I based my action upon a knowledge that all the Governments here represented are in favor of what I proposed" (114). The international system led by the Great Powers had decided the matter:

> I know that the Great Powers are in favour of this proposal because they believe that to unmix the populations of the Near East will serve to secure the true pacification of the Near East and because they [the Great Powers] believe an exchange of populations is the quickest and most efficacious way of dealing with the grave economic results which must result from the great movement of populations which has already occurred. (114)

A sense of urgency underpinned Nansen's report. To begin rebuilding the Greek and the Turkish economies, the exchange needed to take place as soon as possible, ideally in time for the massive displaced rural populations to take to the fields in their new countries in time for spring planting. As we saw, most of the exchange had already occurred by the time of Nansen's report, transforming a "minority" problem into a "refugee" problem. Of those peoples who remained where they did not "belong," speedy migration seemed inconsistent with voluntary migration. For the majority of migrants, the real issue was preventing them from returning

[140] See Harry J. Psomiades, *Fridtjof Nansen and the Greek Refugee Crisis, 1922–1924* (Bloomingdale, IL: Asia Minor and Pontos Hellenic Research Center, 2011).

[141] "Territorial and Military Commission: Minutes of the Eighth Meeting, December 1, 1922, at 3:30 p.m., under the Presidency of Lord Curzon," *Lausanne Conference*, 113–17.

whence they came.[142] From the need to preclude any right of return came the need to make the exchange compulsory.

Through it all, the League of Nations itself, meeting in nearby Geneva, maintained its focus on mitigating the effects of the exchange. It did, however, maintain the fiction that most of the migrants were not "refugees," but rather the objects of forced "repatriation." Paradoxically, emphasizing humanitarian concerns had the effect of reinforcing the centrality of Nansen in the whole matter. As early as the Assembly meeting on September 19, 1922, Arístides Agüero y Betancourt of Cuba called on the best instincts of the League: "If we use all our endeavors to create a favorable public opinion I am certain that the funds which are necessary to assist our brothers in the East will be forthcoming for Dr. Nansen from every part of the world."[143]

Similar appeals for humanitarian aid would echo through both the Assembly and the League Council in the ensuing weeks. The League Council debated the matter regularly, but from the narrow perspective of providing funds to support Nansen's relief efforts. For example, following a September 19 Assembly resolution in support of the forced migrants, Arthur Balfour lamented "that a great calamity had undoubtedly occurred, and that it was the duty of the League to do what it could to relieve the distress," though he added that no formal means existed inside or outside the League to raise the necessary funds.[144] In the end, the Council found 100,000 Swiss francs in its own budget to send to Nansen, a small sum under the circumstances.[145]

It would prove a short step from relying on Nansen to manage relief in Greece and Anatolia to identifying Nansen as the author of the exchange itself. Both Nansen and the League Council resisted this elision. In his report to the League Council in February 1923, Nansen reminded his readers that back in November 1922, "I had accepted an invitation from the representatives of the Principal Powers to negotiate between the Governments of Turkey and Greece for an exchange of population and of prisoners of war. In accepting this invitation, I acted in according with what I was officially informed were the wishes of both Governments interested."[146] The convention on the Greek–Turkish exchange implicated the League only through the designated responsibility of the League Council to name three of the seven members of the mixed commission from countries that had not fought the Great War (Article 11). In December 1923, Viscount Ishii of Japan, as president of the League Council, responded to a complaint about the Greeks from İsmet Paşa (shown in Figure 6.2) by reminding his colleagues that "the Council, in accepting responsibility for appointing three members of the

---

[142] Article 1 of the convention expressly forbade return to the country of origin without the express permission of the relevant government.

[143] Eleventh Plenary Meeting, Tuesday, September 19th, 1922, 139.

[144] "Ninth Meeting (Public), Held at Geneva on Tuesday, September 19th, 1922, at 4:30 PM," *League Council: JO* (1923), 1195.

[145] Worth approximately $222,000 in 2015. www.historicalstatistics.org/Currencycoverter.html [accessed July 13, 2017].

[146] "Report by Dr. Nansen, High Commissioner of the League for Refugees, Submitted to the Council on February 2nd, 1923," *League Council: JO* (1923), 383.

Figure 6.2. İsmet Paşa (front, right of center) and entourage, Conference of Lausanne.
gallica.bnf.fr/Bibliothèque nationale de France.

mixed commission, has assumed no responsibility for the execution of the Convention regarding the exchange of populations."[147]

How, then, to assess the role of the League of Nations and its instruments in this most sordid of population policies resulting from the Great War? All the state agents wanted it, or at least proved willing to accept it. None of them wanted responsibility for it. The League, as Viscount Ishii had reminded his colleagues, had no direct role in either writing the exchange convention or implementing it. Nevertheless, the role of the League in mitigating the human catastrophe of the exchange, by definition, attached it to carrying out that policy. The personal, dual, and highly visible role of Nansen, as interlocutor for the Great Powers and as High Commissioner for Refugees, obscured the implication of the League and more importantly, the states the League represented. As on so much else, the League on population exchange became what states made of it.

CONCLUSION: WHAT WAS THE LEAGUE OF NATIONS?

From the first days of the League of Nations to its last, and indeed long thereafter, specialists in international law debated just what the Paris Peace Conference had created in creating the League. Of particular interest was whether the League

---

[147] "First Meeting (Private) Held at Paris on Monday, December 10th, 1923, at 11 a.m.," *League Council: JO* (February 1924), 324.

acquired legal personality under international law. Was the League itself a locus of sovereignty? Could the League make and implement international agreements, and could it work its will in the resolution of international disputes? Did it even have its own will to work in the first place? As noted, P.E. Corbett questioned whether the League had an identity distinct from the sum total of the identities of the states that it comprised. Alfred Zimmern pressed the question further by asking whether states were even the same agents they had been before the Great War.

Wilsonian sovereignty underpinned the Covenant of the League of Nations as written. Collective intentionality would guide state behavior, according to a direction set by a global liberal compass and guaranteed by a transnational community of liberal citizens. By the time the League formally existed in January 1920, the idea of Wilsonian sovereignty had surely faded, though it had not altogether disappeared. In the end, Wilsonian sovereignty would rule the world, or it would not. If it would not, it is pointless to expect the League to have become anything other than what it was. I have argued here that visibly "Wilsonian" traces in various forms remained, at any rate through the early years of the League. The League existed to try to change state identities.

Many scholars at the time believed that the League possessed some kind of legal personality. Lassa Oppenheim wrote shortly before his death: "The League of Nations seeks, through a written constitution, to organize this community of states [previously referred to as the community of 'civilized states'], up to that time remaining unorganized." The existence of a written constitution, he argued, rendered the League "a union of a kind that had never before existed."[148] Corbett argued that the League possessed none of the standard attributes of state personhood, but had a kind of personality as a confederation: "The League of Nations is but a looser species of this genus, established to comprise an indefinite number of self-governing political communities."[149] On the other hand, French expert Fredinand Larnaud emphasized the political rather than the legal character of the League: "The League of Nations is nothing more than a new form of international political life."[150] Whatever its legal personality or lack thereof, the Wilsonian character of the League died hard. In 1934, with the League already descending into the Manchurian crisis that would herald its demise, John Fischer Williams called attention to the ways in which the League sought to transform sovereignty. International relations and international law had hitherto recognized only states. In contrast, as he put it, the League is "something different from a mere agglomeration of States; it is a construction which looks to individuals, those subjects whose welfare is the ultimate aim of all sound political international organization."[151] In 1934, Williams still understood the radical liberal origins of the League.

---

[148] Lassa Oppenheim, "Le Caractère essentiel de la Societé des Nations," *Revue générale de droit international public* 26 (1919): 238. Brackets in original.

[149] Corbett, "What is the League of Nations?," 148.

[150] M.F. Larnaude, *La Société des Nations: Conférences faites à MM. les officiers du Centres des Hautes Études Militaires de l'École supéreire de Guerre et de l'École superiéur de Marine les 20 28 février et 12 mars 1920* (Paris: Librairie de la Société du Recueil Sirey, 1920), 8.

[151] Sir John Fischer Williams, *Some Aspects of the Covenant of the League of Nations* (London: Oxford University Press, 1934), 44.

Zimmern described the League as "an instrument of cooperation," but of cooperation in a new sense.[152] To him, the League "presupposes a transformation of Power-Politics into Responsibility-politics, or, at the very least, a sincere and consistent effort on the part of the Great Powers to begin to face the innumerable tasks of adjustment which such a transformation would carry with it." The League would not abolish states, but would seek to change them as they worked together to preserve the peace. "By itself," he argued as late as 1936, "it [the League] is nothing. But the peoples regard it as Something." Zimmern, like Williams, returned to the Wilsonian origins of the League to define its success or failure: "It is their will [of the peoples of the member states] and their will alone which can make the League a living reality."

This chapter has explored the ways in which the League of Nations sought some form of existence in the international system after the Great War. It certainly aspired to some form of legal personhood, at least in the long run. On security, the League worked to shape state behavior in the direction of collective security. At the very least, Great Powers had to treat the League as a partly autonomous entity in the "unmixing" of lands and peoples, if only because they had turned to it for help in the first place. In the mandates, the League endorsed a teleology of eventual independence, however distant in the future, and the accountability of mandatory powers in the interim. "Empire" simply did not make sense in the same way once the international system accepted mandates, and the League kept the resulting contradictions visible in the international public sphere. All this said, state interests shaped the League more than the League shaped state interests.

It would be rhetorically challenging, and probably pointless, to write a triumphalist narrative of the first years of the League of Nations. But this chapter concurs with recent scholarship insisting that historians can no longer conflate the undignified end of the League with its whole history. The League was both an agent and a structure, both an entity seeking a role in the system and a formal structure in which states could work together. It came into being through an internal contradiction. It rested on Wilsonian sovereignty as written, and on state sovereignty in practice. The League could capably help adjudicate those aspects of international relations consistent with state sovereignty when states chose to make use of it. But the League could neither make nor enforce new law on anything in the absence of Wilsonian sovereignty. Nor is there any reason to have expected it to. This became painfully clear once Great Powers, first Japan and then Italy, challenged the League in the 1930s.

---

[152] Zimmern, *League of Nations*, 283–85.

Conclusion
History, IR, and the Paris Peace Conference

Two priorities have driven this book; showing that there was more to peacemaking after the Great War than establishing a new balance of material power; and seeking in modest ways to deepen the encounter between history and international relations (IR) theory. Every historian believes IR could benefit from a more thorough grounding in what "actually happened." Realism and IR liberalism continue to exert considerable influence over the most thoughtful studies of the Paris Peace Conference and its aftermath. Historians' use of both IR schools contributed to a long fixation on "success" or more commonly "failure" in Paris. The historical specificity of the conference and the impassioned debates that took place there—in other words, its "then-ness"—have tended to get lost in the study of the conference looking forward, particularly to how its results unraveled in the interwar period. The Rankean task of understanding the Paris Peace Conference "as it was," however epistemologically foredoomed, requires engaging IR differently. It may also require acknowledging that IR will always change much faster than historians' attempts to keep up with it.

Historians often work best with theory—whether cultural theory or social science theory—by embedding it into explanation. IR scholars may find this frustrating, as embedding theory can make it practically invisible. As the "culture wars" of the 1990s among historians died down in the new millennium, historians felt less of a need to provide elaborate expositions of theoretical positions. Its debt to pieces of constructivism notwithstanding, this book has taken an eclectic approach to IR. This book itself makes no claim to theoretical contribution to the field. Michel de Certeau memorably characterized reading as "poaching," a practice of everyday life, and an unpredictable exercise in appropriation.[1] Perhaps I have read and poached IR in this way. I have done so toward the end of recapturing some of the "then-ness" of peacemaking after the Great War.

While generations of historians have relied on "anarchy" as imagined in realist and liberal IR, there remains something dissatisfying about it. Anarchy structures history by an absence, the absence of some overarching power sufficient to keep the peace. Of course, this absence is not really an absence. Self-interested states seek security to fill it in, providing familiar agents and structures across time. This book

---

[1] Michel de Certeau, *The Practice of Everyday Life*, Steven Rendal, trans. (Berkeley: University of California Press, 1984 [originally published in French in 1980]), 166–75.

has never denied the "reality" of realist security. Rather, it has argued that security and its pursuit does not tell us everything we need to know about what happened. Instead of "anarchy" as an overarching concept, I have chosen "sovereignty." Sovereignty at the Paris Peace Conference was about filling in the absence of anarchy. The conference sought to create sovereignty over the international system in ways that sovereignty previously had not existed. Doing so meant deciding what there was to decide on a host of particular issues.

The most important new discourse seeking to create sovereignty in Paris was the unstable amalgam of ideas known as Wilsonianism. This book has sought neither to praise nor condemn Wilson or Wilsonian liberalism as such. Rather, I have sought to add some much-needed critical distance, and to explore how this ideological revolution made sense, and failed to make sense, to so many intelligent people at the time. It is hardly news that liberalism operates historically through exclusion as well as inclusion, of peoples as well as states. I have argued that Wilsonianism sought to create a radically new kind of sovereignty over the international system, based in a radicalized, transnational liberal individual. Peoples and states, at any rate those included in the system, would find guidance through a common moral compass. Accepting this discourse had consequences, whatever the intent of the peacemakers doing so. "The world," meaning the Great Powers that had won the war—not to mention the Central Powers, which had lost it—accepted Wilsonianism as the foundational discourse for a redesigned international system. Public positions taken by states and their leaders mattered. From the beginning of peacemaking after the Great War to the end, words spoken and written down could take on their own reality.

Yet the record of Wilsonianism at the Paris Peace Conference tells a long tale of messengers losing control over the message. Certainly, Wilson's own views took paths he had not foreseen. The global embrace of Wilsonianism in the heady days of late 1918 and early 1919 had implications for what would happen in Paris. Britain and France appeared to embrace Wilsonianism in the Middle East in November 1918, only to face decades of resistance from people who took it much more seriously. Germany sought to instrumentalize Wilsonianism in asking for an armistice, only to see it redeployed against the post-Kaiserreich republic to create a new, criminalized state identity. Moreover, Wilsonianism helped legitimize the ethno-national successor state. I have argued that the pursuit of concurrent "ethnic" and "historic" state identities was not the same thing as a realist pursuit of security, though it was certainly no less disruptive, and perhaps in the end no less Hobbesian. But thinking of successor states in this way helps us see them as historically contingent.

Much of this book has recounted how the conference sought to reconcile competing discourses, and through doing so assert its own authority as provisional sovereign over the international system. Wilsonianism implied a "sovereignty of justice," that the conference debated and decided along lines of morality, compensation, and criminal prosecution. The conference sought to "unmix" lands and peoples, and thus to define them. It had many more discursive than material means of doing so. "Unmixing" proved a messy business that would long outlast the Paris Peace

Conference. Freshly minted "experts," geographers, professional diplomats, politicians, nationalists, and outright demagogues would create knowledge that the conference would try to adjudicate, all the while looking to its own interests. The conference would turn to population policies when and where it could not draw boundaries that would solve more problems than they created. The conference would hold the most brutal of these policies, population exchanges, at arm's length.

The conference embraced, resisted, and sought to master "revolution." Any new international system, by definition, would overthrow the existing order of how states related to one another. Millenarian aspirations as to how to do so after the Great War had circled the globe. Bolshevism constituted a discursive and in certain places material challenge to the Paris Peace Conference. The conference created the International Labour Organization in part to master the Bolshevik challenge by incorporating workers' concerns into the international system. The Mandate System exemplified a Janus-like approach to revolution. On the one hand, the original Mandate Principle had become so compromised by the time it was written down in the Covenant that particularly B- and C-class mandates had come to look quite a lot like colonies from the previous century. But on the other, empire itself simply did not make sense in the same way once the Mandate Principle became part and parcel of the international system. Why should some imperial domains have a trajectory toward independence and not others? How could the system of racial classification make sense when it simply recoded a compromise on territorial annexation?

The conference and the imperial powers came up with unsatisfying answers to these questions. Domains under "unjust" German or Ottoman rule were subject to the Mandate Principle, domains under "just" allied rule were not. But if just rule was inherently tutelary, as most of the most avid imperialists who sought mandates boasted, what was the argument for placing the former domains of the Central Powers under the mandatory rule and not those of the allies? Why should Muslim, Arabic speakers in Syria and Lebanon be on a fast track toward independence and Muslim, Arabic speakers in Tunisia, Algeria, and Morocco not? If religion and/or language made a people, why should Muslims in Syria be encouraged to develop under the Mandate Principle and Muslims in South Asia not?

Nineteenth-century imperial practices neither predominated nor were eradicated in Paris. At the same time, any kind of Mandate System at all would have been inconceivable among European imperialists before the Great War. Imperial power after 1918 had to wear different clothes. However narrow, twisting, and filled with roadblocks the paths to independence under the Mandate System, it set empire on a new and uncharted course. In their turn, the messengers of the Mandate System would not be able to control the message.

The power of the Paris Peace Conference to recognize or decline to recognize new states was both discursive and "real." Recognition determined access to the international system. The conflict between successor Hungary and successor Romania demarcated the limits of recognition by the conference. But in the end, the conference proved able to compel even the most recalcitrant successor states in Central and Eastern Europe to accept treaties for minority protection as the price of recognition. Even successor Turkey, victorious after the Chanak Affair of 1922, permitted minority protection in the Treaty of Lausanne. In addition, Turkey agreed to a plan to repay the Ottoman debt, all as the price of admission to the international system. Bolshevik Russia, which had rejected the international system created in Paris as much as that system rejected Bolshevik Russia, would eventually accept socialization.

The founders of the League of Nations envisaged it as the institutional successor to the peace conference ending the Great War. It would keep the peace established by exemplifying and guaranteeing the new international system. States were first, last, and always the heart and soul of the League. The League of Nations was always going to be what states made of it. The issue was the identity of states in the new system. As written in the Covenant, the League was supposed to function according to the collective intentionality imagined under Wilsonianism. States and Great Powers would exist, but would be guided by a common moral compass and accountable to a transnational community of liberal citizens. Wilsonian sovereignty would exist or it would not. If it would not, the League would become something else through the interactions of its member states, in their various identities.

Consequently, viewing the League of Nations as either a powerless talking shop or a tragic victim of human weakness, true or not, is somewhat beside the point. Like the I.L.O., the League of Nations reflected the international system that created it. The Paris Peace Conference left the League a great deal of unfinished business. The Covenant created an executive body and assembly with exactly the same charges and little guidance as to the relationship between them. Talented, hard-working individuals labored for years to play the impossible hand dealt to the League of Nations by the Paris Peace Conference. The League could create knowledge and advise—on collective security, borders, and plebiscites. As administrator of the Mandate System, it could keep alive the distinction between mandates and conventional imperial domains. It could even exercise modest levels of local governance, in Danzig and the Saar. Mostly, however, the League in practice provided a means for states of myriad identities to cooperate when they found it desirable to do so. Great Power support created the League in 1919. Great Power opposition to the League destroyed it. Japan in Manchuria and Italy in Ethiopia essentially ruined the League of Nations before the expansionism of Nazi Germany got serious.

Establishing the historical specificity of peacemaking after the Great War has been of paramount importance here. The war created what Masaryk referred to as that "vast cemetery" over which the Paris Peace Conference constituted a laboratory. This laboratory conducted experiments in finding a better way. Whatever they actually believed, the peacemakers operated in the context of a publicly affirmed consensus that something ought to replace realist anarchy as the foundational principle of the international system. New kinds of agents would inhabit that system, and they would interact according to new structures. I have argued that this amounted to the creation of a new kind of sovereignty within and over that system.

We can judge these experiments historically in numberless ways. Some, surely, were noble at least in their intent, such as the League of Nations. Some seem foredoomed, such as creating discursively a criminalized, once-and-future Great Power. Others seem well-intentioned if fanciful, such as encouraging Poles to believe that a successor Poland could combine characteristics it simply could not. Others, such as drawing borders and holding plebiscites, inevitably struck thousands of people as arbitrary. Some experiments seemed cruel and cynical, such as the arm's-length approval of the population exchanges and, to many, the Mandate System itself. In 1891, more than two decades before the Great War, Clemenceau said in a famous speech before the Assemblée Nationale: "The French Revolution is a block that must be accepted or rejected in its entirety, because the revolutionary struggle continues." He meant that posterity must take the good with the bad—here, the Declaration of the Rights of Man and Citizen along with the Reign of Terror. Though there is no evidence that he did so, Clemenceau could have said much the same about the Paris Peace Conference. Just as Wilson is too important to leave to Wilsonians or anti-Wilsonians, the Paris Peace Conference is too important to leave to its supporters or its far more numerous critics.

Historians and IR scholars look for what the academy still sometimes calls "truth" along different and often mutually uncomprehending paths. IR seeks truth through conceptual consistency and sophistication. Some of the most thoughtful questions raised by IR in recent decades come from pondering deep issues in the philosophy of social science. Though there is no reason to expect it to do so, this approach to IR shows little interest in history at all. Flesh-and-blood people staggering through confused times are largely absent. Historians, on the other hand, embrace the sticky and often incoherent details of actual human behavior, and poach from myriad bodies of theory—literary, cultural, social scientific, often all of the above—in order to try to make sense of that behavior. We often sacrifice consistency in doing so, and fall back on expansive narrative forms such as tragedy. For a century, the historiography of the Paris Peace Conference as guided by realism or liberalism has told tragic stories of unstable balances and dashed hopes. This book has embraced the contributions of this historiography. It argues simply that these frameworks do not tell us all we need to know about this extraordinary time in the development of international relations.

The history of most anything struggles to find the appropriate mix between seeing things clearly and seeing them whole. This book has tried to find its own mix, toward the end of thinking about the Paris Peace Conference in different ways. The historiography of international relations in the interwar period has gone a long way toward showing how the treaties written in Paris and Lausanne were not destiny. The carnage of World War II was not written into them, or even foretold as inevitable to historians who knew how to read these treaties properly. Historians have thus restored agency to international relations between the wars. This book has tried to restore agency to the conference itself. Understanding the "then-ness" of the Paris Peace Conference would surely suggest a need to rethink its relationship to problems that afflict our world today. At least for now, I am content to leave that task to historians more present-minded than myself. But what the "then" has to tell us about the "now," must begin with a proper understanding of the "then."

Index